ID0984263

THE FATHERS
OF THE CHURCH

A NEW TRANSLATION

VOLUME 131

REGIS COLLEGE LIBRARY
100 Wellesley Street West
Toronto, Ontario
Canada M5S 2Z5

THE FATHERS
OF THE CHURCH

A NEW TRANSLATION

EDITORIAL BOARD

David G. Hunter
University of Kentucky
Editorial Director

Andrew Cain
University of Colorado

Joseph T. Lienhard, S.J.
Fordham University

Brian Daley, S.J.
University of Notre Dame

Rebecca Lyman
Church Divinity School of the Pacific

Susan Ashbrook Harvey
Brown University

Wendy Mayer
Australian Catholic University

William E. Klingshirn
The Catholic University of America

Robert D. Sider
Dickinson College

Trevor Lipscombe
Director
The Catholic University of America Press

FORMER EDITORIAL DIRECTORS
Ludwig Schopp, Roy J. Deferrari, Bernard M. Peebles,
Hermigild Dressler, O.F.M., Thomas P. Halton

Carole Monica C. Burnett
Staff Editor

ST. GREGORY OF NYSSA

ANTI-APOLLINARIAN WRITINGS

Translated, with an introduction, commentary, and notes by

ROBIN ORTON

REGIS COLLEGE LIBRARY
100 Wellesley Street West
Toronto, Ontario
Canada M5S 2Z5

BR
60
F3
G8
v.2
2015

THE CATHOLIC UNIVERSITY OF AMERICA PRESS
Washington, D.C.

Copyright © 2015
THE CATHOLIC UNIVERSITY OF AMERICA PRESS
All rights reserved
Printed in the United States of America

The paper used in this publication meets the minimum requirements of the
American National Standards for Information Science—Permanence
of Paper for Printed Library Materials, ANSI z39.48-1984.

∞

English biblical quotations that are not otherwise marked or do not
constitute an intrinsic part of a patristic text have been drawn from the
New Revised Standard Version Bible, copyright 1989, Division of Christian
Education of the National Council of the Churches of Christ in the
United States of America. Used by permission. All rights reserved.

Library of Congress Cataloging-in-Publication Data
Gregory, of Nyssa, Saint, approximately 335–approximately 394.
[Works. Selections. English]
Anti-Apollinarian writings / St. Gregory of Nyssa ; translated, with an
introduction, commentary and notes, by Robin Orton.
pages cm. — (The fathers of the church, a new translation ; volume 131)
Includes bibliographical references and indexes.
ISBN 978-0-8132-2807-5 (cloth : alk. paper) 1. Jesus Christ—
History of doctrines—Early church, ca. 30–600. 2. Gregory, of Nyssa, Saint,
approximately 335–approximately 394—Correspondence.
3. Apollinaris, Bishop of Laodicea, –approximately 390—Correspondence.
4. Theophilus, patriarch, Archbishop of Alexandria,
–412—Correspondence. I. Orton, Robin, 1942– translator,
writer of supplementary textual content. II. Title.
BT1340.G74 2015
230'.14—dc23
2015009765

To my wife, Morwenna

CONTENTS

Abbreviations   xi
Notes to the Reader   xiii
Select Bibliography   xv
Preface   xvii

INTRODUCTION

Introduction   3

1. Apolinarius of Laodicea and his Christological
   teachings: A Historical Sketch   3

   Some problems in the historiography of Apollinarianism   3
   The life of Apolinarius of Laodicea   5
   The early history of Apollinarianism   7
   Apollinarianism at Antioch   12
   Apolinarius seeks allies   17
   Apolinarius condemned in Rome   17
   The tide begins to turn in the East, 378–381   19
   The Council of Constantinople, 381   21
   Gregory Nazianzen's struggle with Apollinarianism, 382–387   23
   Further moves against Apollinarianism in the East after 381   25
   The composition of the *Apodeixis*   27

2. Gregory of Nyssa and Apollinarianism   28

3. The Date and Circumstances of the Composition
   of *antirrh* and *Theo*   35

4. The Method of Composition and Structure
   of *antirrh*   38

5. The Adequacy of Gregory's Reporting of the Text
   and Argumentation of the *Apodeixis*   41

6. Reconstructing the Structure and Argument of
   the *Apodeixis*   43

   Introduction: Defending an orthodox Christology against
   Judaizers and Hellenizers   44

Christ both divine and human 44

A defense of the unity of Christ's person against those who
teach "two Christs" 45

Who were those who taught "two Christs"? 47

Why Christ's manhood cannot have been complete, that is,
have included a human mind 49

Apolinarius's trichotomous anthropology 50

Its Christological application: Christ as "enfleshed mind" 51

Christ's will 54

Christ's flesh 55

Christ's glorified body 58

7. Gregory's Argumentative Techniques in *antirrh* 58

8. Gregory's Use of Scripture in *antirrh* 62

9. Gregory's Critique of Apolinarius in *antirrh* 67

Critique of Apolinarius's trichotomous anthropology 68

Critique of Apolinarius's "enfleshed mind" Christology:
Introduction 68

Critique of Apolinarius's "enfleshed mind" Christology:
Christ's divinity 69

Critique of Apolinarius's "enfleshed mind" Christology:
The anthropological structure of Christ's person 70

The origin of Christ's human flesh 72

10. Gregory's own Christology as set out in *antirrh* 73

Christ is not a "God-filled man" 73

Christ is God 74

Christ is fully man 74

The unity of Christ's person: His virginal conception 75

Christ's will 78

The unity of Christ's person: His glorification 79

Christ's glorified body 81

11. Gregory's Soteriology as set out in *antirrh* 82

12. An Overall Assessment of *antirrh* 86

13. The Christological Arguments in *Theo* 86

ANTI-APOLLINARIAN WRITINGS

Refutation of the Views of Apolinarius:
Translation and Commentary 91

1. Introduction 91

2. The title of Apolinarius's work 93

3. Apolinarius's critique of the notion of Christ
   as a "God-filled man": Introduction   97

4. First excursus: Gregory attacks Apolinarius's alleged
   theory that the divine Logos died on the cross   100

5. Apolinarius's critique of the notion of Christ
   as a "God-filled man": Its origin and its
   condemnation by orthodox synods   102

6. Apolinarius's critique of the notion of Christ
   as a "God-filled man": The "man from earth"
   and the "man from heaven"   103

7. Apolinarius's trichotomous anthropology
   and the implication for Christology   107

8. Apolinarius's critique of the notion of Christ
   as a "God-filled man": Implications of the
   Nicene definitions   112

9. The first Adam and the second Adam   115

10. Apolinarius's teaching on the pre-existent
    Christ and the identity of Jesus with him   120

11. Second excursus: Gregory's teaching on how
    we are saved through Christ's humanity   126

12. Apolinarius's teaching on the pre-existent
    Christ and the identity of Jesus with him
    (continued): Zechariah 13.7 and Hebrews 1.1–3   130

13. Third excursus: Gregory's reflections on
    Philippians 2.5–11   136

14. Apolinarius's teaching on the pre-existent
    Christ and the identity of Jesus with him
    (continued): Philippians 2.5–11   140

15. The divinity of Jesus: The divine mind,
    eternally enfleshed   147

16. The divinity of Jesus: "Enfleshed mind" and
    "God-filled man"   151

17. The divinity of Jesus: The divine mind,
    eternally enfleshed (continued)   156

18. The divinity of Jesus: Arguments from Scripture   161

19. The relationship between Christ's divinity
    and his humanity: Arguments from Scripture   169

20. The enfleshment as the assumption of a man
    by God   175

21. More on Apolinarius's trichotomous anthropology and the "enfleshed mind"   177

22. Christ as wisdom: The "God-filled man" again. Apolinarius's first and second syllogisms   181

23. Soteriological arguments for the concept of Christ as "enfleshed mind." Apolinarius's third, fourth, and fifth syllogisms   189

24. The unity of Christ. Apolinarius's sixth, seventh, and eighth syllogisms   204

25. More on Apolinarius's trichotomous anthropology and the implication for Christology   219

26. Christ's death and resurrection   233

27. The eternal Christ   237

28. Fourth excursus: Gregory defends his Christology   238

29. The eternal Christ (continued)   248

30. Christ's ascension and glorification   251

31. Final arguments   254

32. Conclusion   258

To Theophilus, Against the Apollinarians:
Translation and Commentary   259

APPENDIX AND INDICES

Appendix: A Reconstruction of the Possible Structure of the *Apodeixis*   271

General Index   275

Index of Holy Scripture   283

ABBREVIATIONS

(Full bibliographical details in Select Bibliography
if not provided here)

antirrh	Gregory of Nyssa, *Antirrheticus adversus Apolinarium*
Carter	T. Carter, *Christologies* (2011)
Cod Theod	*Codex Theodosianus* (Theodosian Code)
Eng. trans.	English translation
Eun	Gregory of Nyssa, *contra Eunomium*
GNO	*Gregorii Nysseni Opera*, the Brill "Jaeger" edition of Gregory of Nyssa's works
Grelier	H. Grelier, *L'argumentation* (2008)
in illud	Gregory of Nyssa, *In illud: Tunc et ipse Filius*
J.[number]	Page number in *GNO*, vol. III.I
L.[number]	Fragment number in H. Lietzmann, *Apollinaris* (1904)
Lietzmann	H. Lietzmann, *Apollinaris* (1904)
Lietzmann, *History*	H. Lietzmann, *A History of the Early Church*, vols. 3 and 4. Translated by Woolf (1961)
LXX	Septuagint
M.[number]	Column reference in PG 45
Mühlenberg	E. Mühlenberg, *Apollinaris* (1969)
NPNF	Nicene and Post-Nicene Fathers, Second Series. Edited by Philip Schaff and Henry Wace. Peabody, Massachusetts: Hendrickson Publishers, Inc., 1994. Consulted at http://www.newadvent.org/fathers/index.html or http://www.ccel.org/node/70

NRSV New Revised Standard Version of the Holy Bible

ODCC *Oxford Dictionary of the Christian Church.* Edited by F. L. Cross, third edition, edited by E. A. Livingstone. Oxford: Oxford University Press, 1997

or cat Gregory of Nyssa, *oratio catechetica*

PG Patrologiae cursus completus, series graeca. Paris: Migne, 1857–66. Consulted at http://graeca.patristica.net/#t042

PL Patrologiae cursus completus, series latina. Paris: Migne, 1841–1855

Raven C. Raven, *Apollinarianism* (1923)

ref Gregory of Nyssa, *refutatio confessionis Eunomii*

Silvas Gregory of Nyssa, *Letters.* English translation by Anna Silvas (2007)

Theo Gregory of Nyssa, *Ad Theophilum adversus Apolinaristas*

Winling Gregory of Nyssa, *antirrh.* French translation by R. Winling (2004)

Zacagnius Laurentius Alexander Zacagnius, the Latin translator of *antirrh* in PG 45

NOTES TO THE READER

Note One

An earlier version of some of the material in the preface and in the introduction to this translation has appeared in Robin Orton, "'A Very Bad Book'? Another Look at St Gregory of Nyssa's *Answer to Apolinarius*," *Studia Patristica* 72 (2014): 171–89.

Note Two

The present volume represents a departure from the customary format of the Fathers of the Church series in that much of the translator's commentary on the text has been interposed in italics between sections of the translated text. Normally such commentary is confined to the introduction and footnotes. It is the complexity and frequent opacity of Gregory of Nyssa's arguments that compels the translator and editor to take such an unusual step.

SELECT BIBLIOGRAPHY

Carter, Timothy John. *The Apollinarian Christologies: A Study of the Writings of Apollinarius of Laodicea.* Ph.D. diss., Heythrop College, University of London, 2010. London: Hamley King Publishing, 2011.

Cattaneo, Enrico. *Trois homélies pseudo-chrysostomiennes sur la Pâques comme œuvre d'Apollinaire de Laodicée: Attribution et étude théologique.* Théologie historique 58. Paris: Beauchesne, 1981.

Chadwick, Henry. *The Early Church.* The Pelican History of the Church. Harmondsworth: Penguin Books, 1967.

Daley, Brian E. "Divine Transcendence and Human Transformation: Gregory of Nyssa's Anti-Apollinarian Christology." In *Re-Thinking Gregory of Nyssa,* edited by Sarah Coakley, 67–76. Oxford: Blackwell Publishing Ltd, 2003.

Drecoll, Volker Henning. "Antirrh." In *The Brill Dictionary of Gregory of Nyssa,* edited by Lucas Francisco Mateo-Seco and Giulio Maspero; translated by Seth Cherney, 48–50. Leiden: E. J. Brill, 2010.

Gregory of Nazianzus. *Letter 101.* PG 37:176A–193B.

———. *Letter 102.* PG 37:193B–201C.

———. *Letter 202.* PG 37:329B–333C.

Gregory of Nyssa. *Ad Theophilum adversus Apolinaristas.* Edited by Friedrich Müller. *GNO* vol. 3.1. Leiden: E. J. Brill, 1958.

———. *Antirrheticus adversus Apolinarium.* Edited by Friedrich Müller. *GNO* vol. 3.1. Leiden: E. J. Brill, 1958.

———. *Antirrheticus adversus Apolinarium.* French translation. In Raymond Winling, *Le Mystère du Christ: Contre Apollinaire (IVe siècle), le défi d'un Dieu fait homme,* 137–284. Les Pères dans la Foi. Paris: Migne, 2004.

———. *Contra Eunomium III.* Edited by Werner Jaeger. *GNO* vol. 2. Leiden: E. J. Brill, 1960.

———. *In illud: Tunc et ipse Filius.* Edited by J. Kenneth Downing. *GNO* vol. 3.2. Leiden: E. J. Brill, 1987.

———. *The Letters.* Translated with an introduction and commentary by Anna Silvas. Supplements to Vigiliae Christianae 83. Leiden: Brill, 2007. Consulted at http://ixoyc.net/data/Fathers/102.pdf.

———. *Oratio catechetica.* Edited by Ekkehard Mühlenburg. *GNO* vol. 3.4. Leiden: E. J. Brill, 1996.

Grelier, Hélène. *L'argumentation de Grégoire de Nysse contre Apolinaire de Laodicée: Étude littéraire et doctrinale de l'*Antirrheticus adversus Apolinarium *et de l'*Ad Theophilum adversus apolinaristas. Thèse en langues, histoire et civilisations des mondes anciens, sous la direction de Olivier Munnich, présentée et soutenue publiquement le 19 novembre 2008. Lyon: Université Lumière, Institut Fernand Courby et Institut des sources chrétiennes (n.d). Consulted at http://theses.univ-lyon2.fr/documents/getpart. php?id=1183&action=pdf; N.B. that in this version some of the footnotes have disappeared and some tabular material has been corrupted.

Hübner, Reinhard M. *Die Einheit des Leibes Christi bei Gregor von Nyssa: Untersuchungen zum Ursprung des "physischen" Erlösungslehre.* Leiden: E. J. Brill, 1974.

Kelly, J. N. D. *Early Christian Doctrines.* Fifth edition, revised. London: A & C Black, 1993.

Lietzmann, Hans. *Apollinaris von Laodicea und seine Schule: Texte und Untersuchungen, I.* Tübingen: J. C. B. Mohr, 1904.

———. *A History of the Early Church,* vols. 3 and 4. Translated by Bertram Lee Woolf. Cleveland, Ohio: Meridian Books, 1961.

Ludlow, Morwenna. *Gregory of Nyssa, Ancient and (Post)modern.* Oxford: Oxford University Press, 2007.

Meredith, Anthony. *The Cappadocians.* Crestwood, New York: St. Vladimir's Seminary Press, 1995.

———. *Gregory of Nyssa.* The Early Church Fathers. London: Routledge, 1999.

Mühlenberg, Ekkehard. *Apollinaris von Laodicea.* Göttingen: Vandenhoek & Ruprecht, 1969.

Norris, R. A. *Manhood and Christ: A Study in the Theology of Theodore of Mopsuestia.* Oxford: The Clarendon Press, 1963.

Orton, Robin. "Garments of Light, Tunics of Skin and the Body of Christ: St Gregory of Nyssa's Theology of the Body." Ph.D. diss., King's College, University of London, 2009.

———. "'Physical' Soteriology in Gregory of Nyssa: A Response to Reinhard M. Hübner." *Studia Patristica* 67 (2013): 69–75.

———. "'A Very Bad Book'? Another Look at St Gregory of Nyssa's *Answer to Apolinarius.*" *Studia Patristica* 72 (2014): 171–89.

Raven, Charles E. *Apollinarianism: An Essay on the Christology of the Early Church.* Cambridge: The University Press, 1923.

Stevenson, J., ed. *A New Eusebius: Documents Illustrating the History of the Church to AD 337.* Revised with additional documents by W. H. C. Frend. London: SPCK, 1995.

———, ed. *Creeds, Councils and Controversies: Documents Illustrating the History of the Church AD 337–46.* Revised with additional documents by W. H. C. Frend. London: SPCK, 1995.

Theodosius (Emperor). *Codex,* Book 16. Consulted at http://ancientrome.ru/ius/library/codex/theod/liber16.htm.

Winling, Raymond. *Le Mystère du Christ: Contre Apollinaire (IVe siècle), le défi d'un Dieu fait homme.* Les Pères dans la Foi. Paris: Migne, 2004.

Young, Frances M., with Andrew Teal. *From Nicaea to Chalcedon: A Guide to the Literature and its Background.* Second edition. London: SCM Press, 2010.

Zachhuber, Johannes. *Human Nature in Gregory of Nyssa: Philosophical Background and Theological Significance.* Supplements to Vigiliae Christianae 46. Leiden: Brill, 2000.

PREFACE

The Christological teaching of Apolinarius[1] of Laodicea and his followers was the target of two polemical works by St. Gregory of Nyssa.[2] The question of precisely what that teaching was, at any rate in the form in which Gregory encountered it, will be considered later. For the moment, suffice it to say briefly that Apolinarius suggested that while Christ's flesh and the "animal" part of his soul were fully human, the divine Logos, the Second Person of the Trinity, took the place of his rational soul, that is, that he had no human mind. This was partly on soteriological grounds but also because Apolinarius wished to address the Christological conundrum of how Christ can be both God and man, without there being two separate Christs.

The shorter (by far) and less elaborate of Gregory's two anti-

1. For the spelling "Apolinarius," see Hélène Grelier, *L'argumentation de Grégoire de Nysse contre Apolinaire de Laodicée: Étude littéraire et doctrinale de l'*Antirrheticus adversus Apolinarium *et de l'*Ad Theophilum adversus apolinaristas, thèse en langues, histoire et civilisations des mondes anciens, sous la direction de Olivier Munnich, présentée et soutenue publiquement le 19 novembre 2008 (Lyon: Université Lumière, Institut Fernand Courby et Institut des sources chrétiennes; consulted at http://theses.univ-lyon2.fr/documents/getpart. php?id=1183&action=pdf), 11, n. 1. Ἀπολινάριος, with one lambda, is the normal Greek spelling; "Apollinarius" (with two "l"s) is more common, though not universal, in the Latin sources. The *Gregorii Nysseni Opera* (henceforth *GNO*) edition, however—Gregory of Nyssa, *Ad Theophilum adversus Apolinaristas* and *Antirrheticus adversus Apolinarium,* edited by Friedrich Müller, *GNO* vol. 3.1 (Leiden: E. J. Brill, 1958), 117–233—uses only one "l" in the works' Latin titles. Like Grelier, I use the spelling "Apolinarius" (except when quoting directly from a source that uses the spelling "Apollinarius"), but I use "Apollinarian" or "Apollinarist" for the adjectival form and "Apollinarianism" for the doctrine.

2. Henceforth generally "Gregory," but I sometimes use "Nyssen" and "Nazianzen" when it is necessary to distinguish him from St. Gregory of Nazianzus.

Apollinarian works is the letter *To Theophilus, against the Apollinarians* (Πρὸς Θεόφιλον κατὰ Ἀπολιναριστῶν, *Ad Theophilum adversus Apolinaristas*). It seeks to provide Theophilus, who became bishop of Alexandria in 385, with arguments against "those who advocate the doctrines of Apolinarius" in the former's diocese.

The other work, much longer and much weightier, is called in Greek Πρὸς τὰ Ἀπολιναρίου ἀντιρρητικός—*Refutation of the Views of Apolinarius*—and is known in Latin, not quite accurately, as the *Antirrheticus adversus Apolinarium, The Answer to Apolinarius*. It is a polemical critique of a work by Apolinarius entitled "The demonstration (ἀπόδειξις) of the divine enfleshment (σάρκωσις)[3] according to the likeness of a human being."

The *Antirrheticus* (henceforth *antirrh*) has not had a good press. Charles E. Raven, in his 1923 monograph on Apollinarianism, calls it "a very bad book." He accuses Gregory of being "noisy and self-satisfied, pettifogging and vulgar." He castigates him for his "fatal tendency to substitute rhetoric for logic," for his "pathetic display[s] of incompetence," for his "febrile petulance," for his "mastery of the less reputable tricks of sophistry which is by no means edifying in a saint."[4]

Raven is not alone among modern writers in his low opinion of *antirrh*. Johannes Zachhuber calls the work "wordy," criticizes the "poor quality of the writing," and suggests that "if Gregory in his anti-Eunomian writings was not a fair polemicist, he is considerably less so in his anti-Apollinarian treatise."[5] T. J. Car-

---

3. Gregory himself points out (J.133) that the word σάρκωσις is not found in Scripture. (References to the text of the *Antirrheticus* and of *ad Theophilum* will be given in the form "J.[number]," where the number is the page in the *GNO* edition.) The obvious translation would be "incarnation," and the participial form of the verb, σαρκωθέντα, is the word used for "and was incarnate" in the Nicene Creed. But the English word "incarnation" seems to me to carry possible connotations of later (Chalcedonian) orthodoxy, which is often not appropriate in these works, so I have avoided it and translated σάρκωσις as "enfleshment."

4. Charles E. Raven, *Apollinarianism: An Essay on the Christology of the Early Church* (Cambridge: The University Press, 1923), 262–65. This work is henceforth referred to as "Raven."

5. Johannes Zachhuber, *Human Nature in Gregory of Nyssa: Philosophical Background and Theological Significance,* Supplements to Vigiliae Christianae 46 (Leiden: Brill, 2000), 220–21.

ter calls *antirrh* "a long and verbose work" and refers to Gregory's "rather pedestrian approach" and his "relative ineptitude as a polemicist."[6]

Its poor reputation no doubt helps to explain why *antirrh* has received far less attention from modern scholarship than Gregory's other major works. There has been no adequate complete translation into English,[7] and indeed the only complete published translation into a modern language seems to be that into French by Raymond Winling.[8] (There is a skillful and perceptive seventeenth-century Latin translation by Laurentius Alexander Zacagnius, prefect of the Vatican Library, reprinted in Migne's Patrologia Graeca).[9]

The work has now, however, for the first time, been made the subject of a learned monograph in the form of a doctoral thesis in French by Hélène Grelier, submitted in 2008 and accessible online,[10] in which she provides her own French translation of many of the key passages. She also provides, in an appendix, a French translation of the letter to Theophilus[11] (henceforth *Theo*).

It is certainly true that *antirrh* is not, at first sight, a very ap-

---

6. Timothy John Carter, *The Apollinarian Christologies: A Study of the Writings of Apollinarius of Laodicea* (Ph.D. diss., Heythrop College, University of London, 2010; London: Hamley King Publishing, 2011), 103–5. This work is henceforth referred to as "Carter."

7. The version by Richard McCambley, on *The Gregory of Nyssa Homepage*, "Against Apollinarius by Gregory of Nyssa: Introduction and English Translation," http://www.sage.edu/faculty/salomd/nyssa/index.html, is of limited value, although I have made use of it to provide an initial template for my own translation. Dr. Brian Duvick of the University of Colorado at Colorado Springs generously showed me an early draft of his as yet unpublished English translation of *antirrh* and *Theo*. This saved me from a number of errors.

8. In Raymond Winling, *Le Mystère du Christ: Contre Apollinaire (IVe siècle), le défi d'un Dieu fait homme*, Les Pères dans la Foi (Paris: Migne, 2004), 137–284. This translation is henceforth referred to as "Winling."

9. PG 45:1123–1270, henceforth "Zacagnius." Migne took it over from an earlier reprint in volume 7 of Galland's *Bibliotheca Veterum Patrum et Antiquorum Scriptorum Ecclesiasticorum*, 14 vols. (Venice, 1765–81). The Latin translation of *Theo* (PG 45:1269–1278) is by the French patristics scholar Fronton du Duc (Fronto Ducaeus, 1559–1624).

10. H. Grelier, *L'argumentation* (see n. 1); henceforth "Grelier."

11. Grelier, 622–41.

pealing work. The style is often breathless; the syntax is often knotty and obscure. The polemical tone is often violent and unattractive.

Moreover, the overall impression is of a work thrown together in some haste and without a great deal of planning or care. As will be argued later, this impression is not substantially falsified by more detailed scrutiny. *Antirrh* is often very repetitious, and its structure is far from easy to discern. It takes the form of a hostile commentary on Apolinarius's "The demonstration of the divine enfleshment according to the likeness of a human being" (which will henceforth be referred to as the *Apodeixis*), of which few if any other fragments have survived, and it is frequently unclear whether Gregory is quoting verbatim, paraphrasing more or less faithfully, or giving a biased summary of what he thinks or claims to think Apolinarius means. In any event it is clear that Gregory more often than not fails to discuss the citations from the *Apodeixis* in their proper context. It is often apparent either that he has made little attempt to understand the underlying rationale of Apolinarius's teaching or that he is deliberately misrepresenting it. All too often he is reduced to making cheap debating points at Apolinarius's expense.

But despite all these defects, there is nevertheless much that can be said in *antirrh*'s favor. Grelier's very detailed and substantial study, of which I have made considerable use, takes a generally sympathetic, though far from uncritical, view of the work.

As will be seen, much of Gregory's scriptural exegesis in *antirrh* is ingenious and original. Regarded also from the strictly theological point of view, I hope to show that it is a work of considerable interest. As Volker Drecoll has suggested, it is "an important contribution to the Christology of the fourth century, rather undervalued by scholars at this point."[12] This is not only because it accurately identifies, though admittedly not usually in the clearest and most elegant way, some important objections that can be leveled against Apolinarius's Christological thesis, but also because it gives us a useful sketch of Gregory's own

12. Volker Henning Drecoll, "Antirrh," in Lucas Francisco Mateo-Seco and Giulio Maspero, eds., *The Brill Dictionary of Gregory of Nyssa*, trans. Seth Cherney (Leiden, 2010), 50.

Christology, in its strengths and its limitations. Raven is quite wrong when he says of Gregory in *antirrh:* "it is difficult to discover what his own beliefs are: he is too busy refuting Apollinarius to have much thought for consistency or the definition of his own Christology."[13] Zachhuber is similarly unfair when he suggests that "only rarely is the flux of rhetorical arguments and slander interrupted by a passage containing positive teaching."[14] There are in fact three substantial sections of *antirrh*[15] where Gregory temporarily abandons his detailed critique of Apolinarius and uses an excursus to develop his own Christological and, as we shall see, soteriological ideas in a suggestive and interesting way.[16]

It is with a view to giving English-speaking readers the opportunity of taking a balanced view of the strengths and weaknesses of *antirrh* (and of its companion work *Theo*) that I have produced this translation. The form in which *antirrh* is cast and its polemical strategy mean that those who are reading the work for the first time are likely to feel the need for some reasonably detailed guidance through what might otherwise appear at first sight to be the trackless morass of Gregory's argument. It is for this reason that I have chosen to interleave my translation with a commentary, rather than, for example, just inventing some chapter headings to serve as occasional signposts, as Winling does. In doing so I have aimed to make the translation helpful and informative not only for Gregory specialists but also for those with a broader and more general interest in the history and theology of the early church.

I have also provided a substantial introduction to the works. This starts with an overview (not elsewhere, so far as I can ascertain, readily accessible in any recent publication in English) of the life and career of Apolinarius and of the development of his characteristic Christological teachings, and discusses what

13. Raven, 265.   14. Zachhuber, 221.
15. J.151–54; J.158–62; J.219–27.
16. See Grelier, 85: "... l'ouvrage est plus qu'une simple refutation (ἀντίρρη-σις): il est aussi l'occasion pour Grégoire d'élaborer sa doctrine christologique et de proposer des exposés personnels non pas particulièrement anti-apolinaristes, mais destinés au lecteur dans une perspective plus spirituelle."

can be deduced about the background to the composition of the *Apodeixis*. I then summarize what is known about Gregory's career during the period immediately prior to the composition of *antirrh* and *Theo,* and about any previous contacts he may have had with Apolinarius and his doctrine. Against that background, I discuss the vexed question of the date of *antirrh* and, in particular, whether it was written before or after *Theo.*

I next examine the method that Gregory seems to have adopted in composing *antirrh* and what can be said about its structure. I consider the extent to which Gregory can be trusted faithfully to have reported the text and the arguments of the *Apodeixis*. In the light of that, I offer (in the appendix to this volume) a suggestion of what the structure of the *Apodeixis* may have been, or, at least, what the main sections were into which it seems to have been divided. I then give a synthetic account of the theological arguments that, so far as we can judge from Gregory's account, Apolinarius advanced in that work.

I then turn to an analysis of Gregory's response to Apolinarius's arguments. I first discuss Gregory's argumentative techniques and the striking and often original way in which he uses Scripture in his polemical dialogue with Apolinarius. I then give a synthetic account of the theological arguments that Gregory advances, under three headings: first, his critique of Apolinarius's arguments; secondly, what he says about his own Christology; and, finally, what he has to say in *antirrh* about the separate although obviously closely related issue of soteriology.

Having given a brief overall assessment of Gregory's achievement in *antirrh,* I conclude with a synthetic account of the Christological arguments in *Theo.*[17]

In my translation I have generally, for both works, followed the text in the Leiden ("Jaeger") edition.[18] On the (not infrequent) occasions when I have decided for any reason not to do so, this is explained in a footnote. If the translation significantly departs from a word-for-word rendering of the Greek, I have usually put a more literal version in a footnote. I have not, how-

17. For the reasons why I discuss *Theo* after *antirrh,* see section 3 of the introduction.

18. See n. 1 above.

ever, usually drawn specific attention to the many places where, for the sake of clarity and comprehensibility, I have split up Gregory's long and complicated sentences into shorter ones.

Finally, there are a number of people I would like to thank. Dr. Anthony Meredith, SJ, and Professor Richard Price at Heythrop College, University of London, initially stimulated and fostered my interest in patristics. At King's College, London, Dr. Steve Holmes helped and guided me when I started to explore some of the complexities of early Christian Platonism, and I was fortunate to have had Professors Oliver Davies and Paul Janz as supervisors of my Ph.D. research project on Gregory. In my more recent work on Gregory's anti-Apollinarian works, I have benefited from Professor Markus Vinzent's support and encouragement and also from that of my King's contemporary and friend Dr. Janet Sidaway. I would also like to thank Dr. Carole Burnett, my editor at the Catholic University of America Press, for her efficiency, helpfulness, and friendly support, of which I cannot speak too highly.

My dear wife Morwenna, as always my closest companion and confidante, was a wonderful "doula" during the prolonged labor pains that eventually brought forth this work. I am honored now to have the opportunity to dedicate it to her.

INTRODUCTION

INTRODUCTION

1. Apolinarius of Laodicea and his Christological
Teachings: A Historical Sketch

In order to put Gregory's critique of the Christological views held by Apolinarius and his disciples into context, I have provided a sketch of the historical and theological background to those views, and the controversy about them, up to about the middle of the 380s, that is, roughly the time when, as will be seen, Gregory composed his two anti-Apollinarian works. But, before that, a few words are needed to explain some difficulties that arise when any attempt is made to give an account of the history of the origin, development, and condemnation of "Apollinarianism."

Some problems in the historiography of Apollinarianism

As will be seen, Apolinarius and his Christological doctrines were condemned by the church (first in the West, then in the East) and then by the imperial government, initially rather hesitantly but finally quite fiercely, on several occasions between 377 and 388. These early condemnations, made when Apolinarius was still alive, help explain why there are few sources for his life. We know that his disciple Timothy of Beirut wrote a history of the times from an Apollinarian perspective; this is now lost, but it seems to be the source of much of the (quite sparse) material about Apolinarius and his disciples that is found in the church historians Socrates and Sozomen.[1] There is also valuable (though often tantalizingly fragmentary) contemporary material in the works of the Cappadocian Fathers, in particular in the

---

1. Hans Lietzmann, *Apollinaris von Laodicea und seine Schule: Texte und Untersuchungen, I* (Tübingen: J. C. B. Mohr, 1904), 43–45; henceforth "Lietzmann."

letters of Gregory's brother St. Basil ("the Great") of Caesarea.

Most of Apolinarius's writings have not survived, and most of those that have did so because they were falsely attributed, presumably by the Apollinarians themselves, to "orthodox" writers.[2] We also have fragments of some other works; in some cases, including (thanks mostly to Gregory) the *Apodeixis,* these are quite extensive. All the surviving dogmatic works and the fragments were assembled by Hans Lietzmann in 1904, in his seminal *Apollinaris von Laodicea und seine Schule: Texte und Untersuchungen.*[3]

One of the factors that make it difficult to give a clear account of the history of Apollinarian Christology is that, particularly in its earlier years, it seems only occasionally to have been in the doctrinal spotlight. It developed, as it were, "under the radar" at a time, during the period between the Council of Nicaea in 325 and the Council of Constantinople in 381, when the big theological guns were being deployed in the battles not about the nature of Christ but about the doctrine of the Trinity, between what later developed into the settled Niceno-Constantinopolitan orthodoxy and various forms of Arianism. As we shall see, Apolinarius seems from the outset to have been firmly in the Nicene, anti-Arian camp. The extent to which the Christology of him and his followers was criticized, condoned, or condemned seems to have depended partly on where its defenders or opponents were positioned in the struggle against Arianism and in the various political maneuvers that, for different reasons, became associated with it.

---

2. And as such claimed as "orthodox" authorities in the fifth-century Christological debates by both St. Cyril of Alexandria and his opponent Eutyches. The *Kata meros pistis* ("Confession of Faith in Parts") was attributed to St. Gregory Thaumaturgus; *De unione, De fide et incarnatione,* and the first letter to Dionysius, to Pope St. Julius of Rome; and the letter to Jovian, to St. Athanasius. The spuriousness of these attributions became known, however, after about 450. Only Apolinarius's dogmatically harmless psalm paraphrases have survived under his own name (but their authenticity is now challenged; see Frances M. Young, with Andrew Teal, *From Nicaea to Chalcedon: A Guide to the Literature and its Background,* 2d ed. [London: SCM Press, 2010; henceforth "Young"], 252). See Lietzmann, 79–83, 91–93, 103–5.

3. Lietzmann. See n. 1 above for full reference.

The life of Apolinarius of Laodicea

Apolinarius was born, perhaps in about 310,[4] in Laodicea in Syria (the modern port of Latakia, and not to be confused with the Phrygian Laodicea, which features in Colossians and Revelation). His father, Apolinarius the elder, came from Alexandria, and this may perhaps help to explain what we shall see is the "Alexandrian" flavor of his son's theology. He moved first to Beirut, where he worked as a teacher of grammar, and then to Laodicea, where he married and became a priest.[5]

Both father and son sat at the feet of the pagan sophist Epiphanius. Their presence at the recitation of a pagan hymn to Bacchus composed by him was the ostensible cause of their temporary excommunication by Theodotus, the bishop of Laodicea; perhaps, as Lietzmann suggests,[6] the fact that Theodotus, like the other Syrian bishops at the time, had Arian sympathies and that the younger Apolinarius, with his Alexandrian background, subsequently became known as a supporter of Nicaea, may also have some bearing on this episode. At any rate, the younger Apolinarius was again excommunicated, this time permanently, by Theodotus's Arian successor George, who became bishop of Laodicea between 332 and 335. The trigger for this was the visit of St. Athanasius, the leader of the pro-Nicene party, to Laodicea in 346, on his way home to Alexandria from his second exile. That Apolinarius became friendly with him was, so far as George was concerned, an inadmissible action on the part of one of his priests.[7]

It is clear that by the time of the synod held in Alexandria in 362 (discussed later) Apolinarius was nevertheless a bishop in Laodicea, perhaps heading a strictly pro-Nicene faction in opposition to the officially recognized George and his "semi-Arian" or "homoiousian"[8] successor Pelagius, although the circumstances

4. See Raven, 129–30, and Grelier, 28, n. 65. (See entries in the Abbreviations list and the Select Bibliography.)

5. Lietzmann, 1.   6. Lietzmann, 2.

7. Lietzmann, 2–3.

8. That is, a subscriber to the belief that the Son was "of like being" to the Father rather than "one in being" (*homoousion*) with him, as in the Nicene formula.

of his election can only be guessed at.[9] At some stage he appears to have been recognized by Rome. According to St. Epiphanius of Salamis, the celebrated writer on heresy, he had a period of exile because of his pro-Nicene views, but we do not know under which Arianizing emperor this was imposed, Constantius (who died in 361) or the later Valens (364 to 378).[10]

In the early sixties it appears that he was in friendly correspondence with Basil the Great on Trinitarian issues.[11] He again appears as a staunch defender of Nicene orthodoxy, but uses arguments emphasizing the unity of God's nature in order to defend the *homoousion* against Basil's preference, at that time, for more "homoiousian" terminology to characterize the relationship between the Father, the Son, and the Holy Spirit. Such arguments seem later to have been perceived as (or at any rate presented as) "Sabellian"[12] in tendency, and to have contributed to the cooling of relations with Basil to be discussed later.[13]

9. Raven (131) suggests that Apolinarius may have been chosen as bishop by the Nicene party in Laodicea soon after his excommunication in 346. Lietzmann (4) suggests that his election may not have been until 360 and that it may have been triggered by the upheavals following the adoption of a "homoean" (extreme Arian) creed at the council of Seleucia in 359 (when, in Jerome's famous words, "the world groaned to find itself Arian"); see Henry Chadwick, *The Early Church,* The Pelican History of the Church (Harmondsworth: Penguin Books, 1967; henceforth "Chadwick"), 142. His homoiousian rival Pelagius was in communion with Meletius of Antioch (see later) and recognized by Basil (see n. 13 below).

10. Lietzmann, 4–5.

11. Basil, *epp.* 361 and 362. If this correspondence is genuine, it can be dated to 360/61. Lietzmann (20–21) thinks it is apocryphal, but its authenticity is defended by Raven, 133–36; by Ekkehard Mühlenberg, *Apollinaris von Laodicea* (Göttingen: Vandenhoeck & Ruprecht, 1969; henceforth, "Mühlenberg"), 38–43; and, according to Young, 252, by Prestige and Riedmatten.

12. That is, as "failing to do justice to the independent subsistence of the Son" and as holding that "in the Godhead the only differentiation was a mere succession of modes of operations." See *ODCC,* s.v. "Monarchianism."

13. In 375–76 Basil was involved in "the Eustathius affair": his old friend Eustathius of Sebaste, with whom he had fallen out over the issue of the Trinitarian status of the Holy Spirit, had accused him of having been in correspondence with Apolinarius on Trinitarian matters and of having endorsed the latter's alleged Sabellianism. Basil makes it clear that he is not currently in communion with Apolinarius and that he has recognized Pelagius as the legitimate bishop of Laodicea. See Lietzmann, 21, and Mühlenberg, 25–45.

Information about Apolinarius's later life is fragmentary. Such inferences as can be tentatively drawn from his surviving writings will be touched on later in this introduction. Otherwise we have a few pieces of more or less hard information. During the pagan reaction under the emperor Julian (361–63) we are told that he and his father sought to circumvent the ban on Christians teaching classics by translating Scriptures into antique forms, the results of which were apparently widely admired. At about that time he appears to have been the author of a "philosophical" apology for Christianity—now lost—which was sent to Julian by the bishops (but to which the emperor responded, "read, understood, rejected").[14] We know that he was teaching in Antioch (an early stronghold of his Christological doctrine, as we shall see) in 377/78, although why he had left Laodicea we do not know; the young St. Jerome sat at his feet there and detected nothing heretical in his teaching.[15] We know that Apolinarius was still alive when Gregory wrote *antirrh* (some time in the 380s, as will be seen later). He must have died before 392, when St. Jerome wrote *de viris illustribus* and reported Apolinarius as having died during the reign of Theodosius.[16]

The early history of Apollinarianism

It is for his heterodox Christological views that Apolinarius is chiefly known to church history. But it should be borne in mind that there were other aspects of his teaching that also concerned his contemporaries. The alleged Sabellianism of his Trinitarian theology has already been mentioned. He was also accused of Judaizing tendencies, and of a belief that the animal sacrifices of the Temple would be restored in the Millennium.[17]

So far as his characteristic Christological doctrines are concerned, there are major uncertainties in establishing when and in what circumstances Apolinarius began to develop them, and when they began to be an object of suspicion to his Nicene allies. Gregory of Nyssa's friend Gregory of Nazianzus dates the

14. See Lietzmann, 9–10; Raven, 136–38.
15. Lietzmann, 15.
16. Grelier, 41, citing Jerome, *de viris illustribus* 104.
17. In Basil's *ep.* 263 and elsewhere; see n. 54 below.

beginning of the Apollinarian heresy to the 350s,[18] but we have no other evidence for that. The evidence from the 360s and most of the 370s is fragmentary and ambiguous.

It should be mentioned at the outset that according to the church historian Rufinus (c.345–411),[19] there were in fact two distinct chronological stages in the development of Apolinarius's Christological teaching, although he does not give any indication of the date of the transition from one to the other. Rufinus locates this distinction within the development of the teaching that the divine Logos replaced, in whole or in part, what would otherwise have been Christ's human soul. As will emerge in more detail later, there is no doubt that this doctrine is, or became, a central element in Apollinarian Christology, though it should be noted that it does not always seem to have been either the most prominent or the most important. According to Rufinus, Apolinarius's initial teaching was that Christ "assumed a body and not a soul at all,"[20] that is, that the divine Logos fulfilled the role not just of his higher or rational soul, that is, his mind (νοῦς), but also of what would otherwise have been his lower or "animal" soul (ψυχή). Later, however, says Rufinus, Apolinarius modified his position to that which is represented in the *Apodeixis*, that is, that Christ possessed both a human body and a human animal soul and that only his mind, which Apolinarius also calls his spirit (πνεῦμα), was divine. It was suggested by nineteenth-century scholars that this development in turn reflected a change in the anthropological model that Apolinarius used to support his Christology, from "dichotomy" (distinguishing only body and soul) to "trichotomy" (distinguishing body, soul, and spirit).[21] More recently, however, scholars have

18. *Ep.* 102, PG 37:200C.

19. Dates from *ODCC, s.v.* "Rufinus, Tyrannius or Tirrranius."

20. Rufinus, *Historia ecclesiastica* 2.20, quoted by Raven, 169.

21. A version of the theory that over time Apolinarius developed two separate versions of his Christology was proposed by Lietzmann (5–6). See Raven, 169–76, for an exhaustive discussion of the issue.

Raven points out that Rufinus's account was copied by Socrates (*Historia ecclesiastica* 2.46) and by St. Augustine (*de dono perseverantiae* 67). Lietzmann also attributes it to St. Epiphanius of Salamis; Raven (169) suggests that this is "on the strength of [Epiphanius's] statement that these two theories were

generally concluded that although he may not be consistent in his use of anthropological terms, such a clear-cut distinction cannot be discerned in what is extant of Apolinarius's writings,

---

held by different people who may or may not have been pupils of Apolinarius": see Lietzmann, 11. In *adversus haereses* 77 (PG 42:643A–B), dating from 377 (Mühlenberg, 51), Epiphanius seems in fact to refer to three separate views among the pupils of Apolinarius who came to Cyprus. "Some of them (τινὲς μὲν γὰρ αὐτῶν) dared to say that the body of Christ had been brought down from heaven. This strange doctrine remained in people's consciousness and brought about a progression to something even more terrible. Others of them (ἄλλοι δὲ ἐξ αὐτῶν) denied that Christ assumed a soul. Some (τινὲς δὲ) also dared to say that the body of Christ was consubstantial with his divinity." Although, as will be seen later, it might be possible to associate each of these opinions with developments (or misunderstandings) of various aspects of what we know of Apolinarius's teachings, there seems no reason to assign them to different chronological stages thereof.

So far as the supposed first stage is concerned, some nineteenth-century scholars find specific evidence for this in the *de unione* (Lietzmann, 185–93) and *contra Diodorum* (L.121–46). (N.B. that henceforth "L.[number]" refers to the numbers assigned to the fragments of Apolinarius by Lietzmann.) The arguments against this are perhaps not quite so conclusive as Raven (170–73) suggests: he fails to mention a clear statement in *de unione* 13 (Lietzmann, 191) that shows that, at any rate, when that work was written, Apolinarius does indeed seem to have held that the Logos provided Christ's ψυχή, the principle of his animal life, as well as his νοῦς: "But it is by the advent of spirit and the overshadowing of power that the holy child is constituted from the Virgin; it is not the seminal material that produces the divine life but the spiritual and divine power which brings about the divine conception in the Virgin, graciously conferring the divine infant."

As for the supposed second stage (the form of his Christology with which Apolinarius is chiefly identified in histories of Christian doctrine), Lietzmann is right to point out (163) that, apart from the *Apodeixis*, there is very little specific evidence for this. The only other place where Apolinarius clearly states that Christ had a human ψυχή, i.e., gives evidence for the supposed "second stage" of his Christology, is in the pseudo-Athanasian *Quod unus sit Christus* (if, as Lietzmann, 159, suggests, it is by Apolinarius himself rather than a disciple); see in particular §11 (Lietzmann, 301). L.2, from an otherwise unknown περὶ ἑνώσεως ("On Union"), implies a "trichotomous" anthropology; that is, it distinguishes ψυχή and νοῦς, but states clearly that Christ did not have a human ψυχή. Lietzmann's speculation (138) that this therefore represents an intermediate stage between the first and the second implies a greater consistency in Apolinarius's use of anthropological terms, and a closer dependence of his Christology on precise anthropological theories, than can be justified.

the order of composition of which is in any event impossible to establish in many cases.[22]

Whether or not two distinct stages can be identified in the development of Apolinarius's Christology, there are nevertheless three documents bearing, or possibly bearing, on that Christology which may date from the early 360s and which can therefore be taken as evidence for a comparatively early form of his teaching.

The first is his letter to Sarapion (probably the bishop of Thmuis in Egypt and a friend of Athanasius). But the date of this is disputed. Raven puts it in 360–61, Lietzmann ten years later.[23] In any event, the Christology reflected in the surviving fragments of the letter shows no sign of the views about Christ's human soul for which Apolinarius would eventually be condemned. It endorses Athanasius's letter to Epictetus of Corinth, in which various Christological errors are denounced (including the view that "the Word has descended upon a holy man as

22. See discussions in R. A. Norris, *Manhood and Christ: A Study in the Theology of Theodore of Mopsuestia* (Oxford: The Clarendon Press, 1963; henceforth "Norris"), 82–94, and in Grelier, 416–21. See also Young, 249–50. Most recently, however, Carter (*passim*) has revived the idea of two successive stages in Apolinarius's Christology, but has argued that the differences can best be characterized in terms of a progression from a "compositional" concept (σύνθεσις) of the unity of Christ's person, found mostly in the (earlier) works, which reflect a "dichotomous" anthropology, to the concept of the Word's "assumption" (πρόσληψις) of the flesh, which is developed in the (later) "trichotomous" works, including the *Apodeixis*, which he dates (415–16) to 377–83. For Carter see entries in the Abbreviations list and the Select Bibliography.

23. Lietzmann, 147; Raven, 103–10; Mühlenberg (218) seems to put it in 373. It seems clear that it was written soon after Athanasius's *ad Epictetum* (or at the same time: Raven suggests—it is not clear on what grounds—that Athanasius sent Apolinarius a draft of his letter for his approval and comments). Raven argues that the only grounds for putting *ad Epictetum* later in Athanasius's career are that the errors it is directed against are Apollinarian (notwithstanding that Apolinarius endorses the letter in his to Sarapion!) and so must date from a time when Apollinarianism had been condemned. He suggests that this is not necessarily the case, and that the target of the letter is rather various forms of docetism and "Ebionism" ("God-filled man" Christology) among Epictetus's congregation in Corinth. He argues further that the absence of any reference in the letter to Athanasius's synod in Alexandria of 362 and the *tomus ad Antiochenos* (see below) means it must pre-date them.

upon one of the prophets,"[24] which is reminiscent of the "God-filled man" Christology which Apolinarius later condemns in the *Apodeixis*). In particular Apolinarius joins with Athanasius in deploring the view that Christ's flesh is consubstantial with God, that is, part of the eternal nature of the second Person of the Trinity. He calls this notion "much madness";[25] Christ's flesh is consubstantial with ours, although it becomes divine by virtue of its union with God.[26] As will be seen, this is the same view that he advances in the *Apodeixis,* although in *antirrh* Gregory does his best to show that his adversary in fact believes that Christ's flesh is divine in origin.

The second is Athanasius's *tomus ad Antiochenos* of 362, which will be discussed shortly in the context of the relationship between early Apollinarianism and the ecclesiastical schisms at Antioch.

The third is a letter about Christology which Apolinarius wrote to Julian's short-lived successor Jovian (363–64), who favored the Nicene faith. Again, there is little of substance to offend later orthodoxy, and no reference to the question of whether or not Christ had a human soul. There is an emphasis on the unity of Christ's person: there are not two Sons but "one nature (φύσιν) of the Word of God which was enfleshed and is worshiped together with his flesh with a single worship."[27] Apolinarius also deals, on the same lines as in the letter to Sarapion, with the question of the origin and status of Christ's flesh; he anathematizes anyone who "says that the flesh of our Lord comes from above and not from the Virgin Mary."[28]

24. *Ep.* 59 *ad Epictetum* 2. Eng. trans. in NPNF 4; see http://www.newadvent.org/fathers/2806059.htm.

25. L.159.

26. L.161.

27. *Ad Jovianum,* Lietzmann, 251, 1–3. The precise theological connotation of terms such as φύσις had not, at this period, yet been established, and φύσις could be used in the sense for which πρόσωπον ("person") or "hypostasis" was later reserved, that is, without necessarily suggesting later "monophysitism," a term used to characterize the view, condemned at the Council of Chalcedon in 451, that in the incarnate Christ there is one "nature" (φύσις) rather than two "natures" in one "person."

28. Lietzmann, 253, 7–8.

Apollinarianism at Antioch

In terms of firm historical evidence, much of our knowledge of the history of Apollinarianism during the 360s and 370s is filtered through one particular prism, that is, the information that we have about the complicated schisms within the church in Antioch, whose bishop had acquired a "patriarchal" primacy among the churches of Asia and Syria.[29] Partly because of the close involvement of Basil of Caesarea in those schisms and the attempts to heal them, that information is quite extensive, particularly for the 370s. It is clear that the teachings of Apolinarius and his disciples played a significant, though not necessarily central, role in Antiochene affairs during this period. But it may be that the growth of Apollinarianism in other places, about which our information is far more fragmentary, may have been at least as significant in forming the background against which Gregory was writing in the next decade.

Ever since the 320s there had been two separate church communities in Antioch. A succession of Arianizing bishops had been officially in charge, but there had also been a small group who remained faithful to the Nicene tradition; it was now led by the presbyter Paulinus. Paulinus's doctrine was, however, itself constantly under suspicion in some quarters; he was a friend and supporter of Marcellus of Ancyra, who was accused of "Sabellianism" and had been anathematized in the East during the 340s.[30]

At the beginning of the 360s there was a further schism. In 360 St. Meletius, previously bishop of Sebaste in Armenia, had been appointed official bishop of Antioch, but he was soon discovered to be opposed to Arianism and to be a friend and adherent of Basil of Ancyra, the leader of the homoiousian party. So he was quickly replaced by Euzoius, a safe Arian, and sent

29. Recognized in the sixth canon of the council of Nicaea: Eng. trans. in J. Stevenson, ed., *A New Eusebius: Documents Illustrating the History of the Church to AD 337*, revised with additional documents by W. H. C. Frend (London: SPCK, 1995), 340. See Chadwick, 131.

30. For "Sabellianism" see n. 12 above. For Marcellus's Trinitarian theology, see Young, 56–61. He taught that there was only one hypostasis in God and (to use rather anachronistic terminology) tended to see the Trinity in "economic" rather than "immanent" terms, which is why he was accused of "Sabellianism."

into exile. But Meletius's homoiousian followers remained loyal to him and split off from Euzoius's communion.[31]

So as well as the official, Arianizing church under Euzoius, there were two separate anti-Arian communions at Antioch: the "old Nicenes" under Paulinus (who, to complicate matters further, was consecrated bishop in 362 by an anti-Arian bishop and friend of Athanasius called Lucifer of Calaris); and a homoiousian group owing loyalty to the exiled Meletius. Much effort was devoted over the next twenty years to reconciling these two groups, notably by Athanasius and by Basil the Great after he had become bishop of Caesarea and metropolitan of Cappadocia in 370. Those efforts were complicated by the fact that Paulinus was recognized by the bishops of Alexandria (Athanasius, then Peter, who succeeded him when he died in 373) and Rome, while Basil was suspicious of Paulinus's alleged Sabellianism and took the view that in the long term the future lay with the (homoiousian) Meletian party.[32]

Until Meletius returned to Antioch after the recall of the Nicene exiles upon the accession of the emperor Julian in 362,[33] the Meletian party was under the leadership of two priests, Diogenes and Vitalis.[34] In due course a distinct Apollinarian party, under the leadership of Vitalis, broke away from the Meletian communion, thus increasing the number of separate groups at Antioch from three to four. But there is no evidence for such a breach as early as 362, when Athanasius, back in Alexandria from his third exile, as a result of Julian's amnesty, convened a synod at Alexandria, perhaps with a view to trying to unify the anti-Arian factions in Antioch. Following this synod, Athanasius reported its conclusions to the church at Antioch in his *tomus ad Antiochenos*.[35]

31. Chadwick, 147; Lietzmann, 8.

32. In 363 Meletius and his party at Antioch adopted the Nicene creed, but only if the *homoousion* could be interpreted as *homoios kat' ousian* ("like as regards being"). The West seems to have recognized Meletius's orthodoxy in the early seventies (Basil, *ep*. 67). See Lietzmann, 13.

33. He was twice exiled again, under the Arianizing emperor Valens, from 365 to 366 and from 371 to 378; *ODCC, s.v.* "Melitius, St."

34. Mühlenberg, 45.

35. To be found at PG 26:796A–809C. See Young, 68, for a summary of

It is difficult to assess the precise bearing of this document on the state of the ecclesiastical parties in Antioch at that time. It seems to show at least that the issues of a kind that we know characterized the controversies about Apollinarian Christology and that we shall find debated in *antirrh*—condemnation of the notion of Christ as a "God-filled man," an insistence on the unity of Christ as against the advocates of "two Christs," and debate about the nature and origin of Christ's soul and mind—were probably by then very much live ones in the Antiochene church. But there is no reason to believe that at this time clear theological distinctions could be drawn between a hypothetical "Apollinarian group" among the Meletian party at Antioch and the Nicene "mainstream" (if it is fair so to characterize the views of Athanasius).[36]

---

some recent views suggesting that in fact the *tomus* "never intended to address itself to the fundamental split in the Antiochene Church" and that the synod of 362 "is likely to have been a local reunion of exiled bishops, without the universal character ascribed to it."

36. For discussions of the *tomus* and its possible bearing on the Apollinarian issue, see Raven, 110–14; Hans Lietzmann, *A History of the Early Church*, trans. Bertram Lee Woolf, vols. 3 and 4 (Cleveland, OH: Meridian Books, 1961; henceforth Lietzmann, *History*), vol. 3, 267–69, 271–72; Chadwick, 147; Mühlenberg, 60–61. Citations below are from the Eng. trans. in Stevenson, ed., *Creeds, Councils and Controversies*, 80–83.

We know from the *tomus* that Apolinarius sent some monks to represent him at this meeting, and it must be assumed that they were in agreement with its conclusions. In the main, those conclusions bore on Trinitarian issues, but there is also a statement about the person of Christ. All parties agreed that "the Word did not, as it came to the prophets, so dwell in a holy man at the consummation of the ages, but that the Word Himself was made flesh, and being in the Form of God, took the form of a servant ... ; that the Savior had not a body without a soul, nor without sense or intelligence; for it was not possible, when the Lord had become man for us, that His body should be without intelligence: nor was the salvation effected in the Word Himself a salvation of body only, but of soul also."

There was also agreement on the unity of Christ's person and the inseparability of his human and divine natures: "Wherefore neither was there one Son of God ... that raised up Lazarus, another that asked concerning him; but the same it was that said as man, 'Where does Lazarus lie?'; and as God raised him up ..."

Much of this is in line with what we know Apolinarius taught, typically in the *Apodeixis*. Like the letter to Sarapion discussed above, it seems to be aimed at those who believed that Jesus Christ was merely a "God-filled man" and as

The secession of the Antiochene Apollinarians under Vitalis seems in fact to have happened by the mid-seventies, but the precise chronology and historical context are unclear.[37] We know that Vitalis made a visit to Rome, probably in 376, with a view to getting Pope St. Damasus's approval to a confession of faith, the content of which is unknown. His aim may have been to enable the Apollinarian party to bypass the Meletians and be reconciled with Paulinus, whom Rome recognized as the orthodox bishop of Antioch; it may have been that growing suspicions about Apollinarian Christology made it particularly desirable at this time to get it endorsed by the West[38] (which was seen as a stronghold of Nicene orthodoxy throughout this period)[39] and that, given Rome's support for Paulinus rather than Meletius, Vitalis decided it would be right for him and his party to transfer allegiance from the latter to the former.[40]

---

such indistinguishable as regards his nature from the holy men of the Old Testament. And, like the letter to Jovian, also discussed above, it emphasizes the unity of Christ's person.

But it also seems on the face of it to condemn what subsequently emerged as the characteristic Apollinarian teaching, that Christ did not have a human soul, or at any rate a rational one. Does that mean that such views were already current in Antioch and that the synod found them sufficiently dangerous to merit issuing a warning against them? If so, it may be that the particular terms that were chosen to express that warning were designed to be deliberately ambiguous, in order to provide the Antiochene "Apollinarians" (if it is yet appropriate to refer to them by that name) with some room for maneuver, to enable them to interpret them as meaning that although Christ did indeed have a soul, perhaps including a rational one, it was, as Apolinarius taught, constituted by the divine Logos rather than being part of his human nature. Apolinarius himself certainly interpreted the *tomus* in this sense when he quoted it, with approval, in his letter to the Diocaesarean confessors (on whom see later) in the mid-370s (*Epistula ad Diocaesareenses*, Lietzmann, 255–56). Indeed, it is possible that Athanasius himself did not interpret the formula in the *tomus* as an affirmation of the presence of a human mind or soul in Christ; see Young, 249.

37. See the detailed accounts in Lietzmann, 15–20; Lietzmann, *History*, vol. 4, 27–28; Mühlenberg, 45–56.

38. See Mühlenberg, 54.

39. A synod called by Pope Damasus in 372 had accepted the *homoousia* of all three Persons of the Trinity—Damasus's *confidimus* (see Lietzmann, *History*, vol. 4, 24–25).

40. See Mühlenberg, 48; Basil of Caesarea's *ep.* 129 (beginning of the year 376) implies that Vitalis was still in Meletius's party.

Initially Damasus agreed to recognize Vitalis's orthodoxy—indeed he provided him with a certificate to that effect,[41] of which Vitalis was able to make use later—and to commend him to Paulinus on that basis. On receiving further information, however, he instructed Paulinus[42] to require of the Vitalians subscription not only to the Nicene creed, but also to certain Christological principles: a recognition that Christ assumed a complete man, and the condemnation both of the doctrine of two Sons (which, however, as we have seen, Apolinarius also condemned) and, more significantly, of the doctrine that the Logos indwelt Christ's human body as a mind. This is the first unambiguous and more or less datable reference to (and condemnation of) the doctrines that we know informed Apollinarian Christology in its mature form,[43] that is, as set out in the *Apodeixis*.

Any possibility of reconciliation between Vitalis and Paulinus now seemed to have been removed. This may be what prompted Apolinarius to consecrate Vitalis as a bishop, perhaps later in 376.[44]

It may have been shortly after this that the heresy expert Epiphanius of Salamis visited Antioch. He makes no mention of the Meletians, and his aim seems to have been that they should be supplanted as the representatives of Nicene orthodoxy by a union of the Paulinian and Vitalian parties. He found that Vitalis was indeed teaching unorthodox Christology and maintaining that Christ had a human ψυχή but not a human νοῦς.[45] But Epiphanius hesitated about not recognizing Vitalis. He asked Basil of Caesarea to intervene, but the latter declined to do so; the Meletians were the only party he recognized at Antioch, but he may in any case have wanted at this stage to avoid causing further bad blood, and thus prejudicing the possibility of an eventual comprehensive settlement, by challenging the orthodoxy of the Vitalians.[46]

41. Lietzmann, 18.
42. In *per filium:* see Lietzmann, 19.
43. Unless the (much vaguer) *tomus ad Antiochenos* counts as such; see above.
44. Mühlenberg, 53.
45. *Adversus haereses* 77.22–23 (PG 42:672B–673C).
46. See Lietzmann, 16–17; Mühlenberg, 52–53.

Apolinarius seeks allies

Meanwhile Apolinarius, following Vitalis's unsuccessful attempt to obtain endorsement from Rome, was seeking allies elsewhere. He sought, without success, recognition from Jerome, whom Vitalis or his representative visited.[47] It may be that it was at this time that he wrote to Terentius, the new imperial Count of the East, to demonstrate his orthodoxy by again making it clear (as in the letters to Sarapion and Jovian; see above) that he believed neither in two Christs, nor that the flesh of Christ came down from heaven or is consubstantial with God.[48]

He also corresponded with a group of pro-Nicene bishops who had been exiled from Egypt and were now based in Diocaesarea (earlier called Sepphoris) in the Galilee region of Palestine. (Their leader, Peter of Alexandria, also exiled, was now in Rome). They were currently in communion with Paulinus of Antioch, as well as with the church at Ancyra, which continued to espouse the allegedly "Sabellian" doctrines of the now deceased Marcellus. Apolinarius tried to persuade them to abandon these unorthodox alliances and to accept communion with him instead, on the basis that his Christology was identical with that of Athanasius.[49] But they were able to examine some of Apolinarius's writings, became suspicious of his teaching, and rejected his approaches.[50]

Apolinarius condemned in Rome

It was in 377 that Basil decided that the time had come to seek a formal condemnation from the West of various schisms and heterodox doctrines that had arisen within the Nicene camp and that were hindering his efforts to build a united front against the Arians in the East. The Apollinarian schism was only one of these; also in his sights were his old friend Eustathius of Sebaste (who denied that the Holy Spirit was consubstantial with the Father and the Son)[51] and the "Sabellians," both the Ancyrans and

47. Mühlenberg, 54.
48. L.162–63, 254–55. See also Lietzmann, 147, and Mühlenberg, 54.
49. In the *Epistula ad Diocaesareenses;* see n. 36 above.
50. Lietzmann, 22–23; Mühlenberg, 55.
51. See n. 13 above.

Paulinus at Antioch, who was, or was shortly to be, in communion with them.[52] Using language reminiscent of that which Gregory would use of the Apollinarians in *antirrh*[53]—complaining that "men clad in sheep's clothing, and presenting a mild and amiable appearance, but within unsparingly ravaging Christ's flocks, find it easy to do hurt to the simpler ones, because they came out from us"—he asked Rome to attend or at least support a synod at which these trouble-makers would be condemned.[54]

What happened next is unclear. There seems to have been a synod in Rome at which the doctrines that concerned Basil were indeed condemned.[55] We have fragments of a letter of Damasus in which the sort of Christology that we know to have been held by Apolinarius is criticized in reasonably explicit terms: he condemns those "from among our own people" who "venture to say that [Christ] took from the Virgin Mary human nature incomplete, that is, without mind," and argues that he came to save humanity "in soul and body, in mind and in the whole substance of its nature."[56] But specific names do not appear to have been mentioned.

It appears that Apolinarius may have sent his disciple Timothy, bishop of Beirut, to represent him at this Roman synod. He

52. Lietzmann, *History*, vol. 4, 31.
53. See J.131.
54. Basil, *ep.* 263; see Lietzmann, 26, and idem, *History*, vol. 4, 29. Basil's complaints against Apolinarius's teaching are mostly that he is a Judaizer, that "he has written about the resurrection, from a mythical, or rather Jewish, point of view; urging that we shall return again to the worship of the Law, be circumcised, keep the Sabbath, abstain from meats, offer sacrifices to God, worship in the Temple at Jerusalem, and be altogether turned from Christians into Jews" (Eng. trans. in NPNF 7; see http://www.newadvent.org/fathers/3202263.htm). Similar ideas are attributed to Apolinarius by Gregory Nazianzen (*epp.* 101, PG 37:189D–191A, and 102, PG 37:197C) and by Jerome in his commentary on Daniel (reproduced in Lietzmann, 266–67).
Basil adds some rather vague complaints about Apolinarius's Christology as a sort of afterthought: "Then, further, he has made such confusion among the brethren about the incarnation, that few of his readers preserve the old mark of true religion; but the more part, in their eagerness for novelty, have been diverted into investigations and quarrelsome discussions of his unprofitable treatises."
55. Lietzmann, *History*, vol. 4, 30.
56. Damasus, *ep.* 2, frag. 2, translated in Stevenson, *Creeds*, 94–95.

was rejected, on the basis that he recognized only Vitalis as the lawful bishop in Antioch, and because he accused Basil, Peter of Alexandria, Paulinus, Epiphanius of Salamis, and Diodore of Tyre (now the bishop of the Alexandrian exiles in Diocaesarea and a protégé of Paulinus)[57] of heresy. Subsequently, both he and Apolinarius himself (*in absentia*) were formally anathematized, perhaps first by Peter of Alexandria (who, as noted above, was now in Rome and whose advice Pope Damasus seems largely to have followed at this time) and then by Damasus himself.

But, from Basil's perspective, the overall outcome, in terms of achieving union among the Eastern anti-Arians, was unsatisfactory; Rome refused to abandon Paulinus at Antioch, to condemn the Marcellans at Ancyra (because of their links, referred to above, with the Diocaesarean exiles and therefore with Rome's ally Peter of Alexandria, who, as noted above, had been their leader), or to condemn Eustathius. Indeed, Meletius, who, although currently in exile again,[58] was of course supported by Basil in the Antiochene context, was condemned for having been illegally translated to Antioch from Sebaste in 360, and was ordered to return to that Armenian city in a subordinate position to Eustathius,[59] who was now again bishop there.[60]

The tide begins to turn in the East, 378–381

All this happened at the end of 377 or the beginning of 378.[61] Basil died, his great project unfulfilled, perhaps in January 379.[62] But momentous changes in the Christian world were now under

57. See Mühlenberg, 55.

58. See n. 33 above.

59. Eustathius had disliked Meletius since the time, many years before (before Meletius had been called to Antioch), when he had supplanted him (Eustathius) as bishop of Sebaste. See Lietzmann, *History,* vol. 4, 22.

60. For this paragraph and the previous one, see Lietzmann, 26–28; Lietzmann, *History,* vol. 4, 29–31; Mühlenberg, 56.

61. Mühlenberg, 46, 56; Lietzmann, 29.

62. The traditional date, but for the (disputed) chronology of this period (the return of the exiled bishops, the death of Basil, and the synod at Antioch nine months later), see Gregory of Nyssa, *The Letters,* with introduction, translation, and commentary by Anna M. Silvas, Supplements to Vigiliae Christianae 83 (Leiden: Brill, 2007), 32–39 (available at http://ixoyc.net/data/Fathers/102.pdf). Silvas argues that Basil died in late September 378.

way. Arianism was about to be finally outlawed within the empire; Apollinarianism too was to be formally condemned in the East, as it already had been in the West, but in what seems to have been a more half-hearted way and with less conclusive effect.

The Arianizing Eastern emperor Valens died fighting the Goths in August 378. It appears that he had granted some kind of concession to the anti-Arians earlier in that year and that the exiled bishops, including Gregory of Nyssa, began to return to their sees.[63] In January 379 Valens's nephew and successor Gratian appointed the Spanish general Theodosius, who supported Nicaea, to be Augustus, that is, his coadjutor, in the East.[64] Before doing so, Gratian had issued a decree of toleration to all except Manichaeans and followers of Photinus (that is, "Sabellians"—Photinus was a follower of Marcellus of Ancyra) and of Eunomius (Arians); Apollinarianism was not mentioned. Meletius, back from exile, was recognized as legitimate bishop of Antioch by the imperial commissioner Sapor and won over the majority of Paulinus's followers. Both Paulinus and Vitalis, however, persisted in their claims, on the basis that they had been recognized by Pope Damasus,[65] and we know that there was an Apollinarian synod in Antioch in 379.[66] Vitalis seems indeed to have remained a dissident bishop in Antioch until at least 388.[67]

Meletius, too, called a synod, which was attended by 153 bishops, including, it appears, Gregory of Nyssa.[68] It asserted its sub-

---

63. See Lietzmann, *History*, vol. 4, 33, and Silvas, 39.

64. Gratian was assassinated in 383 and was succeeded in the West by his half-brother Valentinian II.

65. Lietzmann, 29. For Vitalis's recognition by Damasus, see above. According to Theodoret (*Historia ecclesiastica* 5.3.9–16, translated in Stevenson, *Creeds*, 103–4), Sapor's decision to endorse Meletius followed a debate held in his presence and chaired by the Antiochene presbyter Flavian (who later became bishop of Antioch himself; see n. 72 below), in which Apolinarius himself, Meletius, and Paulinus participated. All three claimed communion with Damasus. But Paulinus denied that there were three divine ὑποστάσεις, thus revealing his "Sabellianism," and Apolinarius did not deny that he "deprived our intelligence of its salvation" by refusing to accept that Christ had assumed our nature "in its perfection."

66. Lietzmann, 28; idem, *History*, vol. 4, 36; Mühlenberg, 46, 56.

67. Mühlenberg, 59.

68. For this synod, see Lietzmann, 28 and 53–56. In *de vita Sanctae Macrinae*,

scription to the Nicene faith as held and promulgated by Pope Damasus, and the Western condemnation of those who taught that Christ assumed an incomplete humanity was endorsed, although neither Apolinarius nor anyone else was specifically condemned by name.

It was clear, however, that still firmer and more decisive action was necessary to overcome the continuing divisions in the Eastern church. Probably in February 380, Theodosius accordingly issued an edict to the effect that all his subjects should adhere to the faith—specifically, the Trinitarian formula—confessed by Pope Damasus and Peter, bishop of Alexandria. [69] But now again Apollinarianism was not specifically mentioned.

In November 380, Theodosius entered Constantinople for the first time. The Arian bishop Demophilus refused to subscribe to his edict and left; Meletius, now the most influential churchman in the East, came to the capital and became the emperor's mentor and guide. Yet another new law was promulgated, in January 381, providing that all dioceses should be handed over to orthodox bishops (orthodoxy being again defined in purely Trinitarian terms, with no mention of Christology) and that heretics could no longer conduct public worship. Theodosius also decided to convene a council of the Church from throughout the whole empire, with a view to a final settlement.[70]

The Council of Constantinople, 381

The council met in Constantinople in the summer of 381. It was initially under the chairmanship of Meletius, but he suddenly and unexpectedly died. The chair was then taken—after he

---

GNO 8.1, 386, and PG 46:974C, Gregory says he visited his dying sister St. Macrina nine months after his brother Basil's death, on his way home from "a synod of bishops ... gathered at Antioch, in which we also took part." Otherwise the main source for this synod comes from a collection of synodical acts in the *Codex Veronensis LX;* the text is reproduced in Eduard Schwartz, "Über die Sammlung des Cod. Veronensis LX," *Zeitschrift für die Neutestamentliche Wissenschaft* (1936), 19–32. Pelagius of Laodicea (see nn. 9 and 13 above), but not Gregory, is one of the seven bishops specifically mentioned in this document as having been present at the synod.

69. Lietzmann, *History,* vol. 4, 37.

70. Lietzmann, *History,* vol. 4, 41–43.

had been unwillingly elected to succeed Demophilus as bishop of Constantinople—by Gregory of Nazianzus, who had been in the capital since the previous year, trying to build up the Nicene presence in that still Arian-inclining city.[71] Nazianzen faced opposition from both East and West; eventually he abandoned the council and "retired hurt"[72] to his home town of Nazianzus in Cappadocia, where, as we shall see, he was forced to get actively involved in the Apollinarian controversy.

Meanwhile the council continued with Nectarius,[73] Gregory's successor as bishop of Constantinople, in the chair. The acts of the council have not survived, but it seems certain that Apolinarius was not condemned by name. The surviving canon 1 includes the Apollinarians in a list of heresies that are anathematized, but it is possible that this is a later addition. Moreover, it appears that Timothy of Beirut, in all probability the disciple of Apolinarius, was one of the signatories of the council protocol, which shows that any Christological pronouncement made by

71. See Lietzmann, *History,* vol. 4, 38–43. Maximus, a protégé of Peter of Alexandria (who was still hostile to Meletius and his party), had actually been consecrated to succeed Demophilus, but the council declared his consecration to have been void.

72. For the details, see Lietzmann, *History,* vol. 4, 43–45. The emperor had initially been careful not to invite to the council bishops who had been hostile to Meletius, including those from Egypt. As a gesture of reconciliation towards the West (and Egypt), Nazianzen first tried to get the council to nominate the now aged Paulinus to succeed Meletius at Antioch, but this proposal was overwhelmingly opposed by the council fathers, all Easterners loyal to Meletius's memory and still bitter about Rome's attitude to the problems at Antioch and elsewhere during the previous decade. Gregory fell ill; the emperor, concerned about a deepening East/West split, arranged for bishops who were in a position to act as proxies for Damasus of Rome—Timothy, Peter's successor as bishop of Alexandria, and bishops from Macedonia—to join the council. In line, it appears, with Damasus's wishes, they in turn now turned against Gregory and accused him of having been uncanonically elected to Constantinople, being already bishop of Sasima in Cappadocia and therefore forbidden under the canons approved at Nicaea in 325 from translation to another see. Gregory immediately retired from the scene and was replaced by a certain Nectarius, a jurist from Cilicia who may not even have been baptized prior to his selection as bishop. A presbyter of Antioch called Flavian was appointed to succeed Meletius as bishop of that city.

73. See previous note.

the council must have been expressed in terms that he and his master were able to accept.[74] It may be, as Lietzmann suggests, that the message to the Apollinarians was that, provided they made no political trouble and did not set up their own bishops, a blind eye would be turned to their doctrinal peculiarities.

Gregory Nazianzen's struggle with Apollinarianism, 382–387

As we have seen, after the traumas of his experiences at Constantinople in 381, Gregory retired, in poor health, to Nazianzus. Officially Nazianzus had no bishop, but Gregory took up the leadership of the community. He soon, however, left the town for the Cappadocian health spa of Xanxaris, and left a priest called Cledonius in charge.

By the autumn of 382, it seems that Apollinarians were preparing to take over Nazianzus—they may have held some sort of synod[75]—and were challenging his own orthodoxy. Cledonius asked Gregory for some material to counter this. In response, Gregory sent him a long letter (number 101). Much of the account that he gives of Apolinarius's Christological teachings shows a close affinity with that which we shall find in the *Apodeixis,* although he does not mention having consulted any written work by Apolinarius, and some of the Apollinarian doctrines he mentions, in particular those relating to the coming restoration of the Temple and the Millennium,[76] do not appear to have been featured in the *Apodeixis.* Similarly, some of the arguments that he employs against Apollinarianism resemble those that Gregory of Nyssa uses in *antirrh,* although there are few if any direct verbal parallels. They include the celebrated formula to explain why Christ must have assumed a human mind as well as a human body and animal soul, "That which he has not assumed, he has not healed."[77]

74. Lietzmann, 30–31; Mühlenberg, 57.

75. As Lietzmann (35) suggests, on the basis of τῷ νῦν συνεδρίῳ τῆς ματαιότητος ("by their present council of vanity") in the first letter to Cledonius (PG 37:192C); but the fact that "council of vanity" is a quotation from Ps 25 (26).4 makes this perhaps less likely.

76. Also mentioned by Basil and Jerome; see n. 54 above.

77. PG 37:181C.

It appears, however, that Cledonius found this tract too long and learned for his purposes and asked for something snappier, to include an explanation of why Gregory had at one time recognized Vitalis of Antioch as orthodox. Gregory responded with *Letter* 102. On the doctrinal issue, all he could come up with was a reference to the Trinitarian formula of Nicaea and an insistence that the slur of the Apollinarians, that he believed in two Sons rather than one, was unfounded. (As already noted, this was a common Apollinarian charge, and it is one against which, as we shall see, Gregory of Nyssa later defended himself at length in both *antirrh* and *Theo.*) He admitted that he had at one time recognized Vitalis as orthodox,[78] on the basis of the statement of faith that the latter had presented to Pope Damasus (in 376; see above), but pointed out that, although Damasus had originally accepted that statement, on being better informed he had in fact subsequently changed his mind and anathematized Vitalis.[79]

In any event, in the autumn of 383, the Apollinarians took advantage of the *de jure* and *de facto* vacancy at Nazianzus to appoint a bishop of their own. Gregory, still away in Xanxaris, appealed to Olympius, the *praeses* of Cappadocia,[80] apparently without effect. He was forced to return to Nazianzus; his illness precluded him from being bishop himself, but he was eventually able to get an orthodox successor, Eulalius, appointed, although we do not know how successful he was in combating the Apollinarians. In 387 the aging Nazianzen (he died in 389 or 390) wrote to Nectarius, bishop of Constantinople,[81] protesting vigorously about the continuing success of the Apollinarians, and it may have been this which prompted Theodosius to issue his decree against them—the most forceful yet—in 388 (see next sub-section).[82] In this letter, unlike those to Cledonius

78. According to a footnote to the NPNF (vol. 7) translation of *ep.* 102, Vitalis visited Nazianzus on his return from Rome, "where Gregory greeted him as a brother in the faith." The source of this information is not stated. See n. 4723 at http://www.ccel.org/ccel/schaff/npnf207.iv.ii.iv.html.

79. Lietzmann, 33; Mühlenberg, 57–58.

80. *Ep.* 125, PG 37:218C–220B.

81. *Ep.* 202, PG 37:329B–333C.

82. Lietzmann, 33–35; Mühlenberg, 58.

in 383, he refers to a written source, "a pamphlet" (or "book," as opposed to a scroll)[83] "of Apolinarius [which] has come into my hands"; from the summary that he gives of its contents, this could well have been the *Apodeixis*.[84]

Further moves against Apollinarianism in the East after 381

On the broader front, the West was not satisfied that Apollinarianism had been properly dealt with at the Council of Constantinople in 381. Following a meeting of the Italian bishops in 382, St. Ambrose of Milan wrote to Theodosius on their behalf, to the effect that there was still unfinished business, that Apolinarius's doctrines should be explicitly condemned, and that he should be deprived of his bishopric (which he clearly still held, presumably at Laodicea).[85] In response, Theodosius moved the Easterners to hold a further synod in Constantinople later that year. But on this occasion again they refused to grasp the nettle. Apolinarius and his doctrines were not specifically condemned; the bishops merely stated that they held that "the dispensation of the flesh is neither soulless nor mindless nor imperfect" and that they knew "full well that God's Word was perfect before the ages, and became perfect man in the last days for our

83. πτυκτιόν; see G .W. H. Lampe, *A Patristic Greek Lexicon* (Oxford: Clarendon Press, 2004), *s.v.*

84. As Raven (213–14) notes. The pamphlet is said to assert that "the Flesh which the Only-begotten Son assumed in the Incarnation for the remodeling of our nature was no new acquisition, but that that carnal nature was in the Son from the beginning"; that "even before He came down He was the Son of Man, and when He came down He brought with Him that Flesh, which it appears He had in Heaven, as though it had existed before the ages, and been joined with His Essence"; and that "that Man who came down from above is without a mind, but that the Godhead of the Only-begotten fulfils the function of mind, and is the third part of this human composite, inasmuch as soul and body are in it on its human side, but not mind, the place of which is taken by God the Word" (trans. in NPNF 7; see http://www.newadvent.org/fathers/3103a.htm). These are all themes found in *antirrh.*

85. Ambrose, *ep.* 14: Eng. trans. in *The Letters of S. Ambrose, Bishop of Milan, translated with notes and indices,* Library of the Fathers (Oxford: John Henry Parker, 1881). See http://www.tertullian.org/fathers/ambrose_letters_02_let ters11_20.htm#Letter14.

salvation."[86] This went little further than Athanasius's *tomus ad Antiochenos* of 362, and could easily have been subscribed to by Apolinarius and his disciples.[87]

Traces of this strange unwillingness on the part of the orthodox and the imperial government in the East to tackle Apollinarianism head-on seem to have persisted for some years, despite the fact that the heresy seems to have taken firm root; Sozomen states that "the eastern regions … from Cilicia to Phoenicia, were endangered by the heresy of Apolinarius," and Apolinarius "found it easy to attract to [his] party the persons among whom he dwelt."[88] It appears that it may also have spread to northern Asia Minor[89] and that there were Apollinarians in Palestine in about 400[90] and possibly in Egypt in 401–2.[91] It may be that, at any rate in the 380s, the Apollinarians had protectors at the imperial court.[92]

In any case, for whatever reason, although the imperial decree against heresies of July 383[93] outlawed the eucharists of (among others) the Eunomians, the Macedonians (that is, the "Pneumatomachoi," those who did not accept the divinity of the Spirit), and the Arians, the Apollinarians were yet again not mentioned. This was corrected, however, in September,[94] when Apollinarians were included in the list of heretics who were forbidden, throughout the imperial domains, to hold eucharists or ordain clergy. There is an appendix to this decree that seems to suggest that there were "wandering preachers" of these heresies, who should be sent back to their homes. In January 384[95]

86. Theodoret, *Historia ecclesiastica* 5.9. Eng. trans. in NPNF 3; see http://www.ccel.org/ccel/schaff/npnf203.iv.viii.v.ix.html.

87. Mühlenberg, 57.

88. Sozomen 6.27: Eng. trans. in NPNF 3; see http://www.newadvent.org/fathers/26026.htm.

89. Lietzmann, 35.   90. Lietzmann, 36–37.

91. Lietzmann, 37.

92. Lietzmann, 35; see also n. 95 below.

93. *Cod Theod* 16.5.11; see http://ancientrome.ru/ius/library/codex/theod/liber16.htm#5.

94. *Cod Theod* 16.5.12 (see ibid.).

95. *Cod Theod* 16.5.13 (see ibid.); addressed to the *praefectus praetorio per Orientem* but not to the *praefectus urbi* at Constantinople, which Lietzmann (32)

priests and teachers of the specified heresies, including Apollinarianism, were banned from Constantinople.

So, by 385 (the earliest possible date for the composition of *Theo*), Apollinarianism was down, but certainly not yet out. That seems to be the best way of characterizing the overall historical context within which Gregory of Nyssa's anti-Apollinarian works were written. It was not until 388 that there was any further imperial action,[96] when (perhaps in response to the representations of Nazianzen; see above) the fiercest decree yet was enacted against "Apollinarians and those who follow the various other heresies"; they were to be expelled, their eucharists and ordinations were forbidden, their bishops were to be deposed, and they were to be denied access to the imperial presence.[97] But even then, though Apollinarianism was at last clearly, definitively, and officially outlawed in both East and West, there is evidence for its survival into the fifth century—only in 425 were the Apollinarians at Antioch officially reconciled under Bishop Theodotus—and it seems certain that it provided fertile soil for the nurture of the monophysitism which was to trouble the church in that century.[98]

The composition of the Apodeixis

Where the composition of the *Apodeixis* fits into the chronology outlined above, and what the circumstances are in which it came to be written, cannot be ascertained. It seems reasonable to assume that it represents the most mature form of Apolinarius's Christological doctrine,[99] so a date not too long before Gregory's response (which was certainly in the 380s; see below), perhaps the late 370s or early 380s,[100] is plausible. I shall discuss

seems to take as evidence for the influence of supporters of Apollinarianism in the imperial court.

96. *Cod Theod* 16.5.14 (see ibid.).

97. See Lietzmann, 32, 35.

98. Lietzmann, 37–40; Mühlenberg, 58.

99. See above, pp. 3–4, 7–11, for a discussion of the question of the extent to which Apolinarius's Christology may have developed over the span of his career.

100. Thus Carter, 415–16.

later what precisely can be gleaned from Gregory's evidence about the likely form and content of the *Apodeixis* and about the particular doctrinal opponents against whom it was aimed, which has been the subject of much scholarly discussion.

2. Gregory of Nyssa and Apollinarianism

To understand the background to Gregory's two explicitly anti-Apollinarian writings, and, specifically, to try to ascertain when they were written, and in what order, it is necessary to consider what can be said, on the basis of the very limited information now available to us, about the history of Gregory's previous exposure to Apolinarius, his thought and the controversies that it inspired. This will involve looking at some details of Gregory's personal history, although this is not the place for a detailed biography of Gregory or for an attempt to disentangle the difficult and contested issue of the chronology of his literary œuvre as a whole.[101]

To anticipate the outcome of this inquiry, it should be said at the outset that there is very little that can be said with any confidence about how and when Gregory first encountered Apolinarius's characteristic Christological ideas. But we need first to note Johannes Zachhuber's suggestion that, in two of Gregory's works that almost certainly pre-date both *antirrh* and *Theo*, clear evidence can be found of the influence of Apolinarius's thought not on his Christology but on his anthropology. Zachhuber argues that Gregory's homily *On the Lord's Prayer* (*de oratione dominica*) reflects Apolinarius's theory that partaking in human nature is equivalent to being a descendant of Adam.[102] He

101. For a good recent summary, see Silvas, 1–54. (See entries in the Abbreviations list, under the name "Silvas," and in the Select Bibliography, under "Gregory of Nyssa.")

102. Zachhuber, 130–33, 182–83. For Apolinarius's theory, his main evidence is two texts from Apolinarius's commentary on the Psalms preserved in the catena and which he says are numbered as fragments 301 and 227 in E. Mühlenberg, *Psalmenkommentare aus der Katenüberlieferung* (Berlin: Walter de Gruyter, 1975). The date of Gregory's homily *On the Lord's Prayer* (*de oratione dominica*) cannot be conclusively ascertained, but it may come from around the period of the Council of Constantinople in 381: see Ekaterina Kiria, "*or*

also suggests an "almost inevitable" conclusion can be drawn from Gregory's *de hominis opificio* that he was acquainted with Apolinarius's "traducianist" theory that the soul was transmitted to individual human beings through the process of sexual reproduction.[103] But even if this suggestion is correct, we cannot of course know whether Gregory had had direct exposure to Apolinarius or his writings before he wrote these works or whether Apolinarius's influence, as identified by Zachhuber, was mediated to Gregory indirectly through conversation with third persons (who may or may not have been identifiable as "Apollinarians") or through reading their books.

The year 371, when Gregory was in his mid-thirties, is perhaps the best time to start with in reviewing his career in search of direct evidence of contacts with Apolinarius or his followers. It was then that, after a career as a teacher of rhetoric, and probably a short marriage (his wife may have died in childbirth),[104] Gregory had been ordained and become bishop of Nyssa, a small town in western Cappadocia. This was the result of an initiative by his elder brother Basil, who, as already described, had become bishop of Caesarea and metropolitan of Cappadocia the previous year, and was anxious to consolidate his own position as leader of the anti-Arian party in the East (to which, as we have seen, Apolinarius was at this time firmly attached).

Gregory seems to have been definitely, though not notably effectively, associated with Basil's efforts on behalf of Nicene orthodoxy. It seems likely that he was one of the two bishops called Gregory who were included in the thirty-two signatories of the appeal for help from the bishops of Italy and Gaul, which Basil and his ally Meletius put together in 372.[105] About

---

dom," in L. Mateo-Seco and G. Maspero, eds., *The Brill Dictionary of Gregory of Nyssa* (Leiden: E. J. Brill, 2010), 550.

103. Zachhuber, 132, 161. For Apolinarius's traducianism he cites a passage from Nemesius of Emesa's *de natura hominis,* reproduced as Lietzmann's fragment 170, and a passage from Apolinarius's *de unione* (Lietzmann, 191, lines 4–7). For the date of *de hominis opificio,* see below, p. 30.

104. For a discussion of the evidence for Gregory's marriage, see Silvas, 15–25.

105. Basil's *ep.* 92. See Silvas, 30 and 79, and, for the background, Lietzmann, *History,* vol. 4, 24–25.

the same time, he seems to have annoyed Basil (who did not think much of his brother's political or administrative abilities) by taking an initiative of his own to make contact with the "Old Nicenes" associated with Marcellus of Ancyra.[106] In 375 Basil briefly entertained the prospect of sending him as an envoy to Pope Damasus on behalf of the Eastern anti-Arians, but decided that, because his "character is foreign to servile flattery," he was not the right man to negotiate with such a "lofty and elevated personage" as the bishop of Rome.[107]

In the winter of 375/76 Gregory was sent into exile—ostensibly because of a conviction for financial mismanagement in his diocese, but probably really because the pro-Arian government of the emperor Valens wanted to intimidate Basil's party. It is not known where he spent his exile.[108] Following Valens's change of heart towards the anti-Arians and then Gratian's edict of toleration,[109] he seems to have returned from exile in the summer or early autumn of 378.[110] He was in Caesarea for Basil's death and funeral in January 379 (or in autumn 378).[111] His treatises *de hominis opificio* and *in Hexaemeron,* continuing and completing themes initiated by Basil, were probably written soon after the latter's death.[112]

In May-June 379 Gregory attended the synod that Meletius convoked in Antioch, at which Apollinarian teachings were condemned. This is the first occasion for which there is any circumstantial evidence that Gregory might have been personally exposed to those teachings, although it is difficult to believe that he would not have been aware of the consecration of Vitalis as an Apollinarian bishop in Antioch earlier in the 370s and of his and Apolinarius's subsequent condemnation by Rome.[113]

Even though Gregory may at this stage have been recognized by his fellow Nicene bishops as in some sense taking over Basil's role as the defender of orthodoxy, there is no evidence that he

106. Basil's *ep.* 100. See Silvas, 30 and 80.
107. Basil's *ep.* 215. See Silvas, 30 and 81–82; also Lietzmann, 19–20.
108. See Silvas, 31–32.
109. See "The tide begins to turn in the East, 378–381," pp. 19–21 above.
110. Silvas, 39.   111. See n. 62 above.
112. Silvas, 40.
113. See "Apolinarius condemned in Rome," pp. 17–19 above.

was involved with any specific anti-Apollinarian activity in the next two years. At the synod at Antioch, it seems he may have been given some sort of remit to reconcile some followers of the "Sabellian" Marcellus of Ancyra,[114] and the "Galatians" who were causing him problems in Nyssa were probably Arianizers.[115] Nor does it appear that Apollinarianism was an issue in his efforts during 380 to ensure orthodox appointments to the episcopate at Ibora in Pontus and Sebasteia in Armenia Minor (successful in the first case, apparently disastrous in the second).[116]

The year 380 seems to have marked the beginning of a period of five years or so during which Gregory devoted much energy to a series of writings on matters of theological controversy. The first volume and perhaps also the second of his great polemic *contra Eunomium*, against Eunomius of Cyzicus and the form of Arianism that he espoused, probably date from 380/381,[117] and his smaller Trinitarian treatises, *Ad Graecos ex communibus notionibus* and *Ad Ablabium, quod non sint tres dii*, are probably from the same period. His main focus was on Trinitarian issues, and on defending himself from the charges, on the one hand, of Sabellianism and, on the other, of tritheism (leveled against him by Eunomius and the Pneumatomachoi respectively).[118]

This period of literary activity was interrupted by, first of all, Gregory's attendance at the great council of Constantinople in 381. He may have preached his sermon "On His Own Ordination" (*in suam ordinationem*) as its inaugural address,[119] and when, as already described, Meletius, its initial chairman, unexpectedly

114. *Ep.* 5.2; see Silvas, 42, 136–37.   115. Silvas, 42.

116. Silvas, 43–44.

117. Silvas, 44–45. Jerome says that at the 381 council Gregory read to him and Gregory Nazianzen from his "books" against Eunomius; see *de viris illustribus* 128, PL 23:713B; http://books.google.co.uk/books?id=oG3ykZEx-lEC&print sec=frontcover&source=gbs_ge_summary_r&cad=0#v=onepage&q&f=false. This may have referred to *Eun I* and *II* (see Zachhuber, 205) as may Gregory's *ep.* 23, reporting that he had worked on his reply to the first part of Eunomius's *Apologia for his Apologia* (i.e., *Eun I* and *II*; see Silvas, 207, n. 440) on his return from Armenia. Silvas later (49) suggests, however, that he may not have completed *Eun II* until 382.

118. Silvas, 46. For the "Pneumatomachoi," see "Further moves against Apollinarianism in the East after 381," pp. 25–27 above.

119. Silvas, 47, following Daniélou.

died, Gregory was chosen to deliver his funeral oration.[120] Apart
from that, we do not know what contribution he made to its de-
liberations. As already noted, it does not in any case appear that
there was much, if any, discussion of Apollinarianism.

We know that Gregory was one of the three bishops communion with whom the council reckoned would be a proof of orthodoxy in the civil diocese of Pontica.[121] It seems that he was
also commissioned by the council to "undertake the correc-
tion of the church in Arabia,"[122] and it was probably not long
after the council ended in July, perhaps during the winter of
381/82,[123] that he set out on a journey in order to do so, combining with it a visit to Jerusalem "because their affairs were in
turmoil and in need of a mediator."[124]

It is clear from *Letter* 3, addressed to three ascetic women
whom he has met in Jerusalem, that Gregory was involved in
some Christological discussions in Jerusalem, but who his opponents were and what constituted the points at issue are difficult to ascertain. We know of disputes among the monks on the
Mount of Olives during the previous decade, probably about
Christological issues,[125] but there is no evidence about what, if
any, part Apolinarius's doctrine played in them.[126]

The positive points that Gregory seems to have been anxious
to establish in the course of his discussions are very reminiscent
of some of his arguments in *antirrh:* (1) that in Christ the divinity is in no way altered or diminished by virtue of its mixture
(ἀνακράσει) with the humanity; (2) that Christ was not a "kind

120. *De Meletio episcopo.*

121. Silvas, 47, and 114, n. 33. The civil diocese of Pontica included the
provinces of Bithynia, Galatia, Paphlagonia, Pontus, Cappadocia, and Armenia (Silvas, 31).

122. *Ep.* 2.12; Silvas, 120.

123. For a discussion of the date of this journey, see Silvas, 48. As reported
by Silvas, "Tillemont and many following him" placed it after the synod of Antioch in 379; Mühlenberg (90) dates it to 380. Zachhuber, 218, n. 73, links it
to the council of 381 but argues that Gregory may not have left on his journey
immediately after the council finished, and that he may have spent Easter 382
in Jerusalem.

124. *Ep.* 2.12.

125. Basil, *ep.* 258, written about 376.

126. *Pace* Grelier, 61, n. 311.

of phantasm cloaking itself in human form, rather than a true Theophany"; (3) that although human nature is not intrinsically evil, our will is "disabled" by sin, and so God willed in Christ to "transform" (μεταστοιχειώσας) our human nature, which nevertheless remained fully human; (4) that after Christ's death the divinity remained united both with his body (in the tomb) and with his soul (in heaven).[127] But, he goes on to ask,

when we cry aloud these things ... what unrighteousness have we committed and why are we hated? And what is the meaning of this competing array of new altars? Do we *announce another Jesus* [2 Cor 11.4]? Do we even hint at another? Do we bring forth other scriptures [cf. Gal 1.6–9]? Have any of us dared to call "man-bearer" the holy Virgin the God-bearer—which is what we hear that some of them recklessly allege? Do we make up myths about three Resurrections? Do we promise the gluttony of the Millennium? Do we assert that Jewish animal sacrifices shall be restored again? Do we lower men's hopes to the Jerusalem below, imagining it rebuilt with stones of a more brilliant material? Is any such charge brought against us that we should be reckoned as something to be shunned, and that in some places another altar should be erected in opposition to us, as if we *profaned their holy things* [Lv 19.8, 22.15; Nm 18.32; and elsewhere]?[128]

The natural reading of this passage is that Gregory is deploring the range of opinions he came across in Jerusalem ("this competing array of new altars") and their heterodoxy ("another Jesus," "other scriptures") and, through a series of rhetorical questions, contrasting them with his own orthodoxy. Characterizing the various heterodox views he reports in terms of teachings we know of from other sources is, however, difficult. Calling the Virgin Mary "man-bearer" (ἀνθρωποτόκον) suggests not Apollinarianism but rather a "divisive" Word-Man Christology, of the kind of which, as already noted, Apolinarius accuses his opponents in the *Apodeixis*. On the other hand, "myths about three Resurrections" and the references to teachings about the Millennium may have echoes of the doctrines attributed to Apolinarius by Basil, Gregory Nazianzen, and Jerome.[129] It is of course possible that other people than Apolinarius and his fol-

127. *Ep.* 3.11–22.
128. *Ep.* 3.23–24; Eng. trans. Silvas, 130–31.
129. See n. 54 above.

lowers may have independently espoused such teachings. Overall, however, it seems more likely than not, on the evidence of
Letter 3, that Gregory was exposed to some specifically Apollinarian doctrines during his visit to Jerusalem in 381/2.[130] But
there is no reason to believe that he had read or studied any of
Apolinarius's doctrinal works at this stage.

In our brief biographical sketch we have now reached the
period in Gregory's life—between 381 and 383—in which some
have sought to date *antirrh*, as will be discussed further in the
next section. It is clear, however, that the controversy with the
Arian Eunomius, which had begun with *contra Eunomium I* and
II in 380/1 (see above), was still very much at the forefront of
Gregory's mind at this time.

The chronology of his remaining anti-Eunomian works is,
however, as usual, uncertain. The short *In illud: Tunc et ipse Filius*
may have been the first to be written, perhaps in 381.[131] *Contra
Eunomium III* may have appeared in 381/2,[132] or possibly in the
first half of 383.[133] Both *In illud* and *Eun III* contain interesting
material on Gregory's own Christology, particularly in the case
of *In illud*, on its soteriological and eschatological elements, often reflecting themes that recur in *antirrh*. The *Refutatio confessionis Eunomii* can be dated reasonably securely to 383, in the

130. Zachhuber, 219–20, suggests that the reference to the Virgin Mary as
"man-bearer" means that Gregory's "opponents cannot have been Apollinarians of any kind," and that the references to putatively Apollinarian teaching
about the Millennium should therefore be interpreted as indicating that "in
Jerusalem Gregory himself was accused of being an Apollinarian" and that
he accordingly "gives a list of Apollinarian doctrines to which he asserts he
does not subscribe." Zachhuber thinks that this accusation may have been
prompted by the "physical" Christological language that Gregory uses in *Eun
III* (dated by Zachhuber, 205, to 381/2, and thus possibly pre-dating Gregory's
visit to Jerusalem); "… one could argue that this kind of terminology would
presuppose a word-flesh Christology which ultimately could not steer clear of
the Apollinarian heresy."

The need, however, for such a hypothesis disappears if one interprets
Gregory's allusions such as the one to a "competing array of new altars" as
implying that he was faced in Jerusalem with a range of different kinds of heterodoxy—some (possibly) Apollinarian in flavor, and others, at the opposite
extreme, reflecting a "divisive" Word-Man Christology.

131. Zachhuber, 205.   132. Ibid.
133. Silvas, 50.

aftermath of the council that Theodosius called in May of that year to sort out the Eunomians and the Pneumatomachoi.[134]

From 384 onwards Gregory's writings seem to become less controversial in tone. The *oratio catechetica*, his major work of apologetic, may date from this period;[135] it also contains much Christological material. His great "mystical" works, the *Vita Moysis* and *In canticum canticorum* reflect different concerns; they are usually considered to be his last surviving writings, before he disappears from history after 394.[136]

3. The Date and Circumstances of the Composition of *antirrh* and *Theo*

Where can Gregory's explicitly anti-Apollinarian writing best be fitted into the tentative chronological framework sketched out in the previous section?

Theo is addressed to Theophilus as bishop of Alexandria, so it must have been written in 385, which is when he was appointed, or later.[137] There is no similar direct evidence for the dating of *antirrh*. As already noted, we do not know when Apolinarius's *Apodeixis*, to which it is a response, first appeared, so that cannot provide a *terminus post quem*.

There are only two passages in the text of *antirrh* itself that might give definite information about when it was written. In one, Gregory expresses the wish that Apolinarius may be "converted from this outrageous doctrine."[138] That must have been written while Apolinarius was still alive. But as we do not know when he died, other than that it cannot have been after 392,[139] that is not much help. The other is Gregory's vague reference to his travels "in many places" and the "serious conversations" about Christological issues he has had in the course of them.[140]

---

134. Silvas, 51; Zachhuber, 205.
135. Zachhuber, 206, suggests 385; Silvas (52), 386–87.
136. Silvas, 54–57.
137. Lietzmann, 75, citing Socrates 5.12.
138. J.162.
139. See "The life of Apolinarius of Laodicea," pp. 5–7 above.
140. J.135.

This has been held to refer to Gregory's travels, probably in 381 or 382 (see previous section), to the churches in Arabia and Jerusalem. But even if it does, there is nothing in the text to indicate whether or not the travels referred to were recent ones.[141]

On the basis of a comparison of the substantive arguments of the two works, there is an obvious argument for putting *antirrh* after *Theo,* and thus for dating *antirrh* to 386 or later, that is, to the last period of Gregory's writing career. *Theo* does not mention Apolinarius by name, but only the "Apollinarians," and does not quote from Apolinarius or any of his followers. It merely gives a brief summary of three doctrines that it attributes to them: that the pre-existent and eternal Word was "fleshly"; that Christ's divine nature was mortal; and that the Apollinarians accused the "orthodox" of teaching "two Christs," that is, the divine Son of God and the human son of Mary.[142] It makes no mention of Apolinarius's central Christological doctrine, as found in the *Apodeixis,* of the "enfleshed mind." This has suggested to some that *Theo* was written at a time when Gregory's knowledge of Apolinarius's teaching was sketchy and incomplete, and that it must therefore pre-date *antirrh.*[143]

This argument has plausibility. As discussed earlier, there is no hard evidence about Gregory's previous detailed exposure to Apollinarianism. In particular, *Letter 3* gives no indication that Gregory had become aware of Apolinarius's "enfleshed mind" Christology from his discussions in Jerusalem. So it is certainly possible that Gregory had no detailed and exact familiarity with Apollinarian Christology until sometime after 385, and that it was only then that he came to embark upon *antirrh.*

But, against that, it is argued that even if he had acquired such familiarity earlier, in the 370s or early 380s, there was no reason for Gregory to have gone into the details of Apolinarius's own teaching in *Theo;* it is an occasional work designed primarily to provide ammunition against a particular schismatic

141. Thus Grelier, 60–61, criticizing J. Daniélou, "Compte-rendu des *Gregorii Nysseni Opera dogmatica minora I,*" *Gnomon* 31 (1959): 614. Perhaps at any rate some of the "serious conversations" took place wherever it was that Gregory spent his exile in 375–76; see p. 30 above.

142. J.120.

143. Thus Lietzmann, 83–84, and Mühlenberg, 90–91.

group formed by Apolinarius's followers. On that basis it would be plausible, other things being equal, to attribute an earlier date to *antirrh* than to *Theo*.[144]

There is, however, another argument for a later date for *antirrh*. This is Gregory of Nazianzus's reference in his letter of 387 to a "pamphlet" of Apolinarius, which may have been the *Apodeixis*.[145] If it was, and it is assumed that it was not long before writing his letter that Nazianzen acquired it, it is arguably unlikely, though not, I think, impossible, that he would have mentioned it in the terms he did if his friend Nyssen had already written a detailed refutation of it. It would seem more likely that Nazianzen got hold of it first (in 387 or shortly before) and then passed it to Nyssen to write a detailed refutation.

On the other hand, there are also some positive arguments for a date for *antirrh* before 385. It has been suggested that there is sufficient similarity between the arguments and images used and the Scripture passages referred to in *Eun III* (particularly books 3 and 4 thereof), *antirrh,* and *Theo,* to indicate that the three works, and particularly the first two, were composed at about the same time. That would explain why *antirrh* several times compares Eunomius and Apolinarius.[146] Moreover, it has been argued on the basis of a comparison of texts referring to the state of Christ's divinity, body, and soul between his death and resurrection that although *antirrh* must have come after *Eun III*, it must have pre-dated the *Refutatio* (written in 383; see above).[147] The controversial tone of *antirrh* in any case certain-

144. See Zachhuber, 205–6.

145. See "Gregory Nazianzen's struggle with Apollinarianism, 382–387," esp. pp. 24–25 and nn. 83–84.

146. See Grelier, 64.

147. Zachhuber, 206, citing J. Lebourlier, "A propos l'état de Christ dans la mort," *RSPhTh* 46 (1963): 161–80 (178–80). (Lebourlier argues on the same basis that the *Refutatio* must in turn have pre-dated *or cat.*) According to Zachhuber, Lebourlier's argument was subsequently accepted by Mühlenberg. Zachhuber suggests 382–83 as a likely date for *antirrh*.

Others, however, have suggested that, on the contrary, Gregory could not have read the *Apodeixis* when he wrote the *Refutatio*. Eunomius had denied the full humanity of Christ and claimed that the Logos united itself only with a body; *Ref* §172, 384–85, PG 45:544D–545A. Gregory challenges this view in §173–81, arguing from the need for the human reason to be saved, but

ly seems to fit more happily in the pre-385 than the post-385 phases of Gregory's career.

So whether *Theo* or *antirrh* should be accorded chronological priority seems to be a question that cannot, for the moment, be conclusively answered. All we can say with any certainty is that both works date from the 380s and that *Theo* must have been written after 385.[148] To me, however, the balance of the argument seems to support an earlier (that is, before *Theo*) rather than a later date for *antirrh*. It is certainly easier to construct a coherent exposition of Gregory's thought if *antirrh* is read first and *Theo* is then interpreted on the basis of the fuller versions of its arguments to be found in *antirrh*. That is the approach I have adopted.

4. The Method of Composition and Structure of *antirrh*

Having set out in the first three sections of this introduction what can be said about the historical context of the composition of *antirrh*, I devote most of the remaining sections to some general remarks about the work itself, on the basis of an analysis of its text. I begin by considering the overall method that Gregory adopted in order to "refute" Apolinarius's *Apodeixis*, and what implications that has for the structure of his work.

Gregory appears generally to work through the *Apodeixis* more or less (see later) in order. He discusses first the title, then some ninety individual extracts on the basis either of a direct quotation or of his own paraphrase or summary. (The extent to which Gregory's report adequately and fairly represents what Apolinarius actually wrote will be considered further in the next section.) His principal method is to quote a passage and to give a global

without mentioning Apolinarius. That would seem highly unlikely if he had already read and responded to the *Apodeixis*. See Mühlenberg, 90, and Grelier, 61–62.

148. See Grelier, 64: "La seule affirmation prudente à laquelle nous nous rangeons est que le *Contre Eunome III*, l'*Antirrheticus*, la *Lettre à Théophile*, la *Réfutation d'Eunome* et le *Discours catéchétique* appartiennent à une même période de rédaction dans la carrière de Grégoire, après le concile de Constantinople."

critique of it, followed by a detailed word-for-word refutation.[149] He often chooses to start by quoting only the first part of the passage and delaying the "unveiling" of the remainder until later.[150]

He often offers explanations to his readers of how his argument is being structured: when he is passing on to a new point,[151] when he is reformulating or summarizing Apolinarius's ideas,[152] when he is quoting his exact words,[153] when he omits or treats in a cursory manner a passage that he thinks (or claims to think) unimportant.[154] As will be seen, however, the reader needs to be cautious about taking these explanations at their face value.

One feature of Gregory's polemical method is that he gives no indication of what the argumentative structure of the *Apodeixis* was (although, as will be seen later, it is possible speculatively to reconstruct it). The way he selects passages for comment and moves from one to another is not made explicit and often seems haphazard. As a result, although it is possible (though seldom straightforward) to divide *antirrh* up into sections (as in the current translation),[155] each of which seems to be dealing with a series of (more or less) consecutive and related passages from the *Apodeixis*, it is impossible to identify any coherent, independent, argumentative structure in *antirrh* as a whole.[156]

149. As Grelier (83) points out. Gregory states explicitly in J.147 that he is applying this method to L.32. Other examples are in J.138–39 (L.16 and L.17); J.142–44 (L.24–25); J.155–57 (L.38); J.162–64 (L.42); J.166–68 (L.48); J.179–83 (L.63); J.185–86 (L.67 and L.68); J.187–89 (L.70); J.191–92 (L.74); J.203–4 (L.84); J.206–7 (L.87); J.227–28 (L.97); J.228–30 (L.98).

150. J.187–89 (L.70); J.190 (L.71); J.191–92 (L.74); J.194–96 (L.76); J.199 (L.80); J.204 (L.84); J.206–7 (L.87); J.213 (L.89); J.217–18 (L.93).

151. J.138, J.142, J.159, J.191, J.192, J.199, J.204, J.205, J.206, J.208, J.217, J.218, J.227.

152. J.135, J.138, J.208–9.

153. J.143, J.47, J.155, J.162, J.168, J.176, J.188, J.193; J.195, J.199.

154. J.174, J.177, J.192, J.193, J.218, J.228, J.230–31, J.231, J.232, J.233.

155. I have made use of, although not always followed, the *Gliederung* of *antirrh* suggested by Mühlenberg (71–72), and the alternative, more detailed version by Grelier (101–9).

156. Grelier (99) ingeniously suggests that Gregory uses the device of "inclusio" as a way of structuring *antirrh* as a whole. An early passage (J.136–39) on Apolinarius's alleged view that God died in Christ's passion (not linked with any specific fragments of the *Apodeixis*) is designed to "balance" the passage towards the end (J.217–33), where a major (although not the only) theme

Gregory's method inevitably leads to repetitions of various kinds.[157] The most significant of these fall into two main categories. The first is the repetition of an *idea*, a "leitmotiv."[158] One such is Gregory's rejection of any possibility of conceiving human nature without its rational element. Grelier counts twelve recurrences of this motif, whether as part of a logical argument or as a definition or as the outcome of scriptural exegesis.[159] The second—at first sight more embarrassing, suggests Grelier[160]—is the repetition of an *argument,* best exemplified by the six repetitions, in three different forms, of the argument that the divinity of Christ cannot have died in the Passion.[161] Though sometimes tedious, these repetitions are arguably a necessary consequence of Gregory's technique of concentrating on individual passages viewed more or less in isolation; he produces all the arguments he can think of to refute them, which inevitably means that the same ideas and arguments will have to be reused, albeit in different contexts.[162]

---

is what happens to the divinity during Christ's death and resurrection. Enclosed within these two passages, what she characterizes as the second main substantive "movement" in *antirrh,* on Apolinarius's trichotomous anthropology as applied to the "man from heaven" (J.140–47), "balances" the penultimate "movement" (J.208–17), which returns to the same theme. (So one might perhaps characterize the structure not as simple "inclusio" but as chiasmus.)

In my view, however, this phenomenon is more likely to have been the outcome of accident than design. In the case of the two inner "movements," there seems to be no reason to believe that Gregory's structure is not based primarily on the order of the arguments presented in the *Apodeixis.* More generally, the degree of formal planning on Gregory's part that the "inclusive" scheme would require does not appear consistent with what other aspects of the work suggest about his method of composition.

157. Extensively analyzed by Grelier (93–98).

158. Grelier, 94.   159. Ibid.

160. Grelier, 95.   161. Grelier, 95–96.

162. But I would not want to go as far as Grelier (98), who defends Gregory's repetitiousness on the basis that his overall polemical strategy is like a "spiral." What she means is that as Gregory moves circuitously, as it were, towards the central core of his thesis—a central core that, she admits, seems always itself to be shifting its position—he deliberately repeats the same arguments, but in different contexts. This again is arguably giving Gregory credit for deliberately planning an effect that is more likely to have arisen as an unintended consequence of the polemical method he has chosen to adopt.

Why did Gregory cast *antirrh* in this form? Ekkehard Mühlenberg suggests that it is a product of his authorial method; he thinks that Gregory may have got a secretary to read the *Apodeixis* aloud to him, and that he interrupted the reading to dictate a response only when he felt himself to be under attack or where Apolinarius's argument seemed to him to be patently absurd.[163] That might explain the cases, referred to above, where Gregory comments piecemeal on the various clauses of a passage that is clearly meant to be read as a single argument; in at least one of these, this approach results in his critique being less effective than it would have been if he had held his fire until he had unveiled the whole passage.[164] On the other hand, on some occasions, as will be seen, Gregory seems, for reasons that are not always clear, to have departed from a strictly linear approach and to have discussed some passages from the *Apodeixis* in other than their original order.[165] That would suggest that Gregory must have had the text physically in front of him at some stage in the compositional process. But, however the work was actually composed, there must be merit in Grelier's suggestion[166] that Gregory's omissions, and failures to explain the argumentative context of the passages he does quote or summarize, may not have been accidental or at any rate unplanned, but that they may rather have reflected a polemical strategy, aimed at obscuring the structure of his opponent's thought.

5. The Adequacy of Gregory's Reporting of the Text and Argumentation of the *Apodeixis*

Gregory's method of composition inevitably raises the question of the extent to which he accurately and fairly quotes from or summarizes the arguments of the *Apodeixis*.

163. See Mühlenberg, 71. Gregory's introduction to *antirrh* (J.131–32), written in an elaborate literary style, must presumably, on this account, have been composed separately.

164. See particularly J.187–88 and my note 346 thereon.

165. See J.138, J.168–74, and J.193–94. It seems clear from J.133 and 134 that Gregory had actually read the whole of the *Apodeixis* before starting work on its refutation; see my commentary *ad loc.*

166. Grelier, 100.

The fragments of the *Apodeixis* that can be recovered, in whatever degree of intactness, from *antirrh* were first brought together by Lietzmann in his collection of all the surviving texts and fragments of Apolinarius's dogmatic writings, which has already been mentioned.[167] Lietzmann attributes his fragments numbered 13 to 107 to the *Apodeixis;* all but 106 and 107 are taken from *antirrh.*[168] He includes not only what he believes are direct quotations, but also what he believes are summaries by Gregory of what Apolinarius wrote, which he prints in a different typeface.

Müller's *GNO* edition of *antirrh* does not acknowledge Lietzmann's work and consequently does not use his system of numbering. He prints what he identifies as quotations from the *Apodeixis* in a more widely spaced type, including some passages that are clearly not verbatim quotations but summaries or paraphrases by Gregory. His view as to what does or does not constitute a quotation, and where a quotation begins or ends, does not always agree with that of Lietzmann.

Subsequent studies by Mühlenberg, Grelier, and Carter[169] have re-examined Lietzmann's and Müller's work and, in particular, focused on the extent to which Gregory's account of what Apolinarius has written can be shown seriously to distort his intentions.[170] Their conclusions will be discussed in the commentary and notes on individual fragments. Suffice it to say here that there are cases where it seems likely that Gregory is paraphrasing Apolinarius's argument, sometimes in a tendentious

167. Lietzmann, *Apollinaris;* see notes 1 and 21 above.

168. Fragments 106 and 107 are derived from other, later sources; Lietzmann's attribution of them to the *Apodeixis* has been challenged (see translation of *antirrh*, nn. 362 and 366). Lietzmann records testimony from a source other than Gregory for only one of the other fragments of the *Apodeixis,* namely, fragment 63.

169. Notes 362 and 366, pp. 188, 191–92 below.

170. Grelier (114) usefully suggests that the fragments of the *Apodeixis* reported in *antirrh* can conveniently be classified in three ways: authentic textual citations; those that have been reworked but are close to the original; and free summaries, which Gregory sometimes introduces as such, and where there is often doubt as to whether he is accurately recording Apolinarius's real views. I have had this classification in mind in later discussions of the status of particular fragments.

way, without admitting that he is doing so. There are also places where what Gregory has left out is in fact essential to a proper understanding of Apolinarius's argument,[171] including some where he seems to have omitted material without revealing that he has done so.

6. Reconstructing the Structure and Argument of the *Apodeixis*

Whatever the defects of Gregory's account of the *Apodeixis,* he has given us enough information about it to make it feasible to attempt a reconstruction of its structure. Such attempts, all different in detail, have been made by Lietzmann,[172] Mühlenberg,[173] and Carter.[174] In my view, there is enough information in *antirrh* to make it possible to suggest with some degree of plausibility what the main sections were into which the *Apodeixis* was divided, and my tentative suggestions in this regard are set out in the appendix to this volume. I do not, however, believe that it is possible to say anything very much about its overall literary or argumentative structure.

I shall nevertheless attempt in this section to set out a summary of the Christological arguments that Apolinarius deployed in the *Apodeixis,* to the extent that they can be reconstructed. I adopt a synthetic approach; that is, I do not set out Apolinarius's arguments in the order that he himself adopted, which, given the structural uncertainties and obscurities discussed above, would be repetitious and confusing. Instead I have tried to pull together the scattered arguments into a coherent and systematic whole. In doing so, I have been conscious of the need to avoid, so far as possible, misrepresenting them by over-simplification, by ignoring uncertainties or ambiguities, or by being too eager to smooth over rough edges.

171. See, for example, the commentary and notes on the passages in J.192 and J.193, pp. 189–94 below.

172. Lietzmann, 139–41.

173. Mühlenberg, 86–90. For a summary of Mühlenberg's reconstruction, see Grelier, 80.

174. Carter, 110–24.

It needs to be emphasized that I am not here attempting to give a complete account of Apolinarius's Christological views. That would require a survey of the whole corpus of his surviving fragments and has been the subject of various modern studies.[175] I shall in general confine myself to the arguments which he seems to have used in the *Apodeixis*.

Introduction: Defending an orthodox Christology against Judaizers and Hellenizers

Apolinarius began his treatise by stating that his aim was to define the Christian view of the "divine enfleshment." He claims that "unbelievers and heretics" are allowing that view to be assimilated to pagan or Jewish ideas.[176] The main point at issue is that because Jews and pagans believe that God is impassible, while Christ was clearly subject to human passibility, they cannot accept that Christ was divine.[177] It is intriguing to note, however, that, according to Gregory, Apolinarius concluded his treatise by "desperately invoking the pagans in support of his own mythology and other stuff of that kind"[178]—that is, presumably, trying to demonstrate that Christian doctrine constitutes the true conclusion of pagan philosophy.

Christ both divine and human

But for Apolinarius, it is clear that Christ, in order to save humanity, must be God as well as man. He argues in detail for his divinity. Christ "is given the title Lord of glory and is called Lord of hosts in prophecy."[179] He was declared holy from his birth,[180] and Scripture attests to his superhuman wisdom.[181] He spoke and acted in the persona of God.[182] He is the grain of wheat that falls to the earth and dies, and produces a miraculously abundant harvest;[183] the death of a mere man could not have

---

175. Notably Raven, 177–232; Norris, 82–122; Mühlenberg, 108–248. There is a useful survey of recent research in Young, 245–53. Most recently, there is Carter (*passim*).

176. L.13, J.135.	177. L.49, J.168.
178. L.105, J.233.	179. L.48, J.166.
180. L.56, J.174.	181. L.57, J.175.
182. L.48, J.166–67; L.58, J.175; L.61, J.177.	
183. L.62, J.177–78.	

achieved that.[184] He is the pre-existent Word,[185] consubstantial with the Father,[186] and is totally one with him.[187] His power is equal to that of the Father, although that power operates in a distinct way; as Apolinarius put it, there is "a distinction in his operation in the flesh."[188]

But he must also be man. "We cannot," says Apolinarius, "be saved even by God unless he is mixed with us. He is mixed upon becoming flesh, that is, man; as the Gospel says, when he became flesh he came to dwell among us. But no one can abolish the sin of human beings unless he becomes a human being without sin, nor can he do away with the sovereignty of death over all human beings unless he dies and rises again as a human being."[189]

A defense of the unity of Christ's person
against those who teach "two Christs"

But the fact that Christ is both God and man cannot be taken to imply that there are two Christs, two persons (πρόσωπα). That, says Apolinarius, is what his opponents are in effect teaching.[190]

They speak of a human being who is like us in every respect but is "taken to himself" by God.[191] In other words, they maintain that Christ, as well as being God, was a complete man—that is, a man who, as well as having a flesh-and-blood body and a vital principle or "soul," which he shared with other living creatures, also had human reason. But, says Apolinarius, "if God, who is complete, had been joined to a complete man, there would have

184. L.94, J.219.
185. L.55, J.174; L.96, J.219.
186. L.37, J.155, 158, 174 (discussion of Zec 13.7).
187. L.100, J.231 (discussion of Jn 10.25–30).
188. L.59, J.176. Apolinarius adds that it is through this operation in the flesh that "he did not give life to all but only to some, those whom he wished" (Jn 5.21), presumably in contradistinction to the Father, "who raises the dead and gives them life." The precise point that he is making here cannot, however, now be identified; on the face of it, it is in any case difficult to reconcile with his apparent monotheletism (attribution of a single will to Christ), expressed a little later (L.63, J.179; see below).
189. L.93, J.217–18.
190. L.67, J.185.
191. L.66, J.184. "Taking to himself" is πρόσληψις; see n. 224 below.

been two of them, the one Son of God by nature and the other by adoption."[192] "If [Christ] is constituted of two complete things"—that is, if he has all the characteristics of God, as the formula of Nicaea requires, as well as being a human being in exactly the same way as we are—then "insofar as he is God he cannot be man, and insofar as he is man he cannot be God."[193]

For Apolinarius, Christ must be a single person. The divine Christ must be the same person as the enfleshed Christ: Christ "became flesh but ... he was not thereby someone other than he had been without a body; he was the same, even though assimilated to our life in the flesh."[194]

Apolinarius cites the celebrated Christological hymn in Philippians 2.5–11 in support of this thesis. St. Paul says that Christ was originally equal with God, but that afterwards he "emptied himself, taking the form of a slave, being born in human likeness." "What can show more clearly than this does," asks Apolinarius, "that complete man and complete God, two different things, are not joined together?"[195] So the divine enfleshment should be seen not as the combination of two separate entities, but rather as an act of the divine Logos, who, by "emptying himself,"[196] took on "the form of a slave," that is, became human, while remaining, as it were, ontically continuous with his eternal and therefore divine state.

In practice, claims Apolinarius, there are only two ways in which his opponents can model or conceptualize the relationship between the human and the divine in Christ. Neither of them gives an adequate account of Christ as a single person. One is by envisaging God as it were welded on to a complete man, to form a sort of monstrous hybrid or chimera. "If we consist of three parts, but he consists of four, he is not a man but a man-God."[197] The other is by giving up any attempt to maintain that

192. L.81, J.199. For the Aristotelian background to Apolinarius's argument here, see the commentary and notes *ad loc.*

193. L.92, J.216.   194. L.67, J.185.

195. L.42, J.162.

196. But Apolinarius's own solution to the Christological dilemma is not a kenotic theory in the modern sense; it does not say that when Christ became man he renounced any of his divine attributes. See n. 222.

197. L.91, J.214.

the man Jesus is in any sense identical with the divine Logos, and making him instead a "God-filled man," ἄνθρωπος ἔνθεος. The effect of this latter model is to make Jesus basically no different from an Old Testament prophet. As such, he would be someone the Jews and the pagan Greeks would be able to accept.[198] But if just "receiving" God—being inspired or filled by him—were sufficient qualification for being called a God oneself, "there would be many Gods, for many people receive God."[199]

Who were those who taught "two Christs"?

The arguments summarized in the previous section reflect what was clearly a major theme of the *Apodeixis:* to defend the unity of Christ's person in opposition to those who, he claimed, taught that there were "two Christs." This seems to have been a constant concern of Apolinarius throughout his career; as has already been noted, it can already be found in his letter to Jovian, which can be firmly dated to 363–64 and thus may have preceded the *Apodeixis* by nearly twenty years.[200] This is a convenient place to consider who precisely were those theologians against whom Apolinarius was arguing in the *Apodeixis.*

It seems likely that they will have included early representatives of that tendency in Christological thought which, in its more developed form, has been characterized as "Antiochene," that is, a Christology based on the concept of the union between the Logos and a *man.* That doctrine was indeed criticized by its opponents for teaching "two Christs"—for being "divisive" or "dualistic"—and in its extreme form it led to the heresy of Nestorianism. It is in contradistinction to the "Alexandrian" preference for speaking of Christ as a union between the Logos and *flesh,* which in its extreme form led to the monophysite heresy. The Apolinarius of the *Apodeixis* seems firmly located in the "Alexandrian" camp; as we have seen, his father hailed from Alexandria.

The evidence from the fragments of the *Apodeixis* seems indeed to bear this out. The "adoptionist" doctrine that Christ

198. L.51, J.169.
199. L.83, J.202.
200. See "The early history of Apollinarianism," p. 11 above.

was a "God-filled man," with a firm conceptual separation of the God and the man, can be seen as a form of "Antiochene," "dualistic," or "divisive" Christology. Apolinarius actually names three theologians who, he claims, have fallen into this error.[201] The first is Paul of Samosata, a third-century bishop of Antioch, whose Christology was condemned at a synod at Antioch in 268. He is generally seen as an "adoptionist," but was regarded by the opponents of Nestorius as the latter's predecessor, and some modern scholars have seen him as an early representative of "Antiochene" "Word-man" Christology.[202] The second is Photinus, bishop of Sirmium, a pupil of Marcellus of Ancyra of whose doctrines little is known.[203] The third is the "Sabellian" Marcellus of Ancyra himself, who had been condemned in the 330s but lived on to about 374; his Christology seems to have been characterized by his opponents as being "adoptionist" in tendency.[204] The *Kata meros pistis* ("Confession of Faith in Parts"), a work of Apolinarius probably dating from the 360s (and therefore almost certainly earlier than the *Apodeixis*) had been written to counter his views.[205]

Another theologian whom the *Apodeixis* may have had in its sights was Diodore of Tarsus. Diodore, who died in about 390, was associated with the "Meletian" party in the divided church of Antioch (discussed in section 1) and therefore with its Cappadocian supporters. Again, we know that Apolinarius had

201. L.15, J.138. As noted in "Apollinarianism at Antioch," in section 1 above, "God-filled man" Christology had been condemned at Athanasius's synod in Alexandria in 361.

202. See J. N. D. Kelly, *Early Christian Doctrines*, 5th ed., rev. (London: A & C Black, 1993), 140; *ODCC, s.v.* "Paul of Samosata." In L.24, J.142, Apolinarius refers to the synodical condemnation of Paul's notion that "the Lord was deified from heaven," i.e., that it was only after being anointed by the Holy Spirit at his baptism that the man Jesus received the title Christ.

203. His followers had been excluded from Gratian's edict of toleration in 378; see "The tide begins to turn in the East, 378–381," p. 20 above.

204. According to Eusebius, *contra Marcellum* 2.4 (PG 24:821A–B, cited in Mühlenberg, 141), because Marcellus's Trinitarian theology taught that the Word was not separate from God, he held that it acted only as an "effective energy" (δραστικὴ ἐνέργεια) in Christ's flesh, so that Christ was no more than a prophet.

205. Grelier, 493–96, following K. M. Spoerl.

earlier written specifically against him, perhaps in the 370s.[206] Although there is much uncertainty about the precise nature of his Christology,[207] it seems likely that "he did teach a 'two natures' Christology with a strongly dualistic basis"[208] and that his theology "had developed along the lines which in many ways foreshadow the ideas, if not the terminology, of the later Antiochenes."[209]

It is also apparent that Gregory felt that his own Christological views were, rightly or wrongly, being associated with that school of thought and that he was personally under attack in the *Apodeixis*. This emerges even more clearly from *Theo*, which is largely devoted to arguments defending "some people in the Catholic church"[210] from the charge of teaching "two Christs."

Why Christ's manhood cannot have been complete, that is, have included a human mind

Apolinarius has a further objection to his opponents' view that the enfleshed Word was a complete man. This is based on the implication that in Christ there was a human mind as well as the divine Logos.

Apolinarius objects to this on soteriological grounds. His anthropology (see next sub-section) assumes that it is the function of our rational minds to check and control the potentially disruptive impulses of our animal souls and our flesh. Our flesh is "in need of direction and is in the grip of passion, with all its mutability and alteration."[211] In our fallen state, however, our minds—and therefore Christ's human mind, if he had one—are not up to the task of providing such direction: "The flesh needed an immutable mind, one that would not fall subject to the flesh because of the weakness of its knowledge, but that would conform it to itself without any compulsion."[212]

But there could not be two genuine, autonomous minds in a single person. If there were, the so-called human mind would

---

206. See Mühlenberg, 215–22, and Grelier, 58–59.
207. See the discussion in Young, 255–60.
208. Young, 258.   209. Young, 260.
210. J.120.   211. L.78, J.197.
212. L.76, J.195.

have to be a sort of automaton, slavishly following the orders of
the divine mind. God would hardly have allowed such a parody
of a real human mind in his Son.[213]

Apolinarius's trichotomous anthropology

Apolinarius's own Christological thesis seeks to address these
problems. It depends upon a particular anthropological theory,
that is, a philosophical account of how human nature is constituted. That theory posits three separate elements in the human
constitution: the physical body, or what he usually calls "flesh";
the lower or animal soul, that is, the vital principle which humans share with other living things; and the mind or rational
faculty, which he also calls "spirit."[214] In support of this theory,
Apolinarius cites a number of scriptural texts in which distinctions seem to be drawn between some or all of the terms "spirit," "soul," and "body" (or "flesh").[215]

In this theory it is the spirit or rational mind that is the cen-
ter of human personality; the lower soul and the flesh can have
no autonomous existence without it. As Apolinarius says, in one
of the few fragments of the *Apodeixis* that we owe to a source
other than Gregory, "The flesh ... is not a complete living organism in itself but is used as a component to form a complete
living organism."[216] It is the function of the spirit or rational
mind, which is "self-determined and unconstrained,"[217] to guide
and direct the lower part of our nature: as Apolinarius says in
the same fragment, "The flesh is moved by something outside
itself and is subordinate to what moves and drives it, whatever
that may be."[218]

---

213. L.87, J.207: "For a living being with free will, to lose it would mean it
became imperfect. He who created a particular nature would hardly render
it imperfect. So the man is not united with God"; that is, a complete human
being cannot have been assumed by the Logos.

214. The use of πνεῦμα to denote the intellectual faculty, otherwise νοῦς,
goes back to Origen if not to St. Paul (1 Thes 5.23). For Apolinarius it seems
clear that, so far as the structures of his anthropology and his Christology are
concerned, the words are in effect synonymous. See Grelier, 437–44, and n.
223 below, on νοῦς ἔνσαρκος.

215. L.88, J.208–9, 211–13.   216. L.107.
217. L.74, J.192.   218. L.107.

Its Christological application:
Christ as "enfleshed mind"

This threefold constitution applied in the case of Jesus Christ. Apolinarius understands the divine enfleshment as the Second Person of the Trinity "coming down from heaven," as in the Nicene formulation, and becoming the spirit, or rational mind, of the man Jesus, while his flesh and his lower soul were just like ours. So, while constituting an anthropological unity, with all three of the necessary constituent parts, he "is God by virtue of the spirit which was enfleshed, and man by virtue of the flesh which was assumed by God."[219] "Spirit" here refers not to the Third Person of the Trinity,[220] but rather to the divine Logos, which, "by virtue of its union" with Christ's flesh,[221] constituted Christ's spirit, or rational mind. "Christ is God in his spirit, in that he has the glory of God, but is a man in his body, in that he wore the inglorious shape of human beings."[222] Christ is thus characterized as an "enfleshed mind," a νοῦς ἔνσαρκος.[223]

This formula addresses the soteriological issue. Our lower

219. L.19, J.140.

220. Grelier (269–74) notes that for Apolinarius the πνεῦμα of Lk 1.35 is not the Holy Spirit, mediating between God and the Virgin, but the divine element which assumes human flesh, that is, that it is synonymous with the pre-existing Logos. She suggests that Apolinarius is reflecting a *Geistchristologie,* identifying Logos and πνεῦμα—a "Pneuma-sarx rather than a Logos-sarx Christology"— of the kind that arose in the second century under Stoic influence.

221. L.20, J.140.

222. L.43, J.164. Cf. *de unione* 6 (Lietzmann, 188): Christ "emptied himself according to the form of a slave, but according to his divine being he remained unemptied, unchanged, and undiminished."

223. L.25, J.143; L.68, J.185; L.89, J.209, 213; L.91, J.214. The terminology here is potentially confusing. As a rule, Apolinarius tends to use νοῦς, the rational mind, in explicitly trichotomous contexts (with ψυχή, the animal soul, and σῶμα, the body), and also where the infallibility of Christ's intellect is at issue (for example in L.74, J.192; L.76, J.195; L.80, J.199). When he is following a dichotomous scheme, he tends to use Paul's πνεῦμα/σάρξ terminology (L.19, J.140; L.41, J.158). In the νοῦς ἔνσαρκος formula (which is dichotomous in form), however, νοῦς is clearly intended to be equivalent to the Pauline πνεῦμα. It is also clear that, despite using the formally dichotomous νοῦς ἔνσαρκος formula, Apolinarius intends the animal soul to be included within σάρξ. See Norris, 88–91; Grelier, 437–44 and 449; and Carter, 151–53.

nature is joined not to a mutable and unstable mind, but to a superhuman mind—the divine Word—which is innately and immutably virtuous, and which, by "assuming"[224] our flesh and animal soul, is alone able to restore them to their original state.[225] It then appears (although the text of the relevant fragment is disputed) that Christ's "pure virtue" is then "communicated" (by a mechanism that Apolinarius does not elucidate) "to every subordinate mind ... and to all those who are made like Christ as regards the mind and not made unlike him as regards the flesh."[226]

As well as the soteriological issue, the "enfleshed mind" formula addresses the ontological problem—how Christ can, on the one hand, truly be said to be a unitary human person while, on the other hand, he maintains his absolute identity with the pre-existent Logos, so can truly be said to be divine. He is a man, says Apolinarius, because he is constituted in the same threefold way as other human beings. He is "one thing, composed, like each of us, of spirit, soul, and body.... he is one just as a human being is one, from spirit and soul and body."[227] But at the same time the unchangeable Logos constitutes "the most important element in the nature of the God-Man,"[228] and thus is itself the vehicle for the necessary ontic continuity between Christ's states before and after his enfleshment.

But does Apolinarius's Christological formula safeguard this

224. Apolinarius's preferred term for this "assumption" is πρόσληψις, "taking to itself," rather than ἀνάληψις, "taking up." See J.193 in the translation and n. 373 thereon.

225. L.74, J.192: "If, together with God, who is mind, there was also a human mind in Christ, the enfleshment does not do its work in that mind. But if the work of the enfleshment is not done in that mind, which is self-determined and unconstrained, then it is done in the flesh, which is externally determined and activated by the divine mind. That work is the abolition of sin. Our self-determined mind participates in that abolition to the extent to which it conforms itself to Christ."

226. L.80, J.199. See the note *ad loc.* on the textual issue. It appears that Apolinarius's soteriology posits the concept of a universal human nature by means of which salvation is communicated from Christ's humanity to the rest of us; as will be seen, Gregory's soteriology uses a similar notion.

227. L.68, J.185.

228. L.32, J.147. For the use of "nature" here for the later "person," see "The early history of Apollinarianism," p. 11 and n. 27 above.

ontic continuity only at the cost of denying Christ his full humanity? He can claim that it ensures that Christ is at any rate "in the likeness of a man" (as in Philippians 2.7). But he goes on to say that he appeared "as a man, while actually being an enfleshed mind."[229] Christ came into the world "as a man, but not a man, because not one in being [consubstantial] with the man's most important element"[230]—that is, with his rational mind. It seems that he regards the "man from heaven" as a man only in a unique and arguably highly artificial sense, and, as will be seen, this is something which Gregory picks him up on.

Apolinarius implies that his "enfleshed mind" formula is nevertheless the only alternative to that of the "God-filled man," which he attributes to his opponents. He claims that if the mind of Jesus were not the Logos enfleshed, it would merely be a human mind inspired by God's wisdom, which would make Jesus merely a "God-filled man." He would not be the unique Savior of which the Gospel speaks. "If he was not an enfleshed mind ... [but] wisdom in the mind, the Lord did not descend to us, nor did he empty himself."[231]

Apolinarius claims that it is as an "enfleshed mind" that Christ can be referred to as the "man from heaven" (1 Corinthians 15.47)[232] or "the one who descended from heaven" (John 3.13).[233] It was not, as Paul of Samosata taught, that God "came down from heaven" to divinize the man Jesus; what "came down from heaven" was rather Christ himself, or at any rate his "spirit," his rational mind, the part of him that constituted his fundamental identity.[234]

Apolinarius illustrates his view that Christ's spirit or rational mind is identical with the eternal Logos by comparing the first Adam with the second Adam, Christ. In 1 Corinthians 15.45 the former is called a "living soul," the latter a "life-giving spirit." The first Adam's body was created from dust, before the "living soul" (which of course, as Apolinarius makes clear, included a

---

229. L.69, J.186.
230. L.45, J.165; see the note *ad loc.* on the authenticity or otherwise of this fragment.
231. L.70, J.188.   232. L.25, J.143.
233. L.16–17, J.138.   234. L.25, J.142–43.

rational as well as an animal element) was breathed into him. So he can appropriately be called "a man of earth." Christ, on the other hand, the second Adam, is called a "life-giving spirit" rather than "a living soul" because "the heavenly spirit" was enfleshed in him and he had no human mind of his own.[235] In other words, Adam is "a man of earth" because he had an "earthy" body; Christ is "a man from heaven" because his mind was "heavenly."[236] He suffered and experienced passions,[237] but not, as we do, "under the necessary constraints of an unwilling nature ... but as a consequence of [his] nature"; in other words, as God chose to adopt a human body, his human passions were merely a consequence of that choice, rather than, as in our case, inevitable.[238]

Did Apolinarius say in the *Apodeixis* that the union between the divine and the human was so close that it was legitimate to say that in Christ God himself died? Gregory certainly claimed he said so. The question cannot conclusively be determined,[239] but it seems fair to say that Gregory and the other critics of Apolinarius were not too wide of the mark in identifying this as an irresolvable dilemma to which his teaching could be taken logically to lead.

Christ's will

As noted above, Apolinarius denied that there could be two genuine, autonomous minds in a single person.[240] It would appear to follow that Apolinarius believed that there was only one will in Christ. In the context of a discussion of Christ's prayer in Gethsemane (Matthew 26.39 and Luke 22.42, as conflated by Gregory), "If it is possible, let this cup pass from me; yet may your will be done, not mine," Gregory quotes him as saying that "they"—his opponents presumably—"do not mention that this will that is spoken of belongs not to the man from the earth, as

235. L.28–29, J.146.
236. τὸ οὐράνιον ἡγεμονικὸν, L.107 (not quoted by Gregory, and possibly not from the *Apodeixis;* see n. 168 above).
237. L.101, J.231.
238. L.102, J.231.
239. See L.95, J.219, and the note thereon.
240. L.87, J. 207.

they think, but to the God who descended from heaven … [and that it] was taken into unity with him."[241] We have no details of Apolinarius's exegesis of this passage, but this fragment is quoted by later writers in the context of the seventh-century monothelete controversy.[242]

Christ's flesh

It seems that Apolinarius believed that this unique union between God and human in Christ was so close that it is permissible to worship not only the divine element in Christ but also his humanity. Gregory reports him as saying, "The flesh of the Lord is to be worshiped in that it forms, with him, one single person and one single living being."[243]

This notion, that the man Jesus was indivisibly united with or indeed totally identical with the Logos, the second Person of the Trinity, is one that Apolinarius seems to have developed even further. The man Jesus, whom he calls "the man from heaven," can also be said, in some sense, to have existed from eternity. Thus he says that "the man Christ pre-existed, not with the Spirit, that is, God, existing separately from him."[244] Such a statement is clearly open to misinterpretation—Grelier calls it "extrêmement ambiguë, et, pourrait-on dire, maladroite"[245]—unless it is clearly understood that "the man Christ" is to be interpreted as the man's "spirit," his rational mind, the most important part of his nature, and that it was that which pre-existed, by virtue of being identical with the Logos.

Gregory, however, represents Apolinarius as having gone even further than that, and as having applied this concept to the two other parts of Christ's nature, his flesh and his animal soul. In other words, he accuses Apolinarius of believing that Christ's flesh was in some sense co-eternal with his divinity and had its origin in heaven rather than in the womb of Mary. He devotes much space in *antirrh* to ridiculing this view.

Gregory clearly attributes to Apolinarius the view that "the divine enfleshment did not take its origin from the Virgin but

241. L.62–63, J.179, 180, 182.
243. L.85, J.204–5.
245. Grelier, 430.

242. See note *ad loc.*
244. L.32, J.147.

existed before Abraham and all creation,"[246] that "the flesh was not acquired by the divinity ... but shared its very being and nature."[247] He claims that Apolinarius

says that the Son was an "enfleshed mind" that was born of a woman but did not become flesh in the Virgin's womb, instead passing through her, so that what was now manifested was a fleshly God (or, as he says, an "enfleshed mind"), which is what he had been since before all ages.[248]

Later he says:

Since Apolinarius wants the flesh that was born itself to be the Godhead, and to argue that it was not a matter of God simply being revealed in flesh, he says: "... but that God, being enfleshed before the ages, was later born through a woman, and came to experience passions and to be subject to the necessities of human nature."[249]

But in none of these cases can we be confident that Gregory is quoting Apolinarius's actual words. Indeed, the logic of the latter's argument as so far summarized here would suggest that Christ's flesh was "earthy" in origin, like Adam's. He clearly states that "the Son of God [is] from woman,"[250] and also spells out, in words that Gregory actually quotes, that Christ "is not consubstantial with God according to the flesh but according to the Spirit which is united with the flesh."[251] Moreover, in his discussion, already mentioned, of Philippians 2, he notes that Christ "empties himself" and "takes the form of a slave," which

246. L.34, J.150–51. Gregory does not claim here to be reporting Apolinarius's exact words.

247. L.36, J.154, but this again is probably a distorted characterization of Apolinarius's views; see the note *ad loc.*

248. L.48, J.166. Again, probably a misleading paraphrase: see note *ad loc.*

249. L.50, J.169. Again see the note *ad loc.* for a discussion of this fragment. It concludes that the issue of its authenticity cannot be decisively resolved; perhaps Apolinarius did write of a God who was "enfleshed before the ages," but used the expression in a rather loose way to mean the eternal Logos, "the God who was to become enfleshed."

Similarly, in L.53, J.171–72, Gregory claims that Apolinarius says that "God was enfleshed from the beginning"; see the note *ad loc.* Again, it is perhaps possible that the latter did use this expression, but, again, probably not in the sense that Gregory attributes to it.

250. L.18, J.139.

251. L.41, J.158.

is hardly consistent with any notion of Christ's flesh originating in heaven; in fact, he says there explicitly that "the equality of the same Jesus Christ to the Father pre-existed; his likeness to men came afterwards."[252]

Further, even more conclusive evidence can be gleaned from surviving fragments of Apolinarius's other works. In his letter to Sarapion, he says, as already noted, "We charge those who say that the flesh is consubstantial with God with much madness."[253] In his second letter to Dionysius he says, "It is clear from what we have always written that we do not say that the flesh of the Savior is from heaven, nor that the flesh is consubstantial with God in that it is flesh and not God."[254] In his letter to the emperor Jovian, he goes so far as to anathematize anyone who says "that the flesh of our Lord is from above and not from the Virgin Mary."[255]

So Gregory can probably justly be criticized for misunderstanding or deliberately misinterpreting Apolinarius's position. It should be noted, however, that his reading seems to have been shared by Nazianzen, writing in 387 about Apolinarius's "pamphlet," which may in fact have been the *Apodeixis;* as noted earlier, however, there can be no certainty about whether Nyssen or Nazianzen wrote first and therefore about whose interpretation may have influenced the other's.[256] It is possible that Apolinarius was indeed led to use what Raven calls "crude and questionable language" in order to ram home the point that the God-man Jesus was ontically continuous with the eternal Word. Raven himself suggests that his aim may simply have been to show that the divine enfleshment was not something contingent, not a stratagem that the Godhead was induced to adopt as a response to human sinfulness. As Raven put it, Apolinarius may have felt that such an

unforeseen alliance between a man and God implied the idea of mutability, not perhaps in the Incarnate, but in the Creator: the Eternal could not be thus treated as a bungling workman who had to adopt a sudden change of method: the Incarnation in time and space must

252. L.42, J.162.   253. L.159.
254. L.164.   255. §3; Lietzmann, 253.
256. See n. 84 and section 3 (pp. 35–38) above.

be the expression and sacrament of a potentiality inherent in the very
nature of deity, a condition of the life of God.[257]

Christ's glorified body

Whatever Apolinarius may or may not have believed about
the origin of Christ's human flesh, it should be noted that, unlike Gregory (as we shall see), he did not believe that Christ's
humanity became totally absorbed into his divinity after his ascension. "He is glorified as man," he says, "rising up from ingloriousness …"[258] "If he existed as God after the Resurrection
and is no longer man, how can the Son of Man send his angels?
And how can we see the Son of Man coming on the clouds?"[259]
Indeed, Apolinarius believes, his human body is now physically
located in heaven: "His body is in heaven and he is with us until
the consummation of this age."[260]

7. Gregory's Argumentative Techniques in *antirrh*

Having given some consideration to the structure, objectives,
and argumentation of the *Apodeixis,* we now turn to an analysis of
how Gregory responds. Before giving a synthetic account of his
theological arguments, parallel to that suggested in the previous
section for the *Apodeixis,* we look more specifically at the polemical techniques that, within his chosen structure (see section 4),
Gregory chooses to employ in order to construct his ἀντίρρησις.[261]

What immediately strikes the modern reader is the extent to
which Gregory resorts to aggressive, sometimes almost violent
language. This sometimes has an element of wit, and can reasonably be characterized as the sort of mockery that modern taste
would find acceptable in this context, as for example when Apoli-

---

257. Raven, 216. See also Enrico Cattaneo, *Trois homélies pseudo-chrysostomiennes sur la Pâques comme œuvre d'Apollinaire de Laodicée: Attribution et étude
théologique.* Théologie historique 58 (Paris: Beauchesne, 1981), 99: "D'après
[Apollinaire] … l'incarnation et la redemption par le croix ne peuvent pas
être considérées comme des accidents de parcours mais se trouvent inscrites
dans l'hypostase du Fils au même titre que sa génération éternelle."

258. L.47, J.166 and 168.   259. L. 98, J.228.

260. L.104, J.232.

261. This section draws on Grelier, 83–85.

narius and Eunomius are portrayed as competing for the "crown of impiety."[262] But more often Gregory resorts to what can only be called abuse of Apolinarius's opinions and arguments.

Thus he writes of the "screed" (λογογραφία)[263] of the "word-smith" (λογογράφος)[264] and his "idle chatter."[265] He refers sarcastically to "our great and straightforward friend,"[266] to "the founding father of the New Arithmetic,"[267] and "the ineluctable logic of his arguments."[268] In fact, he suggests, Apolinarius has a "weakness in his powers of explanation";[269] his interpretation of Scripture is "feeble and incomprehensible,"[270] a "bizarre dogmatic concoction."[271] "He loses the thread of his argument, like those who speak nonsense in their sleep."[272] "An enchanter and a diviner who can discern the mysteries of dreams" is needed in order to understand him.[273] He is "out of his mind";[274] he writes "deluded rubbish."[275] His arguments are "trackless wastes";[276] they are "childish,"[277] foolish, and stupid;[278] "incoherent and unintelligible";[279] a "stream of rubbish";[280] they appeal only to "exceptionally silly people";[281] they are "nauseating";[282] "vomit," which he "disgorges";[283] and amount to "actual blasphemy against the Father."[284] "He exposes his unorthodoxy by the sloppiness of his advocacy in defense of the untruths that he is proposing."[285] He makes a "slanderous assault"[286] on the orthodox. The reader is invited to weep at the "deceitfulness and vanity"

262. J.206.
263. J.132, J.136.
264. J.134 and *passim*.
265. J.185: τοὺς φληνάφους.
266. J.143: ὁ πολὺς καὶ ἀκέραιος.
267. J.194.
268. J.187. See also J.207.
269. J.147: τῇ ἀτονίᾳ τῆς ἑρμηνευτικῆς δυνάμεως.
270. J.182.
271. J.191: ἡ ἀλλόκοτος αὕτη δογματοποιία.
272. J.166.
273. J.192.
274. J.186, 187; ἔξω διανοίας.
275. J.189: τὸν ὀνειρώδη λῆρον.
276. J.158.
277. J.175.
278. J.214.
279. J.230.
280. J.232: ὕθλον χύδην.
281. J.136: τοῖς ἄγαν νηπίοις.
282. J.199.
283. J.166.
284. J.157. See also J.179: "I do not think that even the father of impiety and lies himself could produce from his sayings anything more terrible by way of blasphemy."
285. J.194.
286. J.174.

of his words[287] and to "move quickly past [their] foul odor." Apolinarius does not attempt to conceal "the outrageous nature of [his] argument ... beneath some rhetorical device," but "explicitly shouts out his impiety."[288]

In Gregory's defense, it should be noted, however, that on occasion he concedes that Apolinarius's views are in some respects sound.[289] And his assaults can mostly be interpreted as being directed towards Apolinarius's arguments, rather than towards his character or personal history. As Grelier points out,[290] he does not in *antirrh* resort to the sort of *ad hominem* attack or hints of moral depravity that elsewhere he directs towards Eunomius.[291]

Leaving aside the sort of material discussed above, Gregory's arguments are for the most part based on a combination of scriptural exegesis (discussed further in the next section) and logical arguments of one sort or another. Thus, for example, he makes use of *reductio ad absurdum*. He demonstrates the ridiculous consequences of assuming that the flesh of Christ is of celestial origin: Mary would be co-eternal with the Father,[292] or Christ must have left some of his flesh behind him in heaven when he became a baby in Mary's womb.[293] The "orthodox" could only consistently believe (as Apolinarius claims they do) that Christ was a "God-filled man," the last in the long succession of Old Testament prophets, if they also believed in a long succession of virgin births, sacrificial deaths, resurrections, and ascensions.[294]

A similar argumentative device is the *aporia*, or irresolvable dilemma. For example, if (as Gregory accuses Apolinarius of believing) the Son is fleshly from eternity, then either he is not consubstantial with the (incorporeal) Father, which would be inconsistent with the Nicene formula, or, alternatively, he is consubstantial with the Father, in which case the Father too would be fleshly.[295]

---

287. J.188.   288. J.148.
289. E.g., J.140, J.142, J.144, J.166, J.168, J.213, J.217.
290. Grelier, 85.
291. See for example *Eun I, GNO* 1 40–41, PG 45:264D–265B.
292. J.148.   293. J.149–50.
294. J.202.   295. J.157–58.

Sometimes, whether by accident or design, Gregory makes use of logical arguments that are clearly invalid. For example, he wrongly accuses Apolinarius of a logical blunder in arguing that if Christ were not "enfleshed mind," he must be "wisdom."[296] And he is himself guilty of a logical howler when he claims that "Bad vision is a consequence of having a disease of the eye" necessarily means the same thing as, "Anyone with a disease of the eye necessarily has bad vision."[297]

There are rhetorical as well as logical devices that are characteristic of Gregory's method of argument. For example, he sometimes turns Apolinarius's arguments back on themselves. If Apolinarius believes that the immutable God could not be associated with a mutable human mind, *a fortiori* he could not be associated with mutable human flesh.[298] Apolinarius cites the story of Elijah as an example of a "God-filled man," but it should actually be read as a type of Christ's Incarnation and glorification.[299] Apolinarius argues that the orthodox model of Christ's nature is like a compound mythological creature such as the Minotaur, but in fact it is his own Christology that invites such comparisons.[300]

Another device is arranging material in the most rhetorically effective order. An obvious example is when Gregory gives his own interpretation of the Philippians 2 Christ-hymn[301] as a "spoiler" before that of his adversary.[302] The fact that Gregory sometimes seems to discuss passages from the *Apodeixis* in other than their original order (see section 4 above) suggests that there may be other examples that would become obvious if we had the complete text of that work in front of us.

Finally, and more positively, mention should be made of Gregory's striking use of *analogy* with natural phenomena as a way of explaining his ideas, such as his comparison of the union of the

---

296. J.187.   297. J.231.

298. J.194–95.

299. J.169–70. On Gregory's use of the figure of Elijah, see also section 8, p. 65, below.

300. J.215–16. On the analogy with the Minotaur, see also "The unity of Christ's person: His virginal conception," in section 10, p. 78, below.

301. J.158–62.

302. J.162–66.

divine and human in Christ to a drop of vinegar absorbed in the sea[303] or to a reed split into parts and reunited.[304] He also uses this device to criticize his opponent, when he uses the analogy of putting different kinds of grain in a common measure to demonstrate how crudely mechanistic Apolinarius's Christology is.[305]

8. Gregory's Use of Scripture in *antirrh*

One of the most striking and effective features of the argumentation of *antirrh* is its use of Scripture. The work is soaked in scriptural references and allusions. Indeed, as Grelier suggests,[306] it can profitably be read as a three-way conversation between Apolinarius, Gregory, and Scripture.

In his elaborate and highly wrought introduction,[307] where Gregory sets out the program for his work, that is, to test whether Apolinarius's teaching is consonant with sound doctrine and whether its effect is to strengthen or undermine the unity of the Church, he develops metaphors drawn from five separate (and, on the face of it, unconnected) scriptural sources.[308] Perhaps this can be read as emblematic of his understanding that Scripture is unequivocally the basis for Christian faith and piety.[309]

303. J.201. On this analogy, see also "The unity of Christ's person: His glorification," in section 10, p. 79, below.
304. J.226. On this analogy, see further in section 11, pp. 84–85, below.
305. J.227–28.
306. Grelier, 149. This section of the introduction draws substantially on Grelier, in particular part II, "L'utilisation de l'Écriture" (149–224). She in turn acknowledges (150) her debt to M. Canévet, *Grégoire de Nysse et l'herméneutique biblique: Étude des rapports entre le langage et la connaissance de Dieu*, Études augustiniennes, Série Antiquité 99 (Paris: Institut d'Études Augustiniennes, 1983).
307. J.131–32.
308. Mt 7.15–16; Jn 12.10; Ps 127 (128).3; Rom 11.17; Gn 30.37–43.
309. See Canévet, 67, cited by Grelier, 150, n. 702: "Grégoire affirme comme ses devanciers, que l'Écriture est canon (*canôn*) et loi (*nomos*) de piété pour les Chrétiens. Ces deux termes, toujours conjoints, indiquent que l'Écriture seule peut servir de point de départ et de référence à une recherche métaphysique." (But this formula of "canon and law" is not found in *antirrh:* Grelier, 151.) Gregory also regards the "holy fathers" as having an authority equivalent to that of the apostles (J.188), as well of course as claiming support from the decisions of church councils such as Nicaea: see J.184 (cited below), J.143, and J.157.

The foundational status of Scripture would of course have been endorsed by Apolinarius, and, as has already been noted, his arguments in the *Apodeixis* were frequently based on scriptural texts. But one of the criticisms that Gregory levels against Apolinarius's Christology is that it is in fact basically unscriptural, that is, that it relies on terminology and concepts drawn from pagan philosophy that cannot be found in the Bible. For example, he claims that neither the term "divine enfleshment" (which Apolinarius uses in the title of his work) nor the latter's notion of Christ as an "enfleshed spirit" has any scriptural warrant.[310] The same applies to his use in Christological controversy of the terms "unity as regards the flesh" (σαρκὸς ἕνωσις) and "taking to himself of the human being" (ἀνθρώπου πρόσληψις):

For as long as no one can produce any of the divine salt of Scripture in order to season our understanding of this mystery, we shall leave aside the tasteless salt of pagan wisdom, to be ignored by the faithful. Which evangelist mentions "unity as regards the flesh"? Which of the accounts by the apostles teaches us of the "taking to himself of the human being," using that term? What law, which prophets, what divinely inspired saying, what synodical doctrine has provided us with any formula like either of these?[311]

Gregory also criticizes Apolinarius on the basis that when he does make use of Scripture he interprets it in a forced and artificial way. In contradistinction Gregory lays down his own principles for scriptural exegesis. "We on the other hand have adopted the simple, unelaborated sense of divine Scripture, and this is how we interpret what it says."[312] He accuses his adversary of contradicting the plain sense of particular texts and ignoring their original context:

If it is allowable for him to force the sacred text into line with his own opinions, and, as interpreters of dreams do, make whatever idea he likes fit in with Scripture, let him attribute this and similar views to the divine writings.... [H]e has no right to fit together things that

310. J.133–34, 146–47.
311. J.184. Gregory fails, however, to point out that these terms are in fact used by Apolinarius (L.66) when he is criticizing his opponents' views rather than expounding his own!
312. J.176.

have nothing in common and to stick irreconcilable things to each other.[313]

Scripture plays several different roles within Gregory's argumentation in *antirrh*. Some passages are in effect his exegeses of scriptural texts. Of these the most striking and detailed is the commentary on the celebrated Christ hymn in Philippians 2.5–11.[314] There are also extended discussions of the passage about the first and second Adam in 1 Corinthians 15.45–47;[315] of Ephesians 1.7, "In him we have redemption through his blood, the forgiveness of our trespasses";[316] and of Matthew 26.39 and Luke 22.42, "If it is possible, let this cup pass from me; yet may your will be done, not mine."[317] Another particularly interesting interpretation is that of Luke 23.43 ("Into your hands I commit my spirit") and 46 ("Today you will be with me in paradise"), which Gregory uses to explain what happened to Christ's soul after his death.[318]

Many of the exegeses referred to above challenge those offered by Apolinarius on the same passage. There are other examples of this. Gregory makes some penetrating criticisms of the mechanical and artificial way in which Apolinarius interprets a string of scriptural texts in order to lend support to his trichotomous anthropology.[319] Other interesting interpretations include

313. J.144. The extent to which Gregory sticks to these principles himself is, however, perhaps arguable. As Grelier (216–17) points out, his use in J.131–32 of the story of Jacob and Laban and the peeled rods (Gn 30.37–43) bears no relation at all to its original context. But perhaps that is excusable, given that he is there using Scripture merely as a source for a metaphor rather than in order to argue a theological point.

314. J.159–62.   315. J.144–47.
316. J.151–54.   317. J.179–82.

318. J.153. The originality of this interpretation is explained in section 11 below. Biblical translations in this paragraph are from the NRSV, as are all biblical quotations unless they are otherwise marked or constitute an intrinsic part of the patristic text.

319. J.208–13. The passages are 1 Thes 5.23 ("May your spirit and soul and body be kept sound and blameless ..."); Dn 3.86 ("Bless the Lord, spirits and souls of the righteous"); Rom 1.9 ("God, whom I serve with my spirit ..."); Jn 4.23 (worship "in spirit and truth"); and perhaps Rom 7.23 ("another law at war with the law of my mind"). Gregory's critique (J.174–78) of Apolinarius's use of a similar string of texts (probably Lk 1.35, Jn 7.15, Mt 13.54, Jn 5.27,

that of Matthew 25.30, referring to "the Son of Man coming on the clouds," which Apolinarius uses to show that Christ retains his humanity after his ascension into heaven; it should rather, thinks Gregory, be understood figuratively as referring to God the Father, as when the latter is symbolized by a man in Christ's parables.[320] We may also note his rebuttal of Apolinarius's typological interpretation of Zechariah 13.7 ("Awake, O sword, against my shepherd and against the man who shares my tribe"), which seems to have been to the effect that the "shepherd" prefigured the eternal Christ and that the term "who shares my tribe" can therefore be applied to his consubstantiality with the Father.[321] (On the other hand, he is quite prepared to use typological exegesis himself: he turns Apolinarius's reference to the prophet Elijah as an example of a "God-filled man" against him by interpreting the story of the prophet's ascent to heaven in a fiery chariot as prefiguring Christ's Incarnation and glorification.)[322]

Another role for Scripture, for Gregory as for Apolinarius, is to provide proof-texts. For example, he uses John 16.15 ("All that the Father has is mine") to show that the divine nature cannot be divided in such a way as to allow the Son to die while the Father remains immortal.[323] Romans 8.7 ("The thought of the flesh is hostile to God; it does not submit to God's law") is used to prove that it is not just the animal soul but mind or spirit, through its power to choose evil as well as good, that opposes God.[324] The characterization of Christ as "son of Adam" in Luke 3.30 proves that his flesh was of earthly rather than heavenly origin.[325] Paul's reference to an "inner" and an "outer" man in 2 Corinthians 4.16 refutes Apolinarius's trichotomous anthro-

---

Mt 21.23, Jn 10.18, Jn 12.24) to prove Jesus's divinity is much less effective, because he is unwilling to accept that this part of Apolinarius's argument is in fact fundamentally orthodox and he is therefore reduced to what is often read as carping or blustering criticisms.

320. J.228–30; Apolinarius's interpretation was discussed in "Christ's glorified body," p. 58 above.

321. J.154–55, 158.   322. 2 Kgs 2.11; see J.169–70.
323. J.137.   324. J.141.
325. J.169.

pology.[326] Solomon's statement in Proverbs 1.5 that "the think-ing person will obtain steering" (LXX) proves that the mind needs "steering" just as much as the flesh.[327] Psalm 44 (45).6–7, "Your throne, O God, is forever and ever ... therefore God, your God, has anointed you with the oil of gladness beyond your companions," proves that Christ, the anointed one, is God for all eternity,[328] as does John 17.5, "the glory that I had in your presence before the world existed."[329]

Sometimes Gregory incorporates scriptural texts into syllo-gisms, for example where he derives a major premise from John 5.21 and a minor premise from John 16.15 and 1 Timothy 2.4 in order to demonstrate that no distinction can be drawn between the wills of the Father and of the (divine) Son.[330] Elsewhere he uses one text to provide confirmatory support to another, for example, when he cites Hebrews 4.15 ("the one who in every respect has been tempted as we are, yet without sin") in order to demonstrate that "as is the man of heaven, so are those who are of heaven" (1 Corinthians 15.48).[331]

Gregory often uses Scripture not so much by way of formal proof but rather to provide examples for illustrating an argu-ment. Instances of this are the list of the various Old Testament epiphanies of the Logos that demonstrate that Christ did not take flesh until he was born of Mary;[332] the various miracles that Elijah was able to perform without being himself divine;[333] examples of people whom Scripture portrays as having ac-quired virtues or talents direct from God without their having been "enfleshed minds";[334] examples of people in Scripture who are enslaved (and so have lost their free will) but never-theless remain fully human;[335] and a summary of the evidence from the Gospel accounts of Christ's human life to show that he must have been fully man.[336] Gregory also uses examples from Scripture in order to illustrate terminological points, to show that there is no distinction between ἀνάληψις, "taking up," and

326. J.185.
328. J.220–21.
330. J.176; see Grelier, 160.
332. J.172.
334. J.192–93.
336. J.167–68.

327. J.197.
329. J.222.
331. J.145–46.
333. J.175.
335. J.208.

πρόσληψις, "taking to himself,"[337] or between "must" and "it is necessary that."[338]

This technique of assembling a series of texts to demonstrate or illustrate a particular theological point is developed further in a striking and original way in the first of the three excursuses that Gregory devotes to more or less extended developments of his own Christological and soteriological views.[339] As already noted, this is nominally an exegesis of Ephesians 1.7, but Gregory structures his exposition by artfully combining the parable of the lost sheep in Luke 15 and Jesus's description of himself as the good shepherd in John 10, together with allusions to Hebrews 2 and Psalm 76 (77). This skillful combination makes the passage more than a chain of separate texts strung together one after another, as in the examples in the previous paragraph. Grelier aptly characterizes it rather as a montage "arranged symphonically"[340] or as a "theological tapestry"[341] where the individual texts can mutually illuminate each other, where Scripture is, as it were, re-forged in the heat of a powerful theological imagination.[342]

9. Gregory's Critique of Apolinarius in *antirrh*

I now return to a theological synthesis of the arguments in *antirrh*, this time Gregory's. First, I outline the negative argu-

337. J.193; see n. 373 thereon. 338. J.231–32.
339. J.151–54. (The other two are in J.158–62 and J.219–27.)
340. "Mis en symphonie" (Grelier, 197, quoting M.-O. Boulnois, "Le cercle des glorifications mutuelles dans la Trinité selon Grégoire de Nysse: De l'innovation exégétique à la fécondité théologique," in M. Cassin and H. Grelier, eds., *Grégoire de Nysse: La Bible dans la construction de son discours, Actes du Colloque de Paris, 9–10 février 2007*, Études augustiniennes, Série Antiquité (Paris: Institut d'Études Augustiniennes, 2008), 40.
341. Grelier, 208.
342. See Grelier, 408: "En somme, nous rejoignons le jugement de M.-O. Boulnois [*loc cit.*]: 'par un certain côté, l'exégèse structure l'argumentation, mais par un autre côté, l'interprétation originale qu'il fait de certains versets montre que la démonstration théologique, y compris réfutative, est 'un puissant creuset de renouvellement de l'exégèse…. On touche ici du doigt la fécondité du cercle herméneutique qui par l'exégèse façonne la théologie, mais aussi enrichit la lecture de l'Écriture par la décision théologique de lire un texte à la lumière d'un autre.'"

ments that Gregory deploys against Apolinarius's Christology. Then the two succeeding sections deal with more positive arguments, in which Gregory seeks to develop his own ideas on, respectively, Christology and soteriology.

Critique of Apolinarius's trichotomous anthropology

As noted above, in support of his trichotomous anthropological model, Apolinarius cites a number of scriptural texts in which distinctions seem to be drawn between some or all of the terms "spirit," "soul," and "body" (or "flesh"). Gregory makes what are for the most part very effective criticisms of his opponent's interpretation of the texts in question, for which the reader is referred to the text and commentary.[343] In some cases he demonstrates, for example, that by ignoring their context, Apolinarius has misread them and attempted to draw anthropological conclusions from them that their authors did not intend.

But Gregory clearly accepts that one cannot prove from Scripture that Apolinarius's trichotomous anthropology must be rejected, and that he was wrong in principle to divide the human soul into a rational and an irrational part. Gregory says, however, that he himself would prefer to keep things simple, and refer to just a (rational) soul and a body (no doubt following the Plato of the *Phaedo,* where emotions are attributed to the corrupting effect on the simple, rational soul of its association with the body); once one starts splitting the soul into different parts (and where would one stop?) there is a danger of jeopardizing the essential unity of the human person.[344]

Critique of Apolinarius's "enfleshed mind" Christology: Introduction

It is one thing, however, to agree that Apolinarius's anthropology is in itself unobjectionable, but quite another to accept it as the basis of his "enfleshed mind" Christology, with the divine Word constituting the enfleshed Christ's mind (which, as

343. J.208–13.

344. J.142. Another place where Gregory says that he is prepared to accept Apolinarius's trichotomous anthropology is in J.213.

we have seen, Apolinarius also calls his "spirit") and with only his animal soul and his flesh being of earthly origin. Gregory deploys a range of arguments against this concept, of varying degrees of effectiveness.

First of all might be mentioned his general point, that in the various ways in which the enfleshment of God is alluded to in Scripture, there is nothing to indicate that it is "spirit" that was enfleshed; Scripture says rather that it was the Word who became flesh, while the Spirit "descended like a dove."[345] This is a fair point, to the extent that Apolinarius's use of the term "spirit" here is ambiguous in terms of Trinitarian theology.[346]

Critique of Apolinarius's "enfleshed mind" Christology: Christ's divinity

But Gregory's main attack is directed at what he argues is the intellectual and theological incoherence of Apolinarius's "enfleshed mind" Christology. The first group of arguments relates to Apolinarius's account of Christ's divinity.

The arguments here are directed mainly against Apolinarius's concern to safeguard the unity of Christ by insisting that the enfleshed Christ remained the same person as the eternal Christ, and that that person therefore was, and continued to be, divine. On Apolinarius's model, the enfleshed Christ is nevertheless tripartite and therefore compound. This means, says Gregory, that Apolinarius is in practice attributing divinity to a compound being. But that would be impossible, because everyone accepts that God's nature must be simple.[347] But, even if it were not, on Apolinarius's account it was God who was subject to physical needs, who suffered, who experienced human emotions, who was not omniscient, and who (if Gregory really did find this in the *Apodeixis*) died and was buried. That, says Gregory, is incompatible with the impassible, immortal nature of God.[348]

Gregory might be accused of overkill in the battery of arguments he deploys to prove that it is clearly impossible to be-

345. J.146–47.
346. See n. 220 above, on L.19, for Apolinarius's *Geistchristologie*.
347. J.185.
348. J.167–68.

lieve that God died when Christ died. To say that Christ's death meant that God died would, he maintains, be like saying that our immortal soul dies when it is separated from our body (which would of course have been an unacceptable notion within the broadly Platonist anthropology which he and Apolinarius shared). And it is not open to Apolinarius to say it was only the Second Person of the Trinity that died; as an opponent of Arius, he cannot believe that there are more than one divine substance, so the implication of his view must be that while Christ was in the tomb there was no God.[349] And, in any case, if it were God who died on the cross, because of the simplicity and indivisibility of the divine nature, all Christ's divine attributes and powers would have been extinguished at the same time. This would have included the divine power which raised Christ from the dead; so the Resurrection would have been impossible.[350]

These arguments are well-founded to the extent that it is true that to say that Christ is one person, but that he is also both man and God, necessarily produces a paradox; in due course the Chalcedonian formula would be devised with the intention of blunting its acuteness. Gregory attempts to avoid the paradox, but arguably, as we shall see, only by just such a "divisive" Christology as Apolinarius accuses the "orthodox" of teaching.

Critique of Apolinarius's "enfleshed mind" Christology: The anthropological structure of Christ's person

Gregory directs some more specific arguments against Apolinarius's νοῦς ἔνσαρκος Christology. One is aimed at the notion that God could be somehow inserted into human nature as a replacement for one of the elements that go to make it up. God and the human mind are, Gregory argues, so ontically disparate that it would be ridiculous to suggest that they are in any sense mutually interchangeable. To claim that God can become the mind of a man implies, Gregory suggests, either that the human mind, even though it is created, is already equal to God in the sense that it can be replaced by him; or it means that, in order to accommodate himself to the natural limitations of such a

349. J.218.
350. J.136–37.

mind, God is able to change.[351] I believe Grelier is correct to suggest that at the heart of Gregory's critique here is his view that Apolinarius's attempts to base Christology on a quasi-scientific anthropological schema (Christ is one part God and two parts man) produce a static and mechanistic formula—"like an operation in arithmetic," as Grelier puts it. Gregory himself rejects this; as we shall see, he prefers a more dynamic approach, which he thinks casts more light on the mystery of the divine enfleshment.[352]

The second type of argument that Gregory deploys against Apolinarius's account of the structure of Christ's person points out that on Apolinarius's account Christ cannot really be said to have been a man. What, on that account, is joined to God is not a human being but only part of one, the flesh and the animal soul. Gregory does not really engage with Apolinarius's contention that, because Christ has all of the three components necessary to make up a human being, he can therefore truly be said to have been a man, even though one of these three components was replaced by the divine Word. For him, as for Christian orthodoxy ever since, to be a man means to have a human mind.

So it is illogical, he says, to characterize Christ as both God and man, if "man" is in this case redefined to mean just a body and an animal soul.[353] That constitutes not a man, but half[354]

351. J.227–28.

352. Grelier, 611: "Réduire à une addition de parties la vision de l'être du Christ par Apolinaire fait disparaître le dynamisme ontologique qu'il concevait dans le Logos incarné, au profit d'une déscription statique, vue comme une opération d'arithmétique et moquée par l'image du bouc-cerf ou du minotaure, où sont unies une substance parfaite et une substance imparfaite dans un être hybride. Mais derrière cette ironie mordante, Grégoire veut dire que l'unité de la divinité et de l'humanité en Christ n'est pas réductible à un schéma formel, à un modèle philosophique." Gregory of Nazianzus, *ep.* 101, in PG 37:188C, accuses the Apollinarians of using "geometrical and necessary proofs" to argue for their views. E. Cattaneo, *Trois homélies*, 228, refers to that passage in making a similar point to Grelier: "Une fois en effet Dieu conçu 'anthropologiquement' dans le Christ comme 'élément constitutive' de son être unique de Dieu-incarné, la notion de mystère ou de transcendence tend à s'estomper, et la porte est ouverte à une christologie 'more geometrico demonstrata.'"

353. J.164.
354. J.172.

or perhaps two-thirds of a man.[355] Was it, he asks, just that half-man, then, that Mary gave birth to?[356] And what sort of union could this have been? Gregory observes that it is difficult enough to envisage God being joined to a corporeal body, and that conceiving of that body as having no human mind does not make it any easier. Moreover, it is less appropriate to envisage God joined to a defective human nature than to a complete one.[357] On Apolinarius's account, because Christ would have had no human mind, he could be said to have been in one sense sub-human; but in another sense, because he would have had God as his rational mind, he could be said to have been super-human.[358] In any case, he would not have been a man. He would have been either an animal, or something resembling a docetic ghost,[359] or some completely novel kind of being, "midway between the human and the divine nature, neither human being nor God but somehow participating in both."[360]

The origin of Christ's human flesh

Finally in this section we come to Gregory's numerous and very repetitive arguments against Apolinarius's alleged view that Christ was enfleshed from before all ages and that his flesh is therefore heavenly rather than earthly. It is not difficult to produce such arguments, and it would be tedious to analyze them in detail here, particularly given the likelihood, as already noted, that Apolinarius did not in fact hold the views that Gregory, for whatever reason, attributes to him. Suffice it to say that Gregory points out the absurdity and impiety of suggesting that there could be a fleshly element in God's eternal nature[361] and how the Scripture makes it clear that it was from Mary (and therefore ultimately from Adam) that Christ derived his flesh.[362]

---

355. J.200; see also J.215.
356. J.185–86.
357. See J.200; also J.214, J.217.
358. J.184.
359. J.165.
360. J.133.
361. J.156–57, J.170–71, J.172, J.204.
362. J.138–39, J.148–51, J.169, J.182–83, J.217–18.

10. Gregory's own Christology as set out in *antirrh*

Of the four passages of varying lengths embedded in *antirrh* that I have characterized as excurses, in which Gregory stands aside from his line-by-line critique of the *Apodeixis,* three[363] are devoted to more or less extended developments of his own Christological and soteriological views. The synthetic account given of those views, in this section and the next, is largely but by no means exclusively drawn from those excurses.

Christ is not a "God-filled man"

It may be noted at the outset that Gregory appears rather disconcerted by Apolinarius's attack on the heretical view that Christ is a "God-filled man." This is no doubt because he recognizes that Apolinarius seems to be attributing a not wholly dissimilar "Antiochene" view to the so-called orthodox, himself presumably included. He nevertheless makes no explicit attempt to dissociate himself from this particular heresy; in fact, his formal response is, rather oddly, to say that he does not believe anyone has actually held it.[364] That is despite later recording both Apolinarius's specific attribution of it to Paul of Samosata, Photinus, and Marcellus, and his statement that it is inconsistent with decisions taken by church synods.[365] This does not inhibit Gregory from arguing that it is merely a straw man that Apolinarius has invented, as an excuse for developing his own theory that Christ was, in effect, not a man at all.[366]

There is one substantive point arising from Apolinarius's discussion of the "God-filled man" hypothesis, which Gregory does not actually engage with or refute, but picks up and uses to illustrate his own Christology. As noted above, Apolinarius claims that if the mind of Jesus were not the Logos enfleshed, it would merely be a human mind inspired by God's wisdom, which

---

363. J.151–54; J.158–62; J.219–27. Raven's criticism (265) is most unfair: "Amid the welter of arguments produced in the *Antirrheticus,* it is difficult to discover what his own beliefs are: he is too busy refuting Apollinarius to have much thought for consistency or the definition of his own Christology."

364. J.135.   365. J.138.

366. J.136.

would make Jesus merely a "God-filled man." He is obviously characterizing "wisdom" here as an intellectual virtue, given by God, but found to varying degrees in all rational creatures. Gregory, however, takes it instead to mean God's supernatural wisdom, the divine Sophia, conceived as an independent hypostasis and identified with the divine Word. He points out that Scripture does in fact call Christ "wisdom" in that sense, and that it is therefore perfectly proper to talk of wisdom descending to us and emptying himself.[367]

Christ is God

Despite claiming not to take seriously the idea of Christ as merely a "God-filled man," Gregory implicitly rejects it and clearly recognizes that Christ is divine as well as human. In saying this he is of course fully in agreement with Apolinarius, but this does not inhibit him from taking every opportunity of trying to identify flaws in the latter's detailed arguments for Christ's divinity,[368] often, it is clear, by raising matters that are quite extraneous to the point that Apolinarius is trying to make. Gregory does not show himself to his best advantage in these passages, which I shall refrain from summarizing here.[369]

Christ is fully man

Gregory's underlying assumption is that when Scripture says that the eternal Son became man, it means what it says. The en-

367. J.187–89. Similarly, Gregory's only other attempt to discuss the substance of the alleged heresy (J.169–70) does not really engage with the substance of what Apolinarius is saying. What he picks up is Apolinarius's view that if Christ were described as a "God-filled man" such as Elijah, the Greeks and Jews would be able to accept Christian teaching. In fact, he says, the story of Elijah does not support Apolinarius's case at all. Pagans would be very skeptical about the literal sense of the account of his ascension to heaven in a fiery chariot. The story is in fact best taken as a prototype of how God's power, having first descended upon the womb of Mary, then raised Christ's humanity to heaven—exactly the opposite of what Apolinarius is arguing.

368. J.174–78.

369. They are no doubt among those that Raven had in mind when he accused the Gregory of *antirrh* of "a pathetic display of incompetence" (263) and of "incoherence and captiousness," which "pitilessly reveal [his] utter failure" (284).

fleshed Word was a complete human being, and, as such, had a human mind. Such a mind must, like his flesh, have necessarily been mutable and potentially fallible.[370] That remains the case even though in fact his flesh "was not subject to any [actual] defilement" and his mind "was not subject to any [actual] change or variation."[371]

Nyssen's primary objection to Apolinarius's νοῦς ἔνσαρκος Christology is a soteriological rather than an ontological one; he would certainly have endorsed the celebrated anti-Apollinarian dictum of Gregory Nazianzen, that what is not assumed cannot be healed.[372] Contrary to what he accuses Apolinarius of implying,[373] the human mind itself is not sin, but it is the case that only a creature with a rational mind can sin.[374] So our minds need healing just as much as our flesh,[375] and the divine Word had to join itself to a complete, albeit damaged, humanity[376] in order to heal it.[377] Gregory claims not to understand, and therefore ignores, Apolinarius's notion that it is soteriologically necessary for Christ to have an immutable divine mind because that alone would have the power necessary to subdue the recalcitrant human flesh with which it is united.[378]

As indicated above, Gregory regards Christ as identical with God's wisdom. He accepts that his divinity is the source of his human wisdom, but points out that that wisdom, like ours, increased as he grew, as evidenced by Luke 2.52 ("And Jesus increased in wisdom and in years ..."). That, Gregory argues, would have been possible only if he had a human rational soul.[379]

The unity of Christ's person: His virginal conception

Apolinarius's Christological formula provides him with a neat solution to the problem of explaining the unity of Christ's per-

---

370. J.195, J.196.

371. J.195.

372. Gregory of Nazianzus, *ep.* 101, PG 37:181C.

373. J.146.   374. J.141.

375. J.197.

376. J.164–65. On the fallenness of the humanity that Christ assumed, see further n. 407 below.

377. J.171.   378. J.192.

379. J.175. This passage is discussed further in n. 401 below.

son. Gregory has a more challenging task in this regard, because of his conviction that Christ was both God and a complete man.

It should be noted at the outset that Gregory seems to accept that the problem cannot be completely solved. It is obvious that if the enfleshed Christ is both God and man, there must be a fundamental duality in his nature; there is a clear conceptual separation between the divine and the human elements, just as there is a conceptual separation between the soul and the body in the constitution of a human person, which is nevertheless in an important sense a unity.[380] Elsewhere he seems to recognize that there is an ontological chasm between the two elements that cannot actually be bridged. "If it can be seen," he says, "that the natures of two things—I mean flesh and divinity—comprise opposite characteristics, how can these two natures be one?"[381] He is unable to accept Apolinarius's answer to this question,[382] but, as I shall now seek to show, his own answer is highly problematical.

Like Apolinarius he uses the Christ-hymn in Philippians 2 as a way into the question of how the union between the two natures in Christ is to be understood. The pre-existent Christ is described as being "in the form of God" and "equal" to God. At Bethlehem he was "born in human likeness and form"; he "took the form of a slave"—that is, a body—and "emptied" himself, that is, accepted the limitations imposed by a corporeal nature.[383] He was "found as a man." Gregory interprets this phrase as meaning that he was not a man "in every way" or "in every respect."[384] On the face of it, that sounds alarmingly close to Apolinarius's interpretation of Philippians 2 to the effect that Christ's flesh-and-blood humanity was in some way "special."[385] But Gregory goes on to make it clear that the only way that Christ differs from us is in respect of the unique way in which he was conceived in Mary's womb.[386]

It is in this miraculous conception that the two elements con-

380. J.205.
381. J.196.
382. See in particular J.216.
383. J.159–60.
384. μὴ δι᾽ ὅλου, οὐ διὰ πάντων: J.160.
385. That is, that "in the likeness of a man" in Philippians 2.7 should be interpreted as meaning that "he appeared as a man, while actually being an enfleshed mind"; see L.69, J.186.
386. J.160.

stituting Christ's person did in a special sense become one. In a similar way to that in which God initially created human beings from matter, when the divine power acted to create the enfleshed Christ, it used Mary's flesh as its material basis, and thus created a New Man who, like Adam, was an organic unity of a human soul and a human body. But he was unlike Adam in that, because of the unique and special way in which he was generated, the divine power "pervaded" (διηκούσης) his whole nature, body and soul.[387] There are other analogies that Gregory uses for this: God "built a dwelling for himself" in the womb of the Virgin; from her flesh he formed a human being, and thus became "mixed" with humanity.[388]

As Gregory's critics have pointed out, there is a lack of ontological precision in such formulations as these. Indeed, it is hardly surprising that models of pervasion, indwelling, and mixture lead Gregory to describe the unity of Christ's person in terms of God being "in" the man Jesus, and to use expressions that Apolinarius could well have taken as evidence for his claim that the "orthodox" doctrine is really that of the "God-filled man." Thus Gregory is prepared to accept Apolinarius's use of scriptural references to the "man from heaven"[389] or "the one who descended from heaven,"[390] but only if they are taken to mean that Christ "receives God into himself."[391] It was the man who suffered on the cross—obviously the divinity in Christ could not do so—but "the divinity is present in him who suffers."[392] It is right to venerate the enfleshed Christ,[393] but, according to Gregory, Apolinarius is wrong to maintain that the divine and the human elements are so closely intertwined that it is right to venerate his humanity as well as his divinity.[394] It is

---

387. J.223–24.

388. J.144; see also J.151, J.154, J.161, J.171, J.207, J.213, J.217, J.221, J.225, J.228.

389. L.25, J.143.   390. L.16–17, J.38.

391. J.214.   392. J.223.

393. J.202.

394. L.85 and 86, J.204–6. Gregory is here out of line with the subsequent dogma, originating at the Council of Ephesus, that both natures in Christ should be worshiped "with one worship" (see the eighth of Cyril's twelve anathemas in his third letter to Nestorius; Stevenson, *Creeds*, 307).

easy to see from arguments of this kind why Gregory has sometimes been accused of Nestorianism *avant la lettre.*

Gregory does, on the other hand, take exception to Apolinarius's characterization of the Christ in whom the "orthodox"
believe as a sort of monstrous hybrid like the Minotaur, with a
complete man being somehow bolted on to God. The divine nature and the human nature are so completely different that it
is absurd to imagine them as being compounded together, like
a man and a bull in the case of the Minotaur, as if they had any
sort of ontic equivalence to each other.[395] The union of man and
God in Christ is not a mere mythological fantasy. What distinguishes it from such pagan concepts is its dynamic nature, the
fact that its whole purpose is to *transform* the human element
in the union[396]—a soteriological conception to which we shall
return shortly.

Christ's will

Gregory is of course clear that the consubstantiality of the
Father and the Son means that the will of the divine Son cannot
be separated from that of the divine Father.[397] He maintains,
however, that there are nevertheless two wills in the enfleshed
Christ, one human and one divine; this is demonstrated by the
accounts in the Gospels of Christ's agony in the Garden.[398] He
does not, however, respond very satisfactorily to Apolinarius on
this point; he does not address the latter's argument that the
"orthodox" doctrine is incoherent in holding that there could
be two guiding principles, a human mind and a divine mind, in

395. But arguably the language of "mixture" which Gregory himself uses
to characterize the relationship between the divine and human natures (see
above) is open to precisely the same objection, so Gregory is not really being
consistent here.

396. J.214–15.

397. J.176.

398. J.181: "Since in Christ the human intention is one thing and the divine another, he who speaks first does so as a human, saying what is appropriate to the weakness of human nature, as one who has made our sufferings
his own; he then adds further words because, for the sake of the salvation of
humankind, he wishes that sublime will that is worthy of God to be fulfilled."
See also J.207.

Christ's nature if that nature is to be regarded as in any sense a unity.

The unity of Christ's person: His glorification

Against this background, Gregory clearly feels vulnerable to Apolinarius's accusation that he is teaching two Christs, and tries to respond further to it. One such response is a tentative sketch of a sort of theory of *communicatio idiomatum* as a way of binding the two natures together. He argues that because of the "mixture" of the two natures, the intimacy of the union between man and God in the divine enfleshment, it can be said that God acquires a name, "Jesus," at whose "name ... every knee shall bend." Conversely, Jesus becomes "*above* a name" and is worshiped by the whole of creation. "As the exalted came to be in the humble, so the humble took on the characteristics of the exalted."[399]

But what precisely is Gregory referring to when he writes of the exaltation of the manhood? There are two passages in *antirrh* where he discusses this. In both of them he is explicitly defending himself against the charge of believing in two Christs. He does so by tacitly conceding some kind of duality to the person of Christ during his earthly life. In effect he postpones the full unification of the person until *after Christ's death,* that is, at his exaltation or ascension into heaven.

In the first passage, he describes how the humanity of Christ is at that stage overwhelmed, dominated, and swallowed up by his divinity. Unity is achieved by the absorption, or virtual absorption, of the former by the latter, as a drop of vinegar is swallowed up in the ocean. "Everything that then [that is, during his life on earth] appeared as an attribute of that flesh (πάντα τὰ κατὰ τὴν σάρκα τότε φαινόμενα) was also changed with it into the divine, immortal nature."[400]

In the second, he describes how the eternal Christ "accepted being mixed with the lowliness of our nature; he took the

399. J.161.
400. J.201. For further discussion of Gregory's use of the image of a drop of vinegar being swallowed up in the ocean (which is also found in *Theo,* J. 126), see commentary and notes *ad loc.*

man into himself and became himself within the man; ... he made him with whom he was mixed what he was himself." But the completion of this process of absorption of the humanity by the divinity occurred only when Christ was risen and glorified. "After the Passion he makes the man whom he has united with him into Christ."⁴⁰¹

401. J. 221–22. Gregory no doubt saw Jesus's Incarnation, Resurrection, and Ascension as separate phases of what was essentially the same divine operation, aimed at restoring fallen human nature, in Christ, to its aboriginal condition of being in the image and likeness of God. See Reinhold M. Hübner, *Die Einheit des Leibes Christi bei Gregor von Nyssa: Untersuchungen zum Ursprung des "physischen" Erlösunglehre* (Leiden: E. J. Brill, 1974), 168: "... die neue Schöpfung nicht ein einmaliger, mit der Inkarnation des Logos oder der Auferstehung abgeschlossener Akt ist, sondern sich vielmehr in einem Prozeß abspielt, der verschiedene Ebenen seiner Darstellung hat.... Jede dieser Ebenen scheint das Ganze zu räpresentieren und wird doch in ihrer Endgültigkeit durch die folgende aufgehoben." This is sometimes presented as a "gradual" process: see Anthony Meredith, *The Cappadocians* (Crestwood, NY: St. Vladimir's Seminary Press, 1995), 113: "*gradually* ... the shadows in and of the cave of our humanity are dispelled by the presence within it of the divine Word, until the work is completed on the cross" (emphasis added) ; Brian E. Daley, "Divine Transcendence and Human Transformation: Gregory of Nyssa's Anti-Apollinarian Christology," in Sarah Coakley, ed., *Re-Thinking Gregory of Nyssa* (Oxford: Blackwell Publishing, 2003), 69: "the point of the Incarnation ... is that the human nature of Jesus ... should *gradually* lose the distinguishing characteristics (ἰδιώματα) of our fallen race" (emphasis added); Sarah Coakley, in "Does Kenosis Rest on a Mistake? Three Kenotic Models in Patristic Exegesis," in C. Stephen Evans, ed., *Exploring Kenotic Christology: The Self-Emptying of God* (Vancouver, BC: Regent College Publishing, 2010), 258: "Rather, what Gregory proposes is a *real*, but gradual, transfusion of divinity into the human, until, as he memorably puts it, the humanity is 'absorbed ... like a drop of vinegar ... in the boundless sea'" (emphasis original).

It is true that *Eun III/4* 157, 736B, uses the growing Jesus's increase in wisdom (Lk 2.52) to argue that it was "as a result of its communion with the Divine" that "the lowliness of the human nature was raised to the height of majesty" (Eng. trans., NPNF, Second Series, vol. 5, 190). But it seems that although Gregory may have viewed Christ's acquisition of wisdom, considered as a purely human process, as a gradual one, he nevertheless saw this process of "deification" of Christ's human flesh rather as a "punctuated" process, with two distinct active "moments," Jesus's conception and his ascension. There seems little evidence that he envisaged that this action continued in any way between these "moments," that, for example, Jesus's human nature became more closely assimilated to the Logos as he grew up physically or acquired more human wisdom or as his ministry developed. See *ep.* 3.16, PG 46:1020C: "Let no one therefore take the Gospel saying in an undue sense, and suppose that our hu-

It has, not surprisingly, been pointed out by modern scholars[402] that this solution can be criticized from the perspective of later Chalcedonian orthodoxy. It can be seen as a clumsy amalgam of (as already noted) a sort of proto-Nestorianism before Christ's resurrection and ascension and a more monophysite model afterwards. But Grelier is right to suggest that its strength is that it focuses on the dynamics of salvation, thus transcending any purely ontological or metaphysical Christological model. The divine plan is that in his resurrection and glorification the characteristics of Christ's human nature should be transformed into those of the divinity; this opens a way for us, too, who share in that human nature, to be transformed and glorified.[403]

Christ's glorified body

Developing this theme of the transformation of Christ's humanity, Gregory argues that to envisage, as Apolinarius does, that

---

man nature that was in Christ was transformed into something more divine by a kind of progress and sequence (κατὰ προκοπήν τινα καὶ ἀκολουθίαν). The saying that *he increased in stature and in wisdom and in favor* is recorded in Scripture (Lk 2.32) in order to prove that the Lord truly came to be in our composition, and to leave no room for those who teach that there was a kind of phantasm cloaking itself in bodily form, rather than a true Theophany" (Eng. trans., Silvas, 128). See also *antirrh* J.175 (already referred to under "Christ is fully man," above), where Gregory makes it clear that the growing Jesus's increase in wisdom is a natural "human" process: "Just as in the case of our bodies, gradual growth, assisted by the intake of food, moves forward towards the maturity of our nature, so in the case of the soul, too, the advance through a devout life to the maturity of wisdom is granted to those who participate in such a life."

402. See D. Karl Holl, *Amphilochius von Ikonium in seinem Verhältnis zu den grossen Kappadoziern* (Tübingen: J. C. B. Mohr, 1904), 224–35; J. R. Srawley, "St. Gregory of Nyssa on the Sinlessness of Christ," *Journal of Theological Studies* 7 (1906): 440; Meredith, *Cappadocians*, 113; Zachhuber, 216–17, 225 (on the "divisive" and "monophysite" Christological tendencies in *Eun III* and *antirrh*).

403. See Grelier, 613: "En somme, Apolinaire propose une solution métaphysique de l'union de l'humain et du divin: il explique l'unité du Christ au niveau de sa constitution anthropologique, en élaborant le modèle du νοῦς ἔνσαρκος ou 'Intellect incarné,' selon lequel l'intellect divin se substitue à la raison dans le composé humain assumé par le Christ. Grégoire, quant à lui, ne cherche pas à résoudre d'un point de vue ontologique le paradoxe d'un Dieu fait homme, mais conçoit la question de l'unité du Christ selon une approche seulement sotériologique, qui engage une réflexion sur le mouvement dynamique de l'incarnation."

after his glorification Christ's physical flesh-and-blood body continued to exist, in all its gross materiality, in heaven is absurd. It is true that Scripture says that the ascended "Son of Man" (a term that on the face of it connotes Christ's human nature) will send his angels at the end of time. But the "Son of Man" here can be understood figuratively, as when God the Father is represented as a man in Christ's parables. And the reference to the Son of Man sending his angels may in any case not be intended to be taken literally: it may be designed merely to impress those who would not accept Christ's divinity. In any event, Scripture also says (Matthew 16.27) that Christ will appear "in the glory of his Father"; that is hardly consonant with his retaining any human characteristics, as the Father's glory can have nothing human about it.[404] He also seems to be arguing (near the end of *antirrh*, where he appears to be getting tired or bored and his arguments become even more difficult to disentangle) that if Christ's body is physically in heaven, he can hardly be with us until the end of time (Matthew 28.20) as he promised to be. In fact, his body has become totally incorporeal and can therefore be present throughout the universe, with us on earth as well as in heaven.[405]

11. Gregory's Soteriology as set out in *antirrh*

Much of the theological interest of *antirrh* lies not so much in Gregory's attempt to refute Apolinarius's account of Christ's nature (the ontological question) or even in his attempt to develop his own orthodox alternative, but rather when he concerns himself with how Christ saves us (the soteriological question).

The starting point for Gregory's soteriology is that the divine Son joined himself to our actual, fallen, sinful human nature, in order to heal and glorify it. "He joined the sinful soul of man to himself."[406] "He took up our filth, but was not himself polluted by the stain; rather, he purified this filth in his own person." He was like a doctor who cures the patient without himself becoming ill.[407]

---

404. J.229–30. 405. J.232–33.
406. J.165.
407. J.171. Gregory certainly believed that, although the humanity that the

What happens then is that through the solidarity between Christ's humanity and ours, that healing and glorifying power is transmitted from his humanity to us. "He who is joined to our nature makes our sufferings his own."[408] Gregory sees human nature as a whole like a body; what happens to one part affects every other. Christ participated in human nature, so that we, as human beings in solidarity with him, might share in his sufferings and in his glorification.[409] Both Adam and Christ are representatives of human nature as a whole. The first Adam was disobedient and brought us death. The new Adam, Christ, was obedient and brings us life. Christ "humbled" himself, but then his human nature is glorified—as God, he is glorified already—and we are glorified with him.[410]

Central to this process is Christ's resurrection. Death means the separation of body and soul, and that is what happened when Christ died. But during the paschal triduum the divinity (itself of course undivided) remained with both body and soul. Christ's body lay in the grave, preserved from corruption, and his soul was admitted to paradise with that of the repentant

---

Word assumed was fallen, Jesus Christ was himself free both from actual sin (see J.145–46) and from πάθος, the inward susceptibility to temptation (see Srawley, 436–48). It seems clear that he also believed that it was from the action of the Logos on that fallen humanity that Jesus's moral perfection was derived. I argue this in detail in R. Orton, *Garments of Light, Tunics of Skin and the Body of Christ: St Gregory of Nyssa's Theology of the Body* (Ph.D. diss., King's College, University of London, 2009), 113–14 and 117–19.

408. J.160.

409. This is Gregory's so-called "physical" soteriology, discussed at length in R. Hübner, *Die Einheit.* I have suggested elsewhere that Hübner's argument to the effect that Gregory's views on this should be interpreted primarily in a "spiritual" rather than a "physical" sense goes too far: see R. Orton, "'Physical' Soteriology in Gregory of Nyssa: A Response to Reinhard M.Hübner," *Studia Patristica* 67 (Leuven, 2013), 69–75. The idea of the whole of humankind as a body, a single living being, is one that Gregory uses on several occasions in different soteriological contexts. See *de perfectione, GNO* 8.1, 197–200, PG 46:272D–273D; *in illud, GNO* 3.3, 19–20, PG 44:1317D–1320A; *or cat, GNO* 3.4, 48–49, PG 45:52A–D. The concept is probably Stoic in origin, but it may also make use of ideas taken from Pythagoreanism and Hippocratic medicine. See Jean Daniélou, *L'être et le temps chez Grégoire de Nysse* (Leiden: E. J. Brill, 1970), 51–73, and R. Hübner, *Die Einheit,* 146–48, 150–51, 246–47, 253–54.

410. J.160–61.

thief.[411] Gregory's doctrine here is interesting in two respects. The idea that the Logos stayed united with Christ's body during its three days in the tomb, rather than just with his soul, which was now in the hands of the Father, is unusual in fourth-century theology.[412] Secondly, there is a consequence of the fact that Gregory distinguishes only between Christ's body and soul, and avoids Apolinarius's threefold anthropology of body, soul, and spirit; it follows that Gregory does not, like earlier commentators such as St. Hippolytus and Origen, envisage Christ's spirit as being in heaven and his soul as preaching to the souls in prison in the underworld. Indeed, he does not mention the descent into hell either in *antirrh* or in other passages, in the sermon *de tridui spatio,* or in his third *Letter,* where he states that Christ's divinity remains with both his body and soul during the triduum.[413]

Then in the Resurrection the divinity brought Christ's body and soul back together again.[414] The divinity did not of course die; but it is possible to say that it rose with the body, because it was the divine healing power that was able to bring together Christ's body and soul in the Resurrection and thus to reverse the natural process of death.[415]

This is the background to the key soteriological point, that it is through our participation in Christ's human nature that we can also participate in that resurrection. That is what it means to be saved through Christ's flesh and blood.[416]

Gregory models the soteriological effects of Christ's resurrection in what appears to be an original way.[417] He uses the image of two ends of a broken reed being joined together to restore the reed to its original state. This image is applied in a double sense. It shows how Christ's body and soul, which were separated in death, are restored to their original union. But it also

411. J.153.
412. See Grelier, 592–94. She points out that this notion of the "bilocation" of the Logos during the triduum is also attributed to Apolinarius in the pseudo-Athanasian treatises *contra Apollinarium.*

413. Grelier, 593–94.   414. J.153–54.
415. J.225–26.   416. J.154.
417. Grelier, 605.

models the way in which the saving effect of Christ's resurrection is extended to the whole of human nature:

Using the model of the reed, through that "end" that was constituted by Adam, our nature was split apart by sin, the soul having been separated from the body by death; but through that "part" that is constituted by Christ, that human nature is restored, the separation having been wholly repaired in the resurrection of Christ's humanity.[418]

But this transmission of the benefits of Christ's resurrection to the rest of humankind is not seen by Gregory as a purely automatic or mechanistic process. We can enjoy those benefits only if we first share in his death; this does not mean through our own natural death but rather through the mystical death effected in our baptism.[419] And this mystical death must be accompanied by an imitation of Christ. "So he who died for us was, in his being, what we are; we who are of the same kind as he are invited to imitate him."[420]

In order to provide an illustrative overview of his soteriological scheme, Gregory uses the parable of the lost sheep in Luke 15 and Matthew 18. The sinful human nature, which, through his enfleshment, the divine Word takes to himself, is represented by the sheep who went astray, but whom Christ lays on his shoulders to bring home. (Gregory takes the opportunity of attacking Apolinarius's notion of Christ as being without a human mind, by pointing out that it is the whole sheep—not just the hide, with the innards left behind—that the Word assumes!) But he then extends the metaphor further. In taking to himself the sheep of our humanity in his enfleshment, Christ the Word in effect becomes a sheep as well as the shepherd. He is the lamb who was slain as well as the shepherd who gives up his life for his sheep. And then there is a further extension. We, too, as individual sinful human beings who seek to follow Christ, are also sheep; we can understand the voice of Christ the shepherd because he shares our sheep-like nature.[421]

418. J.226.
420. J.178.
419. J.226–27.
421. J.151–52.

12. An Overall Assessment of *antirrh*

Taken as a model for polemical theology, *antirrh* has many im-
perfections. It is repetitive, it is too often unfair, and it too often
misses its target. And too often Gregory seems deliberately to re-
fuse to engage with Apolinarius's arguments in their own terms.

Nevertheless, I believe that *antirrh* is a theologically valuable
and important work. Firstly, it correctly, although not always
very clearly or coherently, identifies one of the principal objections that can be raised against Apolinarius's Christological concept of the "enfleshed mind," that is, that it is based on an over-
schematized, static, and artificial ontology. Secondly, it tells us
much about Gregory's own Christology. That Christology is in
many ways awkward, vague, and approximate if it is measured
by the standard of the Chalcedonian definition. But it demonstrates a powerful theological insight into how, by joining himself to our human nature, Christ, through his death and resurrection, could exalt that nature with him into the divine glory
in which he had shared with his Father from before all ages.

13. The Christological Arguments in *Theo*

The Christological issues raised in *Theo,* and Gregory's discussion of them, for the most part correspond closely to those
to be found in the more substantial and comprehensive *antirrh.*
So only a brief introduction is required here.

Gregory again claims, as in *antirrh,* that the Apollinarians
"mak[e] the Son of Man, the Word, the Creator of all ages, into
something fleshly, and mak[e] the divinity of the Son into something mortal."[422] But he does not pursue that issue. The main
thrust of the letter is an attempt to rebut the Apollinarian charge,
again discussed at length in *antirrh,* "that in their doctrine some
people in the Catholic Church profess two Sons, one Son by nature and one who emerged later by way of adoption."[423]

He first deploys against it a complicated, probably unique, but

422. J.120.
423. Ibid.

not very convincing *reductio ad absurdum* based on the notion, common among the Fathers, that the eternal Logos, the "Son by nature," manifested himself to human beings not only when he took flesh in the womb of Mary, but also in the theophanies of various kinds to holy men that are recorded in the Old as well as the New Testament.[424] He argues that the enfleshment of Christ in the womb of Mary was in fact quite different from such theophanies. As in *antirrh,* he appeals to Philippians 2: "the Only-begotten Son appeared to our more fleshly race by becoming flesh, restricting himself to the narrow bounds of what received him, or rather, as Scripture says, 'emptying himself,'" so that human nature could receive him according to its capacity.[425] And, unlike the other theophanies, the appearance of Jesus Christ was not exclusively vouchsafed to, and for the sake of, people of heroic virtue; its purpose was rather to save "an evil and adulterous generation" (Matthew 12.39).[426] Using an image that is also found in *antirrh,*[427] Gregory calls Christ "the true physician"; he who "cured those who were ill by using the treatment that the disease required, has in the same way provided care for the sick by in a way becoming ill himself … and by becoming flesh, flesh that has weakness innate in its own nature."[428]

Now if the divine Word had simply entered into human flesh, without changing it in any way, it would be quite reasonable, Gregory concedes, to talk of two Christs, the eternal Son in his immortality and incorruptibility, and the man Jesus in his weakness and mutability.[429] But, as in *antirrh,* Gregory adopts a dynamic approach to the question of the relationship between the divine and the human elements in Christ's person. The humanity of Jesus was in fact changed by being "mixed" with the divinity, and acquired its characteristics by "becoming that which the Godhead is," that is, sinless and changeless.[430] So Jesus Christ's divinity overwhelms his humanity, with the result that in the end no distinction can be made between them, any more than between a drop of vinegar and the sea into which it

424. J.121–22.
426. J.123–24.
428. J.124.
430. J.125–26.

425. J.123.
427. See *antirrh* J.160, J.171, J.226.
429. J.124–25.

is poured. This produces a total unity between the human and the divine, so there can be no question of two Sons.[431] (Unlike the other two places where Gregory uses this image, he gives here no explicit sign that he is applying it only to Christ's glorified, post-ascension condition, although it seems clear that that is what is meant.)[432] As in *antirrh*,[433] Gregory expresses the resulting intimate union between the two natures in terms of a kind of *communicatio idiomatum*,[434] so that the Crucified One can be called the Lord of glory, and the eternal Son can be called Jesus. There is thus, ultimately, one Son, not two.

431. J.126–27.

432. See discussion in "The unity of Christ's person: His glorification," pp. 79–81 above, and the commentary and notes on J.201 (*antirrh*) and J.126 (*Theo*).

433. J.161–62; see discussion in "The unity of Christ's person: His glorification," pp. 79–81 above.

434. J.127–28.

ANTI-APOLLINARIAN
WRITINGS

REFUTATION OF THE VIEWS
OF APOLINARIUS

TRANSLATION AND COMMENTARY

1. Introduction

Gregory begins (at M.1124 and J.131) with an explanation of why it is necessary to expose false teachers. Instead of adding to the flock, to the number of those who are to be saved, they are like wolves in sheep's clothing; by corrupting sound teaching and introducing novel doctrines, they bring about schism in the Church. This is why Gregory has decided to subject to examination the teaching of Apolinarius of Syria, and, in particular, to criticize his work entitled "Demonstration of the divine enfleshment according to the likeness of a human being."

GOOD[1] INTRODUCTION to our work would be the saying of our Lord that bids us to "beware of false prophets who," he says, "come to you in sheep's clothing but inwardly are ravenous wolves. You will know them by their fruits."[2] It is through their respective fruits that the true sheep is distinguished from the corrupter of the sheep, who creeps surreptitiously into the company of the flock in the shape of a tame beast, and the fierce jaws[3] hidden under that tameness are brought to light. So we should look for the good fruit and the bad, in order to expose the deceitful disguise. As the text says, "You will know them by their fruits." Now as regards any doctrine, in my judgment an addition to the number of those who are to be saved through the Church is good fruit; but de-

1. Καλόν: the first word in the Greek text, a way of attracting the goodwill of the reader at the outset, a "captatio benevolentiae," as Grelier (211) points out.
2. Mt 7.15–16.
3. Literally, "hostile mouth." Gregory has Jn 12.10 in mind here.

taching those already established in the Church constitutes de-
structive and poisonous fruit.

One person may increase the flock by his words [M.1125].
He may extend the vine to all the sides of the house, and plant
around the Lord's table those whom he has converted from
wild olives of error into young cultivated olives.[4] He may place
into the sweet and drinkable stream of teaching those mystic
rods[5] through the agency of which the flock breeds abundantly, so that Laban's possession diminishes while Jacob's share
abounds and increases by giving birth to progeny [J.132] with
a distinctive marking.[6] If someone shows forth such fruit of his
teaching—the fruit, as has been said, being the increase of the
truth—indeed he is a prophet, correctly interpreting, in the
Spirit, God's meaning.

But another may pluck the vine's twigs off and strip God's
table bare by uprooting the plants around it. He may plan mis-
chief to the spiritual watering-troughs, with the result that the
sheep no longer become pregnant under the influence of the
patriarch's rods and so do not increase the flock by giving birth
to progeny with a distinctive marking, but rather stray from
nourishing pastures (that is, from the traditions of the fathers),
are housed outside the fold, and are scattered to alien pastures.
When this is the fruit of his teaching, the form of a wolf hiding
under a sheep's skin will show itself.

So let us now examine what fruit the teaching of Apolinarius
of Syria has brought forth for us—an increase or a decrease in
the flock, a bringing together of the scattered or a detaching
of those already gathered together, a defense of the doctrines
of the fathers or their subversion? If his enthusiasm is directed
towards a good end, he is indeed a sheep, not a wolf. If the opposite—well, "beware of false prophets," says the Lord. There

4. Literally, "young plants (νεόφυτα) of (cultivated) olives"; perhaps Gregory intends a reference to the newly-baptized "neophytes" (thus Winling, 146,
n. 2). For the image in general, see Ps 127 (128).3 and Rom 11.17.

5. The reference to "the Lord's table" and the term "mystic" may be intended to have eucharistic resonances. The expression "stream of teaching" is
used with a eucharistic connotation ("mystic nourishment") by Theodoret in
his *Interpretatio in Psalmos*, PG 80:1124B (reference in Grelier, 216).

6. See Gn 30.37–43.

should be no concealment of the mouth equipped with the sharp teeth of innovation, designed to mutilate or destroy any body that approaches it, and to tear apart the healthy body of the church of God.

To prevent what we have said from being seen as mere abuse, we shall present one of the works of Apolinarius that are in circulation. It is the one whose title is "Demonstration of the divine enfleshment[7] according to the likeness of a human being."

2. The title of Apolinarius's work

Gregory begins by analyzing the title of Apolinarius's work. He first takes objection to the expression "divine enfleshment." It is not, he points out, scriptural. (He does not mention that, as he later concedes, the Nicene/Constantinopolitan creed nevertheless speaks of the Son being "enfleshed"; see J.142–43 below.) He asserts (without really explaining why) that Apolinarius's formulation, "divine enfleshment," is inconsistent with those of Scripture, which present the Godhead as being "revealed in flesh," and "becoming flesh," and taking the "form" and "likeness" of a man.

It may be that if one could precisely expose the meaning of this title, it would not be necessary to resort to the screed itself[8] in order to demonstrate the absurdity of its author's teaching. [J.133] So, "Demonstration of the divine enfleshment according to the likeness of a human being." It would be best to cite divine Scripture to refute this novel formulation. "The Word became flesh."[9] "Glory has dwelt in our land."[10] "God was revealed in flesh."[11]

Through each of these verses [M.1128] we learn that the Godhead, whose substance is always invariable and unchangeable, comes to be in our variable and changeable nature, so that by its own invariability it may heal our tendency to change to-

---

7. σάρκωσις. For the translation of this word, see n. 3 of the preface.

8. δι' αὐτῆς τῆς λογογραφίας. As Winling (148, n. 17) implies, Gregory may well be using λογογραφία here, as he later does λογόγραφος, in a pejorative sense.

9. Jn 1.14.   10. Ps 84 (85).9.

11. 1 Tm 3.16.

wards the bad.[12] But Apolinarius denies that God "was revealed
in flesh."[13] That is the same as saying that "the Word," he who
associated himself with human life in the "likeness" and "form"
of a man, taking on the role of a slave,[14] did not "become flesh."
Instead he envisages some kind of "divine enfleshment" for the
Word.

And what, he goes on to ask, does "enfleshment" mean? That the di-
vinity, in its simple and uncompounded nature, somehow changes and
becomes solid flesh? But that would be absurd. Or, alternatively, that a
new kind of being is produced, combining in a single nature the char-
acteristics of both God and fleshly humanity? (This second alternative
is closer, as we shall see, to how Gregory understands the Christology
that Apolinarius in fact will be advancing in the Apodeixis.*) But that*
would be impossible: such a being could not, by virtue of its compound
nature, participate in the divine nature, nor, as it would not possess
a human soul as well as a human body, could it participate fully in
human nature.

It should be noted that Gregory here assumes the fact, which he has
not yet demonstrated, that Apolinarius held that Christ did not have a
human soul. This seems to show that, even though Gregory's method is
generally to work through the Apodeixis *in order, without paying any*
attention to the overall structure of its argument (see "The Method of
Composition and Structure of antirrh," *in the introduction), he already*
had a good idea of its overall contents before he, or his amanuensis,
actually put pen to paper.

But I do not know what this expression means. A change in
the Godhead from its simple uncompounded nature, with the
latter being converted into the solidity of flesh? Or does the divine substance remain as it is, and something else manifest itself
as "divine enfleshment" midway between the human and the di-

12. This introduces for the first time the soteriological dimension that is so
central to Gregory's Christology. In Jesus Christ the perfect and immutable divinity joined itself to sinful human nature in order to heal and glorify it. See,
for example, J.171, "... the God whose essence is immaterial, invisible, and
incorporeal, out of love for mankind ... mixed himself with human nature in
order to destroy sin."

13. Gregory produces no evidence for any such denial on Apolinarius's part.

14. See Phil 2.7.

vine nature, neither human being nor God but somehow participating in both—to the extent that it is "enfleshment," related
to humanity, but to the extent to which it is "divine," superior to
any human element? But that cannot be God, for the Godhead
is simple and uncompounded by nature. If simplicity is taken
away, it necessarily follows that divinity is, too.

But then again it is not human. A human being is understood
as something composed of a rational soul and a body. Unless
both these elements are included in the concept, how can the
appellation "human being" be appropriate? We speak of a human being's body or a human being's soul, when we are considering each of these as itself; but it is the combination of both of
these that constitutes a human being and is understood as such.

What this "divine [J.134] enfleshment" (to quote the new expression found in the work's title)—neither a human being nor
God—actually is, it is not possible to ascertain from our investi-
gation so far.

*Gregory next objects to the expression "according to the likeness of a hu-
man being," καθ' ὁμοίωσιν ἀνθρώπου. Does this refer to Christ's birth from
Mary? If so, he suggests, it implies that Christ's birth was purely natural—that his mode of generation, rather than his enfleshed nature, was
"like" that of other human beings. (Gregory's unconvincing argument
here is rendered even more so by his failure to recognize that Apolinarius's formulation is quite scriptural in that it is clearly based on Philippians 2.7, "in human likeness," ἐν ὁμοιώματι ἀνθρώπων.)*

*Or, Gregory wonders (on, at this stage, no very obvious grounds—
again, this is an issue that will emerge later), is Apolinarius maintaining that the "enfleshment" of the divine Word "according to the likeness
of a human being" took place before all ages? But that is absurd, because there was then as yet no human being to form the model for that
"likeness."*

"Demonstration of the divine enfleshment according to the
likeness of a human being." What does the phrase "according to
the likeness of a human being" mean? That the "divine enfleshment" is constituted in the same way as a human enfleshment?
When does this come about? In the last days?[15] Then where

15. I.e., the time of Christ's earthly career: see Heb 1.2, Acts 2.17.

does the mystery of Mary's virginity come into the matter? The Lord is not "enfleshed according to the likeness of a human being," as our wordsmith[16] says, but rather by the divine "power" and "the Holy Spirit," as the Gospel states.[17]

Or does this enfleshment occur before time begins? But then how could what exists be made like what does not yet exist? For humanity was made last according to the order of creation, while the Lord is king before time begins. According to whose likeness does this "divine enfleshment" occur if it is pre-temporal? Adam's? He did not yet exist. Some other human being's? But who is this human being, conceived of as existing before Adam, who provided the model for this enfleshment of God? Likeness [M.1129] really does have to be likeness to something that exists, not to something that does not.

And so two absurdities appear in Apolinarius's work. Either something created is posited that is older than its creator; or "the divine enfleshment" is "likened" to what does not exist, because in the beginning divinity existed but Adam did not. So if the divine nature is enfleshed "according to the likeness of a human being," the "divine enfleshment" is "likened" to what does not exist. But what was "likened" to what did not exist would not itself exist at all. But then Apolinarius says that this enfleshment happens in a different way from that of human enfleshment. So what is that "likeness" of two different natures?

So whatever Apolinarius means by the phrase "the divine enfleshment according to the likeness of a human being," it is misleading.

So it is impossible for "the divine enfleshment according to the likeness of a human being" to have happened before time began. And "enfleshment according to the likeness of a human being" did not occur at the end of the days either, when the Lord's provision for humankind was that [J.135] God should be manifested in flesh, for that would leave no room for the mystery of Mary's virginity.[18] So it would be pointless for Apoli-

16. ὁ λογογράφος. See n. 8 above.
17. Lk 1.35.
18. For the (unconvincing) reason given a few lines earlier: i.e., because "likeness" would imply that Jesus's conception and birth were purely natural.

narius to give his work this title, on the basis of either concept. Because his inscription is ill-considered and supported by no consistent thought, I think that for careful readers what we have said already has adequately revealed it for what it is.

3. Apolinarius's critique of the notion of Christ as a "God-filled man": Introduction

Gregory now turns to the actual text of Apolinarius's work. Apolinarius states that Christian faith should be subject to rigorous examination, lest it depart from orthodoxy and become tainted by Jewish or pagan opinions. Specifically, he attacks the notion of Christ as a man, born of a woman and subject to the normal human passions, but who was "God-filled."

It is now time to subject to examination the treatise that appears under this title. I shall first summarize its argument briefly in my own words, except where there is a risk in leaving unexamined anything that Apolinarius has actually written.

He says that only an orthodox[19] faith should be considered good. Eve, he says, did not benefit from her unexamined faith, so it is appropriate for the faith of Christians too to be subject to examination, lest it should imperceptibly be assimilated to the opinions of the pagans[20] or the Jews.[21] [L.13]

He expresses this thought at greater length in his prologue. Then he goes on to say that the view has been current among unbelievers and heretics that God could not become a human being or become involved with passions.[22] This view, he claims,

19. Literally, "pious" (εὐσεβῆ).
20. Literally, "Greeks."
21. J. shows this as a direct quotation, but Lietzmann rightly prints it in small type; Gregory indicates in the following sentence that this is a précis of what Apolinarius says in his prologue.
22. πάθεσιν. Zacagnius (PG 45:1130C) has "humanis passionibus"; Winling (152) keeps the Greek word ("pathè") and comments (n. 28): "*Pathos,* pluriel *pathè,* est difficile à traduire; ce mot désigne globalement les passions, les sensations, les souffrances; le context permet parfois de préciser le sens." Grelier (133) renders it "souffrances," but that seems too specific here. See also next note.

was introduced among the heretics under the form of faith; they say that because of his birth from a woman and because he was subject to passions,[23] Christ was a God-filled man.[24] [L.14]

Gregory's first response is that he does not believe any Christian actually holds this view. Perhaps he means "at the time of writing"; later on[25] he cites (and does not contradict) Apolinarius's statement to the effect that it had been held by Paul of Samosata (in the third century) and by Marcellus of Ancyra and Photius of Sirmium (earlier in the fourth). So far, at any rate, as current controversy is concerned, the "God-filled man" theory is, Gregory argues, a straw man that Apolinarius has invented as an excuse for developing his own Christology in contradistinction to it.

Apolinarius and anyone who has been instructed by him would be able to identify these heresies calling Christ a "God-filled man," which he says he knows! But we have traveled in many places; we have had serious conversations both with those who share our doctrine and with those who disagree with us on controversial issues about the Word; and we have never heard anyone express the view about that mystery that [M.1132] Christ was a "God-filled man."[26] People who want to correct [J.136]

23. διὰ τὰ πάθη. Zacagnius (PG 45:1130D) here has "per quos pertulit cruciatus," "through the sufferings that he bore," and Grelier (134) has "en raison ... des souffrances [qu'il a endurées]." But see previous note.

24. Both Lietzmann and J. show this sentence and the previous one as a direct quotation, as does Carter (340). But Mühlenberg (65) argues that, like the preceding and following (L.15, J.138) fragments, it is a summary by Gregory of what Apolinarius says about the "God-filled man." Grelier (134–35), however, notes that some of the words and expressions used (προτεθρύλλεται, "has become current"; πάθεσιν ὁμιλῆσαι, "become involved with passions") are unusual and not found elsewhere in Gregory, and that the expression ἐπὶ σχήματι πίστεως, "under the form of faith," is reminiscent of ἐν σχήματι πίστεως in L.52 (J.170), which is clearly a direct quotation. She therefore includes this fragment in an intermediate category of "paraphrastic or quasi-textual fragments" where Gregory paraphrases Apolinarius's text but keeps some of his original wording. That seems sensible.

The concept of a God-filled man (ἄνθρωπος ἔνθεος) does indeed have a pedigree in anti-Christian pagan polemic, e.g., in Celsus, Porphyry (who seems to have been prepared to apply it to Christ), and Julian; see Mühlenberg, 117–29.

25. J.138, 142–43.

26. For the possible implication of this passage for the dating of *antirrh*, see

mistaken opinions about doctrine and to introduce more orthodox ones in their place should not invent for themselves things
that do not exist and fight against unrealities, but should take
up arms against what is actually said by their opponents. Skilled
physicians do not apply their art to non-existing ailments but
engage with their knowledge against an illness that has actually
arisen.

So let Apolinarius show us this person who has said that God
was not manifested in the flesh but that Christ was a "God-filled
man." Then we will concede that his work was not written in
vain. Otherwise, until this "illness" is identified, everyone will
agree that it is pointless to wrestle with things that do not exist.

*In particular, Gregory claims, Apolinarius wants to advance the theory
that Christ was indeed divine but that in the "enfleshment" his divine
nature was changed into something mutable and subject to passion, into
something that was mortal and that could and did die. Indeed, mislead-
ingly and perhaps mischievously, Gregory here suggests that defending
this theory is the main aim of the* Apodeixis. *He will go on, in what is
in effect the first of the four excursuses that he introduces into his sequential critique of Apolinarius's text, to attack it, but without, at this stage,
producing any evidence that Apolinarius actually subscribed to it.*[27]

But it was not without purpose that Apolinarius invented the
need to deal with this in his screed. It is rather that, in order to
provide some kind of direction and sequence in establishing his
doctrine, he presented as having actually been said what had
not been said at all. This was so that, by appearing to combat
that view through a contrived refutation, he could establish that
the divine is mortal. The whole thrust of his screed[28] is directed towards this: that the Godhead of the Only-begotten Son is
mortal and that it was not through his humanity that he was
subject to passion but that his impassible, immutable nature

"The Date and Circumstances of the Composition of *antirrh* and *Theo*," pp. 35–
38 in the introduction.

27. L.95 (J.219 below), which may not be a verbatim quotation, is the only
direct evidence that Apolinarius may have advanced this view in the *Apodeixis*.
See n. 493 on p. 236.

28. ἅπας ... αὐτῷ τῆς λογογραφίας ὁ σκοπὸς ... See n. 8 above.

was changed so as to participate in passion. How this reason-ing produces anything of value to him, those who are privy to his mysteries would know. The conclusions that the sequence of his argument demonstrates to exceptionally silly people are of a kind to which the most atheistical pagans would not subscribe.

4. First excursus: Gregory attacks Apolinarius's alleged
theory that the divine Logos died on the cross

Gregory's first argument is that if, as he claims, Apolinarius believed that Christ's nature had been purely divine (albeit, as just suggested, "changed" into a human form) and that it was therefore God who died on the cross, it would follow that, because of the simplicity and indi-visibility of the divine nature, all Christ's divine attributes and powers would have been extinguished at the same time. This would have in-cluded the divine power which raised Christ from the dead; so the Resur-rection would have been impossible.

For if the Only-begotten's divinity itself had died, life, truth, righteousness, goodness, light, and power must have died along with it; for these are what the Only-begotten God both is and is agreed to be, according to a range of different doctrines.[29] Since God is simple, undivided, and uncompounded [J.137], whatever he is said to be he is as a whole. He does not have dif-ferent attributes in different parts. If one attribute exists, all the others can be understood in the light of it; if it does not exist, all the others are erased at the same time. So if the divine per-ished in death, all the characteristics that can be understood as associated with his divinity perished as well.

Christ is not simply power; he is "the power of God and the wisdom of God."[30] If both these had been extinguished in death at the same time as the divinity of the Son, neither wisdom nor power nor life nor any other of those characteristics of God that

---

29. κατὰ διαφόρους ἐπιβολὰς ... Gregory's argument here is virtually iden-tical to that which he uses in *Eun III.*1§80, 31–32 (PG 45:593C), to prove, against the Arian Eunomius, the coeternity of the Son with the Father; see Grelier, 579.

30. 1 Cor 1.24.

we call good would have remained with the Father.[31] For these are all attributes of God, and we believe that all the attributes of the Father [M.1133] are in the Son. So when the Son exists, they exist; when he does not exist, neither do they, because it is agreed that all the attributes of the Father are in him.

If the power was extinguished in death and Christ is the power of God, what kind of power could be summoned back from what no longer existed? The power that existed has disappeared in death, and there is no alternative one left behind. For even our opponents believe that the Father's power is present in the Son. If there is one power, and this was conquered by death and obliterated at the time of the Passion (which was ordained by the providence of God),[32] what other power does Apolinarius invent that is able to recall that power from death?

Against that, Gregory goes on, the Apollinarians might perhaps argue that even if the divine Son died, the power to raise him remained in the Father. But that would be contrary to the statement in John 16.15 that all that the Father has is the Son's, and that in John 14.11 that the Son is in the Father and the Father in the Son. The divine nature cannot be divided in this way. (Gregory does not mention here that such an argument would in effect be Arian, though he does later suggest that Apolinarius's teaching has Arian implications.)[33] Apolinarius fails to see that it was what was human and passible in Christ that died, not what was divine.

If our opponents claim that one power has died while another remains immortal, they no longer accept that the power of the Father is in the Son. As a consequence, they disregard the words of our Lord himself, which attest that everything that belongs to the Father belongs to the Son,[34] and treat them as not being true. For he who possesses everything the Father has must possess in himself the Father's immortality.

And immortality, as the word itself shows, cannot be mixed

31. Literally, "When both these were extinguished … neither wisdom … nor any of those characteristics … that we call good remained with the Father."
32. Literally, "at the time of the economy of the Passion."
33. J.168 and J.174.
34. See Jn 16.15, 17.10.

with[35] or associated with mortality.[36] So if they say the Son's divinity is mortal [J.138], they are affirming that he does not have in himself the immortality of the Father. But the Son speaks the truth when he says that he has the totality of the Father in himself.[37] Anyone who attributes mortality to him in whom the whole eternity of the Father is seen is lying. According to the doctrine of the orthodox, the Father and the Son share a single power, for we see the Son in the Father and the Father in the Son.[38] This clearly shows that it is what is possible by nature that is subject to death; what is not subject to passion exercised its impassibility within what is possible.

5. Apolinarius's critique of the notion of Christ as a "God-filled man": Its origin and its condemnation by orthodox synods

Gregory now returns to the text of the Apodeixis, *and to Apolinarius's attack on the heretical doctrine that Christ was a God-filled man. He first offers a summary of "the next part" of Apolinarius's argument (τὸ ἐφεξῆς τοῦ λόγου); Apolinarius attributes the doctrine, he says, to Paul of Samosata, Photinus of Sirmium, and Marcellus of Ancyra (on whom see "Who were those who taught 'two Christs'?" on pages 47–49 of the introduction), and states that it is inconsistent with decisions taken by church synods. But it appears that, as he may well have done elsewhere,[39] Gregory may be jumping ahead of himself here and discussing Apolinarius's text in something other than its original order. For it is not until a few pages later (J.142), after quoting and discussing some other passages from the* Apodeixis *dealing with matters not directly related to the teachings of Paul of Samosata and the others, that he reports—in*

---

35. ἀμίκτως ... ἔχει. In this translation "mix" and "mixture" normally translate κεράννυμι and κρᾶσις, or compounds and derivatives thereof; I draw attention in the notes to where, as here, μίγνυμι and μίξις, or compounds and derivatives thereof, are used instead.

36. Literally, "And immortality (ἀθανασία), for as long as it is called immortality, cannot be mixed with or associated with death (θάνατον)."

37. Cf. Jn 14.11.

38. See Jn 17.21.

39. See, e.g., J.168–74 and J.193–94 below, and the commentary there.

not much more detail—the specific point actually "summarized" here, to the effect that those teachings had been explicitly condemned.[40]

But let us move on to the next part of the work. Again I will summarize his argument in my own words.[41] He says that to call Christ a God-filled man is contrary to apostolic doctrine and inconsistent with synodical decisions. Paul, Photinus, and Marcellus are, he claims, the authors of this distorted teaching. [L.15]

6. Apolinarius's critique of the notion of Christ as a "God-filled man": The "man from earth" and the "man from heaven"

At any rate, rather than pursuing this further at this stage, he moves on to Apolinarius's next argument, which can reasonably be assumed to have been directed against the "God-filled man" theory. Christ cannot, Apolinarius claims, have been a "man from earth," even though he is clearly a man. This is because he is described in Scripture as "a man who descended from heaven": a rephrasing, perhaps rather an incautious one, of "the Son of Man" who "descended from heaven" in John 3.13. This man, Apolinarius goes on to point out, is called God and Son of God, as well as man and Son of Man.

Apolinarius's principal aim seems to have been simply to demonstrate that Christ was God as well as man, rather than just a "God-filled man." There is nothing here directly to suggest that he intended his formulation "the man who came down from heaven" to be interpreted as meaning that Christ's human nature, his corporal flesh, descended from heaven, that (qua "Son of Man") he was not a "man from earth," any more than the Fourth Gospel does, although he may indeed have held that the unity of his person was such that in some sense the humanity of Jesus, "the man from heaven," existed from eternity. (See "Christ's flesh," on pages 55–58 of the introduction.)

40. L.24. Grelier (141) may be right to suggest that Apolinarius may have given more detail about the condemnation of Paul of Samosata's views than is apparent from either L.15 or L.24.

41. Reading τῇ ἐμαυτοῦ φωνῇ (J.) for τῇ ἑαυτοῦ φωνῇ (PG). J. shows L.15 as a direct quotation, but on the basis of the J. reading here it must be a summary by Gregory in his own words; and indeed Lietzmann, even though he follows the PG reading, prints it in small type.

But Gregory's response here is nevertheless to accuse Apolinarius (as he hinted in his earlier discussions of the title of the Apodeixis, *J.134) of teaching that Christ's human flesh was actually divine in origin and "came down" from heaven. (This reflects a change of polemical stance on Gregory's part. In sections 3 and 4 above, he assumes that Apolinarius's view was that at Christ's "enfleshment" his divine nature somehow changed into flesh.)*

If Christ died, Gregory argues, he must have been a "man from earth," a biological human being. The title "Son of Man" similarly points towards Christ being a "man from earth." Is Apolinarius saying that the title "Son of Man" implies a human father, but that it was the man who descended from heaven who had a human father, in heaven (!)? And if it were true both that Jesus was born of a human mother and that it was as Son of Man that he descended from heaven, how could he have been Son of God as well?

Then, like the fiercest of wrestlers, he grapples close to his interlocutor. Having found the author of the view under consideration, he says: "How can you say that the man who is testified to have descended from heaven is a man of earth, and that he who is called God and Son of God is the Son of Man?" [L.16] But here again the argument so far provides a starting-point for another absurdity: so that he can show that God died, he absolutely rejects seeing anything of earthly nature in him, even though[42] it is apparent that it is [M.1136] from our earthly origin that the sufferings of death are totally derived. "The man who descended from heaven," he says, "is not a man from the earth. But he is a man nevertheless, even if he descended from heaven, and the Lord does not reject this appellation in the Gospels."[L.17]

But how can he maintain consistency in what he has said? If the man is not from the earth but descends from heaven to us, [J.139] how can he who descended from heaven be called Son of Man? For he would presumably at any rate concede that just as on the earth we recognize fathers before we recognize their sons, so it is not accidental that his "man who comes from

42. ἐπειδὴ, literally, "since." Something like "But he must be wrong, [since] ..." needs to be understood in the Greek.

heaven" is called the Son of Man, and he would presumably hold that he was given that title from his father.[43] So he is assumed, on the human model, to have another man as his father in heaven! If Apolinarius relies on the saying of our Lord, "No one has ascended into heaven except the one who has descended from heaven, the Son of Man,"[44] and if he separates the Son of Man from any affinity with the earthly man, saying that the Son of Man has come to us from heaven, he will give us to believe that the one who comes down to us has a human father[45] in heaven, a father of the sort as to lead us to conjecture that in the life of heaven there are human races, peoples, and nations and everything else that pertains to our existence here! If what comes from heaven is the Son of Man, and what comes from Mary of the seed of David is born according to the flesh but is called the Son of a Man from on high, he is falsely called the Son of God by those people, as neither his heavenly nor his earthly element has anything in common with God.

It appears that Apolinarius summed up this part of his argument by asking, "If the Son of Man is from heaven and the Son of God from woman, how can he not be both God and man?" Again, his target seems to be the "God-filled man" hypothesis. Christ is both God and man, but the human element can be called divine ("the Son of man from heaven") and the divine element human ("the Son of God from woman"); so, by virtue of a sort of communicatio idiomatum, *he remains a single indivisible person.[46] Gregory, however, takes this rather elaborate and rhetorical argument in a literal sense (although he himself later propounds a kind of* communicatio idiomatum; *see J.161 below) and accuses*

43. Literally, "For he will at any rate concede that, just as on the earth we recognize fathers before we recognize their sons, so it is not accidental that his 'man who comes from heaven,' since he is called the Son of Man, should be given that title from his father."
44. Jn 3.13.
45. Literally, "another father."
46. A similar concept, though differently expressed, can be found in Apolinarius's (almost certainly) earlier work *de unione*, e.g., in §2 (Lietzmann, 186, lines 2–6): "And it is not possible to call the body in strict terms a created thing, as it is completely inseparable from him whose body it is; rather, it shares the name of the Uncreated and the appellation of God, because it has been joined in union with God, as in the text 'The Word became flesh …'"

Apolinarius of confusing Christ's humanity and his divinity, of deny-
ing that the former came from Mary.

Apolinarius brings his argument to an end by summarizing
what he has said in the following words: "If the Son of Man is
from heaven and the Son of God from woman, how can he not
be both God and man?"[47] [L.18] I assert that I believe that the
same person[48] is both man and God, and that this, rather than
the opinion of our wordsmith, is what is defended by all orthodox believers. For neither is the divinity earthly nor is humanity divine, as he maintains. Rather, the power of the Most High
came from above through the Holy Spirit and was overshadowed[49] in our human nature; that is, it took on form within it;
the fleshly share was contributed by the spotless Virgin,[50] and

47. Apolinarius may expressly have referred to Lk 1.35 here: "The child
to be born ... will be called the Son of God." The fact that Gregory does not
mention that (although he clearly alludes to the same text in his comments in
the next sentence but two) may point merely to an omission on Gregory's part
(thus Grelier, 117–18) rather than casting doubt on whether this fragment
represents a precise quotation from Apolinarius (Mühlenberg, 66).

48. "Person" is not in the Greek.

49. The reading ἐπεσκιάσθη, in the passive voice, is found in all the mss.,
and is very odd given that in Lk 1.35 it is the power of the Most High that does
the overshadowing (ἐπισκιάσει σοι) rather than being overshadowed. Grelier's
suggestion (288–89) that the passage is Platonic in inspiration, with the divinity being "darkened" by its contact with matter, implies a view of Christ's
humanity that is hardly, as she claims, "cohérente avec l'ensemble de la Christologie de Grégoire." Perhaps the least unsatisfactory solution is to assume a
mistake in the original MS, reproduced by later copyists. (Thus apparently
Zacagnius, who, at 1135C, renders the passage "virtus Altissimi per Spiritum
sanctum humanae naturae obumbravit.")

50. ἐκ δὲ τῆς ἀμιάντου παρθένου ἡ τῆς σαρκὸς μοῖρα συνηρανίσθη. This is the
reading of the mss., retained by PG. (See G. Lampe, *Lexicon* [2004], *s.v.* συν-
εϱανίζω, who refers to this passage.) J. corrects συνηρανίσθη το συνηφανίσθη.
On that basis, the clause ought to mean "the fleshly share vanished through
the spotless Virgin." Winling (160) seems to follow the J. text, but translates
it as, "the portion of flesh coming from the immaculate Virgin was overshadowed (*couverte d'ombre*) at the same time," which seems to give an unprecedented sense to συναφανίζομαι. B. Pottier, cited in Grelier, 288, n. 1205, translates
the J. text as, "the deathly fate of the flesh vanished ... ," but, as Grelier points
out, that meaning of μοῖρα is unprecedented in the Fathers.

The mss. reading is perfectly plausible in the context, and indeed seems to
fit better with the contrast between the divine and human natures expressed

so that which was conceived in her was named Son of the Most High. Thus the divine [J.140] power claims as its own the affinity to the Most High, while the flesh claims as its own the kinship with humanity.

7. Apolinarius's trichotomous anthropology and the implication for Christology

Apolinarius seems to have responded to the rhetorical question in fragment 18 by seeking to provide a better explanation of the relationship between Christ's divinity and his humanity than the "God-filled man" theory. He first introduces the concept of "spirit," as opposed to "flesh." Christ "is God by virtue of the spirit that was enfleshed, and man by virtue of the flesh that was taken to himself" (or "assumed" by God; see note 52). He cites scriptural texts to support this distinction. Gregory continues to insist that Apolinarius is nevertheless claiming that Christ's flesh is divine in origin, and again objects that that flesh is in fact the flesh Christ inherited from Adam. But he approves Apolinarius's further statement that it is "by virtue of its union" with God that the Word became flesh. (In fact, as will become clear, Apolinarius and Gregory understand the "union" in different ways: Apolinarius as the anthropological union of spirit (that is, God), soul, and flesh to form the "man from heaven"; Gregory, as the union of God and a complete man, the latter comprising spirit, soul, and flesh).

But[51] "he is God," says Apolinarius, "by virtue of the spirit that was enfleshed, and man by virtue of the flesh that was taken to himself[52] by God." [L.19] But again, what is the "enfleshment of the spirit" except union with our flesh? And what is the origin of the man Christ took to himself, if not the first man, about whose genealogy we are informed by Moses, and whose original

in the last sentence of the paragraph; it is difficult to see why amendment is necessary.

51. I follow Mühlenberg (66) and Grelier (130), against J. and Lietzmann, in attributing "But" to Gregory rather than to Apolinarius.

52. προσληφθείσῃ. Gregory discusses later (J.193) the possible distinction between πρόσληψις ("taking to himself") and ἀνάληψις, ("taking up"). Both words could be rendered "assumption," but to maintain the distinction I have avoided using this word in my translation.

genesis was from earth, not from heaven? God took "dust of the earth" and "formed man."[53] Nobody has told us about another creation of humankind, [M.1137] from heaven.

Then Apolinarius adds to these words, "'The mystery ... was revealed in flesh.'"[54] [L.20] He is right here: this is our teaching. Then he says, "'The Word became flesh'[55] by virtue of its union." [L.21] These words, too, reflect a sound opinion; to say that the Word has been united with the flesh is the same thing as saying that the two have come together in association.[56]

Apolinarius next points out that human flesh is necessarily accompanied by an animal soul, which is naturally at war with the human mind, as in Romans 7.23. (For the relationship between this "trichotomous" anthropology—mind/soul/ body—and the "dichotomous" model which Apolinarius uses elsewhere, see "The early history of Apollinarianism," pages 7–11 in the introduction.) Apolinarius identifies the human mind here with the human spirit. (On the issue of Apolinarius's anthropological terminology, see note 223 of the introduction.) Gregory is content to go along with this trichotomous schema. But its implication is, he argues, that it is necessary, if God is to become truly human, for him to take to himself (assume) the human spirit, that is, the rational human mind as well as the irrational animal soul. As will become clear later, Apolinarius does not accept this.

But he says, "The flesh is not without a soul,[57] for it is said that it makes war on the spirit[58] and that it is 'at war with the law of my mind.'"[59] [L.22][60] What an admirable acknowledgment

---

53. Gn 2.7.   54. 1 Tm 3.16.
55. Jn 1.14.   56. συνδρομήν.

57. ἄψυχος usually = "inanimate," but the etymological link with ψυχή, "soul," is important here. As Carter (343, n. 17) suggests, the term may echo the formula that "the Savior had not an ἄψυχον body" in §7 of Athanasius's *Tomus ad Antiochenos* of 361, which all parties, including Apolinarius's representatives, agreed to. See introduction, n. 36.

58. See Gal 5.17, "For what the flesh desires is opposed to the Spirit."

59. Rom 7.23.

60. The "But" at the beginning of this sentence is again probably Gregory's (thus Mühlenberg, 67; Grelier, 120), although Lietzmann and J. make it part of the fragment, as does Carter (343, n. 17). Grelier (119–20) is probably right to argue, against Mühlenberg, that there is no reason not to regard this fragment as a direct quotation (as in Lietzmann and J.) rather than a paraphrase

of the facts! The flesh that he says was formed around God was "not without a soul." So let us inquire whether the flesh taken to himself by the Word of God was ensouled,[61] as our wordsmith says.

We say that the bodies even of irrational animals are ensouled.[62] To make human flesh, that is, ensouled human flesh, a property of the Word is the same as to join the Word to the whole man. For the only distinguishing feature of the human soul is its rational capacity. All its other features are common to us and to irrational animals: the appetitive element, the irascible element,[63] desire for food, capacity for growth, satiety, sleep, digestion, [J.141] physiological change, the elimination of waste products, are all controlled, both in us and in irrational animals, by some capacity of the soul. So anyone who says that it was man that was taken to itself by the Word, and who grants that this man was ensouled, is necessarily vouching for the fact that the man also has a rational capacity, which is the characteristic of the human soul.

Gregory does not, however, develop this theological argument any further at this stage. Instead he embarks upon a further discussion of Apolinarius's trichotomous anthropology, apparently for its own sake; despite himself, he seems to have found it quite attractive, and indeed he produces some arguments from Scripture to support it. It is indeed the

---

by Gregory, given that the latter quotes the words "not without a soul" again in the next sentence but one.

61. ἔμφυχος.

62. Lietzmann punctuates the Greek in such a way as to combine these words with the previous sentence and make them part of fragment 22. Carter (343, n. 1) also attributes these words to Apolinarius, interpreting them as an explanation of the fact that "not without a soul" and "ensouled" mean the same thing. But it seems preferable to follow J. (that is, to accept the implication of the editor's punctuation), Mühlenberg (66), Winling (161), and Grelier (119) in attributing the words to Gregory. The latter's point seems to be that although all animals have souls, the human soul is unique in that it necessarily incorporates a rational element, or mind; so to say that Christ had a human soul (as Apolinarius concedes) means that he must also have had a human mind.

63. τὸ ἐπιθυμητικόν, τὸ θυμοειδές, the two lower parts of the tripartite soul in Plato's *Republic*.

rational mind, or spirit, Gregory argues, that is the source of the power to make free, rational choices and that is where the origin of human sin is therefore to be found. He points out that later in Romans (8.7) Paul makes it clear that it is not just the animal soul but "the thought of the flesh," that is, mind or spirit, through its power to choose evil as well as good, that opposes God. The fact that in 1 Corinthians 3.3 Paul calls the Corinthians "fleshly" does not mean he is blaming their animal nature for their shortcomings; the jealousy and quarrelling he attributes to them can only originate in the rational mind.

This is evident from the very words of the Apostle Paul, whose writings Apolinarius offers us in his support. When the Apostle says, "The thought of the flesh[64] is hostile to God; it does not submit to God's law,"[65] he is speaking of the manifest characteristics of the capacities of free choice and reason. For whether to behave in an obedient or a resistant way with regard to the law is a matter for free choice, which is what is called "thought." One would not wish to deny that "thought" is the same thing as the operation of thinking.[66] And not even those completely unschooled will deny that "thinking" is the same as "mind."[67]

And how can what is "at war"—and "makes captives"![68]—lack the operation of mind?[69] The fact that in evil people the power of choice moves them towards bad things does not show that they lack mind. They are without sound reason, but they use mental processes all the same.[70] The word of God states that even the serpent, who Scripture teaches us was the originator and inventor of evil, was not without mind; indeed, it witnesses that he was "more crafty"[71] than all other creatures. So the words of his that we have quoted, from the scriptural passages he thinks support his conclusion, demonstrate the heretical nature[72] of his teaching.

64. Τὸ φρόνημα τῆς σαρκός: NRSV translates it as "the mind that is set on the flesh."

65. Rom 8.7.

66. τῆς κατὰ φρονεῖν ἐνεργείας.

67. τῷ νοεῖν.

68. I.e., the flesh: Rom 7.23.

69. τῆς ἐνεργείας τοῦ νοεῖν.

70. νοοῦσι δὲ ὅμως.

71. Gn 3.1.

72. τὸ ἀσεβὲς; see n. 19 above. Gregory seems to have forgotten temporarily that what Apolinarius is arguing for here is his trichotomous anthropology

It is not only in that passage that the Apostle Paul contrasts the flesh with the spirit, that is, the choice of a wicked life with that of [M.1140] a nobler one. In his letter to the Corinthians too, when reproaching them for having succumbed to passion, he says, "You are fleshly."[73] Now when the Apostle wrote to the Corinthians, were those people human beings without a share in the operation of "mind" (as in Apolinarius's triple division of human nature)? Or does the Apostle Paul call such people "fleshly" [J.142] because of their inordinate inclination to the flesh, that is, naming them from what they had in excess? The context supports the latter sense. He advises the following: "For as long," he says, "as there are jealousy and quarreling among you, are you not fleshly?"[74] But jealousy and quarreling are operations of thought.

Gregory concludes this part of his argument by again accepting that there is nothing wrong in principle in dividing the human soul into a rational and an irrational part, as Apolinarius does. He himself would, however, prefer to keep things simple and refer to just a (rational) soul and a body (no doubt following the Plato of the Phaedo *rather than of the* Republic,[75] *where the irrational emotions are explained by attributing them to the corrupting effect on the simple, rational soul of its association with the body); once one starts splitting the soul into different parts (and where would one stop?), there is a danger of jeopardizing the essential unity of the human person.*

Subsequent passages in Apolinarius's screed amount to a demonstration, on the basis of more evidence, that a human being consists of three parts: flesh, soul, and mind.[76] [L.23] This is a view not far from ours. It comes to the same thing to say that man is made of an intellectual[77] soul and a body as to number

---

(which Gregory does not reject) rather than his use of that anthropology to support a heretical Christology.

73. Σάρκινοί ἐστε. Cf. 1 Cor 3.3, σαρκικοί ἐστε. NRSV translates the adjective as "of the flesh."

74. Ibid.

75. See n. 63 above.

76. This should be read not as a separate fragment, but merely as a preview of later discussions of Apolinarius's trichotomous anthropology.

77. νοερᾶς. Literally, "mind-like."

the mind separately and take a threefold view of mankind. But
this latter view gives much scope to the heretics. For, if the rational capacity is counted individually, one could also separate out
the irascible and the appetitive.[78] Indeed, perhaps one could
count all the other impulses of the soul individually and produce a fragmented and complex picture of humankind rather
than a threefold one.

8. Apolinarius's critique of the notion of Christ as a "God-filled man": Implications of the Nicene definitions

*Gregory now returns to the passage where Apolinarius discusses Paul of
Samosata and his "God-filled man" Christology. (From the way Gregory
introduces it below, it seems likely that here, rather than the earlier position suggested by J.138 above, was where it actually came in the Apodeixis.) Against Paul's "adoptionist" view that Jesus "was deified from
heaven," Apolinarius cites the Nicene formula that Christ "came down
from heaven and was enfleshed and was made man." He interprets that
formula as meaning that Christ has God as his spirit—that is, as his
rational mind—but a human (animal) soul. It is in this sense that he
is "a man from heaven" (as in 1 Corinthians 15.49): "a man" in that
he has all the three elements that make up a man; "from heaven," in
that the highest element, the rational mind, is God.*

But let us leave these matters, lest by picking on every single
point we unduly prolong our refutation. Let us move on to the
next passage.

Having spent many words in devising this structure for humankind, threefold or tripartite or whatever else you want to
call it, Apolinarius then recalls some conciliar decrees: the collection of those made against Paul of Samosata, who said, "The
Lord was deified from heaven";[79] and what was promulgated at

78. See n. 63 above.
79. ἐξ οὐρανοῦ ἀποτεθεῶσθαι τὸν κύριον. N. 61 in PG, *ad loc.* (referred to in
G. Lampe, *Lexicon* [2004], *s.v.* ἀποθεόω), seems to assume this means the same
thing as "e caelo descendisse," and points out that is just what Paul of Samosata did not believe. But in fact the phrase surely reflects Paul's adoptionist
view that it was "after being anointed by the Holy Spirit" that the man Jesus

Nicaea, whose actual words he quotes in evidence, as follows: "He came down from heaven and was enfleshed and was made man."[80] [L.24]

He cites these words as if they were preparing the way for what he is to say next. Then he reveals his own sense and purpose, as it were accommodating it to what has already been demonstrated. His [J.143] precise words are: "Since Christ has God as his spirit, that is, as his mind, together with a soul and a body, one may reasonably say that he is a man from heaven." [L.25] What do these words have in common with those that came before? Where [M.1141] can this view be found in the decrees of the council called to deal with Paul of Samosata?

Gregory points out, reasonably enough, that there is nothing in the decrees of Nicaea to support Apolinarius's interpretation. But he rather spoils the argument by again incorporating in it the charge, irrelevant in this context, that Apolinarius believed that Christ's flesh as well as his spirit "came down from heaven."

But let us put aside things that date from before we can remember.[81] What on these lines can be found in the decrees of Nicaea? Faith teaches of him who "came down from heaven and was enfleshed." It knows of no flesh before the "coming down"; it was after the "coming down" that we can speak of him who "was enfleshed and was made man."[82] This is what is proclaimed by all the churches; this is our teaching, or rather the teaching of the Church. Where in the Nicene texts is it said that Christ, in addition to his soul and body, has, for his spirit, that is, for his mind,

---

"received the title Christ" (Raven, 53, quoting from fragments attributed to Paul in pseudo-Anastasius, *Doctrina de Verbi Incarnatione*).

80. "... καὶ σαρκωθέντα ... καὶ ἐνανθρωπήσαντα. Apolinarius obviously interpreted ἐνανθρωπήσαντα in his own way. Brian Duvick, in his private communication (see preface, n. 7), renders it here as "enhumaned"; perhaps "took on human form" would be possible.

81. As Grelier (157) points out, this may be just a rhetorical device on Gregory's part, to enable him to pass swiftly on to the next part of his argument, or it may reflect the fact that he has not got access to the source that Apolinarius is using here.

82. There seems no reason to follow J. and make this sentence and the previous one (a single sentence in the Greek) a question. Grelier (158, n. 750) agrees. Winling (165) also translates it as a statement.

God, and so is called the "man from heaven"? Whether you look at the actual words or at the underlying sense of the text, you will not find such a statement. Indeed, the two assertions "are as far apart as the east is from the west," as the psalmist[83] has it. What do the words of the council have in common with those of Apolinarius? He says that Christ, enfleshed in human flesh, has God within him[84] as his spirit, that is, as his mind. He who bids us not to speak of Christ as a "God-filled man" claims that Christ has God within him, as something quite different from his humanity! So in fact he is the one who takes the lead in devising that doctrine!

Gregory's tone now becomes, for the moment, rather more positive, and he gives a hint of his own theology of "enfleshment." Christ did indeed "come down from heaven," and this is to be interpreted not as movement in space, but as "condescension" (συγκατάβασις), in order to share the lowliness of our nature. God "as he is in himself" was not born of the Virgin (which is what he accuses Apolinarius of implying), but "built a dwelling for himself" in her womb; he formed a human being from her flesh, through which he became "mixed" with humanity.

But what was promulgated at Nicaea is that Christ "came down from heaven." Let our great and straightforward friend think about this "descent" to us from heaven; we do not disagree in any way with such a concept, although thinking about it will reveal its higher meaning, which is not that the divinity, which is everywhere and is in control of all being, "came down" in some quasi-geographical sense. What it signifies rather is "condescension," to share the lowliness of our nature.

But however anyone may wish to interpret "descent," the council adds the words [J.144] "was enfleshed." These are exactly the right words, for how could his birth from a woman be better interpreted? As God, as he is in himself, he was not born

83. Ps 102 (103).12.

84. In fact, the words "within him" do not appear in L.25, quoted verbatim above. As Winling (165, n. 67) points out, Gregory (rather naughtily) inserts them here so that he can go on to argue that Apolinarius does not really believe in the unity of Christ's person, because he has something "quite different from his humanity" within him.

of a woman;[85] he exists before creation and did not receive his actual existence by being born through the flesh. Rather he prepared an entry for his power through the Holy Spirit. He was then short of no material resources for the construction of the appropriate dwelling. As is said of Wisdom, he "built a house for"[86] himself; he made a human being "from the dust of"[87] the Virgin, through which he became mixed with humanity.

9. The first Adam and the second Adam

Apolinarius next seeks to illustrate his view that Christ's spirit or rational mind is identical with the eternal Logos by comparing the first Adam with the second Adam, Christ. He first points out that 1 Corinthians 15.45 calls Adam a "living soul." Gregory seizes on this as implying that Apolinarius did not believe that Adam had a (rational) spirit as well as an (animal) soul, and accuses him of ignoring scriptural evidence that Adam was a rational creature, and of not realizing that Paul is using the word "soul" here to mean, by synecdoche, "human person." But, typically, he is jumping the gun; it will be seen that Apolinarius makes it clear shortly afterwards (L.28, J.146) that he realizes that when Paul calls Adam a "soul," he means this to include a rational as well as an animal soul.

Where in these words of the council can Apolinarius's view be found, that Christ, in addition to his soul and body, has God for his spirit, that is, for his mind, and so can properly [M.1144] be called a "man from heaven"? If it is allowable for him to force the sacred text into line with his own opinions, and, as interpreters of dreams do, make whatever idea he likes fit in with Scripture, let him attribute this and similar views to the divine writings. But if the Apostle Paul says we must at all costs avoid "old wives' tales"[88] and "profane chatter,"[89] he has no right to fit

---

85. This could be read as a rejection of the notion of Mary as θεοτόκος, "God-bearer," but in fact Gregory is happy to approve that expression in *ep.* 3.24 (Silvas, 131; PG 46:1024A). This is further evidence of Gregory's vagueness as to the precise nature of the union of the natures during Christ's earthly career.

86. Prv 9.1.   87. Gn 2.7.
88. 1 Tm 4.7.   89. 1 Tm 6.20.

together things that have nothing in common and to stick irreconcilable things to each other.

Indeed, what he says in defense of his views is in fact on our side of the argument and tends to overturn his teaching. He states that Paul too calls the first Adam a soul with a body[90] [L.26]. This is well said and represents the truth. So did the first man, who, Paul says, "became a living soul,"[91] have a soul that was like that of the animals, without reason?

In fact the historical account bears witness that he was intellectually graced to a significant degree. The animals were brought to him by [J.145] God, and he was responsible for finding names for them, that is, for thinking up a suitable and appropriate one for each.[92] His disobedience too, and his inclination toward unlawful things, and his shame because of what he had done, and his sense that he needed to find a defense against the accusations made against him—all these provide a proof of mental activity.

Why, then, was Paul silent about the thinking aspect of Adam's soul? It is clear that the same term can be applied to both the whole and the part, as when saying, "To you all flesh will come."[93] David means by "flesh" the whole of humanity. Seventy-five "souls" of the house of Jacob sojourned in Egypt,[94] but Scripture is not saying that at that time they were without either minds or flesh.

The body of Adam, the first man, Apolinarius says, was created from dust before he was given a soul (and, as he now makes quite explicit, a spirit), so he can appropriately be called "a man of earth." Christ, the second Adam, is called by Paul (also in 1 Corinthians 15.45) a "life-giving spirit" rather than "a living soul." This means, Apolinari-

---

90. Lietzmann prints this as a direct quotation, but J. does not, and Mühlenberg (67) thinks that is right. Grelier, however, argues (120–22) that this fragment can be regarded as an anticipation of the beginning of the undoubtedly verbatim L.28 (J.146 below), despite the fact that it refers to "the first (πρῶτον) Adam" while the latter calls him "former" (πρότερον), and that it and L.29 (J.146 below) can therefore in effect be treated as (more or less) exact quotations. Carter (345) calls it "verbatim." The point is not, however, of great significance, as the substance of Apolinarius's argument is clear enough.

91. 1 Cor 15.45.   92. See Gn 2.19.
93. Ps 64 (65).2.   94. Gn 46.26–27.

us claims, that "the heavenly spirit" was enfleshed in him and that he
had no human mind of his own. This is why Apolinarius thinks he can
properly be called "a man from heaven": not (it seems reasonable to as-
sume) because his flesh was heavenly—it was as "earthy" as Adam's—
but because his mind (spirit) was. So Adam is "a man of earth" because
he had an "earthy" body: Christ is "a man from heaven" because his
mind (not his body) was "heavenly."

Despite Apolinarius's explicit assertion in L.28 that Adam had a
rational mind, Gregory is perversely unwilling to accept that he real-
ly believed it. He advances, however, two quite reasonable objections to
Apolinarius's argument that Christ was enfleshed spirit and had no
human mind. First of all, he points out that it is clear from Scripture
that we are to become like Christ; it can hardly be that we can do so only
by, literally, losing our human minds. Conversely, Christ became like us,
"yet without sin" (Hebrews 4.15); but the mind is not sin! Secondly, in
the various ways in which the enfleshment of God is alluded to in Scrip-
ture, there is nothing to indicate that it is "spirit" that was enfleshed;
Scripture says rather that it was the Word that became flesh, while the
Spirit "descended like a dove" upon Christ at his baptism.

But our wordsmith says that the second man, from heaven,
is called spiritual, and this is an indication that, for Apolinarius,
the man mixed with God is himself without a mind.[95] [L.27]
But there is a refutation of this strange doctrine to hand, drawing on what Apolinarius himself says. He who said "as is the man
of heaven, so are those who are of heaven"[96] takes us[97] far away
from any such notion. Those who believe in him who has come
from heaven are themselves called "of heaven" by Paul. Those

95. Lietzmann makes the first clause of this sentence a direct quotation
from Apolinarius, and the second a summary by Gregory. J. makes the whole
sentence a direct quotation; Mühlenberg (67) believes that both clauses are
a summary by Gregory. My translation follows Grelier (135–36), who argues
that the second clause is neither a quotation from nor a summary of Apolinarius, but Gregory's interpretation of Apolinarius's argument; she suggests that
Apolinarius would never have described Christ as "without a mind" (ἄνουν),
because for him the incarnate Word did have a mind, but a divine one. So
for clarity I have added the words "for Apolinarius" to the second clause, although these are not in the Greek.

96. 1 Cor 15.48.

97. Reading ἡμᾶς ἀφίστησιν with PG. J. silently omits ἡμᾶς; it is not clear why.

who have transferred, as he says, their "citizenship" to heaven, these, too, are called "of heaven" (like the "man of heaven") by the Apostle.[98] But among those who have embraced the faith there is no one without a mind! This comparison necessarily shows the likeness between the "man of heaven" and human beings and that the former had a (human) mind. "As is the man of heaven, so are those who are of heaven"; so, it must necessarily be agreed, a mind is either in all these or in none of them. Just as we see the attributes of an earthly man [M.1145] in his offspring, so it is necessary that "the one who in every respect," as the Apostle says, as regards our human life "has been tempted as we are, yet [J.146] without sin"[99]—but the mind is not sin!—must share every aspect of our human nature. Thus what the Apostle says is true: if it is accepted that he became like us, we are like him. It is by becoming like us that he makes us like him.

Now let us once again take note of the words of Apolinarius: "So Paul calls the former Adam a soul.[100] Adam had a body, too; that was certainly not something he lacked. Paul applies the word 'soul' to the whole; the meaning of that word includes the 'spirit' as well." [L.28] In saying this he is asserting that human nature has three parts; he attributes an inclusive meaning to the word "soul," with the notions of "body" and "spirit" embraced in the one word. But, he says, Paul calls "the last Adam ... a life-giving spirit."[101] [L.29] The word chosen to describe the first Adam is superior to other possible characterizations in that it expresses his predominant feature; the same applies to that applied to the last Adam.[102] For the word "soul" is used of Adam, because he sinned, while the man who was mixed with God is called only "spirit," because "he did not sin, nor was treachery found in his mouth."[103]

But Apolinarius does not accept this interpretation.[104] He

98. See Phil 3.20.   99. Heb 4.15.
100. 1 Cor 15.45.
101. Ibid. For the status of this fragment, see n. 90 above on L.26.
102. This sentence expresses Gregory's rather than Apolinarius's interpretation.
103. Is 53.9.
104. τὴν τοιαύτην διάνοιαν, i.e., the view that "soul" and "spirit "are used of

says that Adam was "from the earth, a man of dust,[105] because his body was formed of earth and then given a soul."[106] [L.30] But then was not mind, which he calls spirit, combined with the physical form belonging to Adam? Surely it is in that that the likeness of God lies? What else but mind could one believe to be the outflowing of the divine breath?

Apolinarius claims that the second Adam is characterized as "from heaven"[107] because the heavenly Spirit was enfleshed. [L.31][108] Where does Scripture [J.147] speak of such a thing? To which sacred author is the statement that Spirit was enfleshed to be attributed? We have heard nothing of this from the Gospel; we have been taught nothing of this by the resounding voice of the Apostle Paul. The teaching of Scripture is rather that "the Word became flesh";[109] the Gospel narrative says that the Spirit descended in the form of a dove.[110] No one of those who "speak mysteries in the Spirit"[111] says anything about enfleshment of Spirit. "His glory has dwelt in our land";[112] "Truth has sprung up from the earth";[113] "God was revealed in flesh";[114] "Righteousness has looked down from heaven";[115] and there are many other such texts. The divinely inspired Scripture knows nothing of enfleshed Spirit.[116]

Adam and Christ respectively, not in order to draw any ontological distinction between them but to identify their "predominant features."

105. 1 Cor 15.47.

106. Cf. Gn 2.7. As Grelier (136–38) concludes, it cannot be determined with certainty to what extent Gregory is quoting Apolinarius's exact words here. Carter's suggestion (346), that L.30 is merely a misleading summary of Apolinarius's alleged views by Gregory, seems unnecessary: there is no reason why Apolinarius should not have expressed himself in these terms, even though Gregory (deliberately?) misinterpreted what he said as implying that Adam had no rational spirit.

107. 1 Cor 15.47.

108. Again, it cannot be determined how exact this quotation is, although, as Grelier (138) points out, "the spirit ... was enfleshed" has an Apollinarian ring to it.

109. Jn 1.14.   110. Mt 3.16.

111. 1 Cor 14.2.   112. Ps 84 (85).9.

113. Ps 84 (85).11.   114. 1 Tm 3.16.

115. Ps 84 (85).12.

116. There is a play on words between "divinely inspired" (θεόπνευστος) and "Spirit" (πνεῦμα).

10. Apolinarius's teaching on the pre-existent
Christ and the identity of Jesus with him

The next[117] section of the Apodeixis *seems to have been aimed at establishing that since Christ's "spirit," his rational mind, was identical
with the Logos, the second Person of the Trinity, it existed from eternity.
This divine "spirit" was the most important element of the man Jesus's
nature; but it seems that Apolinarius wants to go one stage further and
to argue not only that there was an unbreakable unity between the eternal Logos and the man Jesus, but also that they are in some sense totally identical. In doing so, he uses some expressions about the origin
of Christ's human nature to which it is hardly surprising that Gregory
takes exception and which he is able to use to support his contention that
Apolinarius held that Christ's flesh was of eternal origin.*

*These expressions convey what seem to be ideas similar to Apolinari-
us's earlier references to "the man from heaven" (L.16–18; J.138–40).
He now says explicitly that "the man Christ pre-existed" and that the
"divine Spirit," that is, the Logos, "the most important element in the
nature of the God-Man," did not "exist separately from him."*

"The man Christ pre-existed,"[118] says Apolinarius, "not with
the Spirit, that is, God, existing separately from him; rather the
most important element[119] in the nature[120] of the God-Man[121]
was the divine Spirit." [L.32] These are [M.1148] the wordsmith's exact words. Since, because of a weakness in his powers
of explanation, his thought is not absolutely transparent in its
lucidity, I will first expose the underlying meaning, which lies

117. Perhaps the second main section; see the appendix to this volume.
118. "Cette expression extrêmement ambiguë, et, pourrait-on dire, maladroite" (Grelier, 430).
119. Winling (171) and Grelier (430) translate the clause as, "le Seigneur
est/était Esprit divin"; Carter (348) has, "the Lord is the divine spirit." But, as
Lietzmann (211, n. on line 27) points out, τοῦ κυρίου is the genitive of τὸ κύριον
rather than of ὁ κύριος, "the Lord" (which is how Gregory misunderstands it;
see n. 122 below). (Compare κατὰ τὸ κυριώτατον in L. 45, J.165, where Gregory
gets it right.)
120. "Nature" (φύσει) here is used in a sense that would later be expressed
by "person" (πρόσωπον); see n. 27 in the introduction above.
121. τοῦ θεοῦ ἀνθρώπου. This expression (cf. *deus-homo*) is also used by
Gregory Nazianzen; see G. Lampe, *Lexicon* (2004), *s.v.* θεός, G.1.

buried in the obscurity of his words, and then subject his argument to examination.

"The man Christ pre-existed," he says. He identifies in his thought the Word who was in the beginning and the man who was made manifest, so that the latter existed before his manifestation. He develops this thought in what follows. He says that the Spirit is not something separate from the man, and thus affirms that the Son's divinity is human from the beginning. He makes this clearer by what he says next, that the Lord,[122] in the nature of the God-Man, was divine Spirit. He posits one single nature for God and man, and refers to it as though it were a coalescence of two individuals.[123] [J.148]

He supports this view by citing various passages of Scripture that orthodox interpreters would accept as referring to a pre-existent Christ; but Gregory again focuses on, and satirizes in a heavy-handed way, the view, which he attributes to Apolinarius, that not just the divine Logos but also the man Jesus pre-existed his birth on earth. In that case, he argues, not only Jesus but Mary, from whom he took his flesh, must have existed from eternity! Moreover, Apolinarius's view is contrary to Philippians 2.6–8, which clearly distinguishes between two states of the Logos, when he was "in the form of God" and after he had "emptied himself, taking the form of a slave." And could it have been through a man, sharing the weakness of the flesh, that all things were created in the beginning? If Jesus existed as a (presumably fully-grown) man before his birth on earth, how and why did he become a tiny baby in Bethlehem? Did he leave some of his original flesh behind him in heaven, and then have to grow some new flesh through what he ate on earth? We know that Christ had a real, passible, corruptible body on earth—are we to believe that his pre-existing flesh in heaven was of the same kind?

The meaning of what he says is that what became manifest through the flesh from the Virgin should be envisaged as preceding all things not only as regards the eternity of the divinity, as we all believe, but also as regards the flesh.

As well as what has been said already, Apolinarius cites in sup-

---

122. See n. 119 above.
123. If this is how the obscure καὶ ἀνθρώπων δύο τὴν συναλοιφὴν κατωνόμασεν is to be understood.

port of his opinion the text "Before Abraham was, I am";[124] the words of John the Baptist, "He was before me";[125] "One Lord … through whom are all things";[126] "He himself is before all things";[127] and some words from Zechariah, which I shall omit, as they have been violently distorted with this end in view.[128] [L.33] If the outrageous nature of this argument were concealed beneath some rhetorical device, I would make an effort to refute its hidden content. But since Apolinarius explicitly shouts out his impiety, I do not know what more our words can achieve. If the flesh existed before the ages and if he who was born of Mary had flesh "before Abraham was," then the Virgin was older than Nahor;[129] indeed, Mary existed before Adam. But what am I saying? That makes it look as if Mary was born before the created world itself and is more ancient than the very ages! For if the Son became flesh in the Virgin, and that flesh is called Jesus, and the Apostle Paul testifies that he existed before all creation,[130] then it seems as though our noble author is contriving that Mary, too, should be included in the concept of the Father's eternity. And I remain silent with regard to the extremely bizarre conclusions towards which the absurdity of this novel teaching is developed step by step; the perceptive reader should be able to see from those steps how absurd it is, without my having explicitly to expose its unseemliness.

[M.1149] Let us move quickly past the foul odor of these thoughts. Let us note in passing only that if the flesh existed before the ages, the divinity did not become "emptied," the Son did not exist "in the form of God," and he did not put on the appearance of a slave. Rather, the divinity which [J.149] now

---

124. Jn 8.58.

125. Jn 1.15.

126. 1 Cor 8.6.

127. Col 1.17.

128. Gregory in fact discusses the passage concerned (Zec 13.7) later (J.154 and J.158). He does not mention further Apolinarius's interpretation of any of the other texts listed here. On the other hand, the list does not include some texts that Apolinarius does in fact seem to have referred to in this context and that Gregory does discuss later: Eph 1.7 (J.151–54); Heb 1.1–3 (J.155–57); and Phil 2.5–11 (J.158–66).

129. Abraham's grandfather; Gn 11.21.

130. And if, as Gregory says that Apolinarius is arguing, Christ's flesh as well as his divinity existed from eternity …

appeared was what it was by nature; it was not "humbled."[131] May the Word be indulgent towards such words! I will pass over the rest in silence.

If the flesh existed before all creation, then all things have their origin in weakness, not in power. "The spirit is willing but the flesh is weak."[132] If Apolinarius carries his absurdity to these lengths, who cannot see the further conclusions that logically follow from it? For he attributes all the characteristics of the flesh to the one who existed in the flesh before all ages: fatigue, grief, tears, thirst, sleep, the exigencies of hunger, and even more inappropriate things.

The divine Scripture says that "a child is born for us";[133] Luke says that the shepherds saw the Lord wrapped in swaddling clothes,[134] and that "Jesus increased in years and wisdom and favor,"[135] growing in perfection, following the way of nature until he attained the full stature of adulthood. What will those who claim that his flesh existed before all ages say about this? What were the dimensions of his body before all ages? For Jesus passed through every stage of growth proper to human life. So was that man who existed before all creation a boy, a newborn babe, an adolescent, or with an instantaneously full-grown body?

If they say he was a child, will they at any rate explain how after the passage of so long an age he failed to reach full maturity? If they say he was a full-grown man, we shall expect to learn how, when he was born as a human, he was reduced to the size of an infant. Where did he leave the rest of his body? How was its mass reduced to small dimensions? And then how did he restore the mass of his body to its proper size? Did he reassume the body he had from the beginning, by gradual growth? Or did he [J.150] add some other material to himself through the process of nutrition? If they say he reassumed the old body, they prove that nutrition was altogether unnecessary for him. But if they do not deny that the Lord partook of nutrition, what will

131. See Phil 2.6–7—anticipating Gregory's later discussion of Phil 2.5–11 and Apolinarius's interpretation of it (J.158–66).

132. Mt 26.41.   133. Is 9.6.
134. See Lk 2.12.   135. Lk 2.52.

they say about the flesh left behind in heaven—most likely the greater part of it, as only as much as the Virgin's womb could contain would have been taken from it? In any event they make up fabulous tales about this too, and as a result concoct other teachings to which the logic of their absurd stories inevitably leads them.

But let us pass over those matters. It would not, however, be unreasonable to make further inquiries of those who proclaim as their teaching that the divine enfleshment occurred before the ages. If they think that Christ has always been in the flesh and so say that flesh is God; if all flesh is solid to the touch, and to be solid is to be material and composite, and what is composite is inevitably subject to dissolution; then it is absolutely necessary that Christ should be made of matter and so composed of different things and by nature liable to dissolution.

We know that when he lived among human beings in a human way, he had a body constituted of different elements. This applies to his flesh and bones and blood, which were like those of other people. We know this from the marks of the nails and the blood that was shed as a result of the lance. We know it from what the Lord said to those who did not believe in his appearance: "Touch me and know that spirit[136] does not have flesh and bones as you see that I have."

In short, says Gregory, Christ the eternal Word cannot have had a human body. Rather, he took our flesh "in the last days," in order to deify humanity by joining it to his divinity. Apolinarius, Gregory claims, admits that we are redeemed through the flesh and blood of Christ, but insists that these were part of his divine nature from all eternity.

Therefore, if the divine enfleshment, as Apolinarius [J.151] says,[137] did not take its origin from the Virgin but existed before

136. Lk 24.39. Gregory seems to have written, "... καὶ γνῶτε, ὅτι τὸ πνεῦμα (trans. here as "spirit") ..." rather than "... καὶ ἴδετε· ὅτι πνεῦμα (NRSV: "... and see; for a ghost ...") as in our text of Luke.

137. Grelier (143) suggests that "as Apolinarius says" (καθὼς ὁ Ἀπολινάριος λέγει) and similar phrases tend to indicate that Gregory is paraphrasing Apolinarius's words, often distorting them to polemical effect. But the other examples she cites—L.36, J.154, 26 (καθὼς ἐκεῖνός φησιν); L.48, J.166, 27–28 (καθὼς αὐτὸς ὀνόμαζει); L.82, J.201, 26 and L.97, J.227, 16–17 (καθὼς ὁ Ἀπολινάριος

Abraham and all creation, [L.34] it must necessarily have been like that which the disciples saw, solid and comprising firm flesh and bones. He must have always remained like that; there can have been no descent to our humble condition, but rather what became manifest at the time of his becoming man must have been that which had remained hidden, the divinity of his nature. Did Arius, did the even more malignant Eunomius, think up anything that so undermined the glory of the Only-begotten as what Apolinarius has constructed for us in this screed? God enfleshed before the ages, with bones, hair, skin, sinews, nerves, flesh, and fat, composed of different elements, and not simple and uncompounded! And this is the Word who was in the beginning and was with God,[138] who, by sharing our humble nature, became flesh in the last days out of love for humanity and thus mixed himself with humanity and received all our nature into himself, in order to deify humanity by mixing it with his divinity, sanctifying the entire batch of our human nature by those first fruits![139]

λέγει)—do not seem to me conclusively to support that hypothesis. As she points out, however, there are other grounds for believing that this fragment represents an inaccurate paraphrase of Apolinarius's views on the origin of Christ's flesh; there is a strong resemblance to L.48 (J.166–67), where Gregory more or less admits that he is not quoting Apolinarius verbatim.

138. Jn 1.1–2.

139. The characterization of Christ as the "first fruits" sanctifying and saving the "lump" of the humanity that we share with him, is found in several places in Gregory's writings. The most extended passage is in the anti-Eunomian *in illud*, GNO 3.2, 14–16, PG 44:1313B–1316B, but it also occurs in other anti-Eunomian works (*Eun III*/10, GNO 2 294, PG 45:889C; *ref*, GNO 2, 346, PG 45:504B; *ref*, GNO 2, 386, PG 45:545D; *ref*, GNO 2, 387, PG 45:548C) and in *or cat*, GNO 3.4, 78, PG 45:80B–C. It is also found in *Theo*, J.126. The scriptural basis of the use of this model in a soteriological sense is 1 Corinthians 15.20, "Christ has been raised from the dead, the first fruits of those who have died." But Gregory and his sources (see below) pay as much attention to Romans 11.16, "if the first fruits is holy, then the whole is holy" (although the context there is not soteriological). The model can also be seen to have been influenced by the notion of the action of yeast on a batch of dough, as in Mt 13.33 and Gal 5.9.

For the history of the use of this analogy in a soteriological context, see R. Hübner, *Die Einheit*, 315–25, who argues that it originates in Valentinian Gnosticism; it is found in the second-century Valentinian Theodotus, as well as in Irenaeus.

11. Second excursus: Gregory's teaching on how
we are saved through Christ's humanity

*This is a total misunderstanding, says Gregory. He now temporarily
suspends his critique of Apolinarius and, in a second excursus, proceeds
to explain his own soteriological views. He begins with a powerful and
complex passage that interprets one of the texts cited by Apolinarius,
Ephesians 1.7 ("In him we have redemption through his blood, the forgiveness of our trespasses ..."), using the imagery of Hebrews 2.10–18,
the parable of the lost sheep in Luke 15, and the notion of Christ as the
good shepherd in John 10.*[140] *The key point is that the sheep who went
astray, but whom Christ lays on his shoulders to bring home, represents
the sinful human nature, which, through his enfleshment, the divine
Word takes to himself. (In a witty side-swipe against Apolinarius's notion of Christ as being without a human mind, Gregory makes it clear
that it is the whole sheep—not just the hide, with the innards left behind—that the Word assumes.) But, the argument proceeds, in taking
up the sheep of our humanity, Christ the Word in effect becomes a sheep
as well as the shepherd—the lamb who was slain as well as the shepherd
who gives up his life for his sheep. Then, finally, we too, as individual
sinful human beings, are also sheep; and it is because Christ the shepherd shares our sheep-like nature, that we can understand his voice.*

But I think we should leave on one side the false interpretation that Apolinarius has applied to each of the sacred texts
that he has cited for this purpose, for it would be pointless
[M.1153] to waste words by examining what is quite obvious.
To demonstrate that Christ always existed in flesh and blood, he
cites the Apostle Paul's words to the effect that we have received
"redemption through his blood, the forgiveness" of our sins
through his flesh.[141] [L.35] But I do not believe that intelligent

140. For a detailed analysis of how Gregory uses these texts, see Grelier,
185–98 and 205–8.
141. The passage in quotation marks is from Eph 1.7. Precisely how Apolinarius used this passage in his argument about the eternal existence of Christ
cannot now be determined.
    Grelier (207) suggests that the addition of the reference to Christ's flesh
may be a "contamination" from Heb 2.14, in the passage in Hebrews that is
part of the background to Gregory's argument here (see commentary and

people could doubt that the significance of that passage is quite other. Who does not know that divine mystery, that [J.152] "the pioneer of our salvation"[142] goes after the lost sheep as a shepherd?[143] We human beings are that sheep, we who have strayed through sin from the flock of the one hundred rational sheep. Christ lays the whole sheep on his own shoulders. The sheep did not stray just in one of its parts; since it went away as a whole, it is brought back as a whole. The hide is not taken and the innards left behind, as Apolinarius would have it.

Once the sheep is on the shepherd's shoulders, that is, in the divinity of the Lord, it becomes one with him through this taking-up. So, wanting to seek out and save what had been lost, once the Lord had found what he was looking for, he took up upon himself what he had found. This sheep, which had once erred, did not walk on its own feet; instead, it is carried along by the divinity. So what appears is the sheep, that is, humanity, but, as it is written, God's "footprints were unseen."[144] He who bears the sheep upon himself is marked with no "footprint" of sin or going astray as regards his human life; the "footprints" that are impressed upon him throughout his life's journey are those which are appropriate to God, such as teachings, cures, restoring the dead to life, and other such marvels. When the shepherd takes this sheep upon himself, he becomes one with it and speaks with the voice of the sheep to his flocks. How could

---

n. 160 below): "Since, therefore, the children share flesh and blood, he himself likewise shared the same things, so that through death he might destroy the one who has the power of death ..." (NRSV).

142. Heb 2.10.

143. Lk 15.4–7; Mt 18.12–14.

144. διὰ τοῦτο τὸ μὲν φαινόμενον πρόβατον, τουτέστιν ἄνθρωπος, τὰ δὲ ἴχνη αὐτοῦ, κατὰ τὸ γεγεραμμένον, οὐκ ἐγινώσκετο (Ps 76 [77].19). The translation offered above is similar to Winling's (177) and Zacagnius's (PG 45:1154B); it assumes that ἐστι is to be understood after πρόβατον. If it is correct, "what appears" must be Christ's humanity, which conceals his divinity ("God's footprints were unseen"). This would reflect, though in a slightly convoluted way, Gregory's identification of Christ's humanity with both the shepherd and the sheep. J.'s suggestion *ad loc.*, that there may be a lacuna in the text after ἄνθρωπος (in which case the sentence might be translated: "So the sheep that appears, that is, humanity ... but, as it is written, God's 'footprints were unseen'"), seems unnecessary.

our human weakness be adequate to comprehend an address by
the divine voice? He speaks to us in a human way, that is, as one
might put it, in a "sheep-like" way, saying, "My sheep hear my
voice."[145] So the shepherd who has taken the sheep upon himself and speaks to us through it is both sheep and shepherd.[146]
He is the sheep in that he has been taken up and a shepherd in
that it is he who has done the taking up. Because it is necessary
for the good shepherd to give his life for his sheep,[147] so that by
his own death [J.153] he may destroy death, the author of our
salvation becomes, in his human nature, both priest[148] and lamb;
he is able to share in suffering, and so is able to incur death.[149]

*He then goes on to explain the soteriological function of Christ's res-
urrection. In Christ's death his body and soul were separated (which
is what death means); his body, preserved from corruption, lay in the
grave, and his soul was committed to God's hands, that is, admitted
to paradise, with that of the repentant thief. (For a discussion of this
doctrine, see section 11 of the introduction, pages 82–85.) But the undivided divinity remained with both body and soul; what happened in
the Resurrection is that the divinity brought them back together again.
So, through our participation in Christ's human nature, we also participate in his resurrection. That, rather than what Apolinarius says, is
what it really means to be saved through Christ's flesh and blood.*

Since death is nothing other than the dissolution of body and
soul, he who unites himself to both, that is, to body and soul,
is separated from neither of them. ("For the gifts [M.1156] of
God are irrevocable," says the Apostle Paul.)[150] But having given

145. Jn 10.16.
146. As Zachhuber, 222, points out, Gregory uses this notion as a way of
showing how, although Christ has two natures, there is a sense in which they
are one. Zachhuber says that Gregory's "attempt at a solution [of this central
Christological dilemma]—sheep and shepherd become one—is too forceful
to convince"; but arguably any account of the mystery of the divine enfleshment must necessarily incorporate a paradox of some kind, and the one Gregory has chosen here is no worse than many others.
147. Jn 10.11, 15.
148. Cf. Heb 2.17.
149. Literally, "causes death to come to pass" (ἐνεργήσας τὸν θάνατον).
150. Rom 11.29.

a share of himself to both body and soul, Christ opened paradise for the thief [151] through the soul, while through the body he put a stop to the power of decay. And this is the destruction of death, to take away the power of decay; it disappears in the vivifying nature of Christ. What acts on these two parts of our nature becomes a grace and a benefit to both. Thus he who is in both knits together through his resurrection that which has been separated. He freely gave over his body, as has been written, to "the heart of the earth";[152] his soul he put away from himself, when he says to the Father, "Into your hands I commend my spirit,"[153] and when he says to the thief, "Today you will be with me in paradise."[154] (Both of these latter two sayings are true. It must be assumed that that divine form of life called "paradise" is none other than the Father's capacious palms, as stated by the prophet when, as the mouthpiece of the Lord, he describes the heavenly Jerusalem: "I have painted your walls on my hands, and you are continually before me.")[155]

Thus he both experiences death and is not mastered by death. For what is composite can be split up, while that which is incomposite is not susceptible to dissolution. The incomposite nature remains in the division of what is composite, [J.154] and so, when the soul leaves the body, it is separated from neither. The proof of this is that the divine power, as has been said, produces incorruptibility for the body and life in paradise for the soul. But in this separation he who is simple and incomposite is not himself divided. On the contrary, he creates a unity; by being himself indivisible, he brings what has been divided into a unity.

This is shown by him who said, "God raised him from the dead."[156] In the case of the Lord's resurrection it would not be pious to think of his restoration to life as having been effected by some external power, as in the case of Lazarus[157] or any of the other people who were brought back from the dead. Rather, it was the Only-begotten God himself who raised the man who

151. Lk 23.43.
153. Lk 23.46.
155. Is 49.16 (LXX).
157. Jn 11.43.

152. Mt 12.40.
154. Lk 23.43.
156. Col 2.12; 1 Thes 1.10.

had been mixed with him. After he had separated his soul from his body, he joined them both together again, so that there is salvation for the whole of human nature. Hence he is called "the author of life."¹⁵⁸ For in him who died and was raised for us the Only-begotten God reconciled the world to himself.¹⁵⁹ We were like slaves captured in war, all participating in him through his flesh and blood,¹⁶⁰ whom he bought back with his blood, which was of the same kind as ours. That must be the tenor of the Apostle Paul's saying that "we have redemption through his blood, the forgiveness of our trespasses"¹⁶¹ through his flesh.

It is this meaning, not that of Apolinarius, that we have found in the words of the Apostle that have been cited. Let a careful judge decide which view is more [M.1157] orthodox: whether, as we say, the divine glory dwelt on our earth, as part of God's plan; or whether, as he says,¹⁶² the flesh was not acquired by the divinity for our benefit but shared its very being and nature. [L.36]

12. Apolinarius's teaching on the pre-existent Christ and the identity of Jesus with him (continued): Zechariah 13.7 and Hebrews 1.1–3

Gregory now resumes his critique of Apolinarius's use of Scripture to defend his thesis that the identity of the man Jesus and the Logos was somehow manifested from before the time that Christ appeared on earth, indeed from all eternity.

158. Acts 3.14.

159. 2 Cor 5.19.

160. πάντας τοὺς κεκοινωνηκότας αὐτῷ τῆς σαρκὸς καὶ τοῦ αἵματος ... See Heb 2.14: ἐπεὶ οὖν τὰ παιδία κεκοινώνηκεν αἵματος καὶ σαρκός ... : "Since therefore the children share flesh and blood ..." (NRSV).

161. Eph 1.7; see n. 141 above.

162. καθὼς ἐκεῖνός φησιν. See n. 137 (J.150–51 above) for the possible implications of this formula. Grelier (144) classifies this fragment not as a citation but as a "distorted characterization of an opponent's view"; Carter (350) calls it "Gregory's (mis)interpretative summary of what he thinks Apolinarius means to say on the basis of his proof texts." That seems right. Grelier points out that in no other fragment of Apolinarius is the expression "[sharing] its very being and nature" (συνουσιωμένη καὶ σύμφυτος) used to characterize the relationship between the divinity and the flesh.

The first of Apolinarius's scriptural citations that Gregory mentions is Zechariah 13.7, which, in the version cited here, reads, "Awake, O sword, against my shepherd and against the man who shares my tribe." Gregory postpones until later a discussion of how Apolinarius used this text; he confines himself at this stage to pointing out, reasonably enough, that the "shepherd" here need not be Christ, but could be the leader of the Jewish people in Zechariah's day.

Whether the prophet Zechariah with his [J.155] riddles is to be interpreted in some other sense than these, I do not think it is necessary to ascertain in our argument, nor whether his meaning refers to the Lord or to someone else. He says, "Awake, O sword, against my shepherd and against the man who shares my tribe."[163] We think this text is a warning against those who unjustly raise the sword against those of their own tribe.[164] Apolinarius says the reference is to raising a sword against the Lord, applying the title "shepherd" to him,[165] [L.37] and ignorant of the fact that in many places in Scripture the words "pastor" and "shepherd" are applied to those who are endowed with authority.

Apolinarius's next text is Hebrews 1.1–3. He says that this shows that the "man" (that is, the Son) who "has spoken to us in these last days" is identical with the "radiance of God's glory and the exact imprint of God's very being," rather than just a man who had God "within himself." It is this man who, "by himself, that is, by his flesh, cleansed the world of sins." Gregory again challenges this on the misconceived basis that what Apolinarius is saying is that the eternal Word was, from eternity, joined to Jesus's limited, weak, and passible human flesh, and that it was through this "enfleshed" Logos that the universe was created. That, he argues, is absurd. The human nature that Christ adopted

163. Zec 13.7. Apolinarius and Gregory follow Aquila's Greek text (see Grelier, 234) rather than the LXX, which has "shepherds" (ποιμένας) rather than "shepherd" (νομέα), and "(who is) my citizen" (πολίτην μου) rather than "who shares my tribe" (συμφυλόν μου).

164. Modern exegesis would suggest that in this passage Zechariah is in fact representing God as indicating that disaster will befall Israel and its leaders.

165. Gregory is (almost certainly wrongly) representing Apolinarius as arguing from the term "who shares my tribe" that the incarnate Christ (the "shepherd") was consubstantial with the Father as regards his body and soul as well as as regards his divinity. This is made clear in J.158 below.

must be clearly distinguished from his divine nature. It cannot have been the man Jesus who was "the radiance of God's glory and the exact imprint of God's very being" because that would carry the blasphemous implication that the divine nature itself was fleshly.

Again, when in a slovenly fashion he uses the letter to the Hebrews with the same end in view, the absurdity of his arguments is equally obvious, as anyone with just a modicum of intelligence can easily see. Because the text says that in the "last days God has spoken to us by a Son," having earlier "spoken to our ancestors in many and various ways by the prophets,"[166] he says that this is proof that the human element of the God who appeared to us existed before the ages. Indeed, this is what he says by way of explanation in his interpretation of the Apostle:

By these words it is clear that it was the man who spoke to us of the things of the Father who is himself God, the Creator of the ages, "radiance of God's glory[167] and the exact imprint of God's very being," inasmuch as he was God in his own spirit and did not have God within him as something other than himself, but by himself, that is, by his flesh, cleansed the world of sins. [L.38]

These are Apolinarius's exact words, without any changes made to the text by me.[168]

If it is a man "who spoke to us," and is "the Creator of the ages," as our wordsmith thinks, and if his flesh is the "radiance," and if the "form of a slave"[169] characterizes God's substance, I

166. Heb 1.1–2.

167. Heb 1.3. NRSV has "reflection of God's glory." But see Frederick William Danker, *A Greek-English Lexicon of the New Testament and other Early Christian Literature,* 3d ed., based on Walter Bauer's *Griechisch-deutsches Wörterbuch zu den Schriften des Neuen Testaments und der frühchristlichen Literatur,* 6th ed. (Chicago and London: University of Chicago Press, 2000), s.v., which states that Gregory normally understands ἀπαύγασμα in the active sense as = "radiance." Cf. his use of ἀπαυγαζόμενον as = "shining out" later in this passage (n. 177 below).

168. Grelier (115) records a suggestion by V. H. Drecoll that the last part of this sentence could be taken to imply that on other occasions when Gregory claims to be recording Apolinarius's "exact words" he is not in fact doing so! She argues (116), however, that in fact there is no reason to believe, on the basis of a comparison with other genuine fragments of Apolinarius, that Gregory has in fact tampered with Apolinarius's text in those cases where he explicitly says he is quoting him directly.

169. Phil 2.7.

no longer think there is any point in combatting what Apolinarius has said; rather, we should mourn the obtuseness of those [J.156] who accept such novel teaching. The man was he "who spoke to us" in a human way using our language: that is, he who spat and made clay with his hand,[170] who put his fingers into deaf persons' ears,[171] touched people who were diseased or dead, took rest from his labor by sleeping[172] or sitting down,[173] wept, felt anguish and distress, experienced thirst, desired food, and asked for water. Is it he, actually in his human flesh, who is to be thought of as existing before the creation of the universe? Is the nature of the flesh, composite, solid, and dense as it is, to be called divine? Let all pious ears be [M.1160] blocked! May the pure doctrine of God not be defiled by having fleshly passions insultingly attributed to him by those who bring down the divine to a human level!

For who does not know that, according to orthodox tradition, the God who appeared to us in the flesh both was and is immaterial, invisible, incomposite, that he both was and is boundless and uncircumscribed, and that he is present everywhere and penetrates all creation; but that in his manifestation he was seen as circumscribed in a human way? For every body must by necessity be contained within some surface. The surface is the boundary of the body enclosed within it. Everything surrounded by a boundary is shut up within something that has a defined size. But what is defined cannot be infinite. But then the prophet says, "His greatness has no limit."[174] If the divine nature is flesh, as Apolinarius claims, and so necessarily surrounded by a surface, that is, by a limit, how can God's greatness, as the prophet says, have no limit? How can we think of what is infinite using the concept of finitude, or of what is limitless by the concept of limitation? Or rather, as we [J.157] have already said,[175] how can what is strong come from death? If, as Apolinarius says, "the man who spoke to us" is Creator of the ages and created everything himself by himself, that is, by his flesh,

---

170. Jn 9.6. 171. Mk 7.33.
172. See Mk 4.38. 173. See Jn 4.6.
174. Ps 144 (145).3 (LXX).
175. This seems to be a rather vague reference to the argument in J.153–54.

as in Apolinarius's interpretation, and if, in the divine words, the flesh is called "weak,"[176] what our wordsmith is claiming is that might and strength and power and other exalted notions appropriate to God originate in weakness!

All this so far is not so dreadful, but if the argument is subjected to further logical scrutiny, it involves itself in actual blasphemy against the Father. He says that the man is "the radiance of God's glory" and that in this fleshly god, which he has constructed as an idol through his vain arguments, the "very being of God" is "exactly imprinted." Just as a sunbeam is related to the sun, and the light that is radiated out[177] is related to the lamp that is its source, and the "imprint" of a human being manifests the "very being" of humanity, so if what appears to us "radiated" from the Father's glory and the "exact imprint of his very being" is flesh, it follows that the Father's nature, too, is constituted as fleshly. For the incorporeal could not be said to be "imprinted" [M.1161] on the corporeal, nor could the visible be said to be "radiated" from the invisible. It is clear, rather, that as is the "glory," so is the "radiance," and as is the "exact imprint," so is the "very being." If the second of each pair is body, there is no way the first can be considered incorporeal.

Gregory now returns again to the Zechariah text referred to earlier (J.154–55), which Apolinarius seems to have read as supporting the Nicene doctrine of consubstantiality: "my (that is, God's) shepherd" is Christ, and "of the same tribe" as I am is equivalent to "organically one and consubstantial" with me. Gregory first accuses Apolinarius of claiming that Christ's fleshly nature is consubstantial with his divinity. But Apolinarius goes on to say that Christ "is not consubstantial with God according to the flesh but according to the Spirit which is united with the flesh." Gregory seems tacitly to accept, in a slightly embarrassed way, that this rather undermines his accusation that Apolinarius does not properly distinguish between Christ's divine and human natures. So he bases his attack on the phrase "the Spirit, which is united with the flesh," on the grounds that this must mean, on the basis of what Apolinarius has already said, "eternally united with the flesh," which, he can again argue, is absurd.

176. Mk 14.38.
177. ἀπαυγαζόμενον. See n. 167 above.

But he even mentions the doctrine of Nicaea, that in which the synod of the Fathers acting together proclaimed consubstantiality.[178] [L.39] No one could say that "consubstantial" could be used of things that differ in kind; the term "consubstantial" is applicable only to things that by definition share the same substance. Let us assume the Son is a fleshly God and is flesh by nature even when the expression "from before the ages" is applied to him. Now even our wordsmith does not doubt that he is consubstantial [J.158] with the Father, and things are consubstantial with each other if they are defined as being of the same substance. So Apolinarius must be suggesting that even the Father's nature is human and corporeal, so that he can allow himself to use the word "consubstantial" with reference to both Persons.[179] He is in fact saying one of two things. Either he is saying that the Father is incorporeal and, because the Son's divinity is fleshly, is admitting a difference of substance; or, if Father and Son share the same substance and divinity, he is attributing fleshliness to the divine nature even of the Father.

But he seems to be correcting this absurdity in what he says earlier, when he gives what seems to him to be the correct interpretation of the words of Zechariah, as referring to the person[180] of the Father and his relation with the Son, claiming that the word "of the same tribe" is equivalent to "organically one"[181] and "consubstantial." [L.40] Whether or not this view is correct would require another argument, but the statement he produces is as follows: "Through these words the prophetic utterance makes it clear that he is not consubstantial with God according to the flesh but according to the Spirit, which is united with the flesh." [L.41] But how could his fleshly God be united to flesh before the world came into being, when neither time nor anything else of the created order existed? The flesh is the very last of the things that came to be in creation. What sort of flesh could the Spirit be united with when human nature had not yet come into existence? But Apolinarius knows of some other kind of flesh apart from that of human beings! How can he say that "it was the man who spoke to us of the things of the Father who

178. τὸ ὁμούσιον.
180. προσώπου.

179. "Persons" is not in the Greek.
181. συμφυῆ.

is himself God, the Creator of the ages"?[182] Who will interpret for us the absurdity of these new-fangled riddles? A man before any man came into existence; flesh that is prior to its own creation; what came into existence in these last times being "before the [M.1164] ages": these ideas, and others like them, are what, all confused together, he sets forth in his treatise.

13. Third excursus: Gregory's reflections on Philippians 2.5–11

Apolinarius seems now to have turned to a discussion of Philippians 2.5–11. Before addressing his arguments, Gregory offers his own reflections on this passage.

The pre-existent Christ is described as being "in the form of God"—not "in the image and likeness of God," like Adam, but "equal" to God. This rules out, as Gregory has already argued, any idea that the pre-existent Christ was fleshly. It was only at Bethlehem that he was "born in human likeness and form," that he "took the form of a slave"—that is, a body—and "emptied himself," that is, accepted the limitations imposed by a corporeal nature. He was "found as a man," and that must mean that he was a human being like us, differing from us only in respect of the unique way in which he was conceived in Mary's womb. (But in characterizing this difference, Gregory uses expressions that, on the face of it, come close to the very error he is accusing Apolinarius of. It means, he says, that he was not a man "in every way" or "in every respect"; see "The unity of Christ's person: His virginal conception," on pages 75–78 of the introduction.) That he "humbled himself" implies that his previous condition had been a more exalted one.

But let our wordsmith follow his own way through the trackless wastes of his arguments; we, using the apostolic [J.159] teaching (which he himself refers to) as a means to reproach his sacrilegious opinions, shall move on to the next part of his text. He cites, "... he was in the form of God."[183] This text does not say "he had a form like God," as could be said of him who was made in the likeness of God,[184] but that he existed in the actual form

182. See L.38, J.155, above.
183. Phil 2.6. Throughout this section "form" translates μορφή.
184. I.e., any human being.

of God. For everything that the Father has is in the Son[185]—eternity, absence of quantity, immateriality, and incorporeality—so that the form of the "exact imprint"[186] of the Father can in every respect be preserved in the Son, who is "equal" with God.[187] What sort of concept of distinction or difference does "equality" permit? How can "equality" be properly applied to beings of different natures? If one being is fleshly by nature, and the other is free from the flesh, how could one say that the fleshliness of the one was "equal" to the opposite quality in the other?

"He emptied himself, taking the form of a slave."[188] What is this slavish form? It must be the body; we have received no other doctrine than this from the Fathers. So he who said that the Son took "the form of a slave" (and that form is flesh) is claiming that he is one thing in his divine form, but that the slavish form that he took was something other in its nature. The word "emptied" also clearly shows that what was seen by us had not always existed: in the fullness of his divinity he is equal to God, unapproachable, inaccessible, and unable to be contained within the limitations of our human insignificance; but he became contained within the perishable nature of flesh when, as the Apostle Paul says, he "emptied" himself of the ineffable glory of his divinity and reduced it to the level of our limitations. What he was, was great and perfect and incomprehensible; what he "took" could be measured on the same scale as our nature. He was "born in human likeness and shape,"[189] so clearly he did not possess the likeness of such a nature from the beginning, nor was he shaped according to some bodily pattern.[190] For how could the pattern of a "shape" be applied to what was [J.160] incorporeal? Nevertheless, at the Incarnation he had a "shape," because he adopted a "shape"; that goes with the nature of the body.

185. See Jn 16.15, 17.10.   186. χαρακτήρος. See Heb 1.3.
187. See Phil 2.6.   188. Phil 2.7a.
189. Phil 2.7b. σχῆμα ("form" in NRSV here) and its derivative σχηματιζό-μενος are translated as "shape(d)" throughout this paragraph.
Modern NT texts, followed by NRSV, read ἐν ὁμοιώματι ἀνθρώπου γενόμενος· καὶ σχήματι εὑρεθεὶς ὡς ἄνθρωπος, with a stop after γενόμενος: "... being born in human likeness. And being found in human form (shape)...." But Gregory assumes a stop after σχήματι, which thus becomes dependent on γενόμενος rather than on εὑρεθεὶς. This reading is unique to him (see Grelier, 321–22.)
190. τύπον.

"Being found as a man …"[191] Yes, indeed, a man—but not in every way[192] a man, rather "as a man" by virtue of the mystery of his virgin birth, so that it would be evident that he was not in all respects subject to the laws of human nature, but rather that he entered human life in a divine way, not requiring the assistance of marital [M.1165] intercourse to constitute his physical nature. Because of the unusual way in which he was brought into being, he was "found" not as an ordinary man in every respect,[193] but "as a man" nevertheless.

Why did Christ take flesh in this way? Gregory now develops the soteriological ideas that he adumbrated in his previous excursus. "He who is joined to our nature makes our sufferings his own." Human nature as a whole is like a body, so that what happens to one part affects every other. Christ became part of human nature, so we, as human beings in solidarity with him, share in his sufferings and in his glorification. Adam and Christ both stand for human nature as a whole: the first Adam, by his disobedience, brought us death; Christ, the new Adam, by his obedience, brings us life. After "humbling" himself, Christ's human nature is glorified (as God, he is glorified already), and we are glorified with him.

It was in this way that "he humbled himself,"[194] by becoming a man (though without any alteration). If he had been a man from the beginning, what did his humbling consist of? As it is, the Most High has humbled himself by a union with our humble nature. When by taking "the form of a slave" he united himself to it and became one with it, he made the sufferings of the slave his own. Then it is like when some accident happens to the tip of a nail. Because of the connection between the parts of our body, the effect is extended to the sufferer's whole body as the sensation runs through it. So he who is joined to our nature makes our sufferings his own.[195] As Isaiah says, "He took up our infirmities and bore our diseases,"[196] and sustained blows on our account,

191. Phil 2.7c, but see n. 189 above for the punctuation of this verse.

192. μὴ δι' ὅλου.   193. οὐ διὰ πάντων.

194. Phil 2.8.

195. For the "physical" soteriology underlying this passage, see section 11 of the introduction, pp. 82–85, in particular n. 409.

196. Mt 8.17, based on Is 53.4.

so that "by his bruises we might be healed."[197] Not that it was the divinity that was bruised; it was rather the man joined in union to the divinity whose nature could be made receptive to bruising.

This was so that evil might return by the same route by which it came. Since death entered the world through the disobedience of the first man, for this reason it departed through the obedience of the second man.[198] [J.161] Therefore, "he became obedient to the point of death,"[199] so that through his obedience he might heal the offense caused by disobedience, and so that through his resurrection from the dead he might destroy death, which resulted from our disobedience. For the resurrection of the man from death is the destruction of death.

"Therefore," says Paul, "God also highly exalted him."[200] This is like a sort of seal on the view we expressed earlier. The most exalted one clearly has no need of exaltation; what is exalted is what previously was humble, which now becomes what it was not before. Human nature united with the Lord is exalted together with the divinity; what is exalted is that which is raised from its humble condition. What is humble is "the form of a slave," which, through its exaltation, becomes Christ and Lord.[201]

But Gregory is aware of the danger of suggesting too sharp a distinction between Christ's human and divine natures. He comes up with his own version of the communicatio idiomatum.[202] *Because of the intimacy of the union between man and God in the divine enfleshment—what Gregory calls a "mixture" of the two natures—God acquires a name, "Jesus," at whose "name . . . every knee shall bend." Conversely, in his exaltation, Jesus becomes "above a name" and is worshiped by the whole of creation. "As the exalted came to be in the humble, so the humble took on the characteristics of the exalted."*

As a result of the mystic initiation the Virgin received from Gabriel, the man in Christ is given an individual name in the

197. Is 53.5.   198. See Rom 5.19.
199. Phil 2.8.   200. Phil 2.9.
201. See Acts 2.36.

202. As Anthony Meredith, in *Gregory of Nyssa*, The Early Church Fathers (London: Routledge, 1999), 150, n. 64, points out. There is a similar passage in *Theo*, J.127–28.

human fashion; his human element, as has been said, was called Jesus.[203] His divine nature, on the other hand, cannot be confined by a name, but the two elements became one, through the mixture, so, by virtue of the human element, even God is given a name. "At the name of Jesus every knee shall bend,"[204] and the man becomes "above a name,"[205] which is a characteristic of Godhead as the latter cannot be indicated by any name. [M.1168] So as the exalted came to be in the humble, so the humble took on the characteristics of the exalted. For just as God acquires a name through the man, so the humble that is raised up with God becomes "above a name." And as the dishonor of the slave's condition is put right by the fact that the divine is mixed with the slave, so worship of the Godhead by the whole [J.162] creation is referred to him who is united to the Godhead. Thus "at the name of Jesus Christ every knee shall bend in heaven and on earth and under the earth, and every tongue shall confess that Jesus Christ is Lord, to the glory of God the Father."[206] Amen.[207]

14. Apolinarius's teaching on the pre-existent Christ and the identity of Jesus with him (continued): Philippians 2.5–11

Apolinarius's account of the Christology of Philippians 2.5–11 begins with what seems to be a clear acknowledgment that the human body of Christ did not in fact precede his birth from Mary, when he says that "the equality of the same Jesus Christ to the Father pre-existed; his likeness to men came afterwards." Gregory presents this as an embarrassed U-turn on Apolinarius's part, but argues that he returns to the error of his ways in then proceeding rhetorically to ask, "What can show more

203. See Lk 1.31.   204. Phil 2.10.
205. Phil 2.9.   206. Phil 2.10–11.
207. Grelier (218–19) points out that Gregory also places an "Amen" at the end of his discussion of this passage in his sermon on the nativity of Christ (*In diem natalem salvatoris, GNO* 10.2, 269; PG 46:1149C), but not after his citations of it in his other works. The "Amen" serves to emphasize the special homiletic character of this excursus, thus distinguishing it from the polemical material that surrounds it.

clearly than this does that complete man and complete God, two different things, are not joined together?"

If Gregory is here following the original order of Apolinarius's text (but see note 209), the latter's argument here is indeed far from clear; what he may be trying to say is that Philippians 2.7 ("he emptied himself, taking the form of a slave, being born in human likeness") should be interpreted as meaning not that the Word assumed a complete, that is, perfect man, but rather that, after the enfleshment, it constituted "the most important element in the nature of the God-Man" (see J.147 above), whose other two elements were a body and an animal soul. In other words, it is part of his project to demonstrate that when the Word became enfleshed, he did not cease to be God. What Gregory, however, focuses on (using a rather labored analogy) is that the second sentence of this fragment (assuming the two sentences do indeed form a single fragment; see note 209) is not a logical consequence of the first; if Christ acquired human "likeness" only when he was made manifest on earth, it does not necessarily follow that such "likeness" cannot have been to a "perfect" man.

But it seems that Apolinarius, as if blushing at himself and ashamed of the outrageousness of what he has said, wants in some way to retract his assertions and to maintain that the likeness of the Son to human beings was something that came later. "Now the equality of the same Jesus Christ to the Father pre-existed; his likeness to men came afterwards." [L.42] Here he seems to be repenting of what he has said; if only he did this in his heart and were converted from this outrageous doctrine, then we for our part would stop accusing him![208] But it seems from what he actually argues that he uses the right judgment he has shown here to lay the foundation for another piece of outrageousness.

These are his exact words. "What can show more clearly than this does that complete man and complete God, two different things, are not joined together?" [L.42][209] But it should be clear

208. This sentence is evidence that Apolinarius was still alive when Gregory was writing; see Lietzmann, 83.
209. Lietzmann treats this and the sentence quoted in the previous paragraph as a single fragment (L.42). Mühlenberg (67) agrees. Grelier (87–91,

to anyone who can follow the argument that this statement is in no way consistent with what comes before it. How can the pre-existent equality with the Father and the likeness to human beings, which came later, both of which Apolinarius admits, prove that there could not have been a perfect human being through whom the perfect God became man? It is as if someone, having pointed out that the heaven is a long way from the earth, claimed that the reason that any given volume of lead is heavier than the same volume of tin is because weight is a function of distance from the heaven! Similarly nobody can prove the defectiveness of the [J.163] humanity through which God came to be in our nature from the fact that it is agreed that the likeness of the Son to human beings is something that came later.[210] But for a little while I shall postpone demonstrating the impiety and folly of this opinion. Now, following in order his exact words, I shall try to correct his argument, wherever it is convenient to refute what he says.

It is, says Gregory, presumably the human rather than the divine element of Christ's person that Apolinarius thinks is imperfect; there is an implied rebuke in the suggestion that Apolinarius is vague about this precisely because of his failure to draw a clear distinction between the two elements. But, Gregory goes on, human beings are defined, against other animals, by their rational faculties. So it is illogical to characterize Christ as both

---

103), however, thinks that this citation (the second part of L.42) is discussed here out of sequence, and that its proper context is later, somewhere near fragment 81, also on the issue of whether perfect man could be joined to perfect God, and discussed by Gregory in J.199–200. That would certainly help to explain why Apolinarius's argument here is rather difficult to follow. On the other hand, in his next sentence here Gregory seems explicitly to be saying that the second sentence of L.42 follows immediately on the first. On balance, it seems better to assume that Gregory is not here departing from Apolinarius's order.

210. The point of this rather labored analogy could perhaps be paraphrased as follows. Heaven is distant from earth, and it is therefore obvious that similar volumes of different elements may thus also be situated at different distances from heaven; but that clearly does not logically entail that their relative weights are a function of those distances. Similarly, when Christ acquired human likeness, it is obvious that he assumed some sort of humanity; but that does not logically entail that the humanity he assumed was a defective one.

God and man, if "man" is in this case redefined to mean just a body and
an animal soul. A being without a mind cannot be a man.

He claims that there can be no perfect God with a perfect
man. So far he has left it ambiguous as to which of these two he
calls "imperfect"; because he is [M.1169] unclear about what
he means, the concept could be just as well applied to either.
From what we have heard, it is not possible to find out to what
he thinks the term "imperfect" should be applied: God, the
man, or both together. He says Christ is God in his spirit, in
that he has the glory of God, but is a man in his body, in that he
wore the inglorious shape of human beings.[211] [L.43] He speaks
of God and he speaks of man; but it is clear to all that these
words are not being applied to the same thing but that one is
being used to explain the divinity and the other the humanity.

For God is what always remains the same, the source of all
good things, who has always existed and always will. Human
beings, on the other hand, share the nature of irrational animals and like them are controlled by flesh and the faculty of
perception, while at the same time they are distinguished from
animals by the addition of mind, which is the special characteristic of their nature. No one would define human beings on the
basis of flesh, bones, or senses, or would describe the faculty of
feeding or digestion as the distinctive characteristic of human
nature; rather, reference would be made to their intellectual
and rational faculties. One can give an account of something's
nature by revealing either its name or [J.164] the attributes attached to that nature. So saying "human being" implies "rational," and saying "rational" implies "human" by the very word.
So with Apolinarius: when he uses the expression "God and
man," he may be wishing to convey the meanings found in the
word "God," but that should not contaminate the meaning of
the word "man."[212] The word "man" is an absolutely correct appellation and not a misleading one; but the correctness of the

211. Gregory gives this as a direct quotation in J.164 below.
212. Literally, "Thus, when Apolinarius uses the appellation (ὀνομάσας)
'God and man,' if he includes in this expression the meanings that appear in
the divinity, he should not damage the meaning of 'man' through [that] interpretation."

word consists in its being applied to a rational creature. Rationality is wholly a product of intellect. So if someone is a man, he is necessarily endowed with intellect. If he has no intellect, he is not a man.

Apolinarius "says Christ is God in his spirit, in that it has the glory of God, but is a man in his body, in that he wore the inglorious shape of human beings." "The inglorious shape of human beings" may be an acceptable expression, says Gregory, even if it does not appear in Scripture, but how it should be interpreted is not, as Apolinarius would have it, that the humanity that Christ adopted was incomplete; rather, it was complete, but fallen and therefore damaged and not capable of achieving its proper perfection. The damage was caused by sin, and, Gregory again reminds his readers, only a creature with a rational mind can sin.

But, Apolinarius says, "He was a man in his body, in that he wore the inglorious shape of human beings." [L.43] These words are his own, rather than being taken from the teaching of Scripture; nevertheless, we should examine his argument so that we can refute from his own words what he is anxious to show. He says that Christ "wore the inglorious shape of human beings."

First we shall examine what the glory of human beings is; thus we shall be able to deduce what their ingloriousness is. Now, the glory of a human being—the true glory, anyway—is nothing other than the life of virtue. To define the glory of human beings by good complexion or the bloom of the flesh, or its opposite by physical ugliness, would be to follow the example of the decadent. If [M.1172] virtue is agreed to constitute what is glorious in human beings, then vice is clearly what is inglorious.

Apolinarius, however, says that God adopted "the inglorious shape of human beings." So if what is inglorious lies in vice, and vice constitutes the shame of our free choice; if what freely chooses is the intellect, and the intellect is an activity of mind; then whoever is considering human ingloriousness as it has come into relationship with God will not detach from human intellect the man through whom God took part in human life. And this is consonant with the [J.165] divine Scriptures: that Christ became sin because of us;[213] that is, he joined the sinful

213. See 2 Cor 5.21.

soul of man[214] to himself. "The Lord," he says, "appeared in the shape of a slave."[215] [L.44] Was this slave, whose shape the Lord adopted, perfect, or had his perfection been damaged? One could quite properly apply the term "damage" to some creature that was defective and incomplete as regards the fulfillment of its nature.

Christ appeared "as a man," Apolinarius goes on, but was not a man in that he was not of the same being as, not consubstantial with, the man's most important element. But, says Gregory, if he did not completely share human nature, he cannot logically have been a man at all; he must have been either some sort of docetic ghost or an animal.

"As a man," Apolinarius says, "but not a man, because not one in being [consubstantial][216] with the man's most important element."[217] [L.45][218] But if he is not one in being, he is altogether other in being. If the principle of their being[219] is differ-

214. τοῦ ἀνθρώπου, which could also be translated as "of the man [Jesus]." See introduction, pp. 82–85 and n. 406, for Gregory's belief that it was sinful humanity that the Logos assumed at Jesus's conception and that it was from the action of the Logos on that fallen humanity that his moral perfection was derived. Cf. J.171 below: "He took up our filth, but was not himself polluted by the stain; rather, he purified this filth in his own person."

215. ἐν δουλικῷ φανέντα σχήματι. See Phil 2.7, μορφὴν δούλου λαβών … καὶ σχήματι εὑρεθεὶς ὡς ἄνθρωπος … The status of this fragment can conveniently be considered with that of L.46 below; J., but not Lietzmann, shows them as direct quotations. Mühlenberg (68) says the question cannot be conclusively decided. I follow Grelier (118), who thinks the fact that the phrases are quoted separately, rather than being embedded in Gregory's commentary, means that they are probably direct quotations.

216. ὁμοούσιος.

217. κατὰ τὸ κυριώτατον. See n. 119 on L.32, J.147, above.

218. Mühlenberg argues (68) that this is not a quotation from Apolinarius but rather a deliberate misrepresentation of his position on Gregory's part in order to charge him with docetism. But it is arguably quite consistent with Apolinarius's overall position for him to claim that, although Christ was consubstantial with our nature as regards his flesh and animal soul, he was not "as regards his most important element" (κατὰ τὸ κυριώτατον), that is, his rational mind. He uses similar language in L.41 (J.158 above): "Through these words the prophetic utterance makes it clear that he is not consubstantial with God according to the flesh but according to the Spirit, which is united with the flesh." Carter (354) also rejects Mühlenberg's argument.

219. ὁ λόγος τῆς οὐσίας.

ent, the two concepts can share neither a nature nor a name. The being of fire is one thing and the being of water is another, so the two have different names. But Peter and Paul, because they have the same nature, share a form of being with the same name: each of them is a man.[220] If Christ were anything other than a man in his being, and were only manifested in the shape of a man, and in truth were quite different in his being, then we must say that everything about him is mere appearance and a deceptive illusion; he did not really eat, he did not really sleep, none of his healing miracles happened, there was no cross, he was not placed in the tomb, he did not rise again after his Passion; all these things were appearances, and, according to our wordsmith, what appeared to happen did not really do so. If he were not a man, how is it that these things came to be recorded about him? How could someone whose being was other than that of a man be called a man? He is not, says Apolinarius, "one in being with the man's most important element." By taking away the man's "most important element," that is, mind, he portrays what is left as a beast. But a beast is not a man.

It seems that Apolinarius may at this stage have offered a paraphrase of Philippians 2.8–9, as follows: "He humbled himself according to the flesh; he was highly exalted by God in a divine exaltation." Gregory chooses, perversely, to read this as implying that what was humbled was the flesh (which, as he points out, was already humble, so would need no further humbling) while what was exalted was the divinity (which, as he has pointed out earlier, was already exalted).

He continues, "He humbled himself according to the flesh; he was highly exalted by God[221] in a divine exaltation."[222] [L.46] This is more senseless than what came before, as well as being impious. He is saying that what was "humbled" was other than what was "highly exalted." The flesh, he says, was "humbled," although what is humble [J.166] by nature has no need to be

---

220. As Winling (194, n. 137) notes, Gregory uses elsewhere, in his Trinitarian treatises, "Peter and Paul," who share the οὐσία of humanity, as an illustration of the concept of consubstantiality.

221. See Phil 2.8–9.

222. For the status of this fragment, see n. 215 on L.44 above.

humbled; the divinity, he says, was "highly exalted," although what is already exalted has no need of exaltation. How could the divinity, which transcends everything and is above all exaltation, be "highly exalted"? Whether our wordsmith likes it or not, it is what is by nature humble that is exalted, as was set out when we discussed these matters a little earlier.[223]

But, Gregory concedes, Apolinarius also says, "He is glorified as man, but as the God pre-existing all ages he has glory before the world was made." Typically, Gregory uses this as evidence for Apolinarius's hopeless inconsistency. In fact, it seems more likely that it shows that Gregory's interpretation of the immediately preceding passage (L.46) is tendentious or plain wrong; Apolinarius quite clearly implies there that it is Christ's humanity, not his divinity, that is glorified.

[M.1173] Then again he loses the thread of his argument, like those who speak nonsense in their sleep. He takes over our own arguments and then mixes up his own with what people who think correctly about doctrine might say. He distinguishes him who is glorified from him who has glory, when he says, "He is glorified as man, but as the God pre-existing all ages he has glory before the world was made."[224] [L.47] Right so far; if he restricted what he said to that, perhaps one might forgive him and think that he had moved over into more orthodox opinions.

15. The divinity of Jesus: The divine mind, eternally enfleshed

The next main section[225] of the Apodeixis *seems to have been devoted to developing in more detail arguments for the divinity of Jesus based on Apolinarius's characterization of him as an "enfleshed mind." Gregory starts his discussion with what appears to be a loose paraphrase of what Apolinarius wrote, and it is difficult in places to distinguish Apolinarius's own views from Gregory's interpretation and comments. According*

223. See J.161–62 above.

224. Gregory cites this fragment again later (J.168) in a slightly different, and possibly more accurate, form; see n. 237 below.

225. The third section according to the scheme suggested in the appendix to this volume.

*to Gregory's report, which is almost certainly misleading, Apolinarius
again characterized Christ as a mind (that is, the divine "spirit") that
had been "enfleshed" from eternity, and stated that the divine mind merely "passed through" the Virgin's womb, that is, without having to take
his flesh from her. It is that divine mind enfleshed, Apolinarius goes on
to say, that was crucified; it is as divine mind enfleshed that Christ can
be referred to as God in Scripture and, during his earthly career, can
speak in the persona of God.*

But now, having ridden his argument around the turning-
point[226] of sound opinion, he gallops back into the course of
error. He directs many insults in our direction and equates our
views with those of the Jews and the pagan Greeks, and returns in
his argument to the vomit that he has already disgorged in earlier
passages.[227] [L.48]

In the vanity of his words he clothes Christ in flesh before
all ages. He says that the Son was an "enfleshed mind" that was
born of a woman but did not become flesh in the Virgin's womb,
instead passing through her,[228] so that what was now manifested
was a fleshly God (or, as he says,[229] an "enfleshed mind"), which

226. The καμπτή, the "goal" at the end of a racetrack, where the riders
turned in a two-lap race.

227. Lietzmann (140) found a parallel between this apostrophe against
Apolinarius's opponents and that located at the beginning of the *Apodeixis*
(L.13 and 14, J.135 above), and suggested that L.48 therefore marked the beginning of the second of two parts or books into which the work may have
been divided. Mühlenberg (77–78) accepted this suggestion and speculated
that a characteristic of the second part may have been that the specific target
of Apolinarius's polemic was his "orthodox" contemporaries, including Gregory himself, rather than Paul of Samosata, Marcellus, and Photinus, as in the
first part. There is evidence, however, in the forthcoming section of a certain
amount of reference back to the discussion of Apolinarius's exegesis of the
Philippians Christ-hymn in the previous section, for example, the fact that
fragment 47 is quoted (in different forms) in both sections (see nn. 224 and
237) and the reference in the second part of L.48 (below) to the glorification
of the Crucified One. I therefore follow Grelier (88–93, 103) and Carter (355)
in not necessarily assuming a major change of direction at this point in the
Apodeixis.

228. Nazianzen (*ep.* 101, PG 37:177C) attributes to Apolinarius the view that
Christ passed through the Virgin "as through a channel" (ὡς διὰ σωλῆνος).

229. καθὼς αὐτὸς ὀνομάζει. See n. 137 on J.150–51 above. But here, as

is what he had been since before all ages. He says that he who was crucified is given the title "Lord of glory" and is called "Lord of hosts" in prophecy and that he utters such magisterial and authoritative statements as "I say to you,"[230] "I command you,"[231] "I am working,"[232] and other things with [J.167] an even higher significance. [L.48]

Gregory objects that on this account it was God who was subject to physical needs, suffered, who experienced human emotions, who was not omniscient, who died and was buried. That is incompatible with the impassible and immortal nature of God. He discusses in particular Christ's cry of abandonment on the cross. If Christ is God, to whom is his cry addressed? Only if Apolinarius is an Arian, and believes that the divine Word is not fully God, can he give a coherent answer to that question.

So what is this excellent fellow saying? How does he deal with the breast-feeding, the swaddling clothes, the life that increases and decays, the gradual growth of the body, the sleep, the fatigue, the obedience to parents, the distress, the grief, the desire to eat the Passover supper, the request for water, the consumption of food, the chains, the blows, the stripes from scourging, the thorns worn on the head, the scarlet robe, the insult with the reed, the bitter gall, the vinegar, the nails, the spear, the linen cloth, the burial, the tomb, and the stone? How can such things be appropriate to God? If Apolinarius's "enfleshed God" had always been that which became visible through Mary, and if what was made manifest was the Godhead, the following were all things that the Godhead suffered: it was breast-fed, was wrapped in swaddling clothes, took food, became weary, grew, became full and then empty again, slept, grieved, became distressed, bewailed, experienced hunger [M.1176] and thirst, ran to the fig tree and did not know at what season that tree bore

Grelier herself says (143), this phrase does not indicate that Gregory is paraphrasing but rather the opposite, that the expression "enfleshed mind" is a direct quotation; it is that which leads to the implication that the rest of the fragment is a paraphrase. It is not unreasonable to assume that that paraphrase is misleading to the extent that it attributes to Apolinarius the view that Christ's flesh existed from eternity.

230. Lk 7.14.   231. Mk 9.25.
232. Jn 5.17.

fruit,[233] did not know the "day and hour,"[234] was beaten, was chained, was flogged, was nailed, shed blood, became a corpse, was prepared for burial, and was placed in a new tomb. Does Apolinarius really conceive all these experiences as natural and appropriate to the Godhead, which existed before the ages? Does he believe that the Godhead could not have been brought up without being breast-fed or could not be fully alive unless the recovery of his strength could be encouraged by partaking in food? How can his enfleshed God be ignorant of "that day and hour"? How can he not know the season for figs, that at the time of Passover there is no [J.168] fruit on the tree fit for eating? Let Apolinarius say, who is it that is ignorant? Who is it who grieves? Who is it that is helpless and in sore straits?

Who is it who cried out that he was forsaken by God, if Father and Son are divine in the same way?[235] And by whom had he been abandoned, as he called out on the cross? If it had been the divinity that suffered—it was he who suffered who says, "My God, my God, why have you forsaken me?"[236]—and the orthodox agree that the Son is of the same divinity as the Father, how can the divinity, being one, be divided in the Passion, so that one part forsakes and the other is forsaken; one dies and one remains alive; one becomes a corpse and the other raises up the corpse? Either Apolinarius will not confess that there is one divinity shared by Father and Son, and thus will appear to be an advocate for Arius; or, if he opposes Arius by saying that there is indeed one divinity, he will not agree even with himself, as the account he concocts is an inconsistent one.

In fact, says Gregory, Apolinarius has already exposed his own error and confusion when he conceded earlier (J.166) that Christ "is glorified as man, rising up from ingloriousness; but as the pre-existing God he has glory before the world was made." (Gregory quotes this sentence here in a slightly longer form than before.) It was in his "inglorious" human nature that Christ suffered, died, and was buried.

233. Mk 11.13.   234. Mt 24.36.
235. Literally, "if there is one divinity of the Father and the Son"; but Gregory is of course challenging not the ὁμοούσιον, but the "single nature" Christology of which he accuses Apolinarius.
236. Mt 27.46.

He cannot avoid ascribing to the humanity the passions and the utterances and attitudes characteristic of our humble condition, which we have mentioned; but he must maintain that the immutable and impassible nature of God remains even when it is shared with human passions. He himself testifies to this when he says of the Son, "He is glorified as man, rising up from ingloriousness; but as the pre-existing God he has glory before the world was made."[237] [L.47] For ingloriousness must indeed be identified with the passible nature of the flesh, and eternal glory with the immortal and impassible power.

16. The divinity of Jesus: "Enfleshed mind" and "God-filled man"

In this section and the following one it may be, as Mühlenberg suggests, that Gregory has not exactly followed Apolinarius's order and that he deals with some of the latter's points out of sequence. Mühlenberg argues that in the next passages of the Apodeixis *Apolinarius first returned to the alleged theory of his opponents that Christ was a "God-filled man" (discussed earlier; see sections 3, 5–6, and 8 above), and again sought to refute it, before then turning again to, and seeking to defend, his own doctrine of Christ as "enfleshed mind." (Whether these arguments were directed against the "orthodox" such as Gregory, or whether Gregory wrongly assumed they were, because he realized that his own "divisive" Christology was vulnerable to the points Apolinarius was raising, cannot be conclusively established.)[238]*

First, Gregory cites Apolinarius's observation that pagans and Jews demonstrate their error by "refusing to accept that he who was born of a woman should be called God." But, says Gregory, we already know that Apolinarius does not believe that Christ took his flesh from Mary, but that he was united to it from eternity. Gregory quotes a further statement to this effect (which, on the face of it, would fit better in the next section of Apolinarius's argument, if that was indeed where he set out his own

237. Another version of the fragment that Gregory has quoted earlier (J.166). Grelier (126) may be right in suggesting that this second version is "more authentic," because Gregory's commentary on it, in the next sentence, specifically picks up on the "ingloriousness," which is not in the earlier version.

238. Mühlenberg (78–79) believes the former alternative is more likely.

doctrine rather than that of his opponents; see Mühlenberg's hypothesis
referred to in the previous paragraph): "... God, being enfleshed before
the ages, was later born through a woman, and came to experience pas-
sions and to be subject to the necessities of human nature." (On the
question of the extent to which Gregory is accurately quoting Apolinari-
us here, see note 241.)

Again Gregory argues that if Christ were "enfleshed before the ages,"
he could not have been a real man; Scripture, however, makes it quite
clear that Christ was a real man, a "son of Adam." On the other hand,
if he had a corporeal nature (from eternity), how could he be God?

To avoid appearing to give the impression of having misrep-
resented Apolinarius in what we have said, I will cite his own
words to support the interpretation we have come to by examining their logic. "The Greeks and Jews," he says, "are clearly
faithless by refusing to accept that he who was born of a woman
should be called God." [L.49] Why, in talking about [J.169] the
birth, does he now say nothing about the flesh? Indeed, "what is
born of the flesh" is assuredly flesh, [M.1177] as the Lord says
somewhere.[239] Since Apolinarius wants the flesh that was born
itself to be the Godhead, and to argue that it was not a matter of
God simply being revealed in flesh,[240] he says: "... but that God,
being enfleshed before the ages, was later born through a woman, and came to experience passions and to be subject to the
necessities of human nature."[241] [L.50] In saying this, he does

239. Jn 3.6.
240. Literally, "to argue that God was not revealed in flesh." "For the first
time when he was born of Mary" is implied.
241. J., but not Lietzmann, shows this as a direct quotation; J.'s view seems to
be supported by the syntax of the sentence. If this fragment accurately reports
what Apolinarius said, on the face of it, it supports Gregory's charge that he
believed in the pre-existence of Christ's flesh. Grelier (142) suggests that the
fragment is substantially a verbatim quotation, but that "enfleshed" (ἔνσαρκον)
was introduced by Gregory for (dishonest) controversial purposes (so the original could presumably have been translated as, "He was God before the ages
and was later born of a woman ..."). Her arguments are, first, that there is no
evidence from other fragments that Apolinarius believed in the pre-existence
of Christ's flesh (which of course has an element of circularity in it); and, second, that Gregory in his subsequent commentary does not specifically mention the controversial expression "God, being enfleshed before the ages," as he

not grant that Christ was a man, but makes him subject to passions as if he were a man, without granting that he participates in human nature. For how could it be claimed that someone who did not originate in the earth was a man? For Scripture says that humankind came from Adam and that he, the first man, arose from the earth by God's power.[242] So Luke too, giving the genealogy of him who was thought to be the son of Joseph, says that he was "son of Adam,"[243] using each of his ancestors to trace the origin of his birth. Anyone who is not born as part of the human race must be something quite other than a human being. So let those who are followers or advocates of our wordsmith's error say what this "enfleshed God" of his might be—he who is neither man, since he has no part in the human race, nor God, as he is not incorporeal.

Gregory now returns to Apolinarius's arguments against his pagan and Jewish opponents, where he again attributes to them the concept of the "God-filled man." If, he says, we described Christ "as a 'God-filled man' like Elijah, the Greeks and Jews would accept what we said." In fact, says Gregory, the story of Elijah does not support Apolinarius's case at all. Pagans would be very skeptical about the literal account of his ascension to heaven in a fiery chariot. The story is in fact best taken typologically, as pointing to how God's power, having first descended upon the womb of Mary, then raised Christ's humanity to heaven—exactly the opposite of what Apolinarius is arguing!

"If," he says, "we described him as having been born as a God-filled man like Elijah, the Greeks and Jews would accept what we said."[244] [L.51] And who among the Greeks would

---

would have done if Apolinarius had actually used it (but, against that, Gregory's argument about Christ's flesh coming from Adam arguably assumes that Apolinarius had clearly stated that it came from heaven). The matter cannot be conclusively decided. Perhaps Apolinarius did say θεὸν ἔνσαρκον, but used the expression in a rather loose way to mean the eternal Logos, "the God who was to become enfleshed." See "Christ's flesh," pp. 55–58 of the introduction.

242. Gn 2.7.
243. Lk 3.38.
244. Shown as a verbatim quotation by J. and Lietzmann. Mühlenberg (68) thinks that the indirect style in which Gregory reports it makes this unlikely, but I have followed Grelier, who argues (127–28) that "we" (i.e., "we Chris-

admit the truth of the wonderful things that happened to Elijah?[245] That fire was fashioned into two different forms, the appearance of a chariot and the shape of horses, and then moved downwards from above, the opposite to its natural direction? That while driving the fiery chariot through the air Elijah was preserved unharmed by the fire, with the fire in the horses pulling the fire in the chariot? Anyone who takes this as it should be taken will be convinced by the features [J.170] just described that it should be read in a hidden sense;[246] he will see in the story a prophecy representing typologically the Lord's becoming man, which is prefigured in what happened. As the fire, which naturally rises, descends down to the earth through the divine power, and Elijah, enveloped by the heavenly fire, which then reverts to its natural upward movement, is taken up with it, so the power of the Most High, immaterial and incorporeal in its essence, adopted the servant's form, which took its individual existence[247] through the Virgin and raised it up to his own sublimity, having transformed[248] it into a divine, immortal nature. Anyone who could not believe in this would not accept the

---

tians") formed part of Apolinarius's text, rather than being an editorial addition by Gregory, and that the fragment can be taken as a direct quotation.

245. See 2 Kgs 2.11.

246. εἰ γὰρ ταῦτα τις δέξαιτο καθ' ὃν δεῖ τρόπον, δι' αὐτῶν δὴ τούτων τῶν λόγων πρὸς τὴν τοῦ μυστηρίου παραδοχὴν ἀναδειχθήσεται … From the structure of the sentence as a whole, τις must be the subject of ἀναδειχθήσεται. On the basis of the dictionary definition of ἀναδείκνυμι—see Henry George Liddell and Robert Scott, *A Greek-English Lexicon,* revised Sir Henry Stuart Jones, 9th ed. with a revised supplement (Oxford: Clarendon Press, 1996); Lampe, *Lexicon* (2004)—the latter ought then to mean "will be shown forth," which makes no sense. Most translators give the verb an active meaning: Zacagnius (PG 45:1178C) has "eliceret"; Winling (200), "trouverait"; and Grelier (344), "déclarera." B. Duvick, in his private communication, clearly recognizes the problem posed by the passive voice, but his suggestion, "(he) will be dedicated to (the acceptance of the mystery)," strikes me as improbable. My rendering is *faute de mieux.*

247. "took its individual existence" = ὑποστᾶσαν.

248. μεταστοιχειώσασα, literally, "trans-elemented." Grelier (354) points out that this term is commonly used by Gregory and his contemporaries to characterize the effects of the Incarnation. In *or cat, GNO* 3.4, 98, PG 45:97B, Gregory also uses it to explain how the prayer of the Eucharist divinizes the bread and the wine in the same way that Jesus's flesh-and-blood body is transformed and divinized by the Word at the Incarnation.

miraculous events associated with Elijah; but anyone who first learned a preliminary sketch of the truth in those events would not hold out stubbornly against the truth itself.[249]

Apolinarius now argues that the so-called orthodox like Gregory are as bad as those who call Christ a "God-filled man," because they do not accept that he who was born of a woman and crucified was God, not man. Gregory retorts that Apolinarius's attribution of flesh to the pre-existent God is worse than Arius's subordinationism: at least Arius believed that the pre-existent Word was incorporeal.

Apolinarius now directs abuse against those of us who do not accept the fable he has constructed, and [M.1180] says: "Those who under the appearance of faith do not believe that God was born of a woman and crucified at the instigation of the Jews, are as worthy of shame as those very Jews are." [L.52][250] Everyone knows that it is those who are incapable of proving the point they are arguing for themselves who utter imprecations against their adversary! What we say is that there are two pits lying in wait: on one side, that of the error of Apolinarius; on the other, of that of Arius. Both bring perdition to those who fall in, but in a choice of evils Arius's breach with orthodoxy seems the less serious. They both drag the immortal nature of the Only-begotten down to a lower level. Arius makes the master of the angels [J.171] share in the incorporeal nature of those angels, professing that both he and they fall short of the uncreated nature by virtue of having been created. But Apolinarius presses his outrageous view to the point that he judges Christ to be worthy of only as much honor as is due to man, who is less than the angels,[251] and defines his nature as fleshly. But to the same extent that an incorporeal nature is superior to bodies, so is Arius's unorthodoxy preferable to the error of Apolinarius.

249. Although the use of Elijah as a type of Christ, and of his ascent to heaven as a type of Christ's glorification, is found in, e.g., Origen, it appears that interpreting the fire as a type of the action of the divine power in the Incarnation is original to Gregory. See Grelier, 358–63.

250. Lietzmann adds to the fragment, "and for that reason he himself will be ashamed of them," but this reading is not found in all mss. and is rejected by J. as an interpolation based on Mk 8.38. Mühlenberg (68) agrees.

251. See Ps 8.5; Heb 2.7.

Gregory now again briefly adopts a more positive tone, and summarizes what he believes to be the orthodox position. Again, his approach is soteriological. God is immaterial, but "mixed himself with human nature in order to destroy sin." "He took up our filth, but was not himself polluted by the stain; rather, he purified this filth in his own person." He was like a doctor who cures the patient without himself becoming ill.

Who is it who "under the appearance of faith does not believe" when he explains the mystery of the virgin birth? I shall expose to public attention our wordsmith's caricature of our faith and his own opinion. For our part, we say that the God whose essence is immaterial, invisible, and incorporeal, out of love for mankind at the consummation of the world when evil had reached its peak,[252] mixed himself with human nature in order to destroy sin. It was as if the sun had entered into a gloomy cave and by the coming of its light had banished the darkness. He took up[253] our filth, but was not himself polluted by the stain; rather, he purified this filth in his own person.[254] For, as it is said, the light shone out "in the darkness, and the darkness did not overcome it."[255] It is as in medicine; once a cure has been applied to the disease, it disappears rather than being transferred back into the doctor's art. Such is our position.

17. The divinity of Jesus: The divine mind, eternally enfleshed (continued)

It seems likely that what follows is a hostile paraphrase of Apolinarius's position. What Gregory represents him as saying is, again, that God was enfleshed "from the beginning," that the human body that Christ had in his earthly life, that was born of Mary, grew by natural processes, suffered, and died, was "that which existed before everything that is."

252. As Winling (202, n. 157) and Grelier (543, n. 2300) point out, this is a key idea in Gregory's account of the Incarnation. Cf. J.221 below and *Theo*, J.123–24.

253. Or "assumed": ἀναλαβών.

254. Literally, "in himself." See introduction, pp. 82–85 and n. 407, for the implications of this expression for Gregory's Christology.

255. Jn 1.5.

But Apolinarius says that God was enfleshed from the beginning, so that that visible and palpable body that came to birth in the last days, which grew by gradual increases as a result of human sustenance, was that which existed before everything that is, [J.172] which made human beings and the whole visible and invisible creation. It was that, he says, which experienced fatigue and, in distress, experienced the trials of death.[256] [L.53]

Gregory attacks the idea that "God was enfleshed from the beginning," on lines that are now familiar to the reader. He does not think it is credible that the divine Word, when he created the world and acted miraculously in the world as reported in the Old Testament (as is usual in the Fathers, and as Gregory himself also does in Theo, *he attributes these Old Testament miracles to the Second Person of the Trinity),[257] was clothed in the same weak, passible, human flesh that he assumed in the life of Jesus.*

I do not know how this clever fellow can maintain, on the one hand, that, when the heavens and the earth and all the marvels of creation came into being, their Maker experienced no [M.1181] fatigue, but, on the other, that he did suffer fatigue in making his journey from Judaea to Galilee;[258] or that he who turned the rock into a pool of water for the Israelites[259] asked the Samaritan woman for a drink;[260] or that he who without weariness poured out heavenly food for so many thousands for forty years[261] ran to the fig tree hoping to eat its fruit yet found none.[262]

These are the doctrinal views on each side. Let the intelligent reader judge for himself who "under the appearance of faith does not believe."

---

256. Neither Mühlenberg nor Grelier seems to discuss the authenticity of this fragment. J., but not Lietzmann, shows it as a direct quotation, but, as Winling (203, n. 159) implies, there is little reason to believe that Gregory is here purporting to quote Apolinarius verbatim. It is possible perhaps that the latter did use the expression "God was enfleshed from the beginning," but, as Carter (357, n. 66) suggests, probably not in the sense that Gregory attributes to it; compare n. 241 above, on L.50.

257. J.121–22.   258. Jn 4.6.
259. Nm 20.11.   260. Jn 4.7.
261. Ex 16.35.   262. Mt 21.19.

Gregory now deals with what appears to have been an accusation made by Apolinarius against the so-called orthodox, including Gregory himself, and may be taken from the attack on the "God-filled man" concept, which Gregory criticized in the previous section. Apolinarius seems to be claiming that the "divisive" Christology of his opponents implies that "he who was crucified"—Jesus the man—is completely distinct from the divine Logos and therefore "had in his nature neither what is divine nor that most important thing of all, which is spirit" (by which he must have meant the divine spirit). Gregory responds by pointing out that the orthodox do believe that Christ has a "spirit," if by that is meant a human mind and that it is Apolinarius who believes that Christ was "half a man," without a "spirit" or mind. As Apolinarius recognizes, the orthodox do also believe that Christ has a divine element "in" him; but they believe that it was something over and above his human nature, not implanted into it to fill the space that would otherwise be occupied by his human mind. When "the Word became flesh," it remained "with God," but, in the Virgin's womb, it joined itself to our human nature in its entirety: body, soul, and spirit.

But, according to Apolinarius, we say that he who was crucified had in his nature neither what is divine nor that most important thing of all, which is spirit. [L.54][263] Against such a calumny the obvious defense is simply to deny it. If Apolinarius identifies spirit with mind, no Christian would say that what was mixed with God was half a man, but rather that the whole man is joined to the divine power. One might wish to apply all of the words "mind," "spirit," and "heart" to parts of a human being, for in Scripture all three are used of the governing part:[264] "Create in me a clean heart, O God";[265] "The man of mind will gain direction";[266] no one "knows what is truly human except the human spirit that is within."[267] He who had been overshadowed by the power of the Most High and on whom the Holy Spirit had

263. J., but not Lietzmann, shows these words as a direct quotation. See n. 268 below.

264. τοῦ ἡγεμονικοῦ, a Stoic term for the rational faculty of the soul.

265. Ps 50 (51).10.

266. Prv 1.5, LXX. "Man of mind" translates νοήμων, cognate with νοῦς. (NRSV has "Let … the discerning acquire skill.")

267. 1 Cor 2.11.

come cannot have been without spirit, without mind, or without heart. It is not we who should be rebuked for claiming that the man Jesus came into being without having spirit, [J.173] that is, mind, within himself, but he who is the originator of the rebuke and projects his own disgrace onto us! For if anyone calls spirit mind and says that the man in Christ has no mind, it is he who is saying that the Lord has no spirit.

But what is the charge he brings against us? He says that we are wrong to say that over and above his own nature the man in Christ has something else better than that, the divinity which dwells within him.[268] [L.54] If this counts as an accusation, we do not seek to avoid the charge—Paul the Apostle is being rejected with us! Learning from him, we believe that what, in the intelligible world, is "the form of God," is, in the visible world, in "the form of a slave."[269] If the divine form is more honorable than the person of a slave, what is visible is in no way equal to what is concealed. So what was seen in the flesh and lived among humans had something more honorable than itself within itself; our wordsmith turns this doctrine into an accusation against the faith! But the Apostle says that "in him the whole fullness of deity dwells bodily."[270] When he said "in him," he did not mean in half a person, but by the use of this expression embraced the whole being.

So if it is accepted that it was a human body in which the divinity dwelt, and that a body cannot be without a soul, and that the faculty of mind [M.1184] is a distinguishing characteristic of the human soul—for if this were to be separated off, as we have often said, what is left would be purely animal—then our

268. Neither Lietzmann nor J. shows this as a verbatim quotation. Lietzmann links Gregory's report of Apolinarius's words here and an earlier one in J.172 above into a single fragment (L.54). But what Apolinarius seems here to be accusing his adversaries of claiming is not that the man Christ has no "spirit" or "divinity" within him, as in the earlier passage, but rather that he did indeed "have" something over and above his humanity, "dwelling within him" but quite separate from his humanity (as in the "God-filled man" theory). If that is indeed the substance of what Apolinarius said here, there seems a good case for categorizing it as a separate fragment.

269. Phil 2.6–7.

270. Col 2.9.

excellent friend is bringing his reproaches not against us but against the Apostle Paul, and also against that great text from John, that "the Word became flesh and dwelt in us."[271] Not "in part of us"; by using the plural he signified everything that is thought of as human nature. At the beginning he indicates a distinction between the Word and the flesh; later, as his words show, he speaks of a union [J.174] between them. For the Word remained as itself, "and ... was with God."[272] What God was, the Word was too, for he "was God." But when "he came to what was his own"[273] and shone out "in the darkness,"[274] then "the Word became flesh," becoming flesh by its own power in the Virgin's womb. So let Apolinarius stop his abuse against us, lest he include the saints as well in his insults.

Apolinarius goes on to argue that it is only his Christological model that will enable us to say that the earthly Christ is identical with the pre-existent Logos, that he is truly "of the same tribe" as God, to use the imagery from Zechariah he quoted earlier. Gregory responds that the orthodox do believe in the pre-existent Christ; what they cannot accept is that his human flesh is not of human origin. He takes the opportunity for a (rather belated) side-swipe at Apolinarius's suggestion that "of the same tribe" is an adequate analogy for the substantial relationship between the Father and the Son: that, he points out, is just the sort of language that Arians like Eunomius would be happy with.

Leaving aside the intervening passages in which he seeks to refute those who do not share his opinions about the mystery, I shall note one of the things he says in his slanderous assault on us. He says that unless we say "that,"[275] neither can we say "that Christ existed before his nativity on earth, or that he is before all things, or that he is 'of the same tribe as'[276] God."[277] [L.55]

271. Jn 1.14.   272. Jn 1.1.
273. Jn 1.11.   274. Jn 1.5.
275. I.e., what Apolinarius affirms.
276. σύμφυλον. See J.158 above.

277. J., but not Lietzmann, shows this as a direct quotation. The use of "that" (ἐκεῖνο) without any explicit reference suggests that Gregory may indeed be quoting directly.

Mühlenberg (79) argues that Apolinarius begins a new section here, with L.55, rather than, as suggested below, with L.56. That is possible, but I think it

But we do confess that he existed before his earthly nativity, provided it is not disputed that his flesh was of earthly origin. As for being "'of the same tribe as' God"—what an idea! No Christian would come up with such an expression, so demeaning and so alien to the divine magnificence. It announces that he who in his real being is God is merely "'of the same tribe as' God" and not truly God. Why, Eunomius would not hesitate to use such an expression of the Lord! He denies Christ's true divinity, but would be quite prepared to say that he was "'of the same tribe as' God," as those who accept faith in him become "of 'the same' body" as Christ and "share" in him "in 'the same' way."[278] But they are not identical with the Lord; they participate in him and are therefore called by "the same" name. So, while accusing us of saying things that the orthodox do not profess, Apolinarius adds, by what he says about us, to the evidence for our unimpeachable orthodoxy.

18. The divinity of Jesus: Arguments from Scripture

Apolinarius now produces some arguments based on Scripture in favor of Jesus's divinity. Gregory does not of course disagree with Apolinarius's objective, but nevertheless takes every opportunity for identifying flaws in his detailed arguments.

First, says Apolinarius, Luke 1.35 indicates that Christ was born holy. Gregory points out that Jeremiah 1.5, "Before I formed you I sanctified you in the womb," would have provided better support for the pre-existence of Christ's divinity, which is what Apolinarius is seeking to demonstrate.

Now, pursuing his argument in favor of the divinity being flesh, he adds the following to what he has already said. "Who,"

---

is more satisfactory to link L.55 with the earlier discussion of the passage from Zechariah and the doctrinal arguments about the pre-existence of Christ and his "consubstantiality" with God than with the evidence from Scripture for Christ's divinity set out in the next section (or rather sub-section of the third main section; see appendix to this volume) of the *Apodeixis*.

278. καὶ σύσσωμοι τοῦ Χριστοῦ καὶ συμμέτοχοι. Cf. Eph 3.6, σύσσωμα καὶ συμμέτοχα: "members of the same body and sharers" (NRSV). The translation here aims to bring out Gregory's play on the prefix συ(μ)-, "the same."

he says, "is the Holy One from his birth?"²⁷⁹ [L.56] It appears
he is unaware of the text from the prophet Jeremiah; God says
[J.175] of him, "Before I formed you I sanctified you in the
womb."²⁸⁰ Scripture testifies that Christ was holy not only from
his birth but before his birth as well; he [M.1185] who leapt in
his mother's womb and rejoiced at the voice of the greeting of
the mother of the Lord²⁸¹ was also holy from his birth, as the
words of the angel about him attest, "He will be filled with the
Holy Spirit from his mother's womb."²⁸²

*Next, he points to Christ's extraordinary wisdom, as evidenced in, for
example, John 7.15 and Matthew 13.54. Gregory accepts that Christ's
divinity is the source of his wisdom, but points out that his wisdom, like
ours, increased as he grew, which would have been possible only if he
had a rational soul.*

But Apolinarius adds the following to what he has just said:
"Who is wise unless he has been taught?"²⁸³ [L.57] But we do
not say that the wisdom of God, which is Christ, was taught by
anyone; on the other hand, we do not doubt that the portion
of our flesh that was united with the divine wisdom received the
benefit of that wisdom through participation. This is because we
trust in the Gospel, which states specifically that "Jesus increased
in years²⁸⁴ and wisdom and in favor."²⁸⁵ Just as in the case of our

279. See Lk 1.35.   280. See Jer 1.5.
281. John the Baptist; see Lk 1.41.
282. A verbatim citation of Lk 1.15: καὶ Πνεύματος Ἁγίου πλησθήσεται ἔτι
ἐκ κοιλίας μητρὸς αὐτοῦ. NRSV translates the last five words as "even before his
birth," giving full force to ἔτι, but that would undermine Gregory's argument
that only Christ was holy before his birth.
283. On the face of it, the suggestion that Christ has been taught wisdom is
inconsistent with Apolinarius's thesis that his intellect was divine; see Winling,
207, n. 168. But he may have had Jn 7.15–18 and Mt 13.54–57 in mind, and
may be making the point that Christ's wisdom was so extraordinary that he
must have been taught directly by God rather than by human teachers, in other words, that he must have been perfectly wise by virtue of his divine nature.
284. Or "in stature." See NRSV footnote; also Liddell and Scott, *Lexicon*
(1996), and Danker, *Lexicon* (2000), *s.v.* ἡλικία.
285. Lk 2.52. See "Christ is fully man," "The unity of Christ's person: His
glorification," and n. 401 in the introduction, pp. 74–75 and 79–81, for a discussion of Gregory's use of this passage.

bodies, gradual growth, assisted by the intake of food, moves forward towards the maturity of our nature, so in the case of the soul, too, the advance through a devout life to the maturity of wisdom is granted to those who participate in such a life.

Apolinarius next refers to Christ claiming the authority to perform the acts of God, in such texts as John 5.27 and Matthew 2.23. Gregory argues that ultimately all acts of God are done by God. The fact that the man Jesus performed miraculous acts in itself proves nothing; Elijah did the same.

Apolinarius says, "Who has the authority to perform the acts of God?"[286] [L.58] How can he belittle the inexpressible greatness of the Lord by such childish arguments? For the authority to do the acts of God is given to those human beings who are worthy of receiving the divine power, as when Elijah by authority sent down and held back the rain,[287] brought down fire on his adversaries,[288] made flour grow in the jar and oil well up in the flask,[289] conferred life on a dead person by breathing on him,[290] and did all the other things that Scripture says of him. So nothing lies beyond human reach if the divine power is used to accomplish some miracle by God's authority; but the ultimate power remains God himself. That is what is believed by us and by all those who have received the word in truth.

While asserting that the Son is just as much God as the Father and that they have equal powers, Apolinarius now seems to try to find a way (perhaps, as Mühlenberg suggests, in an excursus)[291] to distinguish between the ways in which, following the divine enfleshment, those powers are actually exercised by the two divine Persons, between their respective ἐνέργειαι or "operations." It seems that as evidence for this distinction he cited John 5.17, "My father is still working, and I also am working." On that basis, it appears that in regard to John 5.21 he distinguished

---

286. Both PG and J. read Τίς ἐν ἐξιουσίᾳ τὰ τοῦ θεοῦ ἐργαζόμενος; But ἐξιουσία is not a word known to Liddell and Scott, *Lexicon* (1996), or to Lampe, *Lexicon* (2004); Lietzmann (L.57) reads ἐξουσίᾳ. See Jn 5.27 and Mt 21.23 (ἐξουσία in both cases).

287. 1 Kgs 17.1. 288. 2 Kgs 1.10–12.
289. 1 Kgs 17.14. 290. 1 Kgs 17.21.
291. Mühlenberg, 79.

between the "operations" of the Father, who "raises the dead and gives
them life," and those of the enfleshed Son, who "gives life to whomever he
wishes," although it is not clear precisely how he interpreted this passage.
Gregory responds that it is clear from 1 Timothy 2.4 that God "desires
everyone to be saved" and that it is wrong to seek to draw any distinc-
tion between the wills of the Father and the Son.

[J.176] It would not be appropriate for us laboriously to
refute the distinction that Apolinarius then goes on unintelli-
gently to make; we leave that to the judgment of the learned.
For what does he mean when he says, "distinguishing an operation in the flesh, while making it equal to one in the spirit ...".?
[L.59] He links this to words in the Gospel that say, "My father
is still working, and I also am working."[292] If there is anyone who
has been commissioned to defend nonsense, let him discharge
his brief and say what our author has in mind when he goes
on to say the same thing again, using these exact words: "What
he has is equality, again, in his power but a distinction in his
operation in the flesh, through which he did not give life to all
but only to some, those whom he wished."[293] [L.60] We, on the
other hand, have adopted the simple, unelaborated sense of divine Scripture, and this is how we interpret [M.1188] what it
says. When we hear the Lord explaining that "the Father raises
the dead and gives them life," and "the Son gives life to whomever he wishes,"[294] we do not conclude from this that some are
excluded from the scope of the will to give life. But since we
have learned, and believe, that everything belonging to the Father belongs to the Son,[295] it is clear that we see the will[296] of
the Father, the same for everybody, in the Son as well. So if the
Father's will is in the Son, and the Father, as the Apostle Paul
says, "wills[297] that everyone should be saved and come to the
knowledge of the truth,"[298] he who has received everything that
belongs to the Father and has the whole Father within himself,

292. Jn 5.17.
293. Or "willed," ἠθέλησεν. Compare nn. 296 and 297 below.
294. Jn 5.21.   295. See Jn 16.15.
296. θέλημα.
297. θέλει. NRSV has "desires everyone to be saved ..."
298. 1 Tm 2.4.

clearly has, as well as the other excellences of the Father, the will to save us. If, then, he is not lacking this perfect will, it is altogether clear that he gives life to those to whom the Father wishes life to be given; he is not, as Apolinarius claims, inferior in his loving will towards humankind in that he wants life to be given to some but not [J.177] to all. For it is not by reason of the Lord's will that some are saved but some perish; otherwise, the responsibility for perdition could be attributed to him; rather, it is through the choice of those who receive God's word that it turns out that some persons are saved and others perish.

Next, as scriptural evidence for Christ's divinity, Apolinarius cites John 10.18, where Christ claims authority to lay down his life (literally, his soul) and to take it up again. Only God could claim such authority, he argues. Gregory picks up the word "soul," and again attacks Apolinarius's notion—not really relevant to the argument here—that Christ's human soul, the vital principle which he "laid down" when he died, was purely animal.

Apolinarius adds to these arguments by saying, "None have died or risen again on the basis of their own authority." In support of this, he cites the words of the Gospel, "No one takes my soul[299] from me.... I have authority[300] to lay it down, and I have authority to take it up again."[301] [L.61][302] What sort of soul is this, rational or irrational? This is what I would say to those who say that it was a soul without a mind that was joined to God. If it is irrational, they are saying that Christ is a beast, not a man; but if it is endowed with reason, what do they suppose thought[303] is, other than reason? "Reason"[304] is not just an arbitrary term; reason starts from and presupposes the activity of thought.[305] So

299. ψυχήν: NRSV has "life."

300. ἐξουσίαν: NRSV has "power," but in J.175 above Gregory distinguished "power" (δύναμις) from "authority" (ἐξουσία).

301. Jn 10.18.

302. The words "None have died ..." could be a verbatim quotation or Gregory's summary, but Mühlenberg (69) is no doubt right in suggesting that in any case they accurately represent Apolinarius's arguments.

303. διάνοιαν, from νοῦς, "mind."

304. ὁ λόγος.

305. νοήματος (again, from νοῦς) κίνησις .

whoever speaks of the rational soul must recognize a soul endowed with mind.[306] If thought is the activity and operation of the mind, and if the soul of the Lord is defined as being without mind, how, as the mind was not present, could there be mental operations? So if the Lord has a soul, which he takes up and lays down on the basis of his own authority, and that soul is not animal and irrational but human in its structure, it necessarily follows that when he took to himself a human soul, he took a soul endowed with mind.

Finally in this section, Apolinarius cites John 12.24, the grain of wheat that falls to the earth and dies in order to bear much fruit. Presumably, although Gregory does not give the details, the argument was that only a divine being could have caused such a miraculously abundant harvest to spring up from death. Gregory uses this as a peg to argue again against Apolinarius's alleged view that the divinity died in the Passion. He points out that it is we, in our flesh-and-blood bodies, who comprise the miraculous harvest, and that we do so because of our solidarity with Christ's flesh-and-blood body; it is that, not the divinity, which died and rose again. We can have no solidarity with his divinity; only other divine beings would be able to do so, in which case Scripture would be talking in terms of a harvest of miraculously resurrected gods!

[M.1189] Next, I shall willingly pass over what he says about the grain of wheat that dies and so can shoot up again with a multiplication of grains,[307] as this supports us and strengthens our argument. [L.62] For who is the seed that has died and that, in the ear in which it is resurrected, raises up in itself a profusion of grains? I do not believe there is anyone so uninitiated into sacred doctrine as not to believe that this points to the mystery of the Passion, fulfilled in Christ's humanity. What this text shows is that we too [J.178] must die, be buried, and rise with him.

It is easy for those who wish to do so to imitate something that is of the same kind as themselves, but to become like something that is more excellent than we are lies beyond our capacity. So if it is the flesh that is subject to death, it must be easier for us

306. ψυχὴν ... διανοητικήν.
307. See Jn 12.24.

who live in the flesh to imitate his death by our own death. But if it is the divinity that died, how can we, who are in the flesh, die with that divinity? It is flesh that dies with his flesh and is resurrected with it. If it is his divinity that suffers, as Apolinarius would have it,[308] we must track down some other divinities who will die and rise with his divinity! [L.62] For, as the Apostle Paul says, just as Christ died and rose, so will we.[309] What are we as regards our nature—divine power, or, as Scripture says, blood and flesh? That is why he, who, for us, came among us, shared, for our sake, our flesh and blood. So he who died for us was, in his being, what we are; we who are of the same kind as he are invited to imitate him.

Gregory goes on to argue again against the notion that the divinity died in the Passion. He starts from the axiom that death, as he again points out, is the separation of immortal soul and perishable body. And mind is an inseparable part of that immortal soul, as the parable of Dives and Lazarus shows. So, on Apolinarius's Christological model, the Logos would similarly be an inseparable part of the soul, which separated from Christ's body when he died.

The argument that Gregory develops from this starting point seems to have two separate elements, which are not clearly distinguished from each other, which are both rather fragile, and which seem to be mutually exclusive. The first is that the Logos could not be said to have "died" at the death of the man Jesus, because it must have remained part of his immortal soul. The second seems to assume that Apolinarius did not in fact believe that the Logos remained part of Jesus's soul; by distinguishing between it and Christ's lower or animal soul, he is in effect fragmenting Christ's soul and implying (one must assume, as this is not spelled out) that it is only the mind, that is, the Logos, that was separated from the other two elements of the human composite when Christ died.[310] So the corollary of Apolinarius's theory is that there was no proper death

308. These words are linked by Lietzmann to the earlier report of Apolinarius's words in J.177 to form fragment 62, but in fact there seems no reason to believe that they constitute anything other than a very general summary by Gregory of what he believes Apolinarius taught.

309. Cf. 1 Thes 4.14; 1 Cor 15.12–23; Rom 6.4–5.

310. Grelier (595) suggests that Apolinarius, like the Arians, did indeed envisage the death of Christ as a separation between the Logos and the body.

*(presumably because the animal soul somehow remained with the body);
and so he is unable to give an adequate account of how the man Jesus,
let alone the divine Logos, can be said to have died.*

The proof of the unorthodoxy of the argument that seeks to
show that Christ's divinity is mortal is what actually happens to
us. In death, which is common to everyone, what is it that dies
and decays? Is it not the flesh that disintegrates in the earth,
while the mind remains with the soul and, as regards its essence,
remains unharmed by the change in the body? A proof of this
is that Dives remembers those left on the earth and beseeches
Abraham on behalf of those linked to him by kinship.[311] No one
would say that to show concern for one's kin when one knew
that one's own fate was unavoidable was an act that did not require a mind.[312]

If, even after death, our mind survives in an impassible and
immutable condition, how could Apolinarius's threefold God
suffer death in the flesh? How could he have died, in what
way could he have suffered the [J.179] dissolution that death
brings? Everyone knows that death is the mutual separation of
soul and body. But how can the soul, that is, the mind, be divided from itself, so that it can experience death in itself?[313] If our
soul is incapable of dying, how can it suffer death? That is what
those who fragment Christ into parts have to explain.

311. Lk 16.27–28.

312. That is, the fact that Dives is able to act rationally even after he has
died shows that his intellectual soul survives death.

313. αὐτὴ δὲ ἡ ψυχὴ καὶ ἡ διάνοια πῶς ἀφ'ἑαυτῆς μερίζεται, ἵνα καὶ ἐν ἑαυτῇ
τὸν θάνατον δέξηται; Both the translation and the interpretation of these two
clauses are problematic. Winling (212) and Grelier (585) translate them as if
the verbs were plural, so that the meaning is, "How are the soul and the mind
separated from each other, so that they can themselves experience death?"
But this seems grammatically unlikely, and I follow Zacagnius (1190D–1192B),
who has: "ipsa autem anima et mens, quomodo a semetipsa disjungitur, ut
et ipsa mortem suscipiat?" In any case, what may lie behind Gregory's argument is the notion that death must involve the separation from the body of
the whole soul: its lower animal soul, not just its higher rational component,
the mind.

19. The relationship between Christ's divinity and
his humanity: Arguments from Scripture

Apolinarius seems now to have discussed two scriptural passages bearing on the relationship between the enfleshed Christ's divinity and his humanity. The first passage he looks at is a conflation of Matthew 26.39 and Luke 22.42: "If it is possible, let this cup pass from me; yet may your will be done, not mine." It appears that he may have thought that this passage caused problems for those who believed in the full humanity of Christ and that he had a separate will; such people, he claims, "are disturbed by the perturbation that infidels experience." To believe that there are two wills in Christ would jeopardize the unity of his person, to which he attached so much importance. In his view there is only one will here, which belongs "not to the man from the earth, as they think, but to the God who descended from heaven."[314]

Gregory's response is to argue that Apolinarius's argument implies that, at any rate in Gethsemane, the first and second Persons of the Trinity could will different things. That, he suggests, would imply that their natures are different, as what one wills is determined by one's nature. So Apolinarius's argument implies that the eternal Christ is not truly divine, which is Arianism. The divine nature could not, as weak human nature does, want two contradictory things at the same time. Indeed, it is incoherent for anyone to pray, "What I want is that what I want should not be done." The true interpretation of the passage is that when he says, "your will," Christ is referring to the will of the Father, which is identical with that of his own divine nature, and that when he says, "my will," he speaks "as a human, saying what is appropriate to the weakness of human nature, as one who has made our sufferings his own."

[M.1192] "But they are disturbed," he says, "by the perturbation that infidels experience." Here he slanders us by calling us "disturbed" and "infidel" because we hold unquestioningly to the words of the Gospel, "If it is possible, let this cup pass from

314. Grelier (582–83) points out, however, that in L.109, from a work entitled *On the Manifestation of God in the Flesh*, Apolinarius seems to suggest that in Mt 26.39 Christ's will, although single, is being exercised in different ways, "divinely" and "according to the economy"; in the latter case it is "asking to be spared death."

me;[315] yet may your will be done, not mine."[316] To this he adds his own words, as follows: "They do not mention that this will that is spoken of belongs not to the man from the earth, as they think, but to the God who descended from heaven."[317] [L.63]

How could people bring themselves to say such a thing? I am not talking now about any of those people who have been condemned for heresy; I do not think that even the father of impiety and lies himself could produce from his sayings anything more terrible by way of blasphemy. Does our wordsmith really know what he is saying? God, who descended from heaven, rejects the will that belongs to his own divinity and does not will that what it wills should come to pass! So the wills of the Son and the Father are separated. How, then, could they have a common will? How, if their wills were different, could the identity of their natures be made manifest?[318] For it is absolutely necessary that the will be in accord with the nature, as the Lord says, "A good tree cannot bear bad fruit, nor can a bad tree bear good fruit."[319] The "fruit" here must be moral choice: good from a good nature, bad from a bad one. So those who hold that the fruit of the will is different [J.180] in the Father and the Son must hold that the nature of each also necessarily differs.

So why is there any quarrel with Arius? Why don't they go over to Eunomius? He distinguishes the nature of the Father and the Son and at the same time separates their wills—a separation that, more than anything else, introduces something that is alien in respect of essence, dividing up the concept of the divine into what is superior and what is inferior.

Let us come back again to what Apolinarius says: "... They do

315. Mt 26.39.
316. Lk 22.42.
317. The last sentence of this fragment is quoted again in J.180 below. It is also cited in the proceedings of the Lateran Council of 649 and the Third Council of Constantinople (680), and by St. Maximus the Confessor, in the context of the monothelete controversy (Lietzmann, 219). Lietzmann links it with another citation in J.182 to form a single fragment (L.63).
318. Gregory's argument is a little over-compressed in these two sentences. It seems to be, "So how could they have a common will, [which is what the doctrine of consubstantiality requires? For] how, if their wills were different, could the identity of their natures be made manifest?"
319. Mt 7.18.

not mention that this will that is spoken of belongs not to the man from the earth, as they think, but to the God who descended from heaven." [L.63] What is this will that our wordsmith is talking about? Clearly that which the Lord does not wish to "be done" when he says to his Father, "May your will be done, not mine." Doesn't he understand the contradiction that his argument has fallen into? The Passion is near, and the betrayer with a mob is on the point of appearing; it is then that this prayer is prayed. Is it [M.1193] man or God who is praying? If he thinks it is God who is praying, he is attributing to God the same degree of weakness as is found in human beings. How could God not have what is good within himself, but have to seek help from above? And how could God reproach his own will? Is what he wished good or evil? If good, then why was what he wished not fulfilled? If evil, how can evil have any relationship with divinity?

As I said, Apolinarius does not understand that he is steering his argument into contradiction. If it was the voice of the Only-begotten God that said, "May your will be done, not mine," that argument is distorted by self-contradiction and has no [J.181] firm foundation. Whoever does not wish his own will to be done wishes precisely this, that what he wishes should not be done. If someone prays, "What I want is that what I want should not be done," how could that prayer be fulfilled? Such a prayer is necessarily re-directed to the opposite of its object, and whoever hears it will be at a loss as to which of the two he is being asked for; whatever he does in response, he will perversely be giving the petitioner, as the outcome of his prayer, what he does not want! Should he do the will of the petitioner? But his prayer is that what he wants should not be done. Should he then not do what he wants? But what the petitioner wants is that what he doesn't want should be done for him. So in whatever way and in whatever sense this idea is taken, it is an incoherent one, contradicting and indeed demolishing itself.

The one solution of this logical impasse is the recognition of the true meaning of this mystery: that fear in the face of suffering is a property of human weakness. As the Lord himself says, "The spirit is willing, but the flesh is weak."[320] But to endure the

320. Mt 26.41.

suffering that comes from God's dispensation is a property of
the divine counsel and the divine power.[321] Since in Christ the
human intention is one thing and the divine another, he who
speaks first does so as a human, saying what is appropriate to the
weakness of human nature, as one who has made our sufferings
his own; he then adds further words because, for the sake of the
salvation of humankind, he wishes that sublime will that is worthy of God to be fulfilled, [M.1196] rather than his human will.
When he says, "not my will," by his words he is referring to his
human nature. But when he adds, "your will," he indicates the
unity of his own divinity with that of the Father. Because of their
common nature, there is no difference between their respective
wills. Speaking of the Father's will, he reveals that of the Son
as well. That will is that "everyone should be saved and come
to the knowledge of the truth."[322] That could not [J.182] have
come to be unless Christ had swallowed the cup of death, that
death that prevents us from coming into true life. The Lord
made his own the lowliness of human fear, both in his words
and in his suffering. Thus he showed that he had truly taken on
our human characteristics; he confirmed his human nature by
sharing in our sufferings.

*Apolinarius added that the will that is spoken of, which belonged "not to
the man from the earth ... but to the God who descended from heaven,"
was "taken into" (or "assumed into," προσειλημμένον) "unity with him."
Gregory professes himself perplexed by this, and, if he is correctly repro-
ducing Apolinarius's words, and Lietzmann's arrangements of the fragments is correct (see notes 317 and 323), the latter does indeed appear
to have expressed himself obscurely. It appears that "him" in the last
clause refers to "the God who descended from heaven," that is, Christ's
divine nature, "into" which his human will, belonging to the "man from
the earth," was "taken," and by which it was accordingly over-ridden or
transformed; but, on the basis of Apolinarius's broader Christological
position, that the "man from the earth" had no rational mind, it is difficult to see how he could have believed that the human Christ ever had a*

---

321. That is, it is only as God that Christ is able to endure the Passion; as
man, he wants the cup to pass from him.

322. 1 Tm 2.4.

will—at any rate, a human will—to be "taken." It seems, however, that it is indeed something on roughly those lines that Gregory, with some difficulty, has worked out that Apolinarius is trying to say. He points out that it implies that it was God who asked for the cup to be taken away from him, and that the Godhead was therefore "subject to passion." It also implies that Christ the man is merely a mouthpiece for God.

"But," says Apolinarius, "what was taken into unity with him[323] did not belong to the man from earth, as they think, but to the God who descended from heaven." [L.63] The feeble and incomprehensible interpretation reflected in these words prevents any rational analysis of the argument contained in them. But his meaning is not totally concealed by the confused way he expresses himself. Those words filled with passion come, he is saying, not from "the man from the earth ... but from God, who descended from heaven." His intention is already clear from what he has said: he conceives the Godhead as being subject to passion. But then he confuses his meaning by the absurd way he expresses himself. To the words "God, who came down from heaven," he adds, "it was taken into unity with him": in other words, to put it more clearly, he who spoke was not a man but rather God speaking through a man, having taken into unity with himself the man who was actually manifested.

Gregory's next argument assumes, however, that Apolinarius is claiming that it was a "man," not just Christ's human will, that was "taken into" the Godhead. Where did this "man" come from, he asks? Gregory seems to be assuming that when Apolinarius denies here that Christ's (single) will belongs to "the man from earth," he is thereby (again) denying that a "man from earth" forms any part of Christ's enfleshed person. This leads Gregory to repeat the argument that the "man" cannot have come from heaven, as there can be no human flesh in heaven. So he must have come from nowhere! In fact, Gregory again reminds us, all the circumstances of Christ's birth show conclusively that Jesus's flesh was of earthly origin.

323. If Lietzmann is right to link three of Gregory's quotations, in J.179, J.180, and J.182, into one fragment (63)—see n. 317 above—"him" must be the divine Logos, and Apolinarius is saying that it is Christ's *will* that is "taken into unity with" him.

So, where was that man from, who was "taken into"? From the earth? No, says Apolinarius. But the human race does not exist in heaven. So the only remaining thing to say is that he was "taken into" from nowhere! That amounts to claiming that what was made manifest was an apparition rather than reality; what originates from nowhere is wholly non-existent. But Apolinarius goes on to say that the man had descended from heaven. But note that Mary existed on earth, that the cave of the Nativity was in the earth, that the manger was an earthly manger. How is our friend able to send his man from heaven to live on the earth? All Scripture gives testimony to the Virgin, the birth, the flesh, [J.183] the swaddling clothes, the suckling, the manger, the human constitution. He puts all this on one side, and his argument fabricates another man who has no grounding in or affinity with our own nature.

Apolinarius's second reference is to Matthew 11.19, where Jesus's opponents accuse him of being "a glutton and a drunkard." According to Gregory, Apolinarius says these terms "must refer to the necessities of the man." How this observation fitted into Apolinarius's argument cannot be known; Gregory again cites them as evidence for the "earthly" nature of Jesus's humanity.

He weaves abuse into the course of his remarks, and thinks he can thereby provide corroboration for his absurd [M.1197] views, the more vehemently to reprove us by his blasphemies. But I believe that the intelligent person should disregard this and leave the judgment to the perception of the readers as to who "the falsifiers of the apostolic faith" are:[324] [L.64] we who, using Paul's words,[325] "knew Christ according to the flesh," but who "know him no longer in that way"; or he who proclaims in his writings that God of his who was always fleshly, both before and after his providential manifestation as a man.

He goes on to repeat the blasphemy that the Jews directed against him, when they said he was "a glutton and a drunk-

324. I follow Lietzmann, who, by printing "the falsifiers of the apostolic faith" in spaced type suggests that that part of fragment 64 may be a direct quotation from Apolinarius, and Winling (218), who also prints them as such.
325. 2 Cor 5.16.

ard,"[326] and says that these refer to the necessary functions of the man.[327] [L.65]. So who is this man who is reproached by the Jews for eating and drinking? Did he partake of food and drink, or not? If he did not, he was a pure phantasm; if he did, what he partook of was earthly; and what is heavenly is not nourished by what is earthly!

20. The enfleshment as the assumption of a man by God

Apolinarius now turns to a critique of what he represents as the "ortho-dox" view, that what happened at the enfleshment was that a (complete) man was "taken to himself" (assumed) by God. Before engaging with Apo-linarius on this, Gregory again makes the point that the latter's "enfleshed mind" account would make Christ in one sense sub-human (because he would have no human mind) and in another sense super-human (be-cause he would have God as his rational mind).

What a contradiction these outrageous ideas produce! Look how Apolinarius falls at the same time into contrary errors! First he says that what appeared in Christ's body was superior to human nature; but then he also demonstrates that Christ was infe-rior to human beings, mutilated in the better part of his nature. For our most excellent part is our mind, and he says that the flesh in which God was manifested did not share in that part. He sets all this out explicitly, if laboriously, in what follows; we will run through this material quite briefly, lest anyone should think it pointless to undertake a careful analysis of such non-sense. [L.66]

Apolinarius characterizes the enfleshment as "unity as regards the flesh," and says that it is wrong to interpret this as "taking to himself (assumption of) the (complete) human being." His objection to that "as-sumption" model is that it implies that there are two Christs, the divine Word who assumes and the man Jesus who is assumed. His "enfleshed

326. Mt 11.19.

327. καὶ φήσιν ἀναγκαῖα εἶναι ταῦτα ἐπὶ τοῦ ἀνθρώπου. Another possible translation would be "and this must necessarily be said of (i.e., refer to) the man" (thus Zacagnius, 1198A, and Winling, 219).

mind" view, on the other hand, emphasizes the continuity, indeed the identity, between the pre-existent Christ and the enfleshed Christ.

Gregory points out that neither "unity as regards the flesh" nor "taking to himself the human being" are scriptural concepts, that both smack of pagan philosophy, and that neither is adequate fully to express the mystery of the divine enfleshment. "Unity as regards the flesh" is ambiguous: it could mean either "unity in respect of itself" (presumably he has the concept of unity of the human person in mind) or "union with something else" (God). "Taking to himself the human being" raises the question of what the origin of the being who is "taken" might be. Both expressions, however, convey something of the truth, in that both contain the idea of a close relationship between two diverse entities.

Again he soaks his arguments in a mass of insults; the charge that he makes [J.184] against us is that those who say that "unity as regards the flesh"[328] is the same thing as "taking to himself the human being"[329] are in error. [L.66] So far as I am concerned, I shall not conceal the truth, even if that means I have to use rather crude expressions; for the unsophisticated nature of our language means that neither of these formulae expresses the concept precisely. To explain simply the difference between "unity as regards the flesh" and "taking to himself the human being" is not easy; unity may be understood in various ways, as expressing unity of number, of form, of nature, of ways of living, of teaching, or of virtuous or vicious characteristics and habits. For this reason we need the help of interpreters to explain "unity as regards the flesh," whether this means "unity in respect of itself" or "union with someone else."[330] And as for how "taking to himself the human being" came about, what kind of "human being" was involved, and whence, how, from whom, and in what way it was assumed, is equally beyond our knowledge. For as long as no one can produce any of the divine salt of Scripture in order to season our understanding of this mystery, we shall leave aside the tasteless salt of pagan wisdom, to be ignored by

328. σαρκὸς ἕνωσιν: literally, "union of the flesh."
329. ἀνθρώπου πρόσληψιν.
330. εἴτε πρὸς ἑαυτὴν εἴτε πρὸς ἕτερον ἑνουμένης.

the faithful. Which evangelist mentions "unity as regards the flesh"? Which of the accounts by the apostles teaches us of the "taking to himself of the [M.1200] human being," using that term? What law, which prophets, what divinely inspired saying, what synodical doctrine has provided us with any formula like either of these?

He attributes one of these two terms to us, and says the other is the one he prefers;[331] but we are still undecided as to which formula is valid in itself. We ourselves make use either of both or of neither, because we can find no difference between one and the other. Union means union with something, and "taking to himself" means taking something. Each signifies a relationship with something else: the taker is united with what is taken, and it is by means of taking that what is united is united.

21. More on Apolinarius's trichotomous anthropology and the "enfleshed mind"

Apolinarius explains that on his account, when the divine Son became man, he did not become a different person, "even though assimilated to our life in the flesh." So, says Gregory, Apolinarius claims that Christ remained the same person before and after his enfleshment, and that that person was divine. He also, Gregory reminds us, claims that Christ is a tripartite being, comprising (divine) mind, soul, and body. But that would imply that a divine person can be composite, whereas everyone accepts that God's nature must be simple.

[J.185] Apolinarius says that we speak of two persons,[332] God and the man taken to himself by God. He claims that what he asserts is that this is not so; what he professes is that Christ became flesh but that he was not thereby someone other than he had been without a body; he was the same, even though assimilated to our life in the flesh.[333] [L.67]

---

331. Literally, "his own" (τὸ ἴδιον). (Apolinarius prefers "unity as regards the flesh.")

332. πρόσωπα.

333. J., but not Lietzmann, shows this as a direct quotation. There is no reason to believe that it is not a more or less accurate summary of Apolinarius's views (thus Carter, 363).

Still he persists in this idle chatter against us, with all these incoherent notions. That fleshly God of his cannot be simple by nature; no one could think of simplicity being a property of flesh; but what is not simple cannot be other than composite. But, he says, he is one thing, composed, like each of us, of spirit, soul, and body.[334] [L.68] So here we are; we have been instructed in a new kind of number; we have learned that one is divided into three parts, each of a different kind!

Apolinarius's difficulties, Gregory goes on, stem partly from his trichotomous anthropology, as he has just indicated (and hinted before; see J.142). It is preferable to follow St. Paul and to distinguish just between the outer man (the body) and the inner man (the soul), rather than trying to make further distinctions within the soul (which is invisible anyway). But in any case, the important point is that human beings are composite, into however many parts their nature is divided, so the objection to Apolinarius's model set out in the previous paragraph stands.

Let us, however, defer until later talking about this spirit that Apolinarius has invented. We have been taught a more rough-and-ready way of dividing up a human being, and use the same distinction as most people; we acknowledge that the human constitution comprises a rational soul and a body in such a way that we may call the two in some sense one. How can we say that the two are one?[335] The Apostle Paul clearly sees two "men" in

334. J., but not Lietzmann, shows this (and similar words used at the end of J.185) as a direct quotation. Carter (363–64) points out that the introduction here of a reference to Apolinarius's "tripartite" model jars slightly, given that the immediately preceding (67) and succeeding (69) fragments are aimed at showing how the concept of the "enfleshed mind" best explains the "enduring singularity of the simple divine person." His suggestion that "Gregory may be responsible for recapitulating the Apollinarian trichotomic analysis here" is a convincing one.

335. πῶς εἴπωμεν τὰ δύο ἕν. PG makes this the beginning of a new sentence (ending at "suggesting the soul"); J. does not, and has no punctuation before πῶς. But, unlike either of them, I take the (new) sentence (which I have split up in my translation) to be an interrogative one. This seems to me to fit better with Gregory's argument (that Apolinarius is incoherently saying that Christ is both one and composite) than if he himself (Gregory) is to be understood as saying "we may call the two in some way one," which presumably is how the clause must otherwise be translated.

each of us. He says that "our outer man is wasting away," referring to the body, while "our inner man is being renewed day by day,"[336] suggesting the soul. On Apolinarius's theory of three "men," two of them are invisible and one is actually manifest. So even if he uses our model to support his, and says that it is two "men" that are really one, Paul contradicts him by using this kind of dualistic terminology to signify that "man" is divided.[337]

Gregory next seeks to show the incoherence of Apolinarius's model of Christ as a sort of mutilated human being of a unique type, a sort of half-man, comprising just body and animal soul, with the divine Word somehow inserted into it in place of a rational mind. Where did this half-man come from? Certainly not from Mary, who in that case could not be said to have given birth to a human child at all. Is Apolinarius claiming that a being of this sort previously existed in heaven?

Since his justification for his teaching is based on his model of the nature of human beings, if the latter is disproved, the former is *ipso facto* refuted too. What he says is in effect this, that he is one just as a human being is one, from spirit and soul and body. [L.68] What I would ask him to establish first is what sort of body, where it [J.186] came from, when it was made; and what sort of soul, whether rational or human [M.1201] or irrational, that is, whether he thinks that Christ the man had an animal soul. If so, was the rational element (which he says is something more than the spirit),[338] what in our case he calls mind and in Christ's case God, inserted into it?

If he had first of all demonstrated to us this creation of a heavenly man in the likeness of an earthly one, we would have been logically obliged to accept his story and to learn from this

---

336. 2 Cor 4.16. (NRSV translates as "outer nature" and "inner nature.")

337. Gregory's argument seems to be that Apolinarius might well be happy to accept his own (Gregory's) bipartite model as an alternative to his (Apolinarius's) tripartite one, on the basis that it is reasonable to recognize a binary distinction between the visible body, on the one hand, and the invisible soul and spirit, on the other. But, Gregory argues, it is no more logical to say that human nature is both one and two than to say that it is both one and three.

338. That is, in Apolinarius's view the "rational element" is, in the case of Christ, not what, in human beings, we call "spirit" (or "mind"), but God, as the second part of the sentence makes clear.

novel wisdom that the earthly race of humans consists of a rational soul and a body, but that there is also a tribe of heavenly human beings, with irrational souls and human bodies and with God mixed in with the constitution of those souls and bodies, taking the place of mind. It is one of this kind of human beings that Apolinarius thinks was manifested on earth as Christ. But Apolinarius has not shown us such a man, because no such man exists. If he did, the doctrine of Christ's birth from the Virgin would have to be rejected, because Christ would not share our nature. I consider it absurd and inconsistent to call something a body that is not a body,[339] and to call something human soul that is not a soul; for to claim that the soul is not rational is to say that it is in no way human. That cannot be right.

Apolinarius accepts of course that Christ was "made in the likeness of a man," by virtue of being "an enfleshed mind." But what sort of likeness can this be, asks Gregory, if Christ has God instead of a rational human mind and if his body and animal soul have no natural human origin but were apparently generated somehow in heaven? The truth is that Christ cannot just have been "like" a man; he must really have been a man. And for there to have been a true "enfleshment," his flesh can only have originated from Mary.

So what is the point of dividing the man Christ into three parts, of which two parts are human and the third is God? Apolinarius says, "For he would not have been made in the likeness of a man[340] unless he appeared as a man, that is, as an enfleshed mind." [L.69] I certainly could not say that the man through whom God reconciled the world to himself was without *a* mind; but that the man who wrote those words was out of *his* mind[341] during the time he was writing them, those words themselves proclaim, even if I do not say so myself. How can something

339. Presumably this is a reference to the fleshly body, which, according to Gregory, Apolinarius believed Christ had from eternity.

340. ἐν ὁμοιώματι ἀνθρώπου. Cf. ἐν ὁμοιώματι ἀνθρώπων in Phil 2.7. "According to the likeness of a human being" in the title of Apolinarius's work is καθ' ὁμοίωσιν ἀνθρώπου. Compare Gn 1.26 (LXX), where ἡμετέραν … καθ' ὁμοίωσιν = "according to our likeness."

341. Nazianzen makes a similar pun at the Apollinarians' expense in *epp.* 101 (PG 37:181C) and 102 (PG 37:196A).

that is other than man and does not share our nature be in the likeness of a man? If humanity is composed of a rational soul and a body, but neither that soul nor that body exists in the man that our author has invented, how [J.187] could that being, which is alien to our nature, have been endowed with our human likeness?

But he says that Christ is not a man but is "as a man, while actually being an enfleshed mind." It is these words that persuade me that the writer is out of his mind. How can what does not partake of the nature be like the nature? What is this "enfleshed mind," which is made one with the flesh and inseparable from it, and remains for ever so? Did it in fact originate from something else of the same kind? For there could not be flesh of the kind produced by human generation unless it came into existence from flesh. As the Lord says, "What is born from the flesh is flesh."[342] In any case, it was later, in time, that Christ was enfleshed. So what kind of flesh did he clothe himself with then? Flesh that already existed? In that case, it must have come into existence from flesh. Flesh that did not already exist? In that case, he could hardly be called "enfleshed"; one could not apply such an epithet to him if it referred to something that did not exist![343]

22. Christ as wisdom: The "God-filled man" again. Apolinarius's first and second syllogisms

The next major section[344] *of the* Apodeixis *seems to have been devoted to a series of eight (probably) syllogisms—or, at any rate, tightly constructed*

342. Jn 3.3.

343. I follow the PG text here. Gregory's (perhaps over-compressed) argument here is rather obscure, but the re-ordering of the different clauses suggested in J.187, lines 9–12, seems, if anything, to make matters worse. The points Gregory seems to be making are that "enfleshed" implies that the Word adopted flesh; that flesh can be produced only by human generation (i.e., from Mary); and that if what purported to be Christ's flesh had somehow been produced out of thin air (or from heaven!) when he was conceived in Mary's womb, it cannot have been true flesh—only "what is born from the flesh is flesh"—and so there can have been no true "enfleshment."

344. The fourth, according to the structure suggested in the appendix to this volume.

deductive arguments—designed to support his "enfleshed mind" Christology.[345]

The first is another version of his attack on the concept of Christ as a "God-filled man" and his advocacy of the "enfleshed mind" concept as the only logical alternative. "If," he says, "the Lord were not an enfleshed mind, he would be wisdom, which illuminates the human mind. But wisdom is what is found in all human beings. So if that is the case, the manifestation of Christ among us is not the coming of God but the birth of a man." In other words, if the mind of Jesus were not the Logos enfleshed, it would merely be a human mind inspired by God's wisdom, which would make Jesus merely a "God-filled man," like the prophets.

Gregory's response starts with a rather puerile debating point based on defective logic. If Apolinarius is prepared to allow only two possibilities, "enfleshed mind" and "wisdom," he must, Gregory (wrongly, of course) concludes, be saying that everything in the created world that is not "enfleshed mind" must be wisdom. So on that basis, a stone or a beetle, as neither of them is "enfleshed mind," must be wisdom! In fact (and here Gregory recovers himself somewhat), there is no reason why Christ could not be both "enfleshed mind" and "wisdom"; the two concepts are not mutually exclusive. Scripture, however, nowhere refers to Christ as "enfleshed mind"; on the other hand, it does call him wisdom. So, if Christ is wisdom, as he undoubtedly is, he cannot in any case, on the basis of Apolinarius's own (faulty) logic, be "enfleshed mind."

There are of course two uses of the concept of "wisdom" in play here. Apolinarius means by it the natural quality found in varying degrees in all rational creatures; Gregory, no doubt as a rhetorical device rather than because of a real misunderstanding, takes it instead to mean God's supernatural wisdom, the divine Sophia, conceived as an independent hypostasis and identified with the divine Word.

[M.1204] But let us take a look at the ineluctable logic of his arguments, through which he compels us to agree with him that the Only-begotten God is an "enfleshed mind." "If the Lord does not have an enfleshed mind, he must be wisdom."[346]

345. For the supposed syllogisms, see Mühlenberg, 73 and 89; Grelier, 93 and 105–7. But, as will be seen, there is uncertainty as to how many of them there are, and about how individual fragments should be assigned to separate syllogisms; see in particular nn. 357, 361, and 380 below.

346. The full syllogism is not given until the end of J.188. The fact that

[L.70] What an irrefutable proposition! He thinks that the Lord must absolutely be one or the other, enfleshed mind or wisdom. So if he is not the former, he must be the latter, since he is not enfleshed mind and everything that is not enfleshed mind is wisdom. But what about a stone? What about a beetle? What about everything else in the visible world? Apolinarius really will classify all of these things as one or the other, that is, either the enfleshed mind or wisdom!

But in fact neither mind nor wisdom has any connection with these things. So our wordsmith's proposition collapses, and his whole fabrication slips away; once his first principle has been undermined, his argument collapses along with it. For it has not been shown that the two concepts are distinguished in such a way that if one is present, the other cannot be, or, conversely, that if one [J.188] does not exist, the other must necessarily do so. But there is no reason why either both or neither should not be present in the same person.

But let us look at his principle the other way round and see how confused it is. If it is held that if Christ is not "enfleshed mind," he must be wisdom, it must also be true, the other way round, that if he is wisdom, he is not "enfleshed mind." But everyone who accepts the faith agrees that Christ is wisdom;[347] as regards the propositions of our wise friend here, what we confess is that Christ is not "enfleshed mind."

So what our wordsmith has demonstrated, on the basis of both his first and his second arguments, and indeed of the one he now puts forward[348]—arguments he uses to fabricate what-

---

Gregory unveils it, and comments on it, bit by bit rather than as a whole (thus arguably blunting the impact of his argument, as Winling [226, n. 213] suggests), is evidence for Mühlenberg's theory (see section 4 of the introduction, p. 41) that Gregory composed *antirrh* by having a secretary read the *Apodeixis* to him straight through and interrupting the reading as soon as he came across a passage that he thought he could refute, without giving much attention to the structure of Apolinarius's argument.

347. That is, the divine Sophia, conceived as an independent hypostasis. Apolinarius, on the other hand, seems to mean by "wisdom" the natural quality found in all rational creatures. It looks as though Gregory is deliberately misunderstanding this.

348. Literally, "the first and the second argument and the one now put

ever he wants—is that the Lord is not "enfleshed mind." This applies both to his original proposition and to the construction he builds upon it.

The conclusion he draws is worthy of them both.[349] What are his words? "The manifestation of Christ among us was not the coming of God but the birth of a man." [L.70] Arrogant people may laugh at these words; as for us, we think the appropriate response is to weep at their deceitfulness and vanity, and we decline to refute his argument any further, lest we may seem to be jesting. For who would not quite properly laugh at the incoherent structure of his argument? I shall set out in order exactly what he says:

> If the Lord were not an enfleshed mind, he would be wisdom, which illuminates the human mind. But wisdom is what is found in all human beings. So if that is the case, the manifestation of Christ among us was not the coming of God but the birth of a man. [L.70]

No orthodox person, led by the words of the holy fathers and apostles, would deny that the Lord is wisdom, [M.1205] raised high above every mind. Paul, too, [J.189] cries out in explicit terms that "he became for us wisdom from God"[350] and that "grace has appeared, bringing salvation, training us to renounce impiety" and in holiness and righteousness "to wait for the blessed hope."[351] This is what we have heard, this is what the Apostle has expounded to us; what we have not heard from any

---

forward" (τὸν πρῶτον καὶ τὸν δεύτερον καὶ ... τὸν νῦν λόγον). It is not clear what Gregory is referring to here or when he writes in the next sentence of "his original proposition" (ἡ πρότασις) and "the construction he builds on it" (ἡ διὰ μέσου κατασκευή). The most likely interpretation is one that does not reflect much credit on the clarity of Gregory's exposition, that is, that "the first and second arguments" refer, in a very imprecise way, to Apolinarius's proposition that "if the Lord does not have an enfleshed mind, he must be wisdom" and the inversion of it, which Gregory has set out in the previous paragraph (which is not in fact of course Apolinarius's argument at all, but Gregory's). In that case, "the construction he builds on it" looks forward to Apolinarius's conclusion, which Gregory is about to quote: "the manifestation of Christ among us is not the coming of God but the birth of a man."

349. That is, presumably, both "the first and the second argument" (see previous note).

350. 1 Cor 1.30.

351. Ti 2.11–13.

of the saints is that the Only-begotten God, he who is above all and through all and in all, is an "enfleshed mind," nor have we found this bizarre neologism anywhere in the holy Scriptures. This is particularly relevant when we consider the objectives of this modern wordsmith of ours; through this insipid creation of his own sophistry he seeks to reject the doctrine that the Lord is to be identified with wisdom—that wisdom through which, we believe, every mind is enlightened—and to introduce in its place this absurd neologism, to call the Only-begotten "enfleshed mind" rather than "wisdom."

If, he says, the Lord is believed to be wisdom, the wisdom, that is, that comes to be in all those who receive grace, we no longer hold that the manifestation of Christ among us is the coming of God[352] [L.70]—as if wisdom were something other than God! [353] Who would not pity the man for this folly? If, he says, we believe that Christ is wisdom, "the manifestation of Christ among us," of that Christ who became wisdom for us from God, will not be "the coming of God but the birth of a man." But what if Christ is indeed wisdom? Have you not heard the prophet crying out that "the virgin shall conceive in her womb and bear a son"?[354] And that "a child is born to us"?[355] And that the Son has "the government on his shoulder,"[356] like the strong and powerful Father, not just of the age that is past but also of that which is to come?

The second syllogism[357] *develops the argument in a rather different way. If Christ were "wisdom in the mind"—the natural quality found, to varying extents, in all rational creatures—he could not have "descended" or "emptied himself." So he cannot have been wisdom, but must have been "enfleshed mind." Apolinarius appeals to St. Paul in sup-*

352. As Lietzmann indicates, these words are a paraphrase of the direct quotation (L.70) in J.188 above.

353. J. makes this phrase—ὡς ἠλλοτριωμένης τοῦ θεοῦ τῆς σοφίας—part of the quotation (or of Gregory's paraphrase thereof; see previous note), but I follow PG, Lietzmann (221), and Winling (227) in taking it as a comment by Gregory.

354. Is 7.14.   355. Is 9.6.

356. Ibid.

357. Mühlenberg (89) seems to combine L.70–72 into a single syllogism; I follow Grelier (105) and Winling (227) in making L.71 the beginning of a new one.

port of the general principle of a human being as an "enfleshed mind";
Christ was indeed a man, but (it is implied) in a special sense, that is,
not, as in the first syllogism, "a mere man."

Gregory again makes the point that Apolinarius's argument, name-
ly, that to be an "enfleshed mind" is incompatible with being "wisdom,"
is false; "wisdom and "mind" are not mutually exclusive opposites, like
life and death, virtue and vice, or health and disease. He also says, with
some justification, that he cannot find any statement in Paul's writings
to the effect that a human being is an "enfleshed mind."

But let us reject this deluded rubbish, which claims [J.190]
that Christ must be said to be an "enfleshed mind" and neither
the wisdom that illuminates us nor God's entry into our life
through birth. Here is another attempt at a proof. "If the Word
was not an enfleshed mind, but wisdom ..."[358] [L.71] What is
wrong with our wise friend now? What has made him contradistinguish mind and wisdom, as if they were logically mutually
exclusive? Those who make accurate distinction between reali-
ties say that words are to be contradistinguished when the realization of one rules out that of the other, as life rules out death
and death rules out life, as vice rules out virtue and *vice versa*,
and all the other concepts that work in the same way. So how
can our author treat [M.1208] wisdom and mind as if they were
opposites and contradistinguish them as if it were impossible
for them to exist in or be attributes of one and the same thing?
That is what leads him to say, "If he was not an enfleshed mind,
he was wisdom" [L.71], on the analogy of saying that if there is
no health, there must be disease.

So what is the argument? "If he was the wisdom in the mind,
the Lord did not descend to us, nor did he empty himself."
[L.71] What unassailable logic! How, by demonstrating that the
Lord was wisdom, can Apolinarius claim that he cannot have
descended? If his descent can be disproved by saying that he is
wisdom, anyone who believes that he descended must necessarily conclude that he is not wisdom. Now the descent is in fact
acknowledged by Apolinarius. But at the same time he professes

358. Lietzmann puts together three separate citations by Gregory—this
and two later in J.190—to form a single fragment; Mühlenberg (69) agrees.

that he who descended was not wisdom. Such are the sophisticated arguments that this splendid fellow marshals against the truth.[359]

Then, arguing incoherently, he adds to this proposition a conclusion based on quite unjustified assumptions. It goes as follows: "So he was indeed a man; for, according to Paul, a human being is a mind in flesh."[360] [L.72] I beseech my readers not to think that this is something we have invented and put into Apolinarius's mouth as a joke to make people laugh. One can see by looking at what he has actually written that these words are an exact rendering [J.191] of what he says. What Paul is this who says that a human being is an "enfleshed mind"? Is he saying he has got another Paul hidden away somewhere? The servant of Jesus Christ who is called an apostle says nothing of this sort in all his writings. So since neither logic nor the evidence of Scripture supports it, how can this bizarre dogmatic concoction be believed in?

It cannot be established precisely where the next fragment that Gregory quotes, to the effect that Christ was both a "man from earth" and a "man from heaven," fits into Apolinarius's supposed syllogistic scheme.[361] Greg-

359. Gregory seems to be assuming that Apolinarius is seeking to prove that the Lord is wisdom ("by demonstrating that the Lord was wisdom") while at the same time denying it (by arguing that "his descent can be disproved by saying that he is wisdom" but that he did in fact descend). He seems to accuse Apolinarius of inconsistency on this basis. But in fact, of course, Apolinarius does not anywhere argue that the Lord is in fact wisdom; he merely seeks to demonstrate the logical consequences of believing that he is. So Gregory's argument seems wholly misconceived.

360. Apolinarius may have been thinking of Romans 7.23 (discussed earlier; see J.140) and 7.25: "I see in my members another law at war with the law of my mind, making me captive to the law of sin that dwells in my members.... So then, with my mind I am a slave to the law of God, but with my flesh I am a slave to the law of sin" (NRSV).

361. Lietzmann (141) and Grelier (105) link it with the preceding material; Mühlenberg (89) does so too, but makes it a separate pendant to the earlier argument. Carter (118–19, 365–66) combines fragments 72 and 73 to form an extra syllogism with an anthropological focus: Christ must be an "enfleshed mind" because that explains his special manhood; that is, it allows him to be like a man in structure, but also God because his mind is from heaven. But that seems rather speculative.

ory has clearly omitted some material.[362] *In any event, he responds merely by repeating earlier arguments. By calling Christ a "man from heaven," he claims, and by making his physical body itself divine, Apolinarius does not give a proper account of the role of Mary in his enfleshment. The divine element in Christ does not manifest itself to the senses, but is recognized only by the mind. In his anxiety to refute those who claim that Christ was merely a "God-filled man," Apolinarius does not acknowledge Christ's real humanity.*

Then he goes on to add another thought to what he has already said. "Since this man of earth was also a man from heaven …"[363] [L.73] I say again, he has forgotten Mary, to whom Gabri-

---

362. Lietzmann suggests (141) that his fragment 106 comes from somewhere near here in the *Apodeixis* (i.e., in the vicinity of fragments 70–73), as it deals with the "second Man."

The fragment comes from a seventh-century florilegium, possibly compiled by Anastasius of Sinai, entitled *Antiquorum patrum doctrina de Verbi incarnatione,* where it is attributed to chapter 12 of Apolinarius's *On the Divine Enfleshment,* which Lietzmann believes should be identified with the *Apodeixis.* It reads: "But now some people have tried to introduce novelty into what has been clearly proved and universally proclaimed; they blasphemously hold that the 'second man' of the apostolic tradition is a man from the earth, like the 'first man,' thus turning the humanity of the Word into an activity found in a man."

The discursive style of this fragment, however, does not seem to fit very comfortably into the "syllogistic" context of this part of the work. Grelier, who accepts that the fragment is from the *Apodeixis,* suggests (145) that it is just as likely that it comes from earlier on, where the "man from heaven" is discussed in more detail (L.16–18, J.138–40). Winling (169, n. 31) attributes (without reference) a similar view to Dräseke. But the *Doctrina* attributes it to chapter 12 of *On the Divine Enfleshment,* which immediately precedes that (13) to which L.107 is attributed (by a different source; see n. 366), and the latter does not fit at all into the earlier context. Carter (129–31) argues persuasively that neither L.106 nor L.107 in fact comes from the *Apodeixis* at all, but rather both are from a separate work entitled *On the Divine Enfleshment,* either a work written by Apolinarius himself or an anthology compiled by his disciples. In the light of the difficulty of finding a suitable "home" for L.106 in the *Apodeixis,* that is an attractive hypothesis.

363. Ἐπειδὴ ἄνθρωπος, φησίν, ἦν καὶ ἐπουράνιος οὗτος ὁ χοϊκός … Mühlenberg (69) comments, "Der Satz ist verstümmelt wiedergegeben, selbst wenn man mit Mühler [the J. editor] nach ἐπουράνιος ein Komma setzt." My translation above suggests it should be read (without the comma) as a subordinate clause, with the main clause omitted by Gregory. Winling (229) and Grelier (124) translate similarly.

el gave the good news, upon whom our faith says that the Holy Spirit came, whom the power of the Most High overshadowed, from whom Jesus was born—Jesus, who "has the government upon his shoulder," that is, who bears the weight of "primacy" upon himself. This "primacy" is of course God the Word, who was in the beginning and is the beginning,[364] as a text from Scripture somewhere says, "I am the beginning."[365] He must either show that the Virgin did not exist on the earth or stop fabricating this heavenly man.

And he must not be afraid because less learned people are misled as regards the divinity; that is, they accept the humanity but do not believe in the divinity as well. Christ's natural generation from a woman makes him human, while the virgin state that attended his birth pointed to what is more than human. So what was generated naturally was human, but the power to make this generation happen came not from human beings but through the Holy Spirit and the power of the Most High. So on a true interpretation [M.1209] Christ is both man and God: in respect of sight he is man; in respect of rational thought he is God. That is not what Apolinarius says; in his conclusions he characterizes the divine by reference to what is seen rather than by what can be known by the mind.

23. Soteriological arguments for the concept of Christ as "enfleshed mind." Apolinarius's third, fourth, and fifth syllogisms

Apolinarius's third syllogism is again reproduced by Gregory only in part; he admits to omitting some "rubbish," which, as Mühlenberg suggests, may in fact have represented a key element in the argument. On the basis of Mühlenberg's speculative reconstruction (see note 366), the argument can be paraphrased as follows. The purpose of the divine enfleshment was to "do the work of abolishing" the sin that is inherent in human flesh. The flesh of human beings is "externally determined" by human

364. "Government," "primacy," and "beginning" all translate ἀρχή(ν). I have not found a way of elegantly rendering Gregory's play on the different meanings of the Greek word.

365. Cf. Rv 1.8.

reason. Now, it will be shown later, in the fifth syllogism (J.194–96), that the human reason is weak and mutable, and therefore incapable in itself of achieving "the work of abolition." But (and this is the putative focus of the argument in this syllogism) if there were nevertheless two reasons (and therefore two wills) in Christ, one human and one divine, they would necessarily always be in conflict, and therefore "the work of abolition" would be unachievable. So it was necessary for "God, who is mind" to be enfleshed in Jesus, in the sense of taking the place of his human reason. Apolinarius adds a soteriological corollary: "Our self-determined mind participates in that abolition to the extent to which it conforms itself to Christ."

Apart from objecting to Apolinarius's identification of God with mind, which he says is unsupported by either Scripture or tradition, Gregory again fails to engage with his opponent's argument here, but merely professes himself unable to understand his novel terminology, "the 'self-determined' and the 'externally determined' mind, the flesh that 'does the work of abolition'" (although, in the case of the last of these expressions, Apolinarius in fact speaks of the "enfleshment," not the "flesh," as "doing the work of abolition").

But let us move on in our consideration to his next argument. "If," he says, "together with God, who is mind, there was also a human mind in Christ ..." [L.74] That is his premiss. But our counter-premiss is as follows. Which of the saints defined [J.192] God as mind? By what Scripture have we been taught that God is the same as mind, so as to induce us to believe in the proposition that the man in Christ has no mind and God constitutes the mind of what would otherwise be non-rational? We must register the totally offensive nature of this proposition.

But I fear we shall be seen by our readers as mere scoffers, bringing the disgraceful ideas of our wordsmith to public attention merely to raise a laugh. What flows from his premiss needs to be demonstrated, but it is necessary only to set out his conclusion; I shall pass over all the intervening rubbish. "If," he says,

together with God, who is mind, there was also a human mind in Christ, the enfleshment does not do its work in that mind. But if the work of the enfleshment is not done in that mind, which is self-determined and unconstrained, then it is done in the flesh, which is externally determined and activated by the divine mind. That work is the abolition of sin. Our self-determined mind participates in that abolition to the extent to which it conforms itself to Christ.[366] [L.74]

366. By accident or design, Gregory has obscured Apolinarius's argument by "passing over all the intervening rubbish" here. Mühlenberg (201–2) suggests that the missing middle term of the syllogism may have been to the effect that if Christ had both a human and a divine mind and will, the former would necessarily have been mutable (τρεπτὸς) and fallible, so the human and divine wills must always have been in opposition to each other. This is an argument that we know Apolinarius used elsewhere: in the version of the text of the *Kata meros pistis* preserved by Leontius of Byzantium (§30, Lietzmann, 178b–179b) and in L.150 (from the letter to Julian). So on that basis the first part of the original syllogism can be tentatively reconstructed as follows: "If, together with God, who is mind, there was also a human mind in Christ, <the mutable human and the immutable divine wills must always have been in opposition to each other. So> the enfleshment does not do [= could not have done] its work in that [human] mind. But if ..."

L.107 has been thought to reproduce, or at least to have been associated with, some part of the omitted material. It is from Justinian's *contra Monophysitas,* and is attributed by him to chapter 13 of Apolinarius's *On the Divine Enfleshment;* as in the case of J.106 (see n. 362 above), Lietzmann thinks that work is to be identified with the *Apodeixis.* The fragment reads:

> The flesh is moved by something outside itself and is subordinate to what moves and drives it, whatever that may be. It is not a complete living organism in itself but is used as a component to form a complete living organism. It comes together into union with what controls it [τὸ ἡγημονικόν, a Stoic term for the rational soul], and is joined with its heavenly controller. As regards its passive element it is assimilated to it; as regards its active element it takes on the divine, which has been brought to inhabit it. Thus it comprises one living organism formed from what is moved and what moves; it is not a duality or formed from two complete or self-moving beings, with the man being a different living organism from God and a slave of God rather than God. If there is some heavenly power present, that is quite consistent; when the flesh becomes the flesh of God, it then becomes a living organism linked into a single nature.

Lietzmann suggests (141) that, as it appears that this fragment 107 (attributed to chapter 13 of *On the Divine Enfleshment*) closely followed fragment 106 (attributed to chapter 12; see n. 362), it must come from "somewhere near" fragment 74 (that is, if fragment 106 is correctly associated with fragments 70–73). It is clearly not in itself the missing middle term of Apolinarius's syllogism, but it could conceivably have preceded it, by way of explaining the anthropological principles that led Apolinarius to suggest that the human and divine wills must always oppose each other. But, again, this does not seem to fit very comfortably with the "syllogistic" style. Moreover, as Grelier (146) points out, the main focus of L.107 is not the role of the reason vis-à-vis the flesh as such, but rather the implications of Apolinarius's Christology for the

Can you see how the conclusions are consistent with the premiss? Perhaps we need an enchanter and a diviner who can discern the mysteries of dreams in order to interpret the novelties of expression in this passage, the "self-determined" and the "externally determined" mind, the flesh that "does the work of abolition." But let us leave this to the cocksure mockery of the young, and move on to the next part of the text.

Apolinarius's fourth syllogism argues that Christ's sinlessness was clearly supernatural in origin, rather than the result of ascetic discipline, and that this is evidence for the divinity of his mind. But Gregory points out some scriptural examples of people who clearly acquired various virtues or talents directly from God; nobody would claim that they were therefore "enfleshed minds."

"If anyone achieves more than someone else," he says, "this comes about through practice and discipline.³⁶⁷ But practice and discipline are not terms that can be applied to Christ. So he had no human mind." [L.75] But how is he taking into account what the divinely inspired Scripture says?³⁶⁸ What "practice and discipline" taught Bezalel his crafts?³⁶⁹ [J.193] Where did Solo-

---

"single nature" of Christ, which is not the issue here. This leads her to suggest that its original context is rather L.80–L.85 (or, on the basis of my ordering, L.81–L.86; see J.199–206), where the question about the extent to which there can be two perfect natures in Christ is discussed. But again that would make it difficult to find a suitable place for L.106 on the assumption that it comes shortly before L.107.

Grelier (146–47) argues that the fact that when Justinian quotes L.81 (which is certainly from the *Apodeixis*), he says it, too, is from *On the Divine Enfleshment*, shows that L.'s attribution of L.107 to the *Apodeixis* must be correct. Carter (131), however, attaches some significance to the fact that, although Justinian gives a chapter number for L.107, he does not do so for L.81; he argues that Justinian drew the latter from the *Apodeixis* and the former from another work with a similar name. As in the case of L.107, and for similar reasons (see n. 362), that is an attractive hypothesis.

367. "Practice and discipline" translates ἄσκησις.

368. *Pace* Grelier (238–39), there seems no reason to believe that Apolinarius himself used the examples that follow, so as "to explain the difference between Christ's ontological perfection and the innate knowledge of the prophets, in order to show that Christ was not a prophet." That would not be relevant to his argument here.

369. Ex 31.1–5.

mon's knowledge of so many things come from? How did Amos, who gashed mulberry trees,[370] acquire such power in prophecy from pasturing goats? None of these descended from heaven; none of them existed in the beginning or were equal to God.

Gregory now moves on to Apolinarius's fifth syllogism, the next part of his soteriological argument. His discussion of it is confusing in two ways. First, he quotes only the conclusion, not the arguments leading up to it. Second, at this stage he quotes only part of that conclusion; only after a diversion on to a discussion of what seems to have been part of the next (sixth) syllogism does he give it in full.

The part of Apolinarius's conclusion quoted here is to the effect that the enfleshment can best be characterized not as God's "taking up" (ἀνάληψις) of a complete human being, including his mind, but rather as the "taking to himself" (πρόσληψις) of just the flesh (see note 373.) Gregory's initial response is that there is no real distinction between ἀνάληψις and πρόσληψις. (Both could be translated as "assumption.") In fact Apolinarius's argument does not depend on such a distinction but on that between the "assumption" of the whole person and the "assumption" just of the flesh.

[M.1212] But let us say no more about the next argument either, particularly in view of what the conclusion attached to it goes on to say, that is, to quote the exact words,[371] that "the human race is saved not by the taking up[372] of the mind and of the whole human being, but by the taking to himself[373] of the

370. τὰ συκάμινα κνίζων, i.e., to make them ripen (Liddell and Scott, *Lexicon* [1996], *s.v.* κνίζω); Am 7.14 (LXX). NRSV has "a dresser of sycamore trees."

371. An attempt to make sense of a very obscure sentence: Ἀλλὰ σιγάσθω καὶ τοῦτο τὸ ἐπιχείρημα μάλιστα διὰ τὸ προσφυὲς τοῦ προτεθέντος αὐτῷ συμπεράσματος οὕτως κατὰ τὴν λέξιν ἔχοντος ... Grammatically, τοῦτο and τοῦ προτεθέντος αὐτῷ συμπεράσματος would more naturally look back to the immediately preceding passage, but there seems no doubt that the συμπέρασμα is L.76 (quoted in a fuller form later, in J.195), which seems to be the conclusion of a syllogism (Apolinarius's fifth) of which Gregory has omitted the hypothesis and the middle term (thus Mühlenberg, p. 83). *Pace* Carter (367), there is no explicit or implicit link with the previous syllogism, and Gregory's argument here seems to assume that a clear line has been drawn under it.

372. ἀνάληψις.

373. πρόσληψις. This distinction between ἀνάληψις and πρόσληψις seems unique to Apolinarius; see Mühlenberg, 200. The former is his preferred "technical term" for describing the "assumption" of flesh by the Logos; see

flesh." [L.76] Such is the conclusion of his argument. But let those who make a study of the minutiae of grammar, so as to instruct schoolchildren in the subtle distinctions between the parts of speech called prepositions, explain the difference between "taking up" and "taking to." For our part, we consider that what is "taken to himself" is "taken up" and do not doubt that what has been "taken up" has been "taken to himself," since we have learned from the Scripture how these terms are used. "You have taken me to yourself with glory," says David.[374] And again elsewhere, "He chose David his servant and took him up from the flocks"[375] belonging to his father. He who was "taken to him" in glory was "taken up," and he who was "taken up from the flocks" was "taken to him." The two expressions refer to the same thing. So anyone who says that the mystery of the Only-begotten providentially becoming man should be explained in terms not of "taking up" but of "taking to himself" will perhaps have difficulty in explaining what he means.

But to avoid submerging reason in the mire of his illogical statements, I will omit most of his nonsense. I think a literal reading of his words is itself a sufficient demonstration of the absurdity of what he says. Those who wish vigorously to attack this heresy should refute its absurdity not so much from [J.194] their own arguments as from what he actually says. He exposes his unorthodoxy by the sloppiness of his advocacy in defense of the untruths that he is proposing.

Gregory now seems to jump ahead somewhat[376] *in order to comment on some words of Apolinarius that he will discuss again in the next section, in what, on the basis of Lietzmann's arrangement of the fragments of*

Carter, 142–48 and 175–85. In the Leontius text of the *Kata meros pistis*, Apolinarius explains that Christ "took flesh to himself (προσλάβοντα σάρκα) from the Virgin Mary" (Lietzmann, 177b, line 7) and that it is wrong to say that God "took up (ἀναλαβών) the whole man" because the "whole man" would necessarily be sinful (Lietzmann, 178b, lines 10–11). For Apolinarius's follower Vitalis's distinction between ἀναλαμβάνειν and λαμβάνειν, see Epiphanius, *adversus haereses* 77.19 (PG 42:668D–670B).

    374. Ps 72 (73).24.
    375. Ps 77 (78).70.
    376. Grelier (105–6) calls it a "digression."

the Apodeixis, *is their proper place, that is, as part of the sixth syllo-gism. In this passage, Apolinarius is again arguing that if Jesus had a human mind as well as being joined with the Word, there would be two Christs: "If the complete God were joined together with a complete man, they would be two." Gregory's response is that Apolinarius's formula-tion, of a complete God joined to an incomplete man, still implies two separate natures, even if one of them is incomplete. (Apolinarius might have conceded that any doctrine of the enfleshment must imply a duality to the extent that it purports to give an account of how Christ is both God and man. He would have gone on to argue that his formula does nevertheless maintain the unity of Christ's person, in that it envisages him as a man with all three of the essential components of human na-ture—mind, animal soul, flesh—even if the place of mind is taken by the divine Word.)*

For he goes on to say, "If the complete God were joined to-gether with a complete man, they would be two." So the incom-plete attached to the complete is not considered by him as a du-ality.[377] [L.81] Has not our distinguished friend seen children counting the fingers of their hands? Anyone who counts things where one is small and the other bigger, counts the larger as one and the smaller as one,[378] but, if he is counting them both together, says nevertheless that there are two of them. Every number is a combination of individual units and indicates a summation of the aggregate of these. If what is being counted, whatever it is, when it is compared with something else that is

377. The first sentence of this fragment is reproduced in an extended and perhaps accurate form in J.199 below. In transcribing the fragment in its form here, Lietzmann (224, line 19) puts a question mark after the second sen-tence, which seems to suggest that it is a rhetorical question by Gregory. ("So does he not consider … ?") J., however, who prints it with a full stop after it but in normal type, seems to assume that it is a straight report by Gregory of Apo-linarius's views. My translation reflects that interpretation. It is supported by the fact that when Lietzmann transcribes a separate version of this fragment, reported by Justinian in *contra Monophysitas* (Lietzmann, 224, lines 22–24), which includes this sentence (without the words "by him"), he seems to accept that the sentence can be attributed to Apolinarius.

378. That is, in the example just given, larger and smaller fingers. The same applies, Gregory argues, when, of two things being counted, one is "com-plete" and the other "incomplete"; there are still two of them.

being counted with it, is of superior magnitude to that smaller thing, that does not mean that the lesser thing does not count as one, even if it is inferior in size. When we assign a number to two things of equal size, we speak of two complete things. But when we count together what is incomplete and what is complete, we still speak of [M.1213] two things, but of one as being defective and the other complete. This fellow, with his great knowledge of arithmetic, says that if each thing is complete as regards its own nature, things so defined should be called two. But if one thing is defective and the other complete, he says they are both one. In some unknown way he fuses together the incomplete element with the superior one, contriving a unity of irreconcilables by means of their opposite qualities. A complete thing could indeed well be linked to another complete thing, or an incomplete thing to an incomplete, because they have completeness or incompleteness in common.[379] But how two opposites, that is, something complete and something incomplete, can be brought into unity, let this founding father of the New Arithmetic tell us.

Gregory now goes back to Apolinarius's fifth syllogism, and to what he presents as his false distinction between "taking up" and "taking to himself." He now summarizes the whole of Apolinarius's conclusion, which seems similar to that of the third syllogism (fragment 74, J.192 above)[380] in that it re-states the point that human flesh needs to be "governed" by the mind. For our (sinful) flesh to be saved, it needs more than

379. Literally, "by virtue of their similarity." As an illustration of Gregory's argument here, perhaps one could think of the handle and the blade of an axe. If they were both complete, one would have a (single) axe; but if, say, the handle were broken, one would have two things, an axe blade and a broken axe handle.

380. Which demonstrated how precarious attempts to identify the structure of the arguments on the *Apodeixis* are. Carter (371) is rightly skeptical about drawing clear distinctions between the various "syllogistic" arguments: he suggests that although "it is not possible to reorganize [the fragments I here attribute to the third and fifth syllogisms] into a singular logical structure to demonstrate that these statements were originally *all* components of a single formal proof for Christ as (divine) νοῦς ἔνσαρκος, ... taken together the fragments do seem to represent a single cohesive complex of soteriological ideas which together justify the Christological conclusion reached in Fr. 76."

a human mind, because it is inevitable that such a mind would "fall subject to the flesh because of the weakness of its knowledge." It needs instead an "immutable mind, one that would not fall ... but that would conform it [the flesh] to itself without any compulsion."

Before actually quoting the relevant passage verbatim, Gregory points out that human nature is inherently "mutable" and that, if Christ really became man, his human nature too must have been "mutable." Moreover, this must apply equally to his human mind as to his human flesh. This remains the case even though in fact his flesh "was not subject to any [actual] defilement" and his mind "was not subject to any [actual] change or variation."

Having then given us Apolinarius's actual words in full, Gregory now again argues that his "enfleshed mind" Christology does not in fact do what it claims to do, that is, to guarantee the unity of the person of Christ. It in fact assumes a duality between the divine mind, which rules, and the fallible flesh, which is ruled. There is no way of getting round the fact that Christ has two natures.

But he does not deem it proper to think of a human mind as being associated with the Only-begotten God. The reason he gives for this is that the human mind is mutable. But follow that argument through: God couldn't [J.195] have flesh either. Even our wordsmith could not deny that the flesh is mutable and that it puts on the various stages of development from youth to maturity, like changes of clothes. How could he not have been mutable, he who was first carried in the arms of his mother, then became a child, then an adolescent, gradually advancing to maturity until he reached the full measure of manhood? If mind is rejected by him because it is mutable, on the same basis he should not allow the flesh. So the whole Gospel will be declared false by him, the proclamation will be made futile, and faith will be in vain. If he does not reject the belief in the manifestation of Christ in flesh, mutable flesh, on the same basis he should not reject Christ's mind. Rather, just as when he came to be in the flesh he was not subject to any defilement, so when he took upon himself a mind, he was not subject to any change or variation.

I shall come back to this same argument by quoting again his precise words:

The human race is saved not by the taking up of the mind and of the whole human being, but by the taking to himself of the flesh, whose nature it is to be governed. The flesh needed an immutable mind, one that would not fall subject to the flesh because of the weakness of its knowledge, but that would conform it to itself without any compulsion. [L.76]

Everybody knows that a being that has needs that must be met is quite different in nature from a self-sufficient one, and that what is born to be governed is different in the principle of its being from that whose nature is to rule. Thus the nature of irrational animals has been constituted so as to make them subject to human beings; the rule over irrational animals is not something that humanity has acquired, but rather its natural property. If, as Apolinarius says, it is natural for the flesh [M.1216] to be ruled and that the nature of divinity is to govern, how can anyone who concedes this pronounce that these two natures are one right from the beginning? For it is clear to [J.196] all that there is one principle of subjection and another of superiority, that there is one kind of thing that is made to be subject to guidance and another whose nature is to govern. If it can be seen that the natures of two things—I mean flesh and divinity—comprise opposite characteristics, how can these two natures be one?

Gregory now seems to move away temporarily from commenting directly on Apolinarius's fifth syllogism, and spends some time "chewing over" its implications; he refers in general terms to other relevant aspects of Apolinarius's teaching (L.77–78) but without quoting him directly.[381] *He seems to imply that it is in an attempt to meet the objection he (Gregory) raised in the immediately preceding passage—that Christ necessarily has two natures—that Apolinarius posits that Christ's flesh was of divine origin and joined to his divinity from eternity. But such divine flesh must, by definition, have been immutable and not turned away towards evil like ours. Therefore, it would have had no need of being saved, and the divine enfleshment loses its point. But he accuses Apolinarius of inconsistency in that he often, as in the passage under discussion here, implies that Christ's flesh is, like ours, mortal and passible and therefore in need of salvation.*

381. I owe this interpretation to Carter, 369–70.

How can he argue for this "divine" and "heavenly" flesh that he has invented? How indeed can he claim that the enfleshment of the Word did not come about when, as provided for in the divine economy, it adopted our form in the last days, but that it was always enfleshed and always remained in the same state? When he says that the flesh is in need of something immutable, of something to rule over it, he is certainly talking about our flesh, which fell into sin because of the mutability of its nature. But if, as he says, it is a celestial and divine body that can be recognized in the Word,[382] [L.77] logically he cannot say that that body is mutable or that it is in need of direction. It is not our saying, but that of the voice of God, that it is not "those who are well" who require "a physician, but those who are sick."[383] For in heaven the disease that arises from sin does not exist; it is we who have fallen into the sickness of sin, who have been weakened by the acceptance of evil; it is we who have been mutable and turned towards evil[384] who need him who is immutable, we who have turned away from the way of salvation who have come to need him who guides us towards the good. So if our wordsmith rightly attributes these characteristics to the flesh adopted by the Lord, that it was natural for it to be ruled and that it needed something immutable to rule over it, he is describing nothing other than our own human constitution. If the divinity is identified with the flesh,[385] and the divine, according to his own definition of the term, does not require anything else to guide it (for it is not susceptible to any change for the worse or any alteration), it is in vain that he has strung together all this pretentious stuff about the flesh, which has just been [J.197] quoted. If that flesh is divine, it is clear that it is immutable; if it is mutable, it is certainly not divine. [L.77]

[M.1217] Who could go all through this dogmatic fiction, confused and inconsistent as it is, and never heading in the

---

382. It is doubtful whether L.77 (here, at the end of this paragraph, and in J.200) constitutes a genuine fragment; see n. 399 below.

383. Lk 5.31; Mt 9.12.

384. "been mutable and" is not in the Greek, but is added to reflect the fact that τρέπειν, "turn," is the root of ἄτρεπτος, "immutable."

385. εἰ δὲ ἐν τῇ σαρκὶ ὁρίζεται τὴν θεότητα, literally, "if he defines [or 'circumscribes'] the divinity in the flesh."

same direction, but, like the fantasies of sleep, appearing in different forms at different times? Now he says the flesh of the Word is divine and co-eternal with it; now he says it is something acquired, which the Word takes to itself; now, that it has a nature different from ours, mortal and passible as it is; and now, that it is itself in need of direction and is in the grip of passion, with all its mutability and alteration, to the extent that he presents it as being without a mind, so that it may be healed by the divinity. [L.78]

On Apolinarius's account, Gregory reminds us, it is only that mortal and passible flesh that needs salvation. Does he believe that God does not love our mind as much as our flesh, and does not think it equally in need of salvation? Scripture suggests otherwise: the mind needs "steering" just as much as the flesh. Moreover, the mind is the part of us that is most like God and therefore the part of human nature that would have been most suitable for Christ to have adopted when he became man.

It is as if he considers the mind as a hindrance to God's care for humans, and that what is irrational is easier for God to love. So if, as he claims, it is the irrational that God takes to himself, [L.78] he must think it is more blessed not to have a mind! So why does he not correct Solomon, who says, "The thinking person will obtain steering"?[386] I think that what "steering" refers to here, in the hidden meaning of the proverb, is our human nature, tempest-tossed and shipwrecked in the midst of evil, being directed by the expertise of the true Steersman into the haven of the divine will. If it is through an absence of the thinking faculty that humanity is saved, how will "the thinking person ... obtain steering"?

To which element of human nature is the divine closest? Towards which does reason suggest that the divine nature most naturally tends? Flesh is gross and solid and has an affinity with the nature of earth, while reason is intellectual and invisible and cannot be pictured. Which of these should be thought more suitable for being linked with God: the gross and earthy or the intangible and unrepresentable?

386. Prv 1.5 (LXX). "Steering" is κυβέρνησιν. NRSV has, "Let ... the discerning acquire skill."

Gregory now seems to return to a sequential discussion of Apolinarius's text. It is here assumed, although there can be no certainty, that the next two fragments are somehow linked to Apolinarius's fifth syllogism.[387]

The first seems to be essentially a paraphrase of an earlier fragment (L.76; see nn. 388–89), which is indeed the core of the fifth syllogism. Gregory asks how Apolinarius can hold the view that Christ's flesh "participates in pure virtue" and is not subject to any "compulsion," while at the same time believing that Christ had no human mind. For virtue implies the power to make a free choice, and there can be no free choice without a rational mind. Flesh without mind could not freely choose to align itself with God.

How, as he claims, can flesh that participates in pure virtue be linked to God "without any compulsion"? [L.79][388] [J.198] For who does not know that virtue is the correct exercise of free choice? The flesh is the tool of free choice, a tool that is involved with the impulse of the mind; the flesh is moved towards whatever that active principle directs it to. Free choice is nothing other than a mental activity, a disposition towards something. If, as he says, the man Christ, in whom there is no mind, participates in pure virtue, what would there be in him that could voluntarily adopt virtue? Perhaps when our wordsmith speaks of what is without compulsion, he is thinking of something that is in fact compelled. For when the body keeps away from evil activities without the mind assenting to a morally commendable principle, what is achieved is the product of necessity, not free choice. But those who choose the good on the basis of a ratio-

387. Thus Mühlenberg, 89, and Grelier, 105–6. But see note 380 on the provisional nature of all attempts to identify the detailed structures of the argument here.

388. Lietzmann makes fragment 79 a direct quotation: "the flesh which participates in pure virtue is linked to God without any compulsion." Mühlenberg, on the other hand, thinks (69) that it is a paraphrase combining elements of L.76 (J.195 above)—"without any compulsion"—and L.80 (near the beginning of J.199 below)—"pure virtue." If, as is suggested below, L.80 has a soteriological focus and is about the transmission of "pure virtue" from Christ to Christian believers, it is difficult to find a "paraphrase" of it in L.79. It may be possible, however, that Gregory borrowed the expression "pure virtue" from L.80 and used it here in a rather different context, i.e., as what is essentially a free interpretation of L.76.

nal judgment are superior to all force and necessity, because they have the disposition towards good within themselves. How can our wordsmith say that what is not freely chosen is not done under compulsion, in the case of someone who has no rational faculty of his own to lead him to do what is good? For what is not [M.1220] done through free choice is considered to be in no way subject to either praise or blame. Otherwise, we should praise those persons who are prevented from evildoing by imprisonment, people whom chains, rather than good judgment, keep from performing bad actions.

But, he says, the divinity takes control of the flesh "without any compulsion."[389] In saying "without any compulsion" he must mean "voluntarily." But how could anyone be willingly taken over by virtue without possessing one's own will? For choosing and willing, espousing what is beneficial and rejecting what is harmful, all these are functions of the reason; and creatures without minds cannot reason. So if the flesh is aligned with God without compulsion, what our wordsmith is asserting is that the flesh is not without the power of choice,[390] nor is it without the power of judgment and reflection about what is beneficial. Nobody would ever describe that as a state of irrationality; for how could the power of reason be present in an irrational being? So by what he says, not only is he agreeing that the human Christ [J.199] possesses mind, but also that that mind is superior to all others. For the free and unconstrained impulse[391] towards the good is evidence for perfection of mind.

The final part of this argument is difficult to follow, not least because the text of the relevant fragment of Apolinarius is contested and its translation is problematical. On the reading and interpretation I have adopted (see note 392), its focus is clearly soteriological. The "pure virtue" of the

389. J. makes the whole of this sentence a direct quotation. Lietzmann (223) prints it as part of fragment 79, in small type, as if it were a paraphrase of what he thinks is a direct quotation in the last sentence in J.197 above (see previous note). But it seems best to follow Mühlenberg (see previous note) and read both passages as paraphrases of L.76.

390. That is, by admitting that Christ's human nature—his "flesh"—voluntarily chose to align itself with God, Apolinarius is in effect conceding that that human nature included a rational human mind.

391. ὁρμή, a favorite term of the Stoics.

Godhead is communicated to "every subordinate mind," that is, to all human beings who subject themselves to Christ; it is shared by all those who are "made like Christ as regards the mind" and "not made unlike him as regards the flesh" (whatever that may mean; perhaps Apolinarius is referring to ascetic self-control of the urges of the flesh). But it needs to be noted that this soteriological argument, describing how believers can obtain the benefits of Christ's saving work, seems to go beyond that made in the earlier fragment (76), which restricts itself to a discussion of Christ's own nature, and that must raise a doubt as to whether this argument was in fact part of the same syllogistic argument (the fifth).

In any event, Gregory does not give an adequate response to either point. On the first, he goes back to Apolinarius's alleged view about Christ's flesh (not, on the face of it, the issue here), that is, that it "participates in virtue" (L.79), and, in effect, he repeats the argument that that would necessarily imply a (human) mind. On the second, he gives up and refuses to comment on the basis that what Apolinarius says is "incoherent and illogical."

And his subsequent words show precisely that alignment with what is better derives from a mental process. These are his exact words: "... communicating pure virtue to every subordinate mind."[392] [L.80] So if it is in the mind that he identifies the purity of virtue, how can he banish the mind from that flesh in which he perceives purity? One of these propositions must be false: either that virtue is a function of mind, or that the flesh that is drawn to virtue without constraint is without mind. What he goes on to say is incoherent and illogical, so it would be superfluous closely to examine what he says on the following lines:

392. That is, to every mind that subordinates itself to Christ. On this interpretation the whole fragment (see next note) is soteriological in focus. My rendering follows the mss. reading, πάντι τῷ ὑποχείριῳ νῷ, as do PG, Lietzmann, and also, it appears, Winling (239), who translates it as "à tout *noûs* soumis." The use of ὑποχείριος in this absolute sense does seem slightly odd, but I am not convinced that it is necessary to adopt J.'s amendment to πάντι τῷ ὑποχείριῳ νοῦ. The natural rendering of that would be "to every subordinate part of mind," which makes little sense in the context. Mühlenberg (180) keeps the soteriological focus by rendering the J. text "allem der Vernunft Unterworfenen (d. h. allen Vernunftwesen)": "everything that is subject to reason (i.e., all rational beings)." But I can find no precedent for the use of the genitive in that sense after ὑποχείριος.

"... and to all those who are made like Christ as regards the mind and not made unlike him as regards the flesh."³⁹³ [L.80]

24. The unity of Christ. Apolinarius's sixth, seventh, and eighth syllogisms

The next two syllogisms of the Apodeixis *seek to establish the unity of the enfleshed Christ's nature, against the "orthodox," who, Apolinarius maintains, teach of two separate Christs.*

In his sixth syllogism Apolinarius argues that two perfect (that is, complete) natures cannot be combined into one: "If God, who is complete, had been joined to a complete man, there would have been two of them, the one Son of God by nature and the other by adoption." It seems clear that Apolinarius is arguing here on the basis of a principle first laid down by Aristotle in the Metaphysics, *that the components of a perfect substance cannot themselves be perfect, because in themselves,* qua *components, they lack the other components that are necessary to constitute that perfect substance. Or, looking at it the other way round, perfection is defined as the total realization of a substance; a perfect being, for example, God or a perfect man, cannot have anything else added to it.*³⁹⁴

In response, Gregory expresses no view as to whether or not it is appropriate to call the man Jesus God's adopted Son. But in any case, for Apolinarius, Gregory again points out, that man would be only half a man—a "half-adopted" Son!—because he has no human mind. Or, he adds satirically, if you divide the animal part into flesh and irrational soul, you could call him a "two-thirds man." It is indeed difficult to envisage God being joined to a corporeal body, but it becomes no easier if that body is conceived of as having no rational mind. Indeed, it is less seemly to envisage God joined to an impaired human nature than to a complete one.

393. This is grouped by Lietzmann with the quotation earlier in the paragraph to form fragment 80.

394. See Grelier, 474–76, giving references to Aristotle, *Metaphysics* Z, 13, 1039A; Δ, 1021B 21–24, 1021A 31–1022A. Nazianzen also attributes to Apolinarius this argument about two perfect natures not being capable of being combined into one, and tries to address it rather more directly than Nyssen does; see *ep.* 101, PG 37:184B–185B.

Let those who admire this deceitful teaching explain these nauseating words; we will pass on to the words that come next: "If God, who is complete, had been joined to a complete man, there would have been two of them, the one Son of God by nature and the other by adoption."[395] [L.81]

I would be glad to learn from the experts on all this, who call the man who is complete and endowed with mind "an adopted son," what they call the "mindless man" (for this is indeed the term they use to denote the man without mind)[396] —what will they say? As the Only-begotten God is in himself complete and lacks nothing, he has the title of true Son; his nature gives him the right to that title. So what name would he have if a half-complete man were joined to him? If Apolinarius says the complete man is the adopted Son, [M.1221] it follows that the half-complete man, insofar as he is man, must clearly be called the "half-adopted" Son, applying to himself only half of the appellation "adopted"! So it would be better to say that it is the complete Son that is the adopted one, and that the other one is [J.200] defective as regards a half—or a third, according to the view of those who divide human beings into three parts. If, on the other hand, it is inappropriate for God to have an adopted son, such inappropriateness applies to an incomplete man in the same way as to a complete man.

But actually, the idea is even more absurd if we are talking about the mutilation of human nature. If, when considered in the context of the divine, even the perfection of human nature is considered disgraceful and beyond any conception of what is worthy of God, how much more disgraceful would it be to envisage Christ's human nature as impaired! If flesh has no mind,

395. A more extended form of the fragment first cited in J.194 above. Grelier argues (127) that this second form, with its reference to the "by nature/by adoption" distinction, is more likely to be what Apolinarius actually wrote, as Gregory specifically comments on the Sonship "by adoption" in his commentary that follows here.

396. ... τὸν ἀνόητον ἄνθρωπον—οὕτω γὰρ πάντως τὸν μὴ ἔχοντα νοῦν ὀνομά-ζουσι ... The reference here is not clear; perhaps "they" are disciples of Apolinarius. Winling (240) has "puisque c'est ainsi ['inintelligent'] qu'il faut nécessairement nommer celui qui est privé de noûs" (emphasis added). That avoids the problem, but arguably only by putting too great a semantic burden on πάντως.

that does not make it easier for it to be joined to the nature of the Father. The whole human being and a part of a human being are equally remote from the essence of the Father[397] so far as the definition of their respective natures is concerned; neither element of our nature, neither the mind nor the body, can be joined with the transcendent nature on the basis of the definition of their respective essences.[398]

Nor does Apolinarius's notion of the eternal Son being clothed in "heavenly flesh" help; the eternal Son must share his Father's immaterial nature, and so cannot have had flesh. But in any case, whether Christ's flesh is of earthly or heavenly origin, it must be totally other than the divine element in his nature. So there must be some distinction within Christ's enfleshed nature on earth; Apolinarius's project of establishing one single nature for Christ is doomed to failure.

Even if Apolinarius's story imagines some heavenly kind of flesh placed around the divine element,[399] [L.77] no one who had considered the matter could believe that such flesh was consubstantial with, of the same essence as, God, as the Father. But if flesh is different in essence from the Father, how can that different thing be the Son? For it is absolutely necessary that whatever comes from something else should be the same in essence as he who begot him. But the Father is not flesh, and so he who comes from the Father could in no way be flesh, for, as it is said, "What is born from spirit is spirit," and not flesh.[400] So if his flesh[401] is not from the Father, he is not the Son.

So what term is to be used to characterize that flesh? Whatever term they propose for that heavenly flesh that our wordsmith

397. ... τῆς μὲν τοῦ πατρὸς οὐσίας ὁμοίως ἄνθρωπος καὶ ὅλος καὶ τὸ μέρος κεχώρισται ... Like Winling (241), I have not found it necessary to follow J. and assume a lacuna after ὁμοίως.

398. Literally, "by the definition of the essence."

399. Lietzmann links this and similar language in the next paragraph with Gregory's reports of Apolinarius's views about Christ's "celestial and divine" body in J.196–97 above, to constitute fragment 77. But, as Mühlenberg remarks (83), it is doubtful whether this passage can properly qualify as a genuine fragment.

400. Jn 3.6.

401. That is, the "heavenly kind of flesh" allegedly envisaged by Apolinarius.

has dreamed up, we must logically apply to the flesh that Christ took up[402] from the human race; his flesh must be characterized in the same way as ours. [J.201] If what is earthly is not the Son, so neither can that heavenly flesh be the Son. If what is earthly is an adopted son, that heavenly flesh must be an adopted Son too. If there are two sons in one case, there must be two in the other too. If the flesh and the divinity comprise one son in one case, so must they in the other. Since all creation is equally far removed from the divine essence, it must be confessed that both earthly flesh and heavenly flesh are similarly outside the Father's nature.

Gregory now seeks to explain his own view of how Christ becomes one (thus defending himself against the charge of believing in two separate Christs). The humanity of Christ, although earthly in origin, is overwhelmed, dominated, and swallowed up by his divinity. Gregory uses the image of a drop of vinegar being swallowed up in the ocean, which is also found in Theo *and in* contra Eunomium III. *(See note 403.) In the last case (but not in* Theo*), it is made explicit that the swallowing-up of the humanity and the consequent unification of Christ's person take place not in the enfleshment in the womb of Mary, but only after Jesus's death, that is, at his glorification. In the present case, although Gregory does not express himself very clearly, it also seems certain that he has Jesus's glorification in mind: "Everything that then [that is, during his life on earth] appeared as an attribute of that flesh was also changed with it into the divine, immortal nature." Gregory in effect postpones the unification of the person until after Christ's death, thus tacitly conceding a duality of natures (not the same thing as "two Christs," of course) during his earthly life. (For a discussion of the theological implications of this "two-stage" Christology, see "The unity of Christ's person: His glorification," pages 79–81 of the introduction.)*

It remains the case that whatever contributes towards the objective of love for humanity should more properly be attributed to God. No special term can be found to characterize this, but it can be identified with what overwhelms and dominates. It is like what happens with the ocean. When someone throws a drop

---

402. Or "assumed": ἀναλειφθείσῃ.

of vinegar into the sea, the drop becomes [M.1224] sea, transformed into the quality of sea water.[403] The same thing happened when the true, Only-begotten Son, who is inaccessible
light, absolute life, sanctification, wisdom, power, every exalted
name and conception, manifested himself to men through the
flesh. The flesh's own nature was changed into the sea of incorruptibility. As the Apostle says, "What is mortal is swallowed
up by life."[404] Everything that then[405] appeared as an attribute
of that flesh was also changed with it into the divine, immortal
nature. Neither weight, form, color, hardness, softness, quantity, nor anything else that was then visible remains: the mixture
with the divine takes up the lowliness of the fleshly nature into
the divine attributes.

*Because he thinks the "orthodox" believe in two Christs, Apolinarius
accuses them of believing in a "Quaternity"—Father, Spirit, and two
Sons—rather than a Trinity, and thus of setting up a mere man, that
is, the human Jesus, as an object of worship. Gregory's reply is again not
very clearly expressed, but the point he seems to be making is that the divine Son was indeed born of a woman and did indeed become a man—
he had to, in order to save humankind—but he was still the divine Son,
and it is therefore quite proper to pay him divine honors.*

So there is no danger, as Apolinarius claims,[406] of our extend-
ing the concept of the Trinity into that of a Quaternity, nor do

403. Gregory uses the same image, of the drop of vinegar absorbed into
the ocean, in *Theo*, J.126, and also in *contra Eunomium III/3* (*GNO* 2, 132–33,
PG 45:703A–C). For recent discussions, including the background in ancient
philosophy to this example of a particular kind of μίξις, see B. Daley, "Divine
Transcendence," 71–72; Morwenna Ludlow, *Gregory of Nyssa, Ancient and (Post)
modern* (Oxford: Oxford University Press, 2007), 100; and Grelier, 508–24. All
argue that Gregory's interpretation of what happens when a drop of vinegar
(or wine) is mixed with a large quantity of water is closer to the Stoic than
to the Aristotelian, that is, that he did not believe that the *nature* of the vinegar (or Christ's human nature) was itself completely obliterated, although the
properties respectively associated with them are totally transformed.
404. 2 Cor 5.4.
405. During Christ's earthly life.
406. καθὼς ὁ Ἀπολινάριος λέγει. See n. 137. Both Mühlenberg (83–84) and
Grelier (143, n. 679) suggest that this may be a reformulation of Apolinarius's words by Gregory, though Grelier argues that the terms "Trinity" (τριάς,

we make angels serve as the man's slaves, which is what he fanci-
fully asserts of us. [L.82] Those who bow down before the Lord
do not enslave themselves to a man, nor are they ashamed to
worship him who made his home in the world through the flesh.
For it is said, "When he brings the firstborn into the [J.202]
world, he says, 'Let all his angels worship him.'"[407] Only one
entry into this world is possible, human birth; it is not possible
to enter into human life other than by using this way of entry.
This is why Scripture calls his birth in the flesh his entry into the
world.[408] If, when he has come into the world, all the angels worship him, and that entry is effected by birth in the flesh, it is not
we who have made beings that are the master's own possession
into his slaves, but rather that the angels' very nature cannot but
recognize the master's power that transcends it. So let Apolinarius stop arguing in this fatuous way that we are putting what is
inferior above what is superior and making the God-bearing angels[409] subject to a God-bearing man. [L.82]

*In his seventh syllogism, Apolinarius reverts to an argument he has used
before, in his discussion of the heretical notion of the "God-filled man":
"If he who received God were true God, there would be many Gods, for
many people receive God." In an eloquent passage, Gregory responds by*

τριάδος) and "Quaternity" (τετράδα) were actually used by Apolinarius. Grelier points out elsewhere (479, n. 2033) that the charge of believing in a "Quaternity" was often leveled by the Apollinarians against the alleged "divisive"
Christology of their opponents. See, for example, *Quod unus sit Christus* (attributed to a disciple of Apolinarius) §3 (Lietzmann, 296, line 9) and Athanasius, *ad Epictetum* §2, where the accusations of the Apollinarians are summarized (PG 26:1053 A).

407. Heb 1.6.

408. εἴσοδον εἰς τὴν οἰκουμένην. The only NT use of εἴσοδος in reference to
Christ's entry into the world is in fact Acts 13.24, "before his coming (εἰσόδου)"
(NRSV).

409. The only parallel in patristic literature for applying the term
"God-bearing" (θεοφόρος) to angels seems to be in Pseudo-Dionysius, who
uses the term to explain why the celestial order of "thrones" is so called (*de
caelesti hierarchia* 7.1, PG 3:205D; see Lampe, *Lexicon* [2004], *s.v.* θεοφόρος, 3).
If Apolinarius, too, applied the term to angels, or accused the orthodox of
doing so (and Gregory offers no direct evidence for this), presumably he did
so to emphasize their exalted status and the consequent inappropriateness of
suggesting they had been enslaved to a mere man.

showing how Jesus's supernatural conception and birth, the wonders he did, and his saving death, resurrection, and ascension, are qualitatively different from what can be seen in the lives of the prophets and other "God-filled men." It was not a question of the man Jesus receiving God, but of God coming into the world, through the divine enfleshment, in a unique way. Indeed, so anxious is Gregory to show his commitment to Christ's divinity, that he arguably downplays the significance of the humanity when he goes on to suggest that its principal function was an interpretative one, to mediate God's message by enabling it to be understood by human beings.

Next, Apolinarius says, "If he who received God were true God, there would be many Gods, for many people receive God." [L.83] So now, what are we to respond to this? The great Paul is adequate authority for saying, "in Christ, God was reconciling [M.1225] the world to himself."[410] If, since we believe that God was actually born among human beings so that "in Christ, God was reconciling the world to himself," our wordsmith thinks that we are therefore introducing a plurality of Gods through our preaching, we offer the following defense. If there were many virgin mothers and Gabriel's mystic revelation came to many women and to each of them the Holy Spirit came down and the power of the Most High was made present; if the prophets made a proclamation of grace about many people, so as to say, in the plural, "For children have been born for us, sons given to us,"[411]and "virgins will conceive in their wombs, and the names of all those who are born will be Emmanuel";[412] if all of these walked on foot upon the waves and with ineffable power fed so many thousands [J.203] in the desert, multiplying the bread by making it grow in the hands of the disciples until there was enough; if they all raised four-day-old corpses from their funeral mounds; if they were all lambs of God and were sacrificed for us as our Passover and nailed sin to the cross and destroyed the power of death and returned to heaven in the sight of the disciples and sit at the Father's right hand; if they are all to come to judge the world in righteousness; and if it is at the name of

410. 2 Cor 5.19.   411. See Is 9.6.
412. See Is 7.14.

all of them that the tongue of those in heaven and on earth and under the earth confesses:[413] then we would concede that there are many Gods, if there were many who displayed these sorts of characteristics.

But if there is one Lord Jesus, through whom all things are—"from him, through him, and in him are all things"[414]—and if it is to him alone that this enumeration of terms appropriate to God refers, what danger is there of our inventing many Gods when we claim that God was made manifest through ensouled flesh? As to whether what was made manifest was a man: who is so ignorant of Gospel teaching as not to know what the Savior himself said to the Jews, "Now you are trying to kill me, a man who has told you the truth"?[415] Do you see in these words what it is that the text[416] is indicating is to be killed, when it says, "You are trying to kill me"? Not the truth, but the man by whom the truth is uttered. For it was not a man who told the truth; it was clearly God who was speaking, while the man mediated to human beings what had been said, using his own voice. So he is called "mediator between God and humankind,"[417] since human nature cannot have direct intercourse with God and so needed a voice of its own kind and in accordance with its own nature, through which the heavenly power could be properly accommodated to it.

The extent to which the expressions that Gregory next goes on to attribute to Apolinarius actually formed part of a single connected piece of prose (perhaps a sort of pendent to the seventh syllogism) is disputed, but it seems that their general tenor was to return to the point that Apolinarius had made earlier, that it would be wrong to worship Christ unless his flesh was totally and indivisibly united with God: otherwise, it would be a man whom we were worshiping. So in worshiping Christ, we are worshiping his flesh, because it is indistinguishable from God.

413. See Phil 2.10–11. 414. Rom 11.36.
415. Jn 8.40.
416. ὁ λόγος. J.'s emendation of the mss. readings, ὅλος or ὅλως. Winling (246) and Grelier (153) translate it as "le Logos," but this seems to anticipate the conclusion reached in the immediately succeeding passage, that it was God who was speaking. There are similar issues about the translation of ὁ λόγος in J.212 (n. 461) and J.215 (n. 477) below.
417. 1 Tm 2.5.

In response, Gregory follows what is by now a well-beaten track. Whether innocently or maliciously, he again claims to interpret Apolinarius's admittedly rather tortuous phraseology as implying that Christ's flesh is as much part of God's nature (and therefore as worthy of worship) as are such divine attributes as goodness, omnipotence, and so on. (For the theological implications of his rejection of Apolinarius's idea that Christ's flesh is to be worshiped, see "The unity of Christ's person: His virginal conception," pages 75–78 of the introduction.) But he (again) accuses him of inconsistency in (inadvertently?) admitting that Christ's flesh was "taken to" (προσληφθεῖσα, "assumed by") God rather than having been joined to him from all eternity.

But let us leave this matter and turn our attention to what follows. [J.204] "Nothing," he says, [M.1228] "can be united to God in the same way as can the flesh which was taken to him."[418] [L.84][419] Well, there's a thoughtful bit of self-justification! "Nothing can be united to God in the same way as can the flesh" [L.84]—not goodness, not eternity, not incorruptibility, not omnipotence, not any other of the concepts that can fittingly be applied to God; all these come second to the flesh, because of its combination with God and the subsequent union between God and the flesh he has acquired! (Our wordsmith admits that the flesh was subsequently acquired: by saying that it was "taken to him," he shows that it was something that came later.)

We pass over this and say nothing about what follows next, as it contains within itself the proof that it is an inconsistent fable and can do no harm to those who read it. He suggests that none of God's characteristics are united with the Lord to the same extent as the flesh that he "took to himself," and concludes that nothing that is not united with God in that way can be worshiped in that way. Then he adds this as a final flourish: "Nothing can be worshiped in the same way as the flesh of Christ." [L.84] We say nothing about the absurdity and folly of this, which would be obvious even to children. Even children sitting

---

418. προσληφθεῖσα.

419. Lietzmann puts together the three separate quotations in J.204 to form a single fragment (84). Mühlenberg (70) expresses doubt as to whether the three sentences were in fact originally together, but says they probably nevertheless reproduce Apolinarius's words.

and playing in the market place[420] would say that if "nothing can be worshiped in the same way as the flesh," then the flesh of Christ is worthy of more reverence than the very majesty of the Father and his omnipotent authority and his rule over all things and anything else that our human nature is able to predicate of the divine power. We would leave off worshiping the Father, the Son, and the Holy Spirit; we would venerate and worship only that flesh to which our friend here gives the primacy of honor, and would ascribe to it power over all things.

"The flesh of the Lord," Apolinarius goes on in the same vein (but see note 422), "is to be worshiped in that it forms, with him, one single person and one single living being." Gregory reads into this (perhaps rather tendentiously) that Apolinarius conceives the unity between Christ's flesh and the divine Word as analogous to that between the body and the soul in a human being, and indeed that it is to this kind of relationship that the phrase in the title of his work, "according to the likeness of a human being," refers. But, Gregory reasonably enough points out, the fact that soul and body constitute a single human person does not mean that body and soul cannot be thought of as separate. The same, he implies, is true of the divine and human natures in Christ.

His next argument is on the same lines. "The flesh of the Lord," he says, "is to be worshiped in that it forms, with him, one single person[421] and [J.205] one single living being."[422] [L.85] He identifies two elements, the Lord and the Lord's flesh, and makes one living being of the two. Now he clearly reveals what is expressed in his work's title, in which he promises to teach about "the divine enfleshment according to the likeness of a human being." Since the soul is joined to the body, and human life is constituted from the mixture[423] and association of these different elements, and the distinguishing mark of our human constitution is this association of soul and body, our wordsmith fondly imagines that the same can be said about the

420. See Mt 11.16.

421. πρόσωπον.

422. Mühlenberg (70) suggests that Gregory has here adapted Apolinarius's words "into the form of a thesis."

423. μίξεως.

divine nature as well. [M.1229] In the very title of his work he gives advance notice of his teaching that the divine too, when it is enfleshed, presents itself "according to the likeness of a human being." In the part of his work currently under consideration, he maintains also that the Lord and his flesh are "one single person and one single living being." It is as if he were saying that, because of the natural conjunction of the soul and the body, the Paul who appears to the senses is the same as the Paul who lies hidden underneath.[424] What arguments, what kind of refutation can be brought against claims like these? How could we avoid being accused of foolishness if we spent time on such false inventions? So let us consider what comes next.

So the implication of Apolinarius's teaching is that Christ's flesh can be worshiped. This is worse than Eunomius's Arianism, retorts Gregory. Both would have us worship creatures. In Eunomius's case, we are to worship the Only-begotten Son, born of his Father before all the rest of creation; but at least for him that creature is like God to the extent that it is a purely intellectual, non-material being. Apolinarius, on the other hand, would have us worship what not only must have been created but is also purely material, that is, the flesh that in his "single" Christ is organically and inseparably linked with his divinity. By saying that Christ's flesh is to be worshiped above all other creatures, he is giving a higher status to a purely material being than to an incorporeal (and to that extent more God-like) creature such as a human soul, which (and here Gregory clearly demonstrates the Platonic presuppositions of his theological anthropology) is clearly an objectionable idea.

"If," he says, "nothing that has been created is to be worshiped alongside the Lord as his flesh is ..." [L.86] Who will decide first place in the competition in impiety between Apolinarius and Eunomius? Which of them will deserve the prize for his struggles against the truth? Perhaps neither of them wins and we are left with a dead heat; perhaps they are equally matched in their impiety. The latter says that the Only-begotten God is something that has been made, but does not deny that he is an intellectual being and without anything material in his nature. But our friend here has concocted the idea that right from the

424. "Paul" is used as the name of a representative person.

beginning the Only-begotten was welded together from two different elements, flesh and divinity, and describes him as "one single living being," according to the likeness of human nature. [J.206] Both writers allow worship of a creature: Eunomius says that what was created was intellectual and non-corporeal by nature, while Apolinarius goes further and attributes a fleshly nature to the creature,[425] and says that it should be worshiped more than other creatures. This implies that even those other creatures are worthy of worship, which is admitted to be impious even by those who support Eunomius. So let him be awarded the victory over Eunomius, and let him celebrate, adorned by the crowns of impiety.

Within human nature the body is inferior to the soul, so among those who worship created things, the person who prescribes the worship of the flesh is, in the scale of impiety, worse than those who revere the intellectual creation—especially if he says that other created things are to be worshiped, too, and that it is by comparison with these that the flesh comes out highest in terms of worthiness to be worshiped. "No created thing," he says, "can be worshiped in the same way as the flesh of the Lord." [L.86] Now, everything within the created order is equally subordinate to the divine power, whether it has a body or not. But within creation distinctions can be made between what is more or less worthy of honor, and the nature of beings without bodies takes precedence over the sensible and corporeal order.

So to the extent that both Eunomius and Apolinarius attribute worship to a created being, there is a dead heat and they are scored equally on the scale of impiety. He, however, who awards first place to the flesh rather than to the intellectual nature is guilty of a greater impiety. Let the followers of this deceitful doctrine learn who it is that their master is in contention with and what the matters in dispute are.

The next fragment of the Apodeixis *that Gregory quotes, which is the eighth of Apolinarius's supposed syllogisms, is difficult to interpret, but its argument can be tentatively reconstructed on the following lines. All rational creatures (angels and human beings) necessarily have the ca-*

425. Christ's flesh.

pacity of free will, and, in the case of human beings, this originates in their minds, which, to use Apolinarius's earlier terminology, "governs" their flesh. But, in the case of Christ, Apolinarius has previously suggested, the flesh needs, if we are to be saved, to be "governed" by an "immutable" mind, that is, by the divine Word. So joining a complete man to the divine Word would work soteriologically only if his human mind, and therefore his human will, were over-ridden by the divine mind. But that would mean that the man would lose his capacity for free will, and would therefore no longer be perfect. But then God would hardly have joined his divine Son to an imperfect man. Therefore, when the Son was enfleshed, he cannot have been joined to a complete man.

[M.1232] Let us now look at the "gyves"[426] (to use the language of Apolinarius's teacher)[427] that he next presents us with, binding us tightly up in syllogistic cords that cannot be untied. He says,

If people think that a man is united with God more than are all other men and angels ...[428] [L.87][429]

We must examine [J.207] the sense of these words, too. But to look for some trace of meaning in them (and I am not even asking for an acceptable meaning—a meaning to support his impious teachings would do!) would be like looking for a soul in a stone or intelligence in a log of wood. Indeed, looking at the context provides even more evidence of the unintelligibility of what he says:

426. ἀλυκτοπέδην, a poetic word for "bonds," found in Hesiod, *Theogony* 521, referring to the binding of Prometheus: Δῆσε δ' ἀλυκτοπέδῃσι Προμηθέα ποικιλόβουλον (consulted at http://www.sacred-texts.com/cla/hesiod/gtheo .htm).

427. J. (note *ad loc.*) suggests this is a reference to the pagan sophist Epiphanius, under whom Apolinarius studied as a young man, and who was accused of "logic-chopping and excessive precision." Alternatively, it might perhaps be an ironic reference, the details of which are now irrecoverable, to the poems in a classical style, but on Christian themes, that Apolinarius is said to have written during Julian's reign, when Christians were forbidden to teach ancient literature. (See "The life of Apolinarius of Laodicea," pp. 5–7 of the introduction.)

428. παρὰ πάντας ἀνθρώπους καὶ ἀγγέλους: "other" is not in the Greek.

429. The quotation continues six lines below, after some commentary by Gregory.

... then they are implying that angels and men[430] lack free will. (The flesh, by itself, could hardly have free will anyway.) For a living being with free will, to lose it would mean it became imperfect. He who created a particular nature would hardly render it imperfect. So the man is not united with God. [L.87]

Gregory, in his usual vein, criticizes all this as unintelligible logic-chopping, or, alternatively, as being like the obfuscatory utterances of a pagan oracle. He does, however, in the end get round to making a substantive response. First, he argues that it is clear from the Gospel account that Jesus, while united (or "mixed") with the divine nature, also had human free will.

Goodness, what irrefutable logic! How indissoluble are the links that bind these arguments together! Union with the divine takes away the free will of men and angels; depriving it of its free will renders a living being with free will imperfect; and, on those assumptions, it is proved that a man cannot be united with God. Are the vatic utterances produced by those who prophesy by ventriloquism or by shouting out from beneath the earth, by those trained in delivering oracles from the inner recesses of their hearts, anything like this? If, it is claimed, humanity is united to God, then men and angels lack free will. Was it not a man who said, "Now you are trying to kill me, a man who has told you the truth"?[431] Was he who demonstrated all the divine power in himself by achieving whatever he wished by an act of free will not mixed with the divine nature? If mutual relationship of the human and the divine in Christ was not of this kind, Apolinarius might as well disregard the evidence of the Gospels.[432] Paul himself will be convicted of lying, as will

430. The best interpretation of this passage seems to be that suggested by Grelier (465), that Apolinarius is here referring to the eventual salvation of all men and angels (cf. *de unione* § 11, Lietzmann, 190, 3–5). So the argument would be that if the man Jesus lost his free will by being united with God, so would all other rational beings who are saved in Christ.

431. Jn 8.40. Gregory has already used this text, in J.203 above, to demonstrate that Christ was truly human. It is difficult to see that it also shows that he had free will.

432. Literally, "If the latter was not in the former [and the former in the latter], let him disregard the evidence of the Gospels." (The words in square brackets are a marginal reading, rejected by PG but incorporated in the text by J.)

the prophets and all who foretold the wonderful deeds of the Lord and those who later described what actually came to pass. But if all this really did happen, and God became manifest in the flesh, and the flesh that was mixed with the divine nature became one with it, then, according to Apolinarius's poetical fable, the free will in human nature was destroyed, and the angels were reduced [J.208] to slavery. As a result, they both forfeited the grace of free will. How absurd this innovative kind of language is!

Then he advances two further arguments, which might be taken as repaying his adversary in his own coin, in that they both rely on sophistical verbal reasoning of a not very convincing kind.

The first of these arguments challenges Apolinarius's notion that having no free will is inconsistent with being a rational living being; that would mean that slaves or those subject to any sort of political authority could not be regarded as rational beings. (That argument depends of course on tacitly conflating two separate, although admittedly overlapping, ideas: the freedom of moral agency and political or economic freedom.) The second makes use of the ambiguity of the word "soul": depending on what anthropological theory is adopted, it can mean "rational mind" or (as in animals) "principle of life" or (as in human beings) a combination of the two. Gregory accuses Apolinarius (without, it appears, any specific evidence) of implying that because Christ's flesh is "mindless" it must also be "soulless." But that must mean, he suggests, that his adversary considers that flesh to be either lifeless (because it lacks the animal principle of life) or bestial (because it lacks a rational mind).

And how about his argument when he says, "For a living being with free will, to lose it would mean it became imperfect"? [L.87] [M.1233] So is a slave not to be counted among living beings, because he is controlled throughout his life without any exercise of his own free will, in thrall to the power of his master? For our wordsmith defines a living being in terms of its having free will; he decrees that anyone without an independent faculty of volition should not be thought of as a living being. So Canaan was dead when he became a slave to his brothers as a result of his irregular behavior;[433] the slave of Abraham was

433. Gn 8.25.

dead;[434] Elisha's servant Gehazi was dead;[435] and in later times
Onesimus was dead;[436] all the centurions under their superiors'
authority[437] were dead. Why do I say this? Because presumably
all those who are subject to the rule of those who have power
over them are dead, because the power of free choice is made
ineffective in them. Even those whom Paul orders to be "subject
to the governing authorities" are dead, even though they are
"souls";[438] they perish because they have no free will and can no
longer be living creatures!

That is the implication of Apolinarius's fable that what is
joined to the God who rules over all things is this "soulless" flesh
that he posits. (It could be "soulless" or "mindless"; his account
would apply equally to either.) But what is "soulless" is dead; and
what is "ensouled" but has no reason is a beast. When our friend
removes free will from this flesh that he posits, he does not recognize the ridiculous implication of his argument and retreat from
it. For what is characteristic of irrational beasts is that they do not
act of their own accord but are subjected to human control.

25. More on Apolinarius's trichotomous anthropology and the implication for Christology

*It appears that the next section of Apolinarius's work[439] was also struc-
tured round a series of syllogisms (or, at any rate, tightly argued logical
arguments)[440] but that he also used scriptural references rather more extensively than in the immediately preceding sections. His aim remains
to defend a Christology based on his tripartite anthropology, with the*

434. Gn 24.   435. E.g., 2 Kgs 4.25.
436. Phlm 10.

437. Literally, "all the enslaved centurions"; perhaps Gregory is thinking
of Mt 8.9 (Lk 7.8).

438. Rom 13.1: "Let every person [NRSV; literally, "every soul"] be subject
to the governing authorities." The argument here and in the next paragraph
depends on the fact that ψυχή ("soul") can mean, among other things, "living
person" and "the principle of life."

439. The fifth in the structure suggested in the appendix to this volume.

440. Grelier (107) brigades the arguments in J.201–17 under the heading
of a "ninth syllogism," but, as will be seen, it appears that in this section Apolinarius in fact produced a number of separate arguments, which may or may
not have been formal syllogisms.

divine Word taking the place of the uppermost of the three parts. Gregory
seeks to show that this does not work; Christ must be a complete man as
well as being God.

The scriptural texts that Apolinarius cites in defense of his tripartite
anthropology are 1 Thessalonians 5.23 ("May your spirit and soul and
body be kept sound and blameless . . ."); Daniel 3.86 ("Bless the Lord,
spirits and souls of the righteous"); Romans 1.9 ("God, whom I serve
with my spirit . . ."); and John 4.23 (worship "in spirit and truth").
He also says that the flesh is at war with the spirit (probably another
reference to Romans 7.23) but that the flesh is not "soulless." (Presum-
ably his argument was that flesh, taken merely as inanimate material-
ity, could not be "at war" with anything, so it must have an animal
soul that is distinct from the spirit.) So human beings comprise three
elements, and "if the Lord is a human being, then the Lord, too, must
comprise these three elements: spirit, soul, and body."

But let us put this on one side and move on to the next part of
the argument; I shall express my adversary's thoughts in my own
[J.209] words, for the sake of brevity. "A human being consists of
three elements," he says: "spirit, soul, and body." This is on the
basis of what the Apostle Paul lays down in his letter to the Thessalonians;[441] he also refers to part of the Song of the Three Holy
Children, "Bless the Lord, spirits and souls of the righteous";[442]
then to Paul serving God "with my spirit";[443] then he adds the
words of the Gospel through which we are taught that those who
worship God should worship him "in spirit."[444] When he has gone
through all this, he adds a further point, that the flesh is at war
with the spirit.[445] He says that the flesh is not "soulless," in order
to show that the spirit is a third entity, in addition to soul and
body. [L.88] "If a human being consists of these three elements,
and the Lord is a human being, then the Lord, too, must comprise these three elements: spirit, soul, and body."[446] [L.89]

441. 1 Thes 5.23.   442. Dn 3.86.
443. Rom 1.9.   444. Jn 4.23.
445. Apolinarius may have referred here to Romans 7.23: "I see in my
members another law at war with the law of my mind, making me captive to
the law of sin that dwells in my members" (NRSV), as in a similar discussion
earlier on (L.22, J.140, above).
446. For the rest of L.89, see J.213 below and n. 466.

Gregory first discusses the passage from 1 Thessalonians. He argues that when Paul distinguishes "soul" and "spirit," he is not drawing anthropological distinctions, but rather referring to different kinds of moral character and moral choices. He supports this view by reference to 1 Corinthians, where Paul distinguishes "persons of spirit," "persons of flesh" (3.1), and "persons of soul" (15.44: ψυχικόν, which NRSV translates as "physical" and is actually applied to the body rather than to a person.) These terms respectively refer, he suggests, to people who "keep their thoughts fixed on divine matters," to those who are "full of passion and concerned with material things," and to those who are in a middle position. They do not, as Apolinarius would have it, imply that the respective natures of the persons concerned are differently constituted.

In order to make clear his errors regarding the interpretation of the divine Scriptures, we will now briefly treat each of these three points. First, let us investigate what the Apostle Paul says. When he [M.1236] writes to the Thessalonians, praying to the Lord that they be entirely sanctified, in body and soul and spirit,[447] he is not, we would maintain, dividing a human being into three sections. [L.88] His argument concerns rather a much loftier philosophical question, about the choices we make during our lives here. This is the case not only in this passage, but also in his letter to the Corinthians. There he recognizes a "person of flesh" and, again, a "person of spirit,"[448] and, halfway between these two, the "person of soul."[449] He calls the person who is full of passion and concerned with material things "of flesh"; he applies the term "of spirit" to those who are not weighed down by the burdensome appendage of the body but who rather keep their thought fixed upon sublime matters; he defines as "of soul" [J.210] anyone who does not fit fully into either category, but has some features of both.

In speaking in this way, he is not saying that the "person of flesh" is deprived of the faculty of mind or of soul, nor does he show that the "person of spirit" is free from involvement

447. 1 Thes 5.23.

448. 1 Cor 2.15, 3.1.

449. τὸν ψυχικόν, which the NRSV translates as "physical" at 1 Cor 15.44 (applied to the body, σῶμα) and as "natural" in the margin at 1 Cor 2.14 ("unspiritual" in the main text).

with the body or the soul, nor does he maintain that the "person of soul" is either mindless or fleshless; rather, he applies the name according to which tendency predominates in a person's moral choices. Those who "discern all things and ... are themselves subject to no one else's scrutiny" are both enfleshed and ensouled but are still called "persons of spirit."[450] A man who, maddened by the passion of the flesh, violates his father's bed[451] is neither "soulless" nor deprived of reason. On the same basis, a person who stands halfway between commendable and despicable behavior partakes of both; he possesses mind, but he is also clothed in a fleshly nature. But, as has been pointed out, Paul's terminology is precisely adapted to the visible indications of a person's life; those who are devoted to enjoyment and love pleasure, those who indulge themselves eagerly in captious strife, are called "persons of flesh"; those who "discern all things" but provide no opportunity to those who wish to "scrutinize" them[452] are given the name "persons of spirit" because their mode of life tends towards the things above; he uses the expression "persons of soul" for those situated between these extremes, as far below the one as they are above the other. He wants the person who is perfect in virtue not only to provide evidence of this in the highest part of his life but also to look towards God when he performs some bodily function and not to abandon God when he does something of an intermediate nature.[453] For, he says, "whether you eat or drink, or whatever you do, do everything for the glory of God";[454] that is, do not let your gaze slip away from the glory of God even when you are performing bodily functions.

So what Paul is praying for in this passage is not three different components of the people concerned, but rather their whole way of living (ἐπιτήδευμα), whether it be carnal, "psychic," or spiritual. On Apolinarius's interpretation of the passage, the prayer that they should be "sanctified entirely" (1 Thessalonians 5.23) included their bodies; but how

450. 1 Cor 2.15.	451. See 1 Cor 5.1.
452. "Discern" and "scrutinize" both translate ἀνακρίνω/ἀνάκρισις, following NRSV in 1 Cor 2.15.
453. I.e., something ψυχικόν, characteristic of the "person of soul."
454. 1 Cor 10.31.

could that have been achieved, given the corruptible nature of the body?
Gregory concedes, however, that the body of "the poor man Lazarus" (see
note 456) was saved "in its entirety," because his "spiritual" way of life
meant that "his reason was not disturbed by the passions of the body."

So, through his blessing, he graciously confers a full sanctification on the Thessalonians, who were universally held to be
already striving towards the good, when he says: "May God sanc-
tify you wholly, and may your entire body and soul and spirit,"
[J.211] that is, your whole way of living, whether this is the life of
body, soul, or spirit, "look exclusively in the direction of sanctification."[455] That is our interpretation. If Apolinarius says [M.1237]
that in these words the mind is being blessed on its own, and that
the power of the blessing falls separately upon the body and the
soul, how can the body, all of which is crumbling completely away
by virtue of the power of death, be kept "entire"? [L.88] How can
what is mortified by abstinence, shriveled up, weakened by harsh
servitude, be "entire"? How could anyone maintain that the poor
man Lazarus, covered with sores and worn out by purulent dis-
charges,[456] did not fail to obtain a blessing?

But, paradoxically, the blessing that Paul speaks of was indeed fulfilled in that body wasted in sores. For, along with his
soul, Lazarus's body was saved in its "entirety" through his "spiritual" way of life, since it was not dragged down by the necessities of the flesh, away from lofty hope to unbecoming thought.
His flesh did not provide distraction to his soul, and his reason
was not disturbed by the passions of the body.

Gregory now turns to a verse of the Song of the Three Holy Children in
Daniel 3.86. He seems to concede Apolinarius's argument to the extent
that he accepts that "souls" could not perform a rational action such as
blessing God unless they had a rational part, a mind or "spirit." But he

455. Based on 1 Thes 5.23.
456. Lk 16.20. It seems that Gregory may be conflating the Lazarus of the
parable with the Lazarus whom Jesus raised from the dead in John 11. Luke 16
does not suggest that in the parable Lazarus's body was in fact "saved" from its
bodily affliction, and indeed in *de anima et resurrectione*, PG 46:68B–69B, Gregory says clearly that it was Lazarus's soul, not his body, that was carried away to
Abraham's bosom when he died.

seems perversely unwilling to concede that this in any way supports Apo-
linarius's anthropological model. Instead he makes the observation—
not really relevant to the point at issue—that angels are pure "spirits"
and that our own "spirits" are entitled to equal honor with them; so the
point of this passage, he suggests, is nothing anthropological but merely
that the souls of the righteous are to join with the angels in blessing God.

When the Song of the Three Holy Children links the "spirits and souls of the righteous" together in its hymn of glory, it
is not first bidding the spirits to praise by themselves and then,
separately, the souls, as Apolinarius states. [L.88] For how could
the soul praise on its own, if the praise is not filled with mind?
For, as I have already often said,[457] the soul separated from the
spirit is animal, and has no faculty of reason or mental activity.
So what separates, as he suggests, our mind from our soul? Let
us agree that praise can be offered to God by spirits, on the basis
of his statement that spirits are mind. If he thinks that spirit is
something other than mind, how could a mindless being praise
God? Why should God be pleased with a hymn offered out of
mindlessness? And what need would the soul have of the mind
[J.212] if it were capable by itself of singing a hymn in praise of
God, and required no cooperation from the mind? But we have
learned nothing of that kind from those who have instructed us.
Souls freed from the chains of the body are like angels, as the
Lord says,[458] so the text of the Song shows, by linking souls and
spirits together, that the former are worthy of the same honor as
angels. Angels are spirits, as the prophet says: he "makes his angels spirits."[459] The Three Holy Children consider that the "souls
of the righteous" are to join with those angels in their hymn.

Gregory next deals with John 4.23. He makes the perfectly reasonable
point that this must be read in its context, which is that of Christ's en-
counter with the Samaritan woman at the well, and that when Christ
says that God is to be worshiped "in spirit and in truth," the point he is
making is not an anthropological one but rather that God is to be wor-
shiped "neither in a particular place nor in a bodily way." Romans 1.9,
he suggests, should be interpreted similarly.

---

457. E.g., in J.140–41 above.   458. Lk 20.36.
459. Ps 103 (104).4 (LXX).

But when the Savior says that we must worship God "in spirit," he is not using the term "spirit" to mean mind; [L.88] rather, he is saying that we should not entertain bodily [M.1240] ideas about God. The Samaritan woman said to the Lord that God should be worshiped on the mountain,[460] in a defined location. That is based upon a bodily notion. The woman has departed from the truth, so in response the text[461] goes on to say that "God is spirit," that is, without a body, and that those who worship him cannot approach the incorporeal in a corporeal way but should perform their worship "in spirit and in truth."[462] The text here offers corrections to two cases of ignorance. First, it contrasts true worship with worship in a particular place; secondly, it separates the concept of spirit from bodily presuppositions. It is on these grounds that Paul says that he worships the Lord neither in a particular place nor in bodily way, but, as the truth requires, in spirit.[463] [L.88]

As a final argument from Scripture, Gregory turns to Romans 8.7, where Paul says that the flesh "does not submit to God's law." Activities such as "submitting," he points out, imply free choice and therefore a rational mind. Apolinarius admits (see above) that the flesh here is not "soulless," but he is wrong to say that the "soul" in question is purely animal; it must have a rational part as well, in order to decide "not to submit." "Flesh," Gregory argues, must be interpreted here as everything that goes to make up a human being.

The statement that the flesh "does not submit to God's law"[464] directly proves the error of these people's doctrine, [L.88] for things like fighting against and taking captive and not submitting are all activities of free choice. [J.213] If there is no mind, there can be no free choice. So when Apolinarius says that the

---

460. Jn 4.20.

461. ὁ λόγος. Winling (257) and Grelier (392) translate it as "le Logos"; Zacagnius (1239A), as "Christus." But this seems unlikely, particularly as all agree that ὁ λόγος eleven lines earlier (J.212, 7) should be translated as "l'Écriture" (Winling, 257), "le discours" (Grelier, 385), or "sermo" (Zacagnius, 1238D). (I render it there as "the text of the Song.") See also n. 416 on J.203 above and n. 477 on J.215 below.

462. Jn 4.24.   463. Rom 1.9.
464. Rom 8.7.

flesh is endowed with soul[465] and with free choice, he is denying that it is devoid of mind. [L.88] Even if one speaks of flesh on its own, it contains the complete specification of humanity within itself; if any one of the elements that make up human nature is taken away, what remains cannot be described as a human being.

In moving on to Apolinarius's next logical argument, Gregory now adopts another tactic. Let us accept, he says, the former's threefold anthropology and his view that Christ, too, was composed of spirit, soul, and body. He also claims, says Gregory, that Christ is "a heavenly man and also a life-giving spirit." These expressions, too, are unexceptionable in themselves. Christ is indeed a "heavenly man" to the extent that his humanity is "mixed with what is heavenly"; and "he who energizes us with his vivifying spirit is indeed a 'life-giving Spirit.'"

"But," he says, "a human being comprises three elements." [L.89] Let that be granted, even though reason does not necessarily compel us to assent to it. "But the Lord himself," he says, "as a man, should also be said to comprise three elements: spirit, soul, and body." [L.89] For the moment we shall not challenge this either; it is quite correct to ascribe to that man all the elements which go to make up our nature. "But he is a heavenly man" (here he is speaking of the Lord) "and also a life-giving spirit." [L.89][466] We accept this, too; it is our view, if its meaning is understood in the right way. For he who is mixed with what is heavenly, and who through that admixture[467] with the better transforms his terrestrial element, would be described as no longer earthly but heavenly. Similarly he who energizes us with his vivifying spirit is indeed a "life-giving Spirit."

But, Gregory suggests, Apolinarius shows his misunderstanding of the true sense of these expressions when he goes on to his next logical step (perhaps the conclusion of a syllogism of which the previous fragment formed the first part), which is to argue that if all three of Christ's constituent elements were like ours, he could not truly be a "heavenly man,"

465. See J.209 above.
466. For the earlier part of L.89, see J.209 above. Mühlenberg (70) suggests, however, that this sentence cannot follow on directly from the first and there must have been some connecting material.
467. ἐπιμίξιας.

but merely an ordinary earthly man who constituted a "receptacle" for
the divine. (Apolinarius no doubt continues to see the specter of the
"God-filled man" lurking behind the "orthodox" formulation.)

Against this, Gregory first repeats an objection he has made before, that
it is offensive to believe that God could join himself only to an incomplete
man, comprising just flesh and animal soul. Then he notes that Apoli-
narius goes on to say: "If the man is a receptacle of the heavenly God, and
God is in heaven above, as Ecclesiastes states …" The point Apolinar-
ius is making here is not clear (particularly as Gregory has omitted the
conclusion of this part of the argument): perhaps that on the "God-filled
man" model, there is no true enfleshment, God and man remain separate,
and God does not "come down from heaven." At any rate, Gregory seems,
understandably enough, to interpret his words in the crude sense that God
cannot be on earth at the same time as he is in heaven, which he considers
a highly questionable notion. But he does not pursue that any further,
and concludes this part of his arguments by repeating the point that it is
quite acceptable from the orthodox perspective to call Christ a "heavenly"
rather than an "earthly man," because he "receives God into himself." (No
doubt Apolinarius would have seized on that particular, on the face of it
ill-chosen, form of words as proving his point that the "orthodox" doctrine
is really that of the "God-filled man": see "The unity of Christ's person:
His virginal conception," pages 75–78 of the introduction.)

But let us see the use to which our wordsmith puts these concepts. "If," he says, "the heavenly man is constituted of all the
same elements as we earthly people, to the extent that his spirit,
too, is like ours, he is not heavenly but a receptacle for the heavenly God." [L.90] [M.1241] There is much that is unclear and
difficult to understand in these words, a result of the weakness
of his powers of interpretation; but it is easy to discover what
he wants to say. For he is claiming that if that man were defi-
cient [J.214] as regards mind, he would be heavenly, but that if
he were a complete man, he would no longer be heavenly, but
would be "a receptacle for the heavenly God"![468]

---

468. I follow Lietzmann (L.90, 227–28) and Grelier (131–33) in assuming
that this sentence is not a new direct quotation from Apolinarius (as J. seems
to suggest); it must rather be a satirical interpretation of the earlier quotation,
demonstrating its absurd implications. (Grelier points out that the word used
here for "complete" is ἄρτιος, rather than Apolinarius's usual τέλειος.)

Which of these two arguments can be more offensive than the other? That completeness should be reckoned an impediment to the divine, with the flesh being more suitable than the mind for union with the Godhead? Or that we should believe that while God is heavenly, he who received the heavenly God into himself is not there where we believe God to be, but in some other place than the heavenly being and that he should be called by some other name?[469] "If," says Apolinarius, "the man is a receptacle of the heavenly God, and God is in heaven above, as Ecclesiastes states ..."[470] [L.90A] But he who receives God into himself is rightly called "heavenly" rather than "earthly," after the one whom he receives. So even if our wordsmith has failed to understand the logic of his own arguments, he clearly maintains the doctrine of truth, and it is confirmed by the wisdom of its adversaries![471]

The next step in Apolinarius's argument is again to make the point that the "orthodox" model of a complete (tripartite) man joined to God

469. That is, some other name than "heavenly."

470. Eccl 5.2. Lietzmann (228) makes this part of fragment 90; following some mss., he inserts "as" (καθὼς) before "Apolinarius says," thus attributing "as Ecclesiastes states" to Gregory. I follow PG and J., who omit "as," and show by their punctuation that they attribute the phrase to Apolinarius, as do Mühlenberg (70) and Winling (259). On this interpretation, the fragment is part of a new logical (perhaps syllogistic) argument (Gregory omits the conclusion), and I have therefore labeled it 90A.

471. The argument in this paragraph is far from transparent. The substance of Apolinarius's point (although rather a lame one) seems to be that if God is "in heaven" (as per Ecclesiastes), the man Jesus cannot have been a "receptacle" for him unless God were in two places at once! Gregory's response seems to be based on the idea that Apolinarius is applying metaphors of space and position in too literal a way. Apolinarius's preferred term of "heavenly man" would be open to precisely the same objection: if Christ is "heavenly," how can he at the same time be on earth?

Grelier (263) understands the sentence beginning "Or that we should believe ..." as the second limb of "une aporie ... , une argumentation par dilemme" (262), the previous sentence being the first limb. She interprets (263) the clause "there where God is believed to be" as "the human part in which the divinity comes to dwell (the intellect)." She summarizes Gregory's argument as being that if there were nothing of humanity in Christ's mind, then the formula "man from heaven" could not be justified, because then there would be no "man" in which the divinity could come to dwell. The whole con-

*produces, instead of a single "man from heaven," a sort of hybrid being.
"If," he says, "we consist of three parts, but he consists of four, he is not
a man but a man-God (ἀνθρωπόθεος)." Gregory represents this as seeking
to turn Christ into a sort of Minotaur-like monster, in an attempt to
get a cheap laugh from scoffers. He argues that what distinguishes the
union of man and God in Christ from such mythological fantasies is the
fact that its whole point and effect is to transform the human element
in the union. He repeats yet again his basic objection to Apolinarius's
model, that it is quite unscriptural to suggest that in Christ God joined
himself to half or two-thirds of a man rather than to a whole one.*

But let us examine the passage that now follows. "If," he says,
"we consist of three parts, but he consists of four, he is not a
man but a man-God."[472] [L.91] Let the reader not deride the
manifest foolishness and stupidity of these words; let him rather
grieve for the deliberate blindness of those who are enslaved
by such irrationality. If the whole of human nature were left
unchanged[473] by the indwelling of the divine power, then God
the Word would be called a man-God. Myths tell of monstrous
animals produced by linking different natures together, and invent shapes and names for them: horse-deer, goat-deer, and so
on; our modern myth-maker, following the lead of those who
have taught him this sort of fiction, scoffs at the divine [J.215]
mystery.[474] The Apostle explicitly cries out that "the resurrection
of the dead has ... come through a human being,"[475] not half
a human being, nor a bit more than a half: his use of the term

---

cept of God "made man" and indeed of a "man from heaven" would need to
be rejected if the "man" were not a complete man. But if that is what Gregory
is saying, he is expressing himself incredibly maladroitly. The interpretation
suggested in the first paragraph of this note seems preferable.

472. ἀνθρωπόθεος, to be distinguished from θεός ἄνθρωπος, "God-man,"
which Apolinarius himself is happy to use; see L.32, J.147, above, and n. 121.

473. σώζηται: Winling (260) and Grelier (525) translate this as "est sauvée," "is saved." This is the more obvious translation, but makes no sense in
this context. I follow Zacagnius (col. 1242C), who has "integra permanserit."
See also *Theo*, J.125, and the note thereon, where a similar issue arises.

474. Perhaps, as Winling (260, n. 283) suggests, Gregory relishes the opportunity to turn back onto Apolinarius's own head his reproach that the "orthodox" have been led astray by pagan Greek ideas.

475. 1 Cor 15.21.

without qualification means that the nature that the word connotes is not a diminished one.

In any case, the divine nature and the human nature are completely different; it is ludicrous to think of them as constituting a "combination" (σύνθεσις, συνάφεια) as if they were ontically equivalent to each other, like a man and a bull in the case of the Minotaur. (Gregory is arguably, however, being inconsistent in criticizing this concept, which seems similar to that of "mixture" between the divine and the human which he himself defends in J.144, J.161, and J.217.)

But by his shameful new coinage this fellow turns the mystery into a monstrous tale of the Minotaur and through his words provides those who are hostile to the faith with many opportunities for scoffing at its teachings. Anyone who wants to make fun of doctrine in order to raise a laugh could hardly fail to notice this absurd combining[476] of words, [M.1244] whether they think our wordsmith's doctrines or our own are more persuasive; for when you talk about both things in this way, you cannot take away the implication that the two natures form a combination.[477]

He who says that the flesh comes down from heaven does not claim that it is not really flesh; and the flesh that is governed by something that has an ensouled nature and contains within itself a vivifying power, as even Apolinarius claims, is properly given the name "human being." But he who took that flesh to himself[478] and manifested himself through it has quite another nature than it. The expression "taking to itself" itself indicates the difference in nature between what takes and what is taken.

Gregory now seems to imply that if anyone is inviting a comparison between Christ and a compound mythological creature, it is Apolinarius himself. Admittedly, such creatures (his chosen example is a "goat-deer")

476. συνθέσεως.

477. τὴν ἐκ τῶν δύο φύσεων σύνθεσιν οὐκ ἀφαιρήσεις τοῦ λόγου. Again the issue arises whether or not ὁ λόγος refers to the divine Word; see J.203 (n. 416) and J.212 (n. 461) above. My translation here follows Zacagnius (col. 1243A) and Winling (261) in assuming that it does not. Grelier's "tu ne pourras exclure du Logos la composition de deux natures" (525) seems to me unlikely.

478. Or "assumed" it: προσλαβόμενος αὐτήν.

do not, like Apolinarius's Christ, comprise the whole of one animal and
half of another; "rather," he claims (although one wonders on precise-
ly what authority), "the combining (σύνθεσις) of the words means that
each in some way participates in the nature of the other." But, even so,
they constitute a new kind of creature with a single nature drawing on
the characteristics of both its constituents—just like Apolinarius's "one-
nature" Christ.

Even so, how could one avoid the insult to the God who was
manifest in the flesh that is implied by this absurd new coinage "man-God," the word that Apolinarius rashly applies to the
God who manifests himself in this way? When the myth uses the
word "goat-deer," it does not mean that half a goat is joined to
a deer, or, if the mixture[479] of animals is the other way round,
that half a deer is joined to a whole goat; rather, the combining[480] of the words means that it in some way participates in the
nature [J.216] of each. So if, in our wordsmith's opinion, God
and the man are one and the same, uniting together in some
way, whether the whole nature enters into the combination[481]
or something less than the whole, he cannot avoid the absurdity of this compound name.[482] If the Greeks learn such teachings from him and then lampoon this mystery of ours, he who
provides the opportunity for such blasphemy will assuredly be
subject to the prophetic curse that says, "Woe to those through
whom 'my name is blasphemed among the Gentiles'!"[483]

Finally in this section,[484] Gregory deals with another bit of deductive
argument by Apolinarius, which takes up an earlier theme, that two
perfect (that is, complete) beings cannot be put together to form a unity.
"If," he says, "[Christ] is constituted of two perfect things, insofar as he
is God he cannot be man, and insofar as he is man he cannot be God."

479. μίξιν.
480. σύνθεσις.
481. συνάφειαν.
482. τοῦ ὀνόματος συνθήκην.
483. Is 52.5.

484. Despite the change in focus (from the application of a trichotomous
anthropology to Christology to the "two perfect beings" issue), I follow Grelier
(107) in linking L.92, and Gregory's critique of it, with what goes before it, that
is, Apolinarius's series of logical arguments in defense of his Christological
model. Mühlenberg (89), however, suggests that it marks the beginning of the
final section of the *Apodeixis*, which he labels, "The divinity of the man Jesus."

In other words, such a combination could not produce a single integrated being, but only the sort of chimera discussed in the previous section, neither man nor God. But, Gregory responds, assuming that the man in such a combination is incomplete rather than complete does not meet that difficulty. He denies, however, that there is in fact a difficulty: there is no problem in describing Christ as both God and perfect man; the two natures should be considered quite separately. (But by arguing thus he is of course failing to meet Apolinarius's contention that the "orthodox" position necessarily implies two Christs.) Then he repeats yet again his attack on the general unseemliness of Apolinarius's notion of God being joined to an "imperfect" (that is, "incomplete") man.

Let us now consider what comes after this passage. "If he is constituted of two complete things," says Apolinarius, "insofar as he is God he cannot be man, and insofar as he is man he cannot be God." [L.92] If on his argument the combination is said to be between one thing that is defective and one thing that is complete, will not those people[485] who are bold enough to share that view equally say that in that he is God he is not man and in that he is man he is not God? The essential principle of humanity is different in every way from that of divinity, and no one would ever suppose that the diminishment of what it is to be human constitutes the definition of the divine nature. That definition is not expressed in terms of whether the human nature is present or present in a less than complete form; each thing has to be conceptualized in its own terms and under its own individual name. When we read "God," we are given by means of this name everything that it is appropriate for us to understand about God; similarly, when we are given the name "human being," the whole of [M.1245] human nature is represented through this word; our understanding experiences no confusion[486] between these expressions, no suggestion that one name should be understood in terms of the other. The former is not signified by the latter, nor the latter by the former; each name carries a fixed meaning that is attached to the respective

485. That is, "even those people."
486. Reading σύγχυσιν with PG, as does Winling, (262, n. 286). J. (first word in line 25) reads ὀνόμασιν, without explanation—a slip (repeat of the first word in line 21)?

nature, and there is no way in which the signification of one can be transferred to the other.

And the terms "imperfect" and "perfect" can each convey different concepts to the reader. What we mean here by "perfect" [J.217] is when the essential principle of something's nature has been fully realized; by "imperfect" we mean the opposite. Neither term on its own can connote either man or God; rather, it suggests that we should think of whatever thing or word the term is applied to as being either complete or incomplete. So, if the man were imperfect, how can Apolinarius imagine that that imperfect entity is divine, on the basis that a man mutilated as regards his nature would be linked more fittingly with the essential principle of divinity?

26. Christ's death and resurrection

In the next section,[487] *Apolinarius seems to have moved to a discussion of the implications for his Christology of Christ's Passion and Resurrection.*

First, he discussed Christ's death. Even though, he says, in order to save us Christ had to be more than just a human being like us—that is, he had to be God—he nevertheless had to become flesh, that is, to be "mixed with us." In order to overcome our sin, he had to become a human being without sin. In order to "do away with the sovereignty of death over all human beings," he had to "die and rise again as a human being."

Gregory responds by agreeing with Apolinarius in saying that the world cannot be saved unless God unites himself with humanity by becoming flesh, and that this union with flesh can properly be called "mixing," even though he wrongly claims—and here Gregory reverts yet again to an earlier theme—that the union took place before all ages, rather than in the womb of Mary. He also accepts what Apolinarius says about Christ dying and rising again as a human being.

He moves on to his next point and says, "The man cannot save the world while he remains a man and is subject to the corruption that is common to human beings." [L.93][488] I agree;

487. The sixth, according to the structure suggested in the appendix to this volume.

488. Lietzmann combines this with the other three quotations in J.217–18 to form a single fragment (93).

for if human nature were sufficient by itself to bring about its own good, the mystery[489] would be superfluous. But since there is no way of passing beyond death unless God provides salvation, the light shines in the darkness through the flesh for the purpose of banishing from the flesh the destruction that arises from that darkness. "But," he says, "we cannot be saved even by God unless he is mixed[490] with us." [L.93] In these words our wordsmith seems sensible, and to be directing his mind towards intelligent thoughts. When he says "mix," he means uniting things of disparate natures. "He is mixed upon becoming flesh, that is, man," he says; "as the Gospel says, when he became flesh he came to dwell among us." [L.93] Nor does this wander away from a sound argument, were it not that he scatters weed seeds in it[491] immediately afterwards. For this is our argument—indeed, it is the argument of truth—that when he became flesh he came to dwell among us and, conversely, when he came to dwell among us he became flesh. So if the flesh dates from the time he came to dwell among us, before the announcement of the good news to the Virgin by [J.218] Gabriel, the Word was not yet flesh. And Apolinarius is lying when he says that the humanity descended to us from above, and that the Word existed as man before the creation of human nature, and that it is through that man that the divine was mixed with humanity.

"But" he says,

no one can abolish the sin of human beings unless he becomes a human being without sin, nor [M.1248] can he do away with the sovereignty of death over all human beings unless he dies and rises again as a human being. [L.93]

Would that he continued to the end in these correct opinions and spoke what the Church professes!

It is difficult to establish precisely what Apolinarius argued next. He seems at any rate to have said that "the death of a man does not do away with death, nor can one who has not died rise again." The first

489. Of the divine enfleshment.
490. ἐπιμιχθέντος. In this section, "mix" translates μίγνυμι or one of its compounds or derivatives.
491. See Mt 13.25.

clause is clearly meant to show how the Christ who died must, in order to save us, also have been divine; the second may be to show that his death must have been a real one. It is possible that Apolinarius went on, as Gregory claims, to draw the explicit conclusion "that God himself died" (see note 493).

At any rate, that is how Gregory, understandably enough, understands the thrust of his argument. He again attacks the absurdity and impiety of any notion that God died. And it is not open to Apolinarius to say it was only the Second Person of the Trinity that died; as an opponent of Arius, he cannot believe that there is more than one divine being, so the implication of his view must be that while Christ was in the tomb there was no God. He adds a further argument based on the analogy (which he attributes to Apolinarius in J.205 above) between the relationship between the divine and the human in Christ and that between the soul and the body in human beings generally. God could not die when Christ died, he argues, any more than our immortal soul dies when it is separated from our body.

But he returns to his own ways and criticizes the teaching of the Church, namely, that, in our view of the matter, it was the man who suffered death. He produces his own argument in refutation of what we assume, as follows: "The death of a man does not do away with death." [L.94] What is he trying to establish in saying this? That it was the Only-begotten One's very divinity, his very power, his very truth, his very life, that were done to death by his suffering on the cross, so that, during that period of time that lasted three days, there existed neither life, nor power, nor justice, nor light, nor truth, nor divinity itself. For he cannot be saying that one divinity died and another was left in existence, as he can often be seen contending with Arius on this point, positing one divinity in Trinity; so if one divinity died, as he is assuming in his argument, there could be no way in which another one could still exist. [L.94]

I cannot understand how anyone could suppose that he does not believe that the divinity is mortal. For[492] human death is no more or less than the dissolution of what is compound. When

---

492. "For" (γὰρ) does not seem logical here. Perhaps some such words as "But his view must be wrong" should be understood before this sentence.

our body has been broken up into the elements of which it is composed, the soul does not perish at the same time as the body is dissolved; rather, that which is composite is dissolved, while that which is incomposite remains undissolved. If death does not affect the soul, only those who do not know what they are talking about can say that the divinity is subject to death.

I shall pass over what follows directly on from this and argues in the same way. For in the next passage he argues that [J.219] the very divinity of the Only-begotten dies. [L.94]. He says:

The death of a man does not do away with death, nor can one who has not died rise again. From all this it is clear

(he says)

that God himself died: this is shown by the fact that it was not possible for Christ to be overcome by death.[493] [L.95]

The absurdity of this is so clear that I think we should leave it aside without examination, since any reasonable person can see by himself the impiety and absurdity of what is explicitly stated here, that God himself died, that in his own nature he succumbed to death.

---

493. It is difficult to be sure that Apolinarius did not make the startling claim that the union between Christ's divinity and his humanity was so complete that God himself can be said to have died. Mühlenberg (70) argues that because Gregory inserts "he says" twice, there must be doubt whether the second sentence of this fragment is reported verbatim. Grelier (558) points out that the logic of "this is shown by the fact that" (καθὸ) is far from clear—why should Apolinarius have felt obliged to distinguish God and Christ here?—and suggests that Gregory may be combining two fragments drawn from different contexts. But neither of these arguments would rule out the possibility of both sentences substantially representing what Apolinarius actually wrote.

It should be noted furthermore that both Gregory Nazianzen (ep. 102, §§ 15–16) and the pseudo-Athanasian contra Apollinarium I (11, PG 26:1112B–1113A; the reference in Grelier, 557, n. 2379, is wrong) accuse Apolinarius of believing that God died on the cross. Grelier (553–75) discusses the issue at length, and concludes that Apolinarius's critics may nevertheless have been attacking not what he actually taught but what they took to be its logical consequence; if the divine Logos constituted the "hegemonic principle," the rational soul, of the God-Man, it must, on the principle of sympatheia between soul and body, have suffered (and died) with Christ's material body.

27. The eternal Christ

The next passage that Gregory discusses seems to attribute to Apolinarius the false charge against the "orthodox" that they "claim that Christ did not exist from the beginning, as God the Word." This may mark the beginning of a new section of the Apodeixis[494] *discussing the different ways in which Christ's nature and status are to be regarded before, during, and after his earthly career.*

If Apolinarius really did say anything on these lines, his point was presumably that the "orthodox," by separating Christ's divinity and his humanity in such a crude way, deny in effect that the Christ who lived and died on earth can be actually identified, in the strict sense that soteriological considerations require, with the Word who existed from before all ages. At any rate, this accusation prompts in Gregory a long section where he moves away from criticizing Apolinarius's text in detail and again develops an account of his own of how Christ's eternal existence as the Second Person of the Trinity can be reconciled with his full humanity.

But perhaps there is one thing worth noting in passing, that he does not exempt from his mendacity the views he attributes to us, but reflects them in the false accusation that he fabricates in order to defame us. He says that we claim that Christ did not exist from the beginning, and that we therefore deny that he was God the Word.[495] [L.96]

---

494. The seventh and last substantive section, according to the structure suggested in the appendix to this volume.

495. μὴ ἐξ ἀρχῆς εἶναι τὸν Χριστὸν παρ' ἡμῶν λέγεσθαι, ὥστε τὸν λόγον εἶναι θεόν. It is not at first sight clear (1) whether ὥστε is governed by (the first) εἶναι or by μὴ ... εἶναι, or (2) what the subject of the second εἶναι is. On (1), Zacagnius (1247D) seems to assume that ὥστε is governed by μὴ εἶναι: "nos dicere Christum ab initio non fuisse, ita ut solummodo Verbum sit Deus," "We claim that Christ did not exist from the beginning, so that it is only the Word that [in our view] is God." Winling (266), on the other hand, seems, more plausibly, to assume that ὥστε is governed by εἶναι: "nous affirmons que le Christ n'a pas été depuis le commencement, de façon à ce que le Logos soit Dieu." Grelier reproduces Winling's translation in her discussion of this fragment on p. 560, but on p. 138 she has "Nous prétendons ... que le Christ n'est pas depuis le commencement de façon à ce qu'il soit le Dieu Logos"—that is, unlike Zacagnius and Winling, she there assumes that, on (2), τὸν Χριστὸν is the subject of

28. Fourth excursus: Gregory defends
his Christology

Gregory first responds to the charge that he does not accept that Christ can properly be called divine by seeking to show that the view attributed to him is untenable. In the enfleshed Christ, God's power, wisdom, light, and life were made manifest. This, he maintains, is equivalent to saying that he can be identified with those divine properties and therefore with God. As these divine properties existed from all eternity, so too must Christ have done. "The Only-begotten God is always God; he does not become God through participation, nor does he come to join the Godhead through a progression from a more humble condition."

But we do not deny that in these last days the power of God, and his wisdom, his light, and his life—and all these things are Christ—became manifest through the flesh. To claim that he who is [M.1249] manifested through these things and on their account is named Lord and Christ was once not identical with them is, in our judgment, just as intolerably impious as denying that name altogether. Anyone who said that Christ did not exist from the beginning—Christ, who is "the power of God and the wisdom of God"[496] and whose name is supremely exalted and totally appropriate to God—would be denying that any of these other things that we know through this great name existed from the beginning. When the term "man" is used, the power of reason and the capacity to understand and all other defining characteristics of human nature are signified at the same time; so that if one said that Christ the man did not exist, the negation of the term "man" would mean that all the other characteristics of human nature were also absolutely denied. In the same way, if Christ is the power, the wisdom, the imprint, and the radiance,[497] [J.220]

τὸν λόγον εἶναι θεόν. That seems to me to make the best sense in the context, and my translation makes the same assumption.

I follow PG and Lietzmann (L.96, p. 229), *contra* J., in not treating this as a verbatim quotation from Apolinarius; Grelier (139) says the question must remain open, but suggests Gregory's report is probably quite close to Apolinarius's text, as it is coherent with the latter's overall doctrine.

496. 1 Cor 1.24.

497. χαρακτήρ, τὸ ἀπαύγασμα. See Heb 1.3.

anyone who denies that he existed from the beginning will also wholly reject all the concepts that are associated with his title.

So, with the divine Scriptures as our guide, we say that Christ always existed, and must be regarded as co-eternal with the Father. The Only-begotten God is always God; he does not become God through participation, nor does he come to join the Godhead through a progression from a more humble condition. Thus the power and the wisdom and every name that is appropriate to God are co-eternal with the Godhead; nothing that was not there from the beginning can be joined by way of addition to the glory of the divine nature.

Gregory next argues that the very title of Christ, the anointed one, proves that he is God from all eternity. He bases this on Psalm 44 (45).6–7, whose divine addressee (that is, the Son of God) is said to have been "anointed with the oil of gladness"— that is, with the power of the Holy Spirit—"beyond his companions" because he "loved justice and hated wickedness." Gregory asserts, with doubtful logic, that if there had ever been a time when the Son had not loved justice and hated wickedness, he could never be said to have been anointed. He adds the further argument that Christ must always have loved justice because, as God, he was justice. (But that is of course begging the question.)

But we say that the name of Christ expresses, from all eternity, the concept of the Only-begotten in a special way; we have been led to this conclusion by the very meaning of the word.[498] Confession of this name implies the Church's teaching on the Holy Trinity, as each of the Persons in whom we believe is, in the way that is appropriate to it, indicated by this title.

So that we do not appear to be speaking solely on the basis of our own opinions, we shall cite the words of prophecy:

> Your throne, O God, is forever and ever;
> the scepter of your kingdom is a scepter of righteousness.
> You have loved justice and hated wickedness;
> therefore God, your God, has anointed you with the oil of
> gladness beyond your companions.[499]

498. Χριστός, Christ, the anointed one.
499. Ps 44 (45).6–7.

The term "throne" means rule over all things. The "scepter of righteousness" means incorruptibility of judgment. The "oil of gladness" represents the power of the Holy Spirit, by whom God is anointed by God, that is, the Only-begotten by the Father, because he "loved justice and hated" injustice. If there had ever been a time when he was not a friend of justice or an enemy of injustice, it would follow that he who is said to have been anointed because he loved justice and hated injustice could be said at one time not to have been anointed. If he was always a friend of justice—as he himself was justice, he can hardly have hated himself—he must always be considered as having been anointed. As [J.221] he who is just cannot be unjust, so the Christ[500] could never be unanointed, and he who had never been unanointed must necessarily always be the Christ. Everyone [M.1252] must believe (or, at any rate, everyone whose heart has not been covered with the veil of the Jews) that it is the Father who anoints and the Holy Spirit who is the anointing.[501]

What Gregory does not believe in is the view he attributes to Apolinarius, that Christ had flesh from all eternity. But he does believe that Jesus remained Lord and Christ after his Passion and glorification.

How can Apolinarius claim that we say that Christ did not exist from the beginning? But it is true that the fact that we confess that Christ is eternal does not mean that we believe that he always had the flesh that Apolinarius has invented. On the other hand, we know that he existed as Lord before all ages, and we confess the same Christ after his Passion; as Peter says to the Jews, "God has made him Lord and Christ, this Jesus whom you crucified."[502]

Gregory next defends himself against the charge of believing in two Christs, by trying to explain the sense in which he understands the enfleshed Christ to be in ontic continuity with the eternal Christ. The eternal Christ became "mixed with the lowliness of our nature," he says; "he took the man into himself and became himself within the man ... he

500. The anointed one.
501. As Winling (268, n. 298) suggests, this casts an interesting light on Gregory's view of the role of the Spirit in the immanent (ontological) Trinity.
502. Acts 2.36.

made him with whom he was combined what he was himself." But Greg-
ory again makes it clear that the completion of this process of absorption
of the humanity by the divinity occurred only when Christ was risen and
glorified. "After the Passion he makes the man whom he has united with
him into Christ." And, interestingly, the glory into which the humanity
is absorbed (Gregory cites John 17.5, "the glory that I had in your pres-
ence before the world existed") is identified with the Holy Spirit.

We say this not because we are claiming that there are two
Christs or two Lords in the one Jesus, but because the Only-
begotten God, who is God by nature, the Lord of all, the King
of creation, the Maker of all who exists, and he who sets aright
those who have fallen—because he, I say, in his great forbear-
ance has undertaken not to deny fellowship with him even to
our nature, fallen as it is through sin, and to restore it to life.
He himself is life itself. When human existence was coming to
an end and the evil in us had reached its peak,[503] in order that
nothing of our wickedness should be left unhealed, he accepted being mixed[504] with the lowliness of our nature; he took the
man into himself[505] and became himself within the man, as he
says to his disciples, "I am in you, and you in me";[506] that is, he
made him with whom he was mixed[507] what he was himself.

He himself was highly exalted in eternity, and in this way
he exalted highly that which was lowly; for he who was exalted
above all things had no need of [J.222] exaltation himself. The
Word was both Christ and Lord, and that is what he who was
combined with him and taken up[508] into the divinity became.
The Word is Lord already; he is not re-ordained into lordship,
but rather the form of the slave[509] becomes the Lord. So the text
"one Lord, Jesus Christ, through whom are all things"[510] applies
similarly to him who before all ages was clothed with the glory
of the Spirit (for that is what his anointing symbolically means).

After the Passion he makes the man whom he has united with him into Christ, making him beautiful with the same

---

503. For this idea, see n. 252 on J.171 above.

504. ἐπιμιξίαν.   505. ἐν ἑαυτῷ λαβών.

506. See Jn 14.20.   507. τὸν ἀνακραθέντα.

508. Or "assumed": ἀναληφθείς.   509. Cf. Phil 2.7.

510. 1 Cor 8.6.

chrism. "Glorify me," he says (it is as if he said "anoint me"), "with the glory that I had in your presence before the world existed."[511] But that glory that is posited here, existing before the world, before all creation, before all the ages, that glory in which the Only-begotten God is glorified, is, in our opinion, no other than the glory of the Spirit. For orthodox doctrine teaches [M.1253] that the Holy Trinity alone exists before the ages. "He who existed before the ages"[512] is what prophecy says of the Father. Of the Only-begotten, the Apostle says, "through him the ages came into being."[513] And the glory attributable to the Only-begotten God, which is posited to exist before all the ages, is the Holy Spirit. Therefore, what belongs to Christ, who was with the Father before the world came into being, also belongs, at the end of the ages, to him who is united to Christ. Scripture speaks of "Jesus of Nazareth," whom "God ... anointed with the Holy Spirit."[514] So let Apolinarius not maliciously misrepresent our views by claiming that we say that the Only-begotten God was not always Christ. [L.96]

This absorption of the humanity by the divinity at Christ's glorification is, again, virtually a total one (as in the earlier image of the drop of vinegar absorbed in the ocean). "For there was no man before the birth from the Virgin, nor after his return to heaven did the flesh retain its own characteristics." The humanity acquires the characteristics of the divinity; it becomes incorruptible, immortal, eternal, and immaterial.

We say that he was always Christ, both before and after God's providential dispensation for humankind.[515] As man he existed neither beforehand nor afterwards, but only at the time of the dispensation. For there was no man before the birth from the Virgin, nor after his return to heaven did the flesh retain its own characteristics. Scripture says, "Even though we once knew Christ according to the flesh, we know him no longer [J.223] in that way."[516] The flesh does not remain, just because God appeared in the flesh; rather, since what is human is mutable, and

---

511. Jn 17.5.   512. Ps 54 (55).19 (LXX).
513. See Heb 1.2.   514. Acts 10.38.
515. Literally, "both before and after the economy" (τῆς οἰκονομίας).
516. 2 Cor 5.16.

what is divine is immutable, the divinity is not susceptible to any change, nor can it be changed into something worse or something better (for it will not admit of what is worse, but, on the other hand, it has nothing better than it); but Christ's human nature experiences a change for the better, that is, from corruption to incorruptibility, from mortality to immortality, from temporal to eternal existence, and from bodily appearance to an incorporeal existence that cannot be manifested in any form.

Gregory next deals with the charge that his account of the Passion—that it is only the man who suffered—proves that he believes in "two Christs." His response is that although it was indeed the man who suffered (clearly the divinity in Christ could not do so), "the divinity is present in him who suffers."

They claim that we say that it is the man who suffers, not the God; let them now hear our response. We confess the divinity to be present in him who suffers, but not that the impassible nature is subject to passion.

He seeks to cast further light on this model of the relationship between God and the man Jesus by giving a careful[517] account of Christ's conception in the womb of Mary. He compares this to the way in which God initially created human beings (which comprised souls as well as bodies) from matter. In a similar way, the divine power acted to create the enfleshed Christ within Mary's womb, using her flesh as its material basis. The New Man thus created was, as in the case of the first creation, an organic unity of soul and body. But he differed from the original creation in that, because of the unique way in which he came into being, the divine power "pervaded" (διηκούσης) his whole nature, body and soul.

To clarify what has just been said, this is [M.1256] the opinion we hold. Human nature, we maintain, has its individual existence[518] by virtue of an intellectual soul being combined with[519] a body. This combination is derived from a certain material

517. Cf. Winling, 271, n. 303: "Ce paragraphe est construit de façon plus soigneuse que d'autres, et sert à exposer une thèse fondamentale, au gré de Grégoire." I have identified some of the key Greek terms, many including the prefix συν-, "with," in the footnotes.

518. "Individual existence" translates ὑπόστασις.

519. συνδραμούσης.

originating principle for its constitution,[520] which has been laid down in advance. That material, made alive by the divine power, becomes a human being. If anyone were to suppose by way of hypothesis that the creative power of God was not involved in[521] the constitution of the human being who was formed, the implication would be that the material element remained inert and immobile, not having been brought to life through this productive activity.

In our own case we perceive this life-giving power acting on the material element, from which a human being, constituted[522] from soul and body, is fashioned. The power of the Most High exercises itself in the same way in respect of the Virgin. It implants itself immaterially, through the life-giving Spirit, into the undefiled body and makes the material of the flesh from the purity[523] of the Virgin, taking up from the Virgin's body a contribution towards the human being who is being formed. And so is created the truly New Man, who first and alone received his individual existence [J.224] in this fashion. He was created in a divine rather than a human way, as the divine power pervaded the whole of his compound nature[524] to the same degree. Neither part of him was without a share of his divinity; it was present in both, that is, soul and body, in a way suitable and appropriate to each.

So the eternal Son "became manifest" in Christ's human form. He was joined in a perfect union with Christ's humanity, both his body and his soul. It was not the divinity that suffered on the cross, but the divinity "appropriated" the Passion to itself. As Gregory has explained earlier,[525]

520. σύστασις. 521. μὴ συμπαρεῖναι.
522. συνεστώς.

523. ἀφθορίαν. For the translation of this word and of ἀμιάντῳ (as "undefiled") in the previous line, see G. Lampe, *Lexicon* (2004) *s.vv.* This passage should not be interpreted as meaning that Christ inherited the (actual) sinlessness of his human nature from that of the Virgin, which would be quite inconsistent with Gregory's view that it was sinful human nature which Christ assumed and which he purified by virtue of that assumption (see introduction, n. 407). "The purity of the Virgin" here is presumably a periphrasis for "the pure Virgin."

524. διὰ πάσης τῆς τοῦ συγκρίματος φύσεως διηκούσης.
525. See J.153 and pp. 82–85 of the introduction.

when Christ died, his body and soul were separated, but the divinity
remained joined both to his body (which remained uncorrupted for three
days in the tomb) and to his rational soul (which accompanied that of
the good thief into paradise). If the distinction between the divinity and
the humanity is modeled in this way, Gregory argues, Christ can be said
both eternally to be Christ and Lord, by virtue of "the kingdom that he
had before all ages," and to have become Christ and Lord, at the time of
his conception and nativity.

When the man Jesus was born, the divinity did not need to
be born, since it had existed before all ages and lasts forever;
but, once it had entered into him, it became manifest with him
in his constitution as a man and in his nativity. In the same way,
the divinity, which lives forever, has no need of rising again,
but it rose in him who was brought back to life through the divine power; the divinity itself was not raised up (for it had not
fallen), but in itself it raised him who had fallen. If the divinity
needs neither birth nor resurrection, it is clear that Christ's Passion is fulfilled not by the divinity suffering, but by the divinity
being in him who suffered, and through the union of the divinity with the sufferer, which thereby appropriated his Passion
to itself. As has been already stated, the divine nature came to
dwell in an appropriate way in the soul and the body, and was
made one with both through the union; because, as Scripture
says, "the gifts of God are irrevocable,"[526] it does not leave either
of them but remains with them permanently. Nothing but sin
can dissolve anyone's bond with God; if anyone's life is without
sin, his union with God is completely indissoluble.

Since the absence of sin extended to both elements, that is, to
the soul and the body, the divine nature was present [M.1257]
to both of them in its own way. But when death brought about
the separation of the soul from the body, what was composite
[J.225] was split up while what was incomposite remained, un-
severed, in both. A sure sign of God's presence in the body is
for the flesh to be kept uncorrupted after death, for God and
incorruptibility are the same thing. That the divinity did not
leave Christ's soul is demonstrated by the fact that it was through

526. Rom 11.29.

that soul that the entry to paradise was opened up to the thief.[527]
The mystery of the divine power is fulfilled by its entering into
both elements of Christ's human nature and through each introducing its life-giving activity into the related part.[528] This is
the flesh in the case of the body, and the soul in the case of the
soul; I mean the intellectual soul, not the irrational soul, for the
non-intellectual element is animal rather than human. Thus the
divinity, which right from the beginning was mixed in with both
body and soul and remains with it forever, is raised up in the resurrection of him who died.

Thus it is Christ who is said to have been "raised from the
dead,"[529] he who both is Christ and becomes Christ. He is Christ
by virtue of the kingdom that he had before all ages; he becomes Christ when the angels brought to the shepherds "good
news of great joy that will be to all the people" at the time of
the nativity of the Savior, who, Scripture says, is "the Christ, the
Lord."[530] He is properly so called on the basis of the words of
Gabriel, that "the Holy Spirit will come upon" the Virgin and
that "the power of the Most High will overshadow" her.[531] So he
who is born is properly called Christ and Lord: Lord, through
the power of the Most High, and Christ, through the Spirit who
anointed him. It was not he who is eternal who was anointed at
that time, but the one of whom Scripture says, "You are my son;
today I have begotten you."[532] The word "today" signifies the
mid-point between the two divisions of time, past and future.

*Gregory goes on to explore further the implications of his Christological
model for Christ's death and resurrection and for soteriology. Although
the divinity did not of course die, it can properly be said to have risen
with the body, in that it was its healing power, which was able to reverse
the natural process of death and to bring together Christ's body and soul
in the Resurrection. Gregory proceeds, as earlier, to draw a soteriological
conclusion from this. Because of Christ's solidarity with human nature*

527. See Lk 23.43: "Today you will be with me in Paradise."
528. I.e., of human nature as a whole, which is sanctified and transformed
through Christ's participation in that nature. Gregory will shortly (J.226) explain this further.
529. Rom 6.4.   530. Lk 2.10–11.
531. Lk 1.35.   532. Ps 2.7.

as a whole, the benefits of this reunion of his body and his soul in his
resurrection are transmitted to all humanity. But in order to appropriate
those benefits, we need first to share in his death, not through our own
natural death but through our mystical death in baptism.

How can he who made all ages be born and anointed in some
moment of time? The implication is that the divinity is raised
up, even though it did not die. It did not die because what is
not formed by composition cannot be dissolved; it was raised because it was present [J.226] in what was dissolved, in him who
had fallen in accordance with the law of human nature. So it is
present to each part, and each part displays its proper characteristics; the divinity heals the nature of the body through the body,
and the nature of the soul through the soul; it restores to unity
what has been separated and rises itself in what is raised up.

It is like (for there is no reason not to use a material metaphor to explain the mystery of the providential dispensation of
the Resurrection) when a reed is divided into two and someone
brings back together into one the ends of each section.[533] If the
ends are fitted together by being joined in a tight ligature,[534]
the whole of each part necessarily fits back together again to
form the whole reed. In a similar way, because of the continuity
of human nature [M.1260], the union in Christ of the body and
the soul, effected through the Resurrection, brings together by
the hope of the resurrection the whole of human nature, divided as it is by death into body and soul, and fits together into
one what had been separate. This is what Paul says: "Christ has
been raised from the dead, the first fruits of those who have
fallen asleep,"[535] and "as we all die in Adam, so we all will be
made alive in Christ."[536] Using the model of the reed, through
that "end" that was constituted by Adam, our nature was split
apart by sin, the soul having been separated from the body by

533. This (rather puzzling) metaphor seems to be original to Gregory: see
Grelier, 605.

534. διὰ τῆς ἐν τῷ ἑνὶ πέρατι συμβολῆς τε καὶ σφίγξεως. Grelier (522) points
out the medical connotations of the rare word σφίγξις, appropriate to this soteriological context: compare the reference to the "healing" (ἐξιάσαιτο) of the
nature of the body a few lines earlier.

535. 1 Cor 15.20.   536. 1 Cor 15.22.

death; but through that "part" that is constituted by Christ, that human nature is restored, the separation having been wholly repaired in the resurrection of Christ's humanity.[537]

So we share the death of him who died for us. I do not mean the death that is necessary and general to our nature. That will happen, whether we want it or not. Rather, because we ought to die willingly with him who died voluntarily, we should have in mind the death that is a consequence of personal choice. An involuntary death [J.227] cannot be an imitation of a voluntary one. The death that is consequent to our nature happens universally to all people, whether they want it or not, and nobody would say that what happened to everyone can be voluntary. So there is another way in which we share the death of him who died voluntarily: by being buried in the mystic water through baptism. Scripture says, "Therefore we have been buried with him by baptism into death,"[538] so that by imitating his death we may also imitate his resurrection.

29. The eternal Christ (continued)

Gregory now returns to the text of the Apodeixis, *and the discussion of the different ways in which Christ's nature and status are to be regarded before, during, and after his earthly career.*

Apolinarius seems next to have posed again the basic conundrum with which he has been wrestling, that is, how, while remaining God, God can "become" man (as opposed to "filling" or "taking over" a man who otherwise remains unchanged as regards his essential nature), and, in the form of a rhetorical question, to have restated his solution: "How can God become man without ceasing to be God unless he is in the man in the place of his mind?"

Gregory responds by agreeing that God cannot "become" man in the sense that God cannot change. His solution is, however, that God comes

---

537. This is obscure. In his earlier use of this metaphor, the two "parts" of the reed seem to represent the body and the soul, split apart in death. Here, however, one "part" seems to be fallen humanity (with Adam as its "end"), and the other "part" is Christ, to whom, presumably, humankind is joined and thereby saved and restored.

538. Rom 6.4, to which Gregory alluded in similar terms in J.177–78 above.

to "be in" man, without changing his own nature in any way; the di-
vine "can be in something else without becoming that something else."

But let us now move on to his next point. "How," he says,
"can God become man without ceasing to be God unless he is
in the man in the place of his mind?" [L.97] But does he understand what he had said? He says that what is divine does not
change, which is right; for what is always the same cannot, by
dint of its nature, become something other than it is. But it can
be in something else without becoming that something else.

He goes on to raise some new objections to Apolinarius's theory. To suggest
that God can become the mind of a man implies either that the human
mind, as a creature, is already equal to God or that God can change, in
order to accommodate himself to the natural limitations of such a mind.
In fact, God and the human mind are such different entities that to sug-
gest that they are in any sense mutually interchangeable is absurd.

So what is that mind that Apolinarius says[539] is "in the man"?
Does it remain in the majesty of its unchangeable nature, or
does it change to a lowly state by circumscribing itself within the
limitations of the man's mind and becoming the same size as it?
The human [M.1261] mind is equivalent to the Godhead if, as
Apolinarius says, the divine nature became a human mind. For
if human nature is equally capable of receiving into itself either
our mind or, instead of that mind, God—that is, if the Godhead
could be enclosed in the same space as is needed to contain the
mind—they are of equal size and weight. It is like when one mea-
sures out grain and then some other kind of seed into an empty
vessel; if they are measured out equally, nobody could deny that
they were the same in quantity. The standard wheat is equal in
quantity to the einkorn wheat[540] when the grains of the former
are emptied out of the corn-measure and it is refilled by the latter. So if [J.228] the divinity takes the place of the mind, it could
not be said that the Godhead was superior to the mind, if the
former as well as the latter can be contained by human nature.

539. καθὼς ὁ Ἀπολινάριος λέγει. See n. 137 (J.150–51).
540. ταῖς ὀλύραις, *triticum monococcum,* an inferior kind of wheat used for
feeding horses.

So either the mind is equal to the Godhead, as Apolinarius believes, and when it is replaced by the divine,[541] it does not change; or, if the mind is inferior to the Godhead, when the divinity becomes mind, it changes[542] into something less significant. But, as everybody knows, everything that can be reckoned as a part of creation is inferior to the unapproachable and inaccessible nature of God. It would amount to the same thing to say that God was changed into mind as to say that he was changed into a creature.

The final part of this argument is difficult to follow, which has led editors to assume that the manuscript text is corrupt (see note 543). The general sense seems to be that Apolinarius cannot argue that when "the Word became flesh" it retained its divine immutability while at the same time maintaining that it adjusted itself to the limitations inherent in constituting the enfleshed Christ's rational mind.

So if Apolinarius thinks that there is a change when the divinity takes the place of mind, he cannot also claim that, if it is mixed with a man who is without a mental faculty, what is blended-in remains unchanged.[543] But if it does not change when it becomes flesh, much more does it remain in its immutable state when it comes to mix itself[544] with mind. If, on the other hand, his contention is that there is a change when it becomes mind,

541. Literally, "[the mind] having changed (μεταστὰς) from this (τούτου) to that (ἐκεῖνο)."

542. Literally, "that which became this (τοῦτο) from that (ἐκείνου) changes …" This sentence is very obscure, but the sense seems to require the assumption that "this" refers to the human mind and "that" to the divinity.

543. Another very obscure sentence. J. reads: ὥστε εἰ τὸ ἐν νῷ γενέσθαι τροπὴν ὁ Ἀπολινάριος <οὐκ> οἴεται, οὐδὲ τὸ δίχα διανοίας καταμιχθῆναι τῷ ἀνθρώπῳ προσμαρτυρεῖ τῷ ἀνακράθεντι τὸ ἀναλλοίωτον. <οὐκ> is a conjecture by Zacagnius (PG 45:1261B), subsequently adopted, without further comment, by J. Zacagnius (n. 64, *ad loc.*) says that the need to "replace" the negative particle here is indicated "not only by the immediately following negation but also by the whole of Nyssen's argument, particularly the last part." This, however, seems to overlook the fact that the "subsequent negation" is in fact a double negative (οὐδὲ … ἀναλλοίωτον). In my view Gregory's argument is less unclear without the insertion of οὐκ, and I have accordingly translated it on that basis.

544. πρὸς τὸν νοῦν ποιησάμενος τὴν ἀνάκρασιν. It is difficult to guess precisely what Gregory meant by this odd expression.

he can hardly avoid admitting that its being accommodated to the flesh[545] also entails change.

30. Christ's ascension and glorification

The argument in the Apodeixis *that Gregory chooses to discuss next concerns Christ's status after his ascension and glorification. He must, Apolinarius argues, have been just as much man then as he was before, as is demonstrated by the scriptural texts about the second coming of the Son of Man. Nor can he have become totally one with God only after his glorification (as Gregory holds); it was during his earthly career that he said, "I and the Father are one," which implies he was totally one with him then.*

He also says (I omit some intervening material),

If he existed as God after the Resurrection and is no longer man, how can the Son of Man send his angels? And how can we see the Son of Man coming on the clouds?[546] How can he have said, before he was united with God and deified, "I and the Father are one"?[547] [L.98]

Gregory responds that to envisage that after Christ's glorification his physical, flesh-and-blood body continued to exist, in all its gross materiality, in heaven is absurd. It is true that Scripture says that, having ascended, the "Son of Man" will send his angels at the end of time. But the "Son of Man" here can be understood figuratively, as when God the Father is represented as a man in Christ's parables. And the reference to the Son of Man sending his angels may in any case not be intended to be taken literally: it may be designed merely to impress those who would not otherwise accept Christ's divinity. In any event, Scripture also says that Christ will appear "in the glory of his Father"; that is hardly consonant with his retaining any human characteristics, as the Father's glory can have nothing human about it.

What he is claiming in these words is that the nature of the human body cannot be changed into what is more divine, that Christ's hair, nails, form, shape, bulk, and [M.1264] other nat-

545. ἡ πρὸς τὴν σάρκα οἰκείωσις.
546. Mt 24.30.
547. Jn 10.30.

ural characteristics remain, whether these are on the surface or hidden inside the body.[548] I think it would be [J.229] superfluous to explain how inappropriate it is to think of these earthly and despised things as attributes of God, seeing that our adversaries' words themselves show the absurdity of this idea. Lest Apolinarius think he can claim the support of Scripture for his fictions, I shall run briefly through each of the things he has said.

Since, he says, he who sends his angels at the consummation of all things is called the Son of Man, he thinks it necessary to believe that Christ has human characteristics until the end of time. He does not remember what is said in the Gospel, where the Lord in his own words refers to the "God over all"[549] as a man. The landlord who leased his vineyard to tenants was a man: the one who, after his servants had been put to death, sent his only-begotten son, whom the tenants threw out of the vineyard and killed.[550] Who is that man who sent his only-begotten son? Who was that son killed outside the vineyard? And is not he who arranged a wedding banquet for his son presented in the text in human terms?[551] Perhaps we ought to go on to say that Christ wanted to give some help to those who in their weakness despised the nature that was like their own and could not therefore believe in his divinity, and so he minimized the effect of the feebleness of their understanding and stiffened it for faith by means of fear; so he says that angels will be sent by the Son of Man at the time of judgment,[552] in order that the expectation of terrible things will correct their failure to believe what they see before their eyes. He also says, "You will see the Son of Man coming on the clouds of heaven with glory and much power."[553] This is consonant with what we have explained above, about the man who planted a vineyard and the man who arranged a wedding banquet for his son, and with the meaning we have given to those passages.

548. Gregory is, on the face of it, over-interpreting what Apolinarius has actually said. Winling (278, n. 318) suggests that he is in fact representing the views of one of Apolinarius's disciples about the nature of Christ's glorified body rather than those of Apolinarius himself.

549. Rom 9.5.
550. Mt 21.33–40.
551. Mt 22.2.
552. See Mt 16.27, 24.31.
553. Mt 24.30.

The meaning of this text [J.230] is far removed from the base opinion of Apolinarius and does not demonstrate that we should assume that the Son of Man referred to has corporeal characteristics, as is clearly proved by the fact that the text is adjacent to one that indicates his appearance at the end of the ages, stating that the Lord will be seen by creation "in the glory of his Father."[554] From these words one of two things must follow: either the Father is to be thought of as having human characteristics, so that the Son may appear in the glory of the Father by appearing in human form; or the magnificence of the Father's glory is untainted by any form that can be envisaged as a visible shape, so that he who, Scripture proclaims, will be seen "in the glory of the Father" cannot be configured in a human way. For the glory of a human being is one thing; the glory of "God over all" is another.

So far as Christ's saying that "I and the Father are one" is concerned, this says nothing about the nature of Christ's humanity during his earthly career, let alone after his glorification. It means merely that the divine Son shares the divine nature and power. (Gregory misunderstands Apolinarius's argument, perhaps deliberately. The latter is using John 10.30 not to prove anything about Christ's earthly career but to rebut any notion of a "two-stage Christology," with Christ becoming fully God only after his glorification.)

But, says Apolinarius, Christ stated, [M.1265] while speaking in the flesh to human beings, that "I and the Father are one."[555] What a foolish idea—to think that if the Lord, speaking in the flesh, said, "I and the Father are one," this proves that in the age to come he will be manifested in human form! So on this basis is he really trying to mount an argument that the Father, too, actually lives in a fleshly form? For if he who said that he was one with the Father was envisaging the unity in a human

554. Mt 16.27.
555. Lietzmann (230) makes this a reference back to L.98 (J.228). Grelier's suggestion (235) that, because the way Gregory introduces it is slightly different and rather more explicit, he may here be citing a separate passage of the *Apodeixis,* which made a more detailed analysis of Jn 10.30, is perhaps introducing an unnecessary complication.

rather than a spiritual way, as Apolinarius maintains, then the Father himself is the same thing as what the Son was seen as being when he was man. But the concept of divinity is far removed from any notion of corporeality. So the unity of the Father with the Son was a matter not of human form, but of their sharing the divine nature and the divine power. That this is the case is abundantly clear from the words he spoke to Philip, "Whoever has seen me has seen the Father."[556] Perfect perception of the majesty of the Son, as it were of an image, produces a vision of the archetype.

31. Final arguments

Gregory now gives the impression that his polemical energy is beginning to flag and that he wants to wrap things up as soon as possible. In consequence, it is even more difficult than usual to identify a common theme in the final passages of the Apodeixis *that Gregory chooses to quote.*

At any rate, he dismisses Apolinarius's next arguments as incoherent, unintelligible, and pointless. It appears from the fragments that Gregory can bring himself to report that they were seeking to develop further the concept of the unity between the Father and the Son during Christ's earthly career, with reference in particular to John 10.25 and following, the passage leading up to Christ's assertion that he and his Father are one ("The works that I do in my Father's name testify to me.... My sheep hear my voice.... No one will snatch them out of my hand.... What my Father has given me is greater than all else, and no one can snatch it out of the Father's hand"). "If," Apolinarius goes on, "Christ is united to the Father before the Resurrection, how can he not be united to the God within him?" (that is, with the divine Word, which constitutes his rational mind and is of course consubstantial with the Father). In other words, the Father and Son are one in seeking the salvation of humankind.

Gregory purports not to understand this at all, and seems (although his argument is far from clear) to be suggesting, rather lazily perhaps, that Apolinarius, having just sought to establish that Christ's humanity

556. Jn 14.9.

(or, at any rate, his flesh-and-blood body) is real and distinct from his divinity, is now being inconsistent in maintaining that he is united with "the God within him." This of course wholly misrepresents the anthropological basis of the unity between the divine Logos and Christ's flesh-and-blood body that Apolinarius posits.

I shall pass over the incoherent and unintelligible material in what comes next, to avoid [J.231] having to linger pointlessly among pointless arguments, arguments that do not enable him to make his meaning clear even to attentive readers of the text. I cannot understand how his argument is helped by referring to the text that says that no one "will snatch out of Christ's hand" the sheep given him by the Father,[557] [L.99] or by saying that Christ draws the sheep to himself by the Father's divinity[558] and that "if Christ is united to the Father before the Resurrection, how can he not be united to the God within him?" Apolinarius, apparently deliberately, inserts this, which appears to refute the story he has invented, into the material he has put together to illustrate the distinction between humanity and God, and their union. "If Christ is united to the Father, how can he not be united to the God within him?" [L.100] So the man in Christ is separate from the God within him and is then united with him!

The penultimate argument of Apolinarius, which Gregory thinks it worth his while to combat, is that Christ did indeed suffer as a human being, but not "under the necessary constraints of an unwilling nature as a human being does, but" solely "as a consequence of that nature." As God chose to adopt a human body, his human passions were merely a consequence of that choice, rather than, as in our case, inevitable. Gregory, however, will have none of this and restricts himself to expressing incomprehension of the distinction between necessity, or necessary constraint, and (logical) consequence. Once again, he fails to engage properly with Apolinarius's Christological model.

I shall treat all this in a cursory manner, as proof that the erroneousness and unsustainability of his opinions are demonstrated

557. Jn 10.28.
558. Apolinarius's argument was in fact probably that the Father and the Son are one in seeking the salvation of humanity, rather than, as Gregory implies, to distinguish the human Christ from God.

just by reading them. I shall just note this one point: "The Savior," he says, "has suffered hunger, thirst, labor, grief, and sorrow." [L.101] Who is this Savior? It is God, as he says earlier,[559] not two persons,[560] one, as it were, God, and the other man. So it is God who has suffered those things that he says were suffered, and "what was incapable of suffering experiences passions not under the necessary constraints of an unwilling nature as a human being does, but as a consequence of that nature." [L.102] Who is up to refuting these vain arguments? Where does he see the distinction between the necessary constraints of a nature and the consequences of a nature?[561] A correct view sees the same meaning in each expression. For example, [M.1268] if I say, "Bad vision is a consequence of having a disease of the eye," and then say the same thing, "Anyone with a disease of the eye necessarily has bad vision," is not the meaning identical in both cases?[562] For someone who [J.232] speaks of necessary constraint is referring to what arises as a consequence, and if they mention a consequence, they mean what is necessary. So why does the wisdom of our wordsmith wish to attribute to the Savior the passions of our human nature not by the necessary constraints of nature but as a consequence of nature? "His passions must be moved," he says, "in the likeness of those of human beings." [L.103] But when someone says "must," are they not clearly asserting necessity? And is this not the usage of Scripture? One can get an explanation of the term from the Gospels themselves: "it is necessary that occasions for stumbling come,"[563] and "for this must take place."[564] Is not the meaning of both words the same?

---

559. See L.67, J.185, above. J., but not Lietzmann, prints this sentence as a direct quotation; as Grelier says (565, n. 2406), there do not appear to be any grounds for doing so.

560. πρόσωπα.

561. In fact, as Grelier (566) points out, "in consequence (ἀκολουθίᾳ) of that nature" is an expression of Stoic origin, and would normally be applied in anthropological contexts to the promptings of the natural law inscribed in man's nature, in contradistinction to what would arise by necessary constraint (ἀνάγκῃ).

562. The correct answer is of course no!

563. Mt 18.7. (NRSV: "Occasions for stumbling are bound to come.")

564. Mt 24.6. It seems unlikely (*pace* Grelier, 237) that Apolinarius cited

When Christ says, "it is necessary that occasions for stumbling come," he is indicating by this term that occasions for stumbling must come; and when he says, "this must take place," he is telling us of what is necessarily bound to take effect.

The last of Apolinarius's assertions with which Gregory engages is that "[Christ's] body is in heaven and he is with us until the consummation of this age." Gregory says he is not bothering to give us the context of this fragment, so it is not clear how it fits into Apolinarius's overall argument. Perhaps, as Mühlenberg suggests, he thought that, although Christ's flesh-and-blood body is in heaven, he remains present to us here in a spiritual way.[565] *Gregory expresses his puzzlement as to how Apolinarius believes Christ can be in two places at once. But he offers his own solution to the conundrum: that Christ's body has now become totally incorporeal and can therefore be present throughout the universe, with us on earth as well as in heaven.*

As for the stream of rubbish that comes next, put together at random on the basis of futile arguments, I will again pass them by. At the end of his treatise he says, "His body is in heaven, and he is with us until the consummation of this age." [L.104] Who is this who is with us? Our wordsmith, dividing what cannot be divided, clearly has no understanding of this. If he locates the body in the heavenly realm, but says that the Lord is here with us, he is clearly indicating, by this antithesis, a certain disjunction and separation. He is not saying that his body is in heaven and with us, but that the body is in heaven without us being in heaven, too. So he believes that there is someone else with us who are here on earth, apart from the body that is in heaven. Such are the sublime teachings of Apolinarius. But what we say is that "when he had said this,"[566] he was taken up, and that he who was taken remains with us, and that there is no division in him; just as he remains in each of us and [J.233] is in our midst,

---

either of these verses; Gregory must surely have found them himself, to prove his point.

565. Cf. *ad Jovianum* (Lietzmann, 252, lines 16–17): the glorified Christ in heaven is "as regards his Godhead incomprehensible, embracing every locality from eternity with the Father, as the ineffable power of the Father."

566. Acts 1.9.

so he reaches the boundary of creation and is manifest in the same way in every part of the universe. If he is present to us corporeal beings in an incorporeal manner, neither is he corporeally present in the heavens.

But, by dividing the Lord in this way, he is saying, incoherently, that he is present to his subjects in two opposite ways: without a body to those who are in the flesh, and in a body to those who are without a body. So Christ settles his flesh in heaven but joins himself [M.1269] in a spiritual way to human beings![567]

32. Conclusion

It seems that Apolinarius may have concluded his treatise by demonstrating that Christian doctrine constitutes the true conclusion of pagan philosophy. But Gregory claims that his arguments are worthless and not worth discussing in detail.

I think I should leave unexamined the material he piles up at the end of his treatise, with baseless ideas which resemble the final panting breaths of a dying man, desperately invoking the pagans in support of his own mythology and other stuff of that kind. [L.105] If there are any who have a taste for getting to know the absolute feebleness of this heresy, let them peruse the actual text. As for us, we do not have the leisure to go into these sorts of arguments in depth; they provide themselves a clear proof of their absurdity, without the need for any examination.

567. J. makes this and the previous sentence a direct quotation from Apolinarius. But Lietzmann does not recognize it as a fragment—Mühlenberg (70) concurs—and it is clearly a satirical representation by Gregory of what he thinks are the implications of Apolinarius's doctrine. Mühlenberg (70) suggests, however, that Gregory is right to attribute to Apolinarius the view that the resurrected Christ "joins himself in a spiritual way to human beings."

TO THEOPHILUS,
AGAINST THE APOLLINARIANS

TRANSLATION AND COMMENTARY

In this text, which begins at M.1269 and J.119, Gregory calls upon Theophilus, as leader of the ancient, venerable church of Alexandria, to oppose the novel doctrines that are threatening the unity of the Church.

ROM GREGORY, TO HIS BROTHER and fellow-minister Theophilus.

The great city of the Alexandrians is not only well-stocked with worldly wisdom, but from olden times the springs of the true wisdom have also welled up among you. So it seems appropriate to me that it is among those who have the most power in furthering what is good that allies in defending the truth of the divine mystery should be found. The sublime Gospel says somewhere, "From everyone to whom much has been given, more will be required."[1] So you would be right to use all the power that you and your church have obtained from the grace of God to oppose "what is falsely called knowledge"[2] of those who are constantly bringing forth something new in contradiction to the truth, through which the concord that comes from God is broken up and the great and noble name of [J.120] Christian can no longer be uttered. For the Church is divided up on the basis of labels given by human beings, and, worst of all, there are people who take delight in using the names of those who have led them into error.

It would be preferable to everyone if the prayer of the prophet were completely fulfilled and "that sinners should disappear

1. See Lk 12.48.
2. 1 Tm 2.20.

259

from the earth, and the lawless, so that they no longer [M.1272] exist."³ But since the words of the lawless have power against the truth through the working of the one who opposes,⁴ and thus prevail, it would be charitable at least to reduce the harm and inhibit the continuing increase in numbers of the worse sort of people.⁵

Gregory accuses the authors of these doctrines, the Apollinarians, of failing to draw a proper distinction between Christ's humanity and his divinity. They for their part, he says, falsely charge the orthodox with teaching that there are two Sons: the eternal Logos, the "Son by nature," and the man Jesus Christ, the "Son by adoption." He urges Theophilus to refute them.

What am I talking about? Those who advocate the doctrines of Apolinarius seek to strengthen their own position by attacking us, making the Son of Man, the Word, the Creator of all ages, into something fleshly,⁶ and making the divinity of the Son into something mortal.⁷ For they allege that in their doctrine some people in the Catholic Church profess two Sons, one Son by nature and one who emerged later by way of adoption. (I do not know where they have heard [J.121] anything like this or who it is they are picking a fight with; I have never heard anyone talking that sort of nonsense.) But since they advance this argument against us and corroborate their theories by seeming to involve us in this absurdity, it would be good if your perfection in Christ, in whatever way the Holy Spirit may direct your mind, could "deny an opportunity to those who are seeking an opportunity"⁸ against us, and persuade those who are making these slanderous accusations against the church of God that there is no such doctrine among Christians, nor will such doctrine ever be preached.

---

3. Ps 103 (104).35.

4. Or "through the working of the Adversary" (ἐν τῇ τοῦ ἀντικειμένου ἐνεργείᾳ); see 2 Thes 2.4, 9.

5. Or, "of the worse evils."

6. Gregory makes this accusation on numerous occasions in *antirrh:* see "Christ's flesh" on pp. 55–58 of the introduction.

7. Another major theme in *antirrh:* see J.219 and the note there.

8. See 2 Cor 11.12.

Gregory now suggests some arguments Theophilus might use against the false accusations of the Apollinarians, by demonstrating that no orthodox Christian could believe in two Christs. His first argument, which appears to be unique to him and to this work,[9] is obviously contrived and makes no attempt to address the actual concerns that, as we know from the fragments of the Apodeixis *that Gregory discusses in* antirrh, *led the Apollinarians to accuse the orthodox of believing in two Christs. (These concerns were to the effect that there was no way in which joining together a perfect man with the perfect God could result in a single unitary person.)[10]*

The argument seems to be directed towards a sort of reductio ad absurdum. *It is based upon the notion, common among the Fathers,[11] that the eternal Logos, the "Son by nature," manifested himself to human beings not only when he took flesh in the womb of Mary, but also in the theophanies of various kinds to holy men that are recorded in the Old as well as the New Testament. It assumes, perversely, that the status and effect of all these theophanies within the divine economy were essentially the same as those of the appearance of Christ "at the end of the ages" as the son of Mary. In that case, it would follow, Gregory suggests, that if an additional "Son by adoption" came into being in Jesus of Nazareth (as the Apollinarians accuse the orthodox of believing), it must have done so in all the others as well. So there would not have been just two Christs, but multiple Christs. That would be absurd, but, Gregory claims (although again on not very obvious grounds), no more so than to assume that Christ's birth of Mary implies two sons.*

The fact that the Maker of all ages[12] was, in the latter days, seen upon the earth and "lived with humankind"[13] does not mean that two Sons are counted by the Church, one the Creator of all ages, and the other revealed in human life through the flesh[14] at the end of the ages. Anyone who took the providential

9. See Grelier, 627, n. 2635.

10. See *antirrh,* J.199 and n. 394.

11. Gregory makes use of it again, in a rather different context, in *antirrh* (J.172).

12. ὁ ποιητὴς τῶν αἰώνων. See Heb 1.2, δι' οὗ καὶ ἐποίησεν τοὺς αἰῶνας ("through whom he also created the worlds," NRSV).

13. Bar 3.37.

14. See 1 Tm 3.16.

manifestation of the Only-begotten Son in the flesh as the pro-
duction of another Son would also have to count within the list
of divine manifestations all the theophanies to holy people that
occurred before the appearance [J.122] of the Only-begotten
Son of God in the flesh, and also those that happened after that
event to those who were worthy, and so would have to assume a
multitude of Sons. The being who had dealings with Abraham[15]
would be one Son; he who appeared to Isaac,[16] another; he who
wrestled with Jacob,[17] another; yet another, he who appeared
to Moses in various manifestations: in light,[18] in darkness,[19] in
a pillar of cloud,[20] in face-to-face encounter,[21] in the view of his
back;[22] still another, he who stood in the line of battle with Moses's successor.[23] Then there is he who conversed with Job from
out of the whirlwind;[24] he who appeared on an exalted throne
to Isaiah;[25] the being in human form described in Ezekiel's writings;[26] later on, he who struck down Paul in the light;[27] and, before that, he who appeared on the mountain in sublime glory to
those with Peter.[28] If it is absurd and wholly impious to assign the
various theophanies of the Only-begotten to a number of Sons,
it is equally impious to use his manifestation in the flesh as an
opportunity to [M.1273] assume that there is a second Son.

*But Gregory now takes a step back and diverts the argument into a com-
pletely different direction, one which does make a real attempt to engage
with the Apollinarians' concerns. He first argues that in fact those other
manifestations of the Logos were quite different in nature from that of
Jesus Christ. They were vouchsafed only to those who were, and to the
extent that they were, morally and spiritually worthy to receive them,
whereas Christ took upon himself the weakness of human flesh in order
to save those who were unworthy, the sinners who shared that flesh.*

[J.123] For in our view it is always in proportion to the ca-
pability of each person who receives a manifestation of the di-

15. Gn 12.1, 7, et alibi.   16. Gn 26.2–5, 24.
17. Gn 32.24–31.   18. Ex 3.2.
19. Ex 19.16–20 and 20.21.   20. Ex 13.21.
21. Ex 33.11.   22. Ex 33.23.
23. Jos 5.13–15.   24. Jb 38.1.
25. Is 6.1.   26. Ezek 1.26.
27. Acts 9.3.   28. Mt 17.1–8.

vine that there is a vision of the supreme nature. That vision is greater and more worthy of God in the case of those who are able to rise to the heights, smaller and less worthy in the case of those who are unable to attain the greater. For that reason it does not manifest itself to the life of human beings in the same way in the case of the providential manifestation in the flesh[29] as it does in the case of the previous epiphanies. For it was because, as the prophet says, "they have all gone astray, they have all been corrupted,"[30] and because, as has been written, there is no one who can understand and seek out the sublimity of the divinity,[31] that the Only-begotten Son appeared to our more fleshly race by becoming flesh, restricting himself to the narrow bounds of what received him, or rather, as Scripture says, "emptying himself."[32] That that generation was guilty compared with those that came before[33] we have learned from the Lord's own sayings, in which he declares that it will be "more tolerable" for the Sodomites[34] and the people of Nineveh than for them, and in which he pronounces that the queen of the South will "condemn that generation"[35] at the resurrection.

If everyone were able, like Moses, to be within the darkness in which he saw things [J.124] that cannot be seen;[36] or, like the sublime Paul, to be raised up above three heavens and in paradise be told "things that are not to be told" about matters that are beyond description;[37] or, like the zealous Elijah, to be raised with the fire to the place up in the sky[38] and not be weighed down by the burdensome appendage of the body; or, like Ezekiel and Isaiah, to see him who is raised above the cherubim[39] and is glorified by the seraphim[40]—then there would be absolutely no need for God's manifestation among us in the flesh,

29. Literally, "the economy through flesh."

30. Ps 13 (14).3.

31. See Ps 81 (82).5; Is 35.2; Rom 11.33.

32. Phil 2.7.

33. For this notion that the Incarnation happened when evil was at its peak, see *antirrh,* J.171 and n. 252.

34. Mt 10.15.   35. Mt 12.42.

36. Ex 20.21.   37. 2 Cor 12.2–4.

38. 2 Kgs 2.11.   39. Ezek 10.1.

40. Is 6.1–3.

because we would all be like them. But since, as the Lord says, that was "an evil and adulterous generation,"[41] ("evil" because at that time, as Scripture says, "the whole world lies under the power of the evil one";[42] "adulterous," because it has turned away from its good Bridegroom and has joined itself to him who debauches its souls through evil)—for this reason, the true Physician, he who cured those who were ill by using the treatment that the disease required, has in the same way provided care for the sick by in a way becoming ill himself with the disease of our nature,[43] and by becoming flesh, flesh that has weakness innate in its own nature: as the divine saying has it, "The spirit is willing, but the flesh is weak."[44]

Now if the divine Word had simply entered into human flesh, without changing it in any way, it would be quite reasonable, Gregory concedes, to talk of two Christs: the eternal Son, in his immortality and incorruptibility, and the man Jesus, in his weakness and mutability.

Now if what is divine had come to be in what is human, and what is immortal in what is mortal, and what is powerful in what is weak, and [J.125] what is unchanging and incorruptible in what is mutable, in such a way as to allow what is mortal to remain in its mortality and what is corruptible to remain in its corruption, and similarly with the other human qualities, it is likely that a duality would be observed in the Son of God, as each opposite quality would be counted separately. But if, when what is mortal came to be in what is [M.1276] immortal, it became immortality, and, likewise, what is corruptible was changed into incorruptibility, and, in the same way, all the other qualities were converted into what is impassible and divine, what justification remains for those who seek to divide the one into two separate elements?

But in fact the humanity of Jesus was changed by being "mixed" with the divinity, and acquired its characteristics by "becoming that which the Godhead is," that is, sinless and changeless.

41. Mt 12.39.
42. 1 Jn 5.19.
43. For Christ as physician, see *antirrh*, J.160, J.171, J.226. But this passage is the only one to say, daringly, that Christ "in a way" (τρόπον τινὰ) became ill himself.
44. Mt 26.41.

For the Word was and is the Word both before it took flesh and after its providential enfleshment, and God is God both before and after he took the form of a slave,[45] and the true light is the true light both before it shone out in the darkness[46] and afterwards. So if every pious conception of the Only-begotten that anyone can form is one of immutability and changelessness, and if he does in himself always possess those same characteristics, how can anyone make us apply the concept of a duality of Sons to his manifestation in the flesh, as if the Son who existed before all ages were one Son and the one who was conceived by God in the flesh were another?

What we have been taught and what we believe through the mystery[47] is that the human nature which was united to the Word was preserved.[48] [J.126] But we have not been taught that a fleshly Son of God can be thought of separately, nor are we induced to believe it by some logical argument. Having, as the Apostle says, become sin[49] and a curse on account of us,[50] and having taken, according to Isaiah's words, our weaknesses upon himself,[51] he did not leave the sin and the curse and the weakness unhealed, but "what is mortal" was "swallowed up by life,"[52] and he who "was crucified in weakness lives by power";[53] the curse was transformed into a blessing,[54] and everything in

45. Phil 2.7.

46. Jn 1.5, 9.

47. Perhaps, as Grelier (635, n. 2672) suggests, "mystery" here means "revealed knowledge."

48. σωθῆναι. See *antirrh*, J.214 and n. 473 *ad loc.* (where I translate σῴζηται as "left unchanged"). Grelier (635) again has "est sauvée," which would be a less improbable translation here than in the *antirrh* passage, given the soteriological context. The fact that Gregory (if my translation is right) is saying here that Christ's human nature "*was* preserved," while in the *antirrh* passage he is saying that it was *not* "left unchanged," is on the face of it an argument against my translation. But it is perhaps explicable by the fact that here he is stressing that it was real humanity that Christ assumed, while in *antirrh* the emphasis is more on that humanity's eventual transformation. On balance, and with some hesitation, I have assumed that σῴζειν in both passages is equivalent to "servare" rather than "salvare," and, in the case of this passage, invoke the support of Fronton du Duc's Latin translation "servatam esse" in PG 45:1275B.

49. 2 Cor 5.21.   50. Gal 3.13.

51. Is 53.12.   52. 2 Cor 5.4.

53. 2 Cor 13.4.   54. Neh 13.2.

our nature that is weak and mortal, having been mixed[55] with the Godhead, became that which the Godhead is. So how could anyone come to believe in this duality of Sons, claiming that they were forcibly led to this theory by the fact of the providential enfleshment?

So Jesus Christ's divinity overwhelms his humanity, with the result that no distinction can be made between them, any more than between a drop of vinegar and the sea into which it is poured. This produces a total unity between the human and the divine, so there can be no question of two Sons.

Gregory uses the image of the drop of vinegar and the sea to illustrate his Christology three times in his writings. This is the only one where he gives no explicit sign that he is applying it only to Christ's glorified, post-ascension condition, although it seems clear that that is what is meant.[56]

For he who is always in the Father, and always has the Father within himself,[57] and is united to him,[58] is and will be what he was before, and there neither was, is, nor will be any other Son but him. For the first fruits of human nature that he assumed[59] have been mixed with the all-powerful Godhead, like (as one might say using a simile) a drop of vinegar in the boundless sea, and are in the Godhead rather than in their own peculiar characteristics.[60] For a duality of Sons could [J.127] logically be acknowledged if some heterogeneous nature could be recognized by its own identifying characteristics within the ineffable divin-

55. ἀνακραθὲν. For this idea of "mixture" in Gregory's Christology, see *antirrh*, J.137 (and n. 35), J.144, J.151, J.154, J.161, J.171, J.207, J.213, J.217, J.221, J.225, J.228.

56. As Grelier (512) argues. For Gregory's use of the image of the drop of vinegar in the ocean, see *antirrh*, J.201, and the commentary and note *ad loc*. For the implications for Gregory's "two-stage" Christology, see "The unity of Christ's person: His glorification," pp. 79–81 of the introduction.

57. See Jn 14.10.

58. See Jn 10.30.

59. For Gregory's use of the image of Christ as first fruits, see *antirrh*, J.151, and the note thereon.

60. ἐν τοῖς ἰδίοις αὐτῆς ἰδιώμασιν is the *GNO* reading. αὐτῆς must clearly refer to "first fruits" (ἀπαρχή) rather than to "Godhead" (θεότητι), so Grelier (512) prefers the variant reading ἑαυτῆς.

ity of the Son, the former being weak, small, corruptible, or temporary, the latter powerful and great and incorruptible and eternal. But as all those characteristics that can be seen to be associated with what is mortal have been transformed into the characteristics of the Godhead, no distinction between them can be perceived; for whatever one can see of the Son is divinity, wisdom, power, holiness, and impassibility. So how could the unity be [M.1277] separated into a duality, since no numerical distinction can be made?

The intimate union between the two natures is reflected in a communicatio idiomatum, *so that the crucified one can be called the Lord of glory, and the eternal Son can be called Jesus. There is thus one Son, not two.*

For God has "highly exalted" what was humble, and to what had been given a human name he "gave the name that is above every name";[61] what was under command and a slave he made lord and king: as Peter said, "God has made him both Lord and Christ."[62] (By "Christ" we understand "king.") And because of the intimate union between the flesh that was assumed and the Godhead that assumed, the names can be exchanged, so that the human can be called divine and the divine human. So the crucified one is called the Lord [J.128] of glory by Paul,[63] and he who is worshiped by all creation, by those "in heaven and on earth and under the earth," is called Jesus.[64] In these passages the true and indivisible union is expounded, because the ineffable glory of the Godhead is referred to by the name of Jesus, when all flesh and "every tongue confesses that Jesus Christ is Lord,"[65] and because he who accepted the sufferings of the cross, who was pierced by the nails and transfixed by the spear, was called the Lord of glory by Paul. So if what is human is not manifested in the characteristics of human nature but is the Lord of glory, and since no one would venture to say that

61. Phil 2.9.   62. Acts 2.36.
63. 1 Cor 2.8.
64. Phil 2.10. Gregory has a very similar passage on the *communicatio idiomatum* in *antirrh,* J.161–62.
65. Phil 2.11.

there are two Lords of glory, as they would have learned that there is "one Lord, Jesus Christ, through whom are all things,"[66] how can those who by accusing us want to present a specious foundation for constructing their own theories attribute a belief in a duality of Sons to us?[67]

Gregory concludes by commending these arguments to Theophilus and inviting him to improve on them.

So these are the arguments we can deploy in our defense. But we look for a greater and more perfect alliance in favor of the truth from your perfection in Christ, so that those who corroborate their own theories by blaming us may have no handle for accusations against the Church.

---

66. 1 Cor 8.6.

67. J. has a comma before "how can those ... attribute ... to us ... (πόθεν ἡμῖν ἐπικαλοῦσι). Grelier (641 and n. 2698) prefers to put a full stop, thus making "no one would venture to say" (οὐκ ἂν δέ τις εἰπεῖν ... τολμήσειεν) the main clause in what then becomes the first of two separate sentences. But in that case the δέ would be syntactically odd. That, combined with the fact that there is no connective particle at the beginning of the putative second sentence (although, as Grelier points out, there is one in the Syriac version), leads me to prefer to follow J.'s punctuation.

APPENDIX AND INDICES

APPENDIX

A RECONSTRUCTION OF THE POSSIBLE
STRUCTURE OF THE *APODEIXIS*

After an introduction,[1] the work seems to have fallen into seven main sections. The first[2] seems to have focused on comparing and contrasting the "God-filled man" Christology, which Apolinarius attributed to his "orthodox" opponents, with his own "enfleshed mind" Christology and the trichotomous anthropology[3] that underpinned it. Christ was a "man from heaven," not a "man from earth,"[4] a view for which Apolinarius finds support in St. Paul's comparison, in 1 Corinthians 15.45–47, between the first and second Adam.[5]

The next section[6] seems to have been devoted to demonstrating, on the basis of a number of scriptural texts,[7] that, as divine Logos, consubstantial with the Father,[8] Christ existed from eternity, and that the unity of his person was such that, in some sense, the humanity of Jesus, "the man from heaven," also existed from eternity.[9]

In the third section,[10] the focus seems to have moved to the human Jesus, to show that he can truly be said to have been divine. Again, a series of scriptural texts are cited in evidence,[11]

1. L.13. 2. L.14–31.
3. L.19–22. 4. L.16–18.
5. L.25–31. 6. L.32–47.
7. L.33, 35, 37–38, 42–47. 8. L.39–41.
9. L.32.

10. L.48–69. For Lietzmann's theory that this section marked the beginning of the second of the two parts or books into which the work was divided, see n. 227 on L.48 (J.166).

11. L.56–62.

and again Apolinarius attacks the "God-filled man" theory of his opponents, which denies that Jesus was God.[12] He again expounds his trichotomous anthropology and "enfleshed mind" Christology and rebuts his opponents' view that the divine Logos "assumed" a complete man.[13] As "enfleshed mind," Christ had only one will, the divine one.[14]

The fourth section[15] seems to have been devoted to a series of syllogisms—or, at any rate, tightly constructed deductive arguments—designed to support Apolinarius's "enfleshed mind" Christology. As will be seen from the commentary and notes, there is, however, uncertainty as to how many of them there are—I believe there are probably eight—and about how individual fragments should be assigned to separate syllogisms. The soteriological aspects of Apolinarius's Christology—how Christ must have had an immutable (that is, divine) mind in order to "govern" the mutable human flesh—are prominent in several of these: explicitly in the third[16] and fifth,[17] implicitly in the fourth[18] and eighth.[19]

The fifth section[20] seems also to have been to a substantial extent syllogistic in its style, but to have focused on providing scriptural proofs for a trichotomous anthropological schema[21] and to have sought to show logically that only an "enfleshed mind" Christology based on that schema can give a defensible account of the relationship between the divine and the human in Christ's person.[22]

The theme of the sixth section[23] seems to have been Christ's death and resurrection and its soteriological logic. In order to save us, the Christ who died and rose again must have been a human being like us, but he must also have been divine. But there was an unbreakable unity between the human and divine elements—so close that Apolinarius may have claimed that it is permissible to say that "God himself died."[24]

12. L.49–52, 54–55.
13. L.66–67, 69.
14. L.63.
15. L.70–87.
16. L.74.
17. L.76, 79–80.
18. L.75.
19. L.87.
20. L.88–95.
21. L.88.
22. L.89–92.
23. L.93–95.
24. L.95 (J.219). See note *ad loc.*

The main theme of the last substantive section[25] was perhaps the continuity of Christ's unique nature before, during, and after his earthly career. He was God from all eternity,[26] and the limitations his humanity imposed on him during his life on earth, though real, were a matter of choice rather than, as in our case, necessity.[27] Nevertheless, he remained separate from the Father; his unity with him during his earthly career was a unity in a common purpose of seeking the salvation of humankind,[28] and his humanity was never absorbed into the Godhead even after his glorification.[29]

The *Apodeixis* seems to have concluded by suggesting that Christian doctrine constitutes the true conclusion of pagan philosophy.[30]

25. L.96–104.   26. L.96–97.
27. L.101–3.   28. L.98–100.
29. L.98, L.104. 30. L.105.

GENERAL INDEX

Abraham, 56, 122, 125, 168, 218, 262
Adam, 28, 53–54, 56, 64, 65, 72, 77,
  83, 85, 96, 107, 115–22, 136, 138,
  152–53, 247–48, 271
adoptionism, 48, 112
ad Theophilum (Gregory of Nyssa): Christological arguments in, xxii, 24, 49,
  70n400, 86–88; date of composition,
  27, 35–38; previous translations of,
  xix; purpose of, xviii; translation and
  commentary, 259–68
Alexandria, 5, 10n23, 13, 19, 21,
  22n71, 22n72, 35, 47, 48n201, 259
"Alexandrian" Christology, 5, 47
Ambrose, Saint, bishop of Milan, 25
Anastasius of Sinai, 112n79, 188
Ancyra, 12, 17, 19, 20, 30, 31, 48, 98,
  102
anthropology: Apolinarius's, 8–10,
  28–29, 39n156, 49, 50, 64, 68, 70,
  84, 107–12, 177–79, 219–20, 226,
  191n366, 271–72; Gregory's, 28–29,
  70, 214–15, 218
Antioch: Apollinarianism at, 7, 12–20,
  24, 27; schisms at, 6n9, 11, 12–20,
  22n72, 32n123, 48; synods at, 20–21,
  30–31, 48
"Antiochene" Christology, 47–49, 73
Antirrheticus (Gregory of Nyssa)
  argumentative techniques in:
    abuse of Apolinarius, 58–60;
    analogy, 61–62; *aporia*, 60; *cap-
    tatio benevolentiae,* 91n1; logical
    arguments, 60, 61; rhetorical
    devices, 61–62
  arguments in, theological synthesis
    of, 67–85
  composition: date of, 35–38;
    method of, 38, 41, 94

Eucharist, allusions to in, 92n5,
  154n248
overall assessment of, xviii–xx, 86
Scripture, use of in: criticism of
  Apolinarius's use of Scripture,
  62–65; exegesis of particular
  texts, 64; illustrative examples
  from Scripture, 66–67; introduction, use of Scripture in,
  62; montage of texts combined
  symphonically, 67; proof texts,
  65–66; syllogisms based on
  scriptural texts, 66
structure of: *inclusio,* 39n156; overall structure, 39; repetitions, 40;
  excursuses, xxi, 67, 73, 99, 100,
  126, 136, 238
translation and commentary,
  91–258
Apodeixis (Apolinarius): accuracy of
  Gregory's reporting of, xx, 41–43;
  arguments, reconstruction of, xvii,
  44–58; date of composition, 10n22,
  27–28; fragments, Lietzmann's
  collection of, 4; Nazianzen, possible reference by, 25, 37; structure,
  reconstruction of, 43, 271–73; syllogisms in, 66, 181–82, 185, 187, 189,
  191n366, 192, 193, 195, 196, 198,
  201, 203, 204, 209, 211, 215, 216,
  219, 226, 228n470, 272; title of, xx;
  whom directed against, 47–49
Apolinarius of Laodicea
  Christology, alleged two stages of
    development in, 8–10
  life: birth and early career, 5–6;
    later career, 7; seeks allies, 17;
    condemned in Rome, 17–19;
    death, 7, 141n208

275

Apolinarius of Laodicea *(cont.)*
  spelling of name, xviiin1
  teaching on non-Christological
    issues, 7, 18n54, 33
  traducianism, 28–29
  works: ad *Diocaesareenses,* 14n36,
    17n49; *ad Dionysium I,* 4n2; *ad
    Dionysium* II, 57; *ad Jovianum,*
    11; *ad Serapionem,* 10, 17, 57;
    Apodeixis (see separate entry);
    contra Diodorum, 8n21; *de fide
    et incarnatione,* 4n2; *de unione,*
    4n2, 8n21, 29n103, 51n222,
    105n46, 217n430; *Kata mer-
    os pistis,* 4n2, 48, 191n366,
    193n373
Apolinarius the elder, 5
Apollinarianism, history of: historio-
  graphical problems, 3–4; early history, 7–11; at Antioch, 12–16; from 378
  to 381, 19–21; at the first Council of
  Constantinople (381), 21–23; and
  Gregory of Nazianzen, 23–25; after
  381, 25–27; at Jerusalem, 32–34
Aquila, 131n163
Arabia, 32, 36
Arian, Arianism, 4, 5, 6, 12, 13, 17,
  19, 20, 21, 22, 26, 29, 30, 31, 34,
  100n29, 101, 149, 160, 167n310,
  169, 214
Aristotle, 204
assumption (of the flesh), 10n22,
  52n224, 107n52, 175–77, 193,
  244n523
Athanasius, Saint, 4n2, 5, 10, 11, 13, 14,
  17, 48n201, 208n406. *See also tomus
  ad Antiochenos;* pseudo-Athanasius

Basil of Ancyra, 12
Basil of Caesarea, Saint: and Apolinarius, 4, 6, 7n17, 18n54, 23n76, 33;
  death, 19, 30; and Gregory of Nyssa,
  29, 30; and the monks of the Mount
  of Olives, 32; and the schisms at Antioch, 9, 12, 13, 15n40, 16, 17, 19
Beirut, 5. *See also* Timothy of Beirut
Boulnois, M.-O., 67n340

Canévet, M., 62n306, 62n309
Cappadocia, 13, 22, 23, 24, 29, 32n121
Cappadocian Fathers, 3

Carter, T. J.
  on Apolinarius's Christology, 10,
    44n175, 51n223
  on the *Antirrheticus:* overall assess-
    ment, xviii–xix
  on the *Apodeixis:* its structure, 43,
    148n227, 196n380; its date,
    27n100; on Gregory's report-
    ing of Apolinarius's text, 42;
    on individual fragments: L.14,
    98n24; L.22, 108n57, 108n60,
    109n62; L.26, 116n90; L.30,
    119n106; L.32, 120n119; L.36,
    130n162; L.45, 135n218; L.48,
    148n227; L.53, 157n256; L.67,
    177n333; L.68, 178n334; L.72–
    73, 187n361; L.76, 193n371,
    193n373, 196n380; L.77–78,
    198n381; L.81, 191n366; L.106,
    188n362; L.107, 191n366
Cattaneo, Enrico, 58n257, 71n352
Celsus, 98n24
Chadwick, Henry, 6n9, 12n29, 13n31,
  14n36
Chalcedon, Council of (451), 11n27
Chalcedonian formula, xviiin3, 70, 81,
  86
Christ: his agony in the garden of
  Gethsemane, 54, 78, 169–72; as the
  Anointed One, 239–40, 242, 246–47;
  his Ascension, 58, 65, 79, 80n401,
  81, 88, 251–53; his birth, 56, 76,
  95–96, 98, 104–5, 114–15, 121–23,
  136–38, 140–41, 148, 151–53, 155–
  56, 157, 161–62, 173–74, 179–80,
  184–85, 189, 208–10, 242, 245–46,
  261; his conception in Mary's womb,
  8n21, 55–56, 60, 74n367, 75–77,
  80n401, 96n18, 106–7, 114, 136,
  145, 148, 153, 158, 160, 181n343,
  207, 210, 233–34, 243–44, 245;
  as "enfleshed mind," 36, 51–54,
  56, 68–72, 86, 114, 147–48, 151,
  156–57, 175, 178n334, 177, 180–81,
  181–82, 183–85, 186–87, 189, 192,
  197, 271–72; as "first-fruits," 125; his
  flesh, alleged pre-existence of, 11,
  17, 25n84, 55–58, 60, 72, 103–5,
  107–8, 113, 120–25, 130–36, 148,
  151–52, 155, 160–61, 173–74,
  180–81, 198–200, 206–7, 212, 230,

234, 240; his glorification, his glory, 58, 79–82, 88, 138, 147, 150–51, 155n249, 207, 240–42, 251–53; as God (divine), 32–33, 44, 52, 64n319, 69–70, 74, 78, 147–49, 151–52, 153, 155, 156, 158–60, 161–63, 165–66; as "God-filled man," 11, 14, 47, 48, 53, 73–74, 77, 97–99, 102–3, 105, 112, 114, 151, 153, 155, 181–82, 188, 209–10, 227, 271, 272; as "man from earth," 103–4, 173, 187, 271; as "man from heaven," 53–55, 77, 103–5, 112–15, 117, 174, 187–88, 229, 271; his mind, xvii, 8, 14n36, 16, 18, 23, 25, 49–50, 51n223, 53, 55, 70–71, 73 75, 78, 85, 109n62, 112–14, 115, 117–18, 126, 143, 145n218, 158–59, 165–66, 167–68, 179–80, 182, 190–92, 195, 197–98, 200, 202, 203, 204–6, 216, 228, 248–50; the "mixture" of his natures, 32, 45, 77, 78n395, 79, 80, 87, 94n12, 102n35, 114, 115, 117, 118, 125, 130, 139–40, 156, 158, 208, 217–18, 226, 230, 233–34, 240–41, 250, 264, 266; as New Man, 77, 243–44; as physician (doctor, healer), 87, 138–39, 156, 199, 247, 264; his Resurrection, 58, 80n401, 81, 83–85, 128–29, 139, 233, 245–48, 251, 254–55, 272; as Son of Man, 25n84, 58, 82, 86, 103–6, 251–53, 260; his soul, xvii, 8, 10, 11, 14, 23, 33, 37, 51–52, 55, 64, 69, 71, 75, 77, 80n401, 83–85, 94–95, 107, 109, 112–13, 128–30, 141, 143, 158–59, 162–63, 165–66, 167–68, 179–81, 244–48; "two Christs," 14, 17, 36, 45–49, 79, 87, 175, 195, 208, 232, 240–41, 243, 261, 264; his will, 45n188, 54–55, 78–79, 164–65, 169–73, 191n366, 215–19. See also assumption, death of God, "God-man," "man-God," triduum
Christology. See Christ
Cilicia, 22n72, 26
Cledonius, 23, 24
Codex Theodosianus (Theodosian Code), 26nn92–95, 27n96
Codex Veronensis LX, 20n68
communicatio idiomatum, 79, 88, 105, 139, 267

Constantinople: bishopric of, 22, 24; city of, 21, 26n95, 27; First Council of (381), 4, 21–23, 25, 28n102, 31, 38n148; synod at, 25; Third Council of (680), 170n317
Constantius (emperor), 6
consubstantial, consubstantiality (ὁμοούσιον), 9n21, 11, 17, 45, 53, 56, 57, 60, 65, 78, 131n165, 134, 135, 145, 146n220, 161n277, 170n318, 206, 254, 271
Cyril of Alexandria, Saint, 4n2, 77n394

Daley, Brian E., 80n401, 208n403
Damasus, Pope Saint, 15, 16, 18, 19, 20, 21, 22n72, 24, 30
Daniélou, J., 31n119, 36n41, 83n409
death of God, Apolinarius's alleged teaching on, 69–70, 99–102, 104, 166–68, 235–36, 247
Demophilus, 21, 22
Diocaesarean confessors, 14n36, 17, 19
Diodore of Tarsus, 48
Diodore of Tyre, 19
Diogenes (priest at Antioch), 13
Dives (in parable), 167–68
docetism, docetic, 10n23, 72, 145
Drecoll, Volker, xx, 132n168
Ducaeus, Fronto (Fronton le Duc), xixn9, 265n48
Duvick, Brian, xixn7, 113n80, 154n246

Ebionism, 10n23
Egypt, 10, 17, 22n72, 26, 116
Elijah, 61, 65, 66, 74 n367, 153–55, 163, 263
enfleshment, as translation of σάρκωσις, xviiin3, 93n7
Epiphanius (sophist), 5, 216n427
Epiphanius of Salamis, Saint, 6, 8n21, 16, 19, 193n373
Eulalius, 24
Eunomius of Cyzicus, Eunomians, xviii, 20, 26, 31, 34, 35, 37, 57, 60, 100n29, 125, 160, 161, 170, 214–15
Eusebius, 48n204
Eustathius of Sebaste, 6n13, 17, 19
Eutyches, 4n2
Euzoius, 12–13
Eve, 97

fall, fallenness, 49, 75, 80n401, 82,
145n214, 241, 245, 247, 248n537
Flavian (bishop of Antioch), 20n65,
22n72
Fronton le Duc (Fronto Ducaeus),
xixn9, 265n48

Geistchristologie, 51n220, 69n346
George (bishop of Laodicea), 5
Gethsemane. *See* Christ
"God-man" (θεός ἄνθρωπος), 52, 57,
120–22, 141, 229, 236n403
Gratian (emperor), 20, 30, 48n203
Gregorii Nysseni Opera, xviin1, xxii
Gregory of Nazianzus, Saint (or "Na-
zianzen"), 7, 18n54, 22, 23–25,
27, 31n117, 33, 37, 57, 71n352,
75, 120n121, 148n228, 180n341,
204n394, 236n493
Gregory of Nyssa, Saint
    and Apollinarianism: history of his
      exposure to, 28–35; influence
      on his anthropology, 28–29
    his life: made bishop of Nyssa, 29;
      helps Basil defend Nicene ortho-
      doxy, 29–30; exiled (375/76),
      30; returns from exile (378),
      20, 30; attends synod in Antioch
      (379), 20, 30; at Basil's funeral
      (378/79), 30; further efforts in
      defense of Nicene orthodoxy,
      30–31; five years of intense
      writing activity, 31; attends First
      Council of Constantinople,
      31–32; journey to Arabia and
      Jerusalem, 32–34; chronology
      of anti-Eunomian works, 34–35;
      later career and death, 35
    his works: *ad Ablabium, quod non
      sint tres dii*, 31; *ad Graecos, ex
      communibus notionibus*, 31; *ad
      Theophilum* (see separate en-
      try); *Antirrheticus* (see separate
      entry); *contra Eunomium I*, 31,
      34, 60n291; *contra Eunomium II*,
      31, 34; *contra Eunomium III*, 34,
      37, 80n401, 81n402, 100n29,
      125n139, 207, 208n403; *de
      hominis opificio*, 29, 30; *de ora-
      tione dominica*, 28; *de perfectione*,

83n409; *de vita Sanctae Macrinae*,
20n68; *epistola (Letter) 3*, 32,
34, 36; *in canticum canticorum*,
305; *in diem natalem salvatoris*,
140n207; *in Hexaemeron*, 30;
in illud, tunc et ipse Filius, 34,
83n409; *in suam ordinationem*,
31; *oratio catechetica*, 35, 37n147,
83n409, 125n139, 154n248;
Refutatio confessionis Eunomii, 34,
37, 125n139; *Vita Moysis*, 35
*The Brill Dictionary of Gregory of
Nyssa*, xxn12, 28n102
Gregory Thaumaturgus, Saint, 4n2
Grelier, Hélène
    on *ad Theophilum*, 261n9,
      265nn47–48, 266n56, 266n60,
      268n67
    on "Apolinarius," spelling of,
      xviin1
    on Apolinarius's anthropology,
      50n214
    on Apolinarius's Christology,
      10n22, 51n220, 51n223, 55
    on Apolinarius's life, 5n4, 7n16
    on Gregory's Christology, 81
    on Gregory's critique of Apolinari-
      us's Christology, 32n126, 71
    on Gregory's reporting of Apoli-
      narius's text, 42
    on Gregory's soteriology,
      84nn412–13, 84n417
    on the *Antirrheticus*: overall as-
      sessment, xx, xxin16; on its
      style and structure, 39n149,
      39nn155–56, 40, 41, 182n345,
      194n376, 219n440; on its
      use of Scripture, 62, 64n313,
      66n330, 67; on its argumenta-
      tive techniques, 58n261, 60; on
      textual, translation, and inter-
      pretative issues, 91n1, 100n29,
      106nn49–50, 113nn81–82,
      126nn140–41, 132n168,
      137n189, 140n207, 154n154,
      154n248, 155n249, 156n252,
      167n310, 168n313, 208n403,
      211n416, 225n461, 228n471,
      229n473, 230n477, 247nn533–
      34; her thesis on, xix, xx

on the *Apodeixis:* its structure,
148n227; its target audience,
48n205, 49n209; individu-
al fragments: L.14, 97n22,
98nn23–24; L.15, 103n40;
L.18, 106n47; L.19, 107n51;
L.22, 108n60, 109n62; L.26,
116n90; L.27, 117n95; L.30,
119n106; L.31, 119n108; L.32,
120nn118–19; L.34, 124n137;
L.36, 130n162; L.37, 131n163;
L.42, 141n209; L.44, 145n215;
L.47, 151n237; L.48, 148n227,
148n229; L.50, 152n241; L.51,
153n244; L.53, 157n256; L.63,
169n314; L.67, 256n559; L.71,
185n357; L.73, 187n361,
188n363; L.75, 192n368;
L.79–80, 201n387; L.80,
204n394; L.81, 205n395; L.82,
208n406; L.87, 217n430; L.90,
227n468; L.92, 231n484; L.95,
236n493; L.96, 237n495; L.98,
253n555; L.102, 256n561,
256n564; L.106, 188n362;
L.107, 191n366
   on the dating of the *Antirrheticus*
   and *ad Theophilum,* 36n141,
   37nn146–47, 37nn146–47,
   38n148

Hesiod, 216n426
Hippocratic medicine, 83n409
Hippolytus, Saint, 84
Holl, D. Karl, 81n402
Holy Spirit, 6, 17, 48n202, 51n220, 96,
   106, 112n79, 115, 158, 162, 189, 210,
   213, 239, 240, 241, 242, 246, 260
homoean(ism), 6n9
homoiousian(ism), 5, 6, 12, 13
Hübner, Reinhold, 80n401, 83n409,
   125n139
hypostasis, 11n27, 12n30, 74, 182,
   183n347

Ibora, 31
impassibility, 44, 69, 99, 102, 149, 151,
   168, 243, 264, 267. *See also* passions
incarnation. *See* enfleshment

"Jaeger" edition. *See Gregorii Nysseni
   Opera*
Jerome, Saint, 6n9, 7, 17, 18n54,
   23n76, 31n117, 33
Jerusalem, 18n54, 32, 33, 34, 36, 129
Jesus. *See* Christ
Jews, Judaizing, 7, 18n54, 33, 44, 47,
   74n367, 97, 131, 148, 151, 152, 153,
   155, 174, 175, 211, 240
Jovian, 11
Julian (emperor), 7, 11, 13, 98n24,
   191n366, 216n427
Julius, Pope Saint, 4n2
Justinian, 191n366, 195n377

Kelly, J. N. D., 48n202
kenotic theory, 46n196
Kiria, Ekaterina, 28n102

Laodicea, 5, 6n9, 6n13, 7, 25
Lateran Council (649), 170n317
Lazarus, 14n36, 129, 167, 223
Lebourlier, J., 37n147
Leontius of Byzantium, 191n366,
   193n373
Lietzmann, Hans
   *Apollinaris von Laodicea und seine
      Schule,* 3n1, 4
   on *ad Theophilum,* 35n137,
      36n143
   on Apolinarius's Christology, de-
      velopment of, 8n21
   on Apolinarius's life: the sources,
      3n1; his early life, 5, 6nn9–10,
      6n13, 7nn14–15; his corre-
      spondence with Basil, 6n11; his
      approaches to Terentius and
      the Diocaesarean exiles, 17n48,
      17n50; his condemnation at
      Rome, 18n52, 18nn54–55,
      19n59, 19n61; his death,
      141n208
   on Apolinarius's works: false attri-
      butions of, 4n2; letter to Sarapi-
      on, date of, 10
   on Apollinarianism, history of: at
      Antioch, 13nn31–32, 14n36,
      15n37, 15n39, 16nn41–42,
      16n46; between 378 and 381,
      20n63, 20nn65–66, 20n68,

Lietzmann, Hans; on Apollinarianism, history of: between 378 and 381 *(cont.)* 21nn69–70; at the Council of Constantinople (381), 22nn71–73, 23; after 381, 26nn89–92, 26n95, 27nn97–98; Nazianzen and Apollinarianism, 23n75, 24n79, 24n82

on Gregory of Nyssa, 29n105, 30n107

on the *Antirrheticus,* 36n143, 42

on the *Apodeixis:* discussion of individual fragments of: L.13, 97n21; L.14, 98n24; L.15, 103n41; L.19, 107n51; L.22, 108n60, 109n62; L.26, 116n90; L.27, 117n95; L.32, 120n119; L.42, 141n209; L.44, 145n215; L.50, 152n241; L.51, 153n244; L.52, 155n250; L.53, 157n256; L.54, 158n263, 159n268; L.55, 160n277; L.58, 163n286; L.62, 167n308; L.63, 170n317, 172, 173n323; L.64, 174n324; L.67, 177n333; L.68, 178n334; L.70, 185nn352–53; L.71, 186n358; L.77, 206n399; L.79, 201n388, 202n389; L.80, 203n392, 204n393; L.81, 195n377; L.84, 212n419; L.90, 227n468, 228n470; L.93, 233n488; L.96, 237n495; L.98, 252n555; L.101, 256n559; L.106, 188n362; L.107, 191n366; supposed fragment in J.233, 258n56; structure of the *Apodeixis,* 43, 148n227, 187n361, 194, 271n10

Lucifer of Calaris, 13

Ludlow, Morwenna, 208n403

"Macedonians." *See* Pneumatomachoi

Macrina, Saint, 20n68

"man-God" (ἀνθρωπόθεος), 46, 229, 231

Manichaeans, 20

Marcellus of Ancyra, Marcellans, 12, 17, 20, 30, 31, 48, 73, 98, 102, 103, 148n227

Mary, the Virgin: as allegedly co-eternal with the Father, 60, 122; and the Holy Spirit, 51n220, 244, 246; as mother of

Christ, 36, 66, 95–96, 105, 139, 140, 149, 152n240, 154, 156, 174, 179, 185, 188, 189, 242, 261; as mother of God, 33, 34n130; as the origin of Christ's flesh, 8n21, 11, 18, 57, 72, 77, 106, 114–15, 121, 124, 148, 151, 180, 181n343, 193n373, 244

Maximus, bishop of Constantinople, 22n71

Maximus the Confessor, Saint, 170n317

McCambley, Richard, xixn7

Meletians, 13, 14, 15, 16, 48

Meletius of Antioch, Saint, 6n9, 12, 13, 15, 19, 20, 21, 22nn71–72, 29, 30, 31

Meredith, Anthony, 80n401, 81n402, 139n202

Millennium, the, 7, 23, 33, 34n130

Minotaur, the, 61, 71n352, 78, 229, 230

monophysitism, 11n27, 27, 47, 81

monotheletism, monothelete, 45n188, 55, 170n317

Mount of Olives, monks of, 32

Mühlenberg, Ekkehard

Apollinarianism, on the history of: early history, 8n21; at Antioch, 13n34, 14n36, 15nn37–38, 15n40, 16n44, 16n46; between 378 and 381, 20nn66–67, 23n74; after 381, 26n87, 27n98; Nazianzen and Apollinarianism, 24n79, 24n82

"God-filled man," on the concept of, 98n24

on Apolinarius's Christology, 44n175

on Apolinarius's life, 6n13, 10n23: his correspondence with Basil, 6n11; his approaches to Jerome, Terentius, and the Diocaesarean exiles, 17nn47–48, 17n50; his condemnation at Rome, 19n57, 19nn60–61

on Gregory of Nyssa: his journey to Arabia and Jerusalem, 32n123; his reporting of Apolinarius's text, 42

on the *Antirrheticus:* its style and structure, 41, 151; its date, 36n143, 37n147, 39n155

on the *Apodeixis*: its structure, 43, 148n227, 151, 152, 160n277, 163, 182nn345–46, 231n484; its target audience, 49n206; individual fragments of: L.14, 98n24; L.18, 106n47; L.19, 107n51; L.22, 108n60, 109n62; L.26, 116n90; L.27, 117n95; L.42, 141n209; L.44, 145n215; L.45, 145n218; L.46, 145n215; L.51, 158n244; L.52, 155n250; L.53, 157n256; L.55, 160n277; L.61, 165n302; L.70–72, 185n357; L.71, 186n358; L.73, 187n361, 188n363; L.74, 189, 191n366; L.76, 193n371, 193n373; L.77, 206n399; L.79–80, 201n387; L.79, 201n388, 202n389; L.80, 203n392; L.82, 208n406; L.84, 212n419; L.85, 213n422; L.89, 226n466; L.90, 228n470; L.92, 231n484; L.95, 236n493; L.104, 257; supposed fragment in J.233, 258n567
Psalmenkommentare aus der Katenüberlieferung, 28n102

Nahor, 122
nature (φύσις), meaning of, 11n27, 52n228
Nazianzus (town), 22, 23, 24
Nectarius, 22, 24
Nemesius of Emesa, 29n103
Nestorianism, 44, 48
Nestorius, Cyril's third letter to, 77n394
Nicaea, First Council of (325), 4, 5, 12n29, 20, 22n72, 24, 46, 62n309, 113, 114, 135
Nicene formula (creed), xviiin3, 5n8, 6, 11, 12, 13n32, 15, 16, 21, 51, 60, 93, 112, 113, 134
Nicene party, 4, 5, 6n9, 7, 13, 14, 16, 17, 22, 29, 30
Norris, R. A., 10n22, 44n175, 51n223
Nyssa (town), 29, 31

Olympius (praeses of Cappadocia), 24
Origen, 50n214, 84, 156n249
Orton, Robin, xiii, 82n407, 83n409

Palestine, 17, 26
passions (παθή), 49, 54, 56, 97, 98, 99, 100, 102, 111, 133, 151, 152, 153, 173, 200, 221, 222, 223, 243, 255, 256
Paulinus (priest, then bishop at Antioch), 12, 13, 15, 16, 17, 18, 19, 20, 22nn71–72
Paul of Samosata, 48, 53, 73, 98, 102, 103, 112, 113, 148n127
Pelagius (bishop of Laodicea), 5, 6n9, 6n13, 20n68
person (πρόσωπον), 11n27, 52n228, 120n120, 213n421. *See also* Christ
Peter (bishop of Alexandria), 13, 17, 19, 21, 22n71
Phoenicia, Apollinarianism in, 26
Photinus, 20, 48, 73, 102, 103, 148n22
Plato, Platonic, 68, 70, 106n49, 109n63, 111, 214
Pneumatomachoi, 26, 31, 35
Pontica, civil diocese of, 32
Porphyry, 98n24
Pottier, B., 106n50
pseudo-Anastasius, *Doctrina de Verbi Incarnatione,* 112n79
pseudo-Athanasius: *Quod unus sit Christus,* 8n21; *contra Apollinarium,* 84n412, 236n493
pseudo-Dionysius, *de caelesti hierarchia,* 209n409
Pythagoreanism, 83n409

Quod unus sit Christus (attributed to a disciple of Apolinarius), 8n21, 208n406

Raven, Charles E.: on the *Antirrheticus,* xviii, xxi, 73n363, 74n369; on Apolinarius's life, 5n4, 6n9, 6n11, 7n14; on Apollinarian Christology and its historical development, 8nn21–22, 10, 44n175, 57, 122n79; on Nazianzen's *Letter 202,* 25n84; on the *tomus ad Antiochenos,* 14n36
reed, broken, image of, 62, 84–85, 247, 248n537
Rome, 6, 13, 15, 17–19, 24n78, 30
Rufinus, 8

Sabellian(ism), 6, 7, 12, 13, 17, 20, 31, 48
sacrifices of the Temple, restoration of, 7, 18n54, 33
Sapor, 30
Schwartz, Eduard, 20n68
Sebaste, 6n13, 12, 17, 19
Sebasteia, 31
Seleucia, Council of, 6n9
semi-Arian(ism), 5
sheep and shepherd, image of, 67, 85, 126–28, 255
Silvas, Anna M., 19n62, 20n63, 28n101, 29 nn104–5, 30nn106–8, 30n110, 30n112, 31nn114–19, 32nn121–23, 33n128, 34n50, 35n134, 35n136, 80n401, 115n85
Socrates (church historian), 3, 8n21, 35n137
soteriology: Apolinarius's, xvii, 49, 51–52, 75, 189–91, 193–94, 196n389, 201n388, 202–4, 216, 237; Gregory's, xxii, 34, 75, 78, 81, 82–85, 94n12, 125n139, 126–30, 138–39, 156, 246–48, 272
Sozomen, 3, 26
Spoerl, K. M., 8n205
Stevenson, J., 12n29, 14n36, 18n56, 20n65, 77n394
Stoic, Stoicism, 51n220, 83n409, 168n264, 191n366, 202n391, 208n403, 256n561
syllogisms, Apolinarius's use of. *See* *Apodeixis*

Teal, Andrew. *See* Young, Frances M.
Terentius (Count of the East), 17
Theodoret, 20n65, 26n86, 92n5
Theodosius (emperor), 7, 20, 21, 24, 25, 35
Theodotus of Antioch, 27
Theodotus of Laodicea, 5
Theodotus (second-century Valentinian), 125n139
theophanies in Scripture, 87, 261, 262
Tillemont, 32n123
Timothy of Beirut, 3, 18, 22
tomus ad Antiochenos (Athanasius), 10n23, 11, 13–14, 16n43, 26, 108n57
triduum, paschal, 83–84

Valens (emperor), 6, 13n33, 20, 30
vinegar, image of drop of, 62, 79, 80n401, 87, 207–8, 242, 266
Virgin Mary, the. *See* Mary
Vitalis, Vitalian, 13, 15, 16, 17, 19, 20, 24, 30, 193n373

Winling, Raymond: his French translation of the *Antirrheticus*, xix, xxi; on interpretation issues, 92n4, 93n8, 109n62, 114n84, 146n220, 156n252, 157n256, 162n283, 174n324, 182n346, 185n353, 185n357, 188n362, 228n470, 229n474, 240n501, 243n517, 252n548; on textual and translation issues, 97n22, 106n50, 113n82, 120n119, 154n246, 175n327, 188n363, 203n392, 205n396, 206n397, 211n416, 225n461, 229n473, 230n477, 232n486, 237n495
wisdom, divine and human, 44, 53, 61, 73, 74, 75, 80n401, 100, 101n31, 115, 123, 162, 163, 181–87, 208, 238, 239, 267

Xanxaris, 23, 24

Young, Frances M., with Andrew Teal, 4n2, 6n11, 10n22, 12n30, 13n35, 14n36, 44n175, 49nn207–9

Zacagnius, Laurentius Alexander, xix, 97n22, 98n23, 106n49, 127n144, 168n313, 175n327, 225n461, 229n473, 230n477, 237n495, 250n543
Zachhuber, Johannes: on Apolinarius's influence on Gregory's anthropology, 28–29; assessment of the *Antirrheticus*, xviii, xxi; on the dating of the *Antirrheticus* and *ad Theophilum*, 37n144, 37n147; on the dating of other works of Gregory, 31n117, 34n131, 35nn134–35; on Gregory's Christology, 81n402, 128n146; on Gregory's visit to Jerusalem, 32n123, 34n130

INDEX OF HOLY SCRIPTURE

Old Testament

Genesis
1.26: 180n340
2.7: 108, 115, 119, 153
2.19: 116
3.1: 110
8.25: 218
11.21: 122
12.1: 262
12.7: 262
24: 219
26.2–5: 262
26.24: 262
30.37–43: 62, 64n313, 92
32.24–31: 262
46.26–27: 116

Exodus
3.2: 262
13.21: 262
16.35: 157
19.16–20: 262
20.21: 262, 263
31.1–5: 192
33.11: 262
33.23: 262

Leviticus
19.8: 33
22.15: 33

Numbers
18.32: 33
20.11: 157

Joshua
5.13–15: 262

1 Kings
17.1: 163
17.14: 163
17.21: 163

2 Kings
1.10–12: 163
2.11: 65, 154, 263
4.25: 219

Nehemiah
13.2: 265

Job
38.1: 262

Psalms
2.7: 246
8.5: 155
13(14).3: 66, 263
25(26).4: 23n75
44(45).6–7: 66, 239
50(51).10: 158
54(55).19: 242
64(65).2: 116
72(73).24: 194
76(77): 67
76(77).19: 127
77(78).70: 194
81(82).5: 263
84(85).9: 93, 119
84(85).11: 119
84(85).12: 119
102(103).12: 114
103(104).4: 224
103(104).35: 260
127(128).3: 62, 92n4
144(145).3: 133

Proverbs
1.5: 66, 158, 200
9.1: 115

Ecclesiastes
5.2: 227, 228

Isaiah
6.1: 262
6.1–3: 263
7.14: 185, 210
9.6: 123, 185, 210
35.2: 263
49.16: 129
52.5: 231
53.4: 138
53.5: 139
53.9: 118
53.12: 265

Jeremiah
1.5: 161, 162

Baruch
3.37: 261

Ezekiel
1.26: 262
10.1: 263

Daniel
3.86: 64n319, 220, 223–24

Amos
7.14: 193

Zechariah
13.7: 45n186, 65, 122, 130, 131, 134–35

New Testament

Matthew

2.23: 163
3.16: 119
7.15–16: 62, 91
7.18: 170
8.9: 219n437
8.17: 138
9.12: 199
10.15: 263
11.16: 213
11.19: 174–75
12.39: 87, 264
12.42: 263
13.25: 234
13.33: 125n139
13.54: 64n319
13.54–57: 162n283
16.27: 82, 252, 253
17.1–8: 262
18: 85
18.7: 256
21.19: 157
21.23: 65n319, 163n286
21.33–40: 252
22.2: 252
24.6: 256
24.30: 251, 252
24.31: 252
24.36: 150
25.30: 65
26.39: 64, 169n314, 170
26.41: 123, 171, 264
27.46: 150
28.20: 82

Mark

4.38: 133
7.33: 133
8.38: 155
9.25: 149
11.13: 150
14.38: 134

Luke

1.15: 162
1.31: 140

1.35: 51n220, 64n319, 96, 106n47, 106n49, 161, 162, 246
1.41: 162
2.10–11: 246
2.12: 123
2.32: 80n401
2.52: 75, 80n401, 123, 162
3.30: 65
3.38: 153
5.31: 199
7.8: 219n437
7.14: 149
12.48: 259
15: 67, 85, 125
15.4–7: 127
16.20: 456
16.27–28: 168
20.36: 224
22.42: 54, 64, 169, 170
23.43: 64, 129, 246
23.46: 64, 129
24.39: 124

John

1.1: 160
1.1–2: 125
1.5: 156, 160, 265
1.9: 265
1.11: 160, 273
1.14: 93, 108, 119, 160
1.15: 122
3.3: 18
3.6: 152, 206
3.13: 53, 103, 106
4.6: 133, 157
4.7: 157
4.20: 225
4.23: 64n319, 220, 224–25
4.24: 225
5.17: 140, 163, 164
5.21: 45n188, 66, 163, 164
5.27: 64n319, 162n283, 163
7.15: 64n319, 162n283

8.40: 211, 217
8.58: 122
9.6: 133
10: 67, 126
10.11: 128
10.15: 128
10.16: 128
10.18: 64n319, 165
10.25: 254
10.25–30: 45n187
10.28: 255
10.30: 251, 253, 266
11.43: 129
12.10: 62n308, 91n3
12.24: 64n319, 166
14.9: 254
14.10: 266
14.11: 101, 102
14.20: 241
16.15: 65, 66, 101, 137, 164
17.5: 66, 241, 242
17.10: 101, 137
17.21: 102

Acts

1.9: 257
2.17: 95
2.36: 139, 240, 267
3.14: 130
9.3: 262
10.38: 242
13.24: 209n408

Romans

1.9: 64n319, 220, 224, 225
5.19: 139
6.4: 246, 248
6.4–5: 167
7.23: 64n319, 108, 110, 187n360
8.7: 65, 110, 225–26
9.5: 252
11.16: 125n139
11.17: 62, 92n4
11.29: 128, 245
11.33: 263
11.36: 211
13.1: 219

1 Corinthians
  1.24: 100, 238
  2.8: 267
  2.14: 221n449
  2.15: 222
  3.1: 221
  3.3: 110, 111n73
  5.1: 222
  8.6: 241, 268
  10.31: 222
  15.12–23: 167
  15.20: 247
  15.21: 229
  15.22: 247
  15.25–47: 64
  15.44: 221
  15.45: 53, 115, 116,
    118
  15.45–47: 64
  15.47: 53, 119
  15.48: 66, 117
  15.49: 112

2 Corinthians
  4.16: 65, 179
  5.4: 208, 265
  5.16: 174, 242
  5.19: 130, 210
  5.21: 144, 266
  11.4: 33
  11.12: 260
  12.2–4: 263
  13.4: 265

Galatians
  1.6–9: 33
  3.13: 265
  5.9: 125
  5.17: 108

Ephesians
  1.7: 64, 67, 122n128,
    126, 130
  3.6: 161

Philippians
  2.5–11: 46, 56, 61, 64,
    76, 87, 122n128,
    123n131, 136–47
  2.6: 136, 137
  2.6–7: 123, 159
  2.6–8: 121
  2.7: 53, 76n385,
    94, 95, 132,
    137nn188–89, 138,
    141, 145, 180, 241,
    263, 265
  2.8: 138, 139
  2.8–9: 146
  2.9: 139, 140, 267
  2.10: 140, 267
  2.10–11: 140, 211
  2.11: 267
  3.20: 118

Colossians
  1.17: 122
  2.9: 159
  2.12: 129

1 Thessalonians
  1.10: 129
  4.14: 167
  5.23: 50n214, 64n319,
    220, 221–23

2 Thessalonians
  2.4: 260
  2.9: 260

1 Timothy
  2.4: 66, 164, 172
  2.5: 211
  2.20: 259
  3.16: 93, 108, 119,
    261
  4.7: 115
  6.20: 115

Philemon
  10: 219

Hebrews
  1.1–2: 132
  1.1–3: 122, 130
  1.2: 95, 242, 261n12
  1.3: 132, 137, 238
  1.6: 209
  2: 67
  2.7: 155
  2.10: 127
  2.10–18: 126
  2.14: 126n141, 130
  2.17: 128
  4.15: 66, 117, 118

1 John
  5.19: 264

Revelation
  1.8: 189

RECENT VOLUMES IN THE
FATHERS OF THE CHURCH SERIES

ST. EPHREM THE SYRIAN, *The Hymns on Faith,*
translated by Jeffrey T. Wickes, Volume 130 (2015)

ST. CYRIL OF ALEXANDRIA, *Three Christological Treatises,*
translated by Daniel King, Volume 129 (2014)

ST. EPIPHANIUS OF CYPRUS, *Ancoratus,* translated by
Young Richard Kim, Volume 128 (2014)

ST. CYRIL OF ALEXANDRIA, *Festal Letters 13–30,*
translated by Philip R. Amidon, SJ, and edited with notes
by John J. O'Keefe, Volume 127 (2013)

FULGENTIUS OF RUSPE AND THE SCYTHIAN MONKS,
Correspondence on Christology and Grace, translated by
Rob Roy McGregor and Donald Fairbairn, Volume 126 (2013)

ST. HILARY OF POITIERS, *Commentary on Matthew,*
translated by D. H. Williams, Volume 125 (2012)

ST. CYRIL OF ALEXANDRIA, *Commentary on the Twelve Prophets,
Volume 3,* translated by †Robert C. Hill, Volume 124 (2012)

ANDREW OF CAESAREA, *Commentary on the Apocalypse,*
translated by Eugenia Scarvelis Constantinou, Volume 123 (2011)

WORKS OF ST. GREGORY OF NYSSA
IN THIS SERIES

Ascetical Works, translated by Virginia Woods Callahan,
Fathers of the Church 58 (1967)

Life of Gregory the Wonderworker, in *St. Gregory Thaumaturgus:
Life and Works,* translated by Michael Slusser,
Fathers of the Church 98 (1998)

Anti-Apollinarian Writings, translated by Robin Orton,
Fathers of the Church 131 (2015)